THEORIES OF PSYCHOLOGY: A Handbook

THEORIES OF PSYCHOLOGY: A Handbook

Ann Neel

SCHENKMAN PUBLISHING COMPANY, INC.
CAMBRIDGE, MASSACHUSETTS

Schenkman Publishing Company, Inc.
Cambridge, Massachusetts

Printed in the United States of America

Library of Congress Catalog Card Number: 68–24265

To Lorenz Misbach—who helped get this book started,

and

Bill McKeachie—who helped get it finished

PREFACE

THIS book is intended to provide a summary acquaintance, a feel, if you will, for the various theories and ideas it presents. It should not be expected to give the detailed knowledge of the expert in any of the fields. The book has been so organized that each theory or each concept could hopefully be studied by itself without reference to the rest. The fact that each section could be used independently has made it necessary to repeat some of the material. The effort has been to avoid duplication, however, and to cast the presentation in that light appropriate to its immediate context.

If the reader finds that the book helps to trace the origin and ramifications of an idea, and either provides him with a pattern into which he can fit the various theoretical concepts, or stimulates him to derive a pattern of his own, then the goal of the writer will have been achieved.

ACKNOWLEDGMENTS

DURING the years that this book has been in process, practically everyone whom I've seen or talked to has been instrumental in the preparation of it. To acknowledge each individual would require a list longer than the book itself. Therefore, I would like to take this means of extending my thanks and gratitude to all the colleagues, friends, graduate students, and secretaries who have read, advised, typed, proofread, and edited this book, and provided the moral support necessary for its completion.

TABLE OF CONTENTS

PART I

INTRODUCTION

CHAPTER 1

AN APPROACH TO THE ORGANIZATION OF PSYCHOLOGICAL THEORY

THEORIES of psychology are in some ways like theories of anything else: they knit a set of facts into a pattern, binding them with laws, postulates, and hypotheses. Each theory forms a different pattern, a different way of relating facts and ideas. While it may be instructive to the scientist to bring conflicting predictions to bear upon his findings, it is frustrating indeed to try to digest and comprehend the body of psychological theory when at times the language and concepts of one system seem completely foreign to another.

This formidable task can be simplified if some shared or common denominators among theories can be discovered. First, all theories have the common goal of being scientific. To this end their author must be concerned with the nature of scientific theory. In fact, to determine what kinds of theories are admissible in science is the job of the relatively new field of study known as the *philosophy of science*, which attempts to set up guidelines for theory.

Once the nature of valid theory is understood, we can inquire into the points different theories have in common. We can then contrast the concepts of one theory with those of another and have a common framework for comparison. All theories must address themselves to the same set of facts; these facts, in turn, will impose a certain order upon the theories.

A. First, each theory must have some basic terms, *basic units*. It must not only organize the whole of psychological information, but must supply some common denominator to aid in this organization. What each theory regards as its *basic unit* therefore offers our first reference point for comparison.

B. Each theory must also spell out its principal concern, what it delimits as its subject matter or field. The *field of study* is therefore our second reference point.

C. A theory not only defines its boundaries, but also establishes the ground rules for studying the material delimited. These set forth the techniques of investigation, the policies which must be followed, and the precautions which must be taken. Data gathered in other ways is not acceptable. Our third reference point for comparing theories is the *methods of investigation* which each theory finds acceptable.

D. In any but the most elementary theories the method of investigation applied to the field leads to the discovery of certain invariable relationships. The theory then proposes these as laws or *principles*; they will provide our fourth general reference point.

The reference points suggested so far apply to theory in any science. The orientation of a theory around these points influences its content. In each science there are certain phenomena which must be investigated no matter what units, fields, techniques, and principles are involved. These processes are the essence of the specific science; for instance chemistry must be concerned with chemicals, astronomy with stars, and psychology with behavior. The science of behavior is further broken down into basic elements which are studied by the field of psychology.

E. In all but the simplest animals, and especially in man, there is good evidence that the organism is to some extent aware of some of the events within and without its body, and not aware of others. Psychologists studying animal behavior can perhaps be less concerned with this awareness, and may even get into animistic difficulties if they call it by name. Those studying human behavior, however, must take this *consciousness* into account, for it is a most salient, if baffling, feature of human function. The matter of consciousness, avoided or not, is a reference concept specific to psychology.

F. A theory of psychology must deal with what happens when a sense organ is stimulated. How does the organism distinguish one stimulus from another? Because *sensation, perception, and discrimination* are matters of common concern, they become another reference point in our presentation.

G. In most organisms there is a good deal of evidence that something besides the stimulus contributes to the response; it appears that the relation of the stimulus to other events, and its implications or consequences, somehow influence behavior. While there is a debate over what terms to apply to these processes in animals, their universal presence in all organisms except the very lowest, makes it necessary for psychological theories to deal with *thinking, cognition, and memory*.

H. All organisms give evidence of being roused by internal and external events and of acting to alter these events. The organism at the same time shows signs of comfort or discomfort, or other states of an emotional nature. Psychological theories have still another reference point in their coverage of *emotion, motivation, and purpose*.

I. Once an organism has been exposed to a stimulus, performed a response, or solved a problem, the reappearance of the same situation is likely to bring forth similar actions. What the organism has learned, and how he has learned it, provide another reference point: *the nature and process of learning*.

J. Consciousness, sensation, perception, thinking, emotion, motivation, and learning are all determinants of behavior. Psychology is also concerned with behavior in its own right, and how it varies from one individual to another. Thus we give the treatment of *behavior* and *personality* as a final reference point.

This book is planned around these common points of scientific theory and of the science of psychology itself. Chapter 2 discusses the essential nature of theory in any science, orients the reader to the goals of psychological theory, and provides criteria against which to judge a theory as to its scientific merit. Chapters 3 through 31 give chronological treatment to a number of theories developed by different investigators in the field of behavior. The treatment of each theory follows our preceding discussion of reference points, in an effort to give a common ground for comparison among the schools of thought. As far as possible the original "flavor" of each theory is retained, although its original order has been altered to conform to the present plan of attack. Each chapter begins with a brief discussion of the social and scientific milieu in which a theory developed, and closes with a summary and critique.

A final chapter is devoted to current theoretical developments which do not seem to be direct outgrowths of some already established system, but appear to have significance for the future of psychology, or which give the current status of an existing theory, but are a sufficient departure from it to be inappropriate for discussion in the chapter where it is treated.

The systems of thought which we have chosen to include were selected for historical significance and apparent heuristic value. Some choices are obvious. Structuralism, Functionalism, Associationism, Behaviorism, Gestalt, and Freudian theories have contributed so heavily to psychology that many of their concepts have become identifying features of the entire field. Historical status aside, other choices were made on the basis of general contribution, significance of trends which evolved, or research that was stimulated. For instance William James's work had a powerful effect on the psychology of emotion and self, and Hull and Tolman's work has determined the activity of experimental psychology for decades. Lewin has done the same for social psychology and motivation. Phenomenology is a rising influence containing remnants of an earlier point of view. Neo-Freudian theorists have reshaped orthodox analytic theory, and the several physiological theories seem destined to guide the future of certain segments of the field. Many other theories which could have been included were not because their views were either restatements of one of the positions discussed or because the research possibilities they suggested were already implied within the parent theory. Neglect of an author is therefore only the inevitable result of a representative sampling procedure.

CHAPTER 2

LOGICAL, PHILOSOPHICAL, AND SCIENTIFIC CONVENTIONS OF THEORY CONSTRUCTION

THE scientist is concerned primarily with establishing cause and effect relationships which will help him understand the significance of the phenomena he observes. He hopes the relationships he discovers can ultimately be stated as laws, expressed in sophisticated mathematical formulae.

There are scientists who adopt the empiricist view, maintaining that the goals of science can be reached only through collecting facts ungarnished by interpretation. The empiricists argue that the value of a fact may not be immediately apparent, but that when enough data has been accumulated, the complex patterns connecting isolated bits of information will be understood. Theories or extrapolations which anticipate the interpretations of these relationships are unscientific.

On the other hand there are scientists who adopt the formal or theoretical approach that the organization of information is as important as obtaining it. Theory gives the scientist an appropriate framework within which to consider new findings. He can then be guided by their implications rather than continuing to record blindly whatever data he comes upon. Theory can add economy and efficiency to research and point up relationships one might not otherwise suspect.

The divergence in attitudes represents not merely a difference in the value placed upon theory, but a basic difference in the way one approaches information. The empiricist uses induction, while the theorist uses deduction. The inductive approach moves from facts to the formulation of laws which describe the facts. The deductive approach begins with a principle or a crude hunch, depending upon the sophistication of the field, and then searches for evidence to support the principle.

For the most part, theories are a product of both approaches. Theoretical systems are induced from an assembly of facts, but in turn elaborate upon the facts. They can only be tested by predictions (deductions) based upon some theoretical proposition. The initial collection of facts further involves some preconception which makes the scientist observe one particular set of facts rather than another. In the last analysis, the empiricist argument must acknowledge the human tendency to interpret and elaborate, and incorporate it into theory in the form of precautions about the limits of interpretation.

The nascent theorist, scientist or layman, frequently suspects the existence of some cause and effect sequence long before he understands its significance. At this point he will attempt crude guesses about the nature of the unknown relationship. An uneducated or primitive man may attempt explanation in terms of casual, semi-superstitious concepts (animistic and anthropomorphic thinking—terms we shall define later in this chapter). The educated layman and the scientist, on the other hand, employ what the experts in logic and theory call *hypothetical constructs* (MacCorquodale and Meehl, 1951; Marx, 1951; Spence, 1951) to account for interactions among events, processes taking place inside the organism, the atom, or the galaxy, processes which they cannot now and may never be able to observe directly. They can, however, observe the *effects* of these hidden processes. The effects and the stimuli which trigger them, and the framework of relevant laws and knowledge help the theorist to infer what he cannot see. Hypothetical constructs are usually tied to each other and to the rest of the theory by hypotheses—sometimes by hunches, and sometimes by laws.

An hypothesis is an inference, derived from either theory or fact, about the relationships among observables or unobservables, processes or interactions. It may be either explanatory or descriptive. Explanatory hypotheses predict that a specific phenomenon will be accompanied by other phenomena, that is, they are causal. They may predict phenomena at various levels of abstraction. Descriptive hypotheses, on the other hand, say something about phenomena at the same level of abstraction as the phenomenon in question. For example, on the basis of a theory that intelligence is the degree of capability at which a person functions and that it is related to past experience, one might hypothesize an abstract explanation that a child with a high IQ comes from a culturally rich background, or a concrete explanation that exposure to specific experiences will produce higher IQ's. Likewise, one might hypothesize descriptively that a child who receives high grades in school will also receive high scores on a test of scholastic aptitude. Once validated, hypotheses assume the status of fact. A *law* is a group of facts tied together by a generalized statement describing their relationship.

Hypothetical constructs, brought to bear upon unobservable organic or psychological processes, are narrower than hypotheses. They suggest that a possible situation is the explanation for a phenomenon. Because they deal with things not observable directly, they can only be validated indirectly. Techniques for empirical proof are often highly refined, and proof of the construct must await the establishment of a body of related facts; often the construct will persist for a long period as a respectable, although unproven and imprecise, statement of a possibility.

Employed in theory and research, the construct is gradually defined more explicitly, and its connotations and the effects of other factors upon it become more obvious. By manipulating the causative factors (i.e., the *independent variables*) and observing variations in the effect (i.e., the *dependent variable*), the scientist makes inferences regarding his postulated process. When the components of the relationship become precise enough, he can then make specific, accurate predictions of events or behavior. He has then reached the point where his postulated relationship can be stated as a precise mathematical formula. This specificity is beyond the capacity of his original hypothetical construct.

He is now employing an *intervening variable* (Tolman, 1951). Intervening variables are processes which, though not observable themselves, can be precisely defined in terms of what must go on when relevant, observable independent variables change in order to account for observable changes in the dependent variables. When all elements of guess work are eliminated, the new relationship can be incorporated into the body of scientific theory as a law.

While intervening variables are scientific laws, they are by no means the only form that laws can take. Laws express invariant relationships of any sort. Intervening variables are only those which describe invariant (and not necessarily observable) events occurring between causative factors and effects. They appear to be the mode through which the causes act to produce the effects.

Laws can either be specific to two events, or so general as to encompass groups or classes of events; that is, laws can be narrow or broad. Constructs and intervening variables also encompass greater or smaller events, but their range of applicability is limited to certain categories of events, and therefore is not as broad as that of a law.

Most psychological concepts have not yet reached the degree of specificity of intervening variables or laws, but remain as hypothetical constructs. Some concepts are still so crude that they possess only a tinge of scientific formality, retaining elements of prelogical myth which complicate their use. Psychoanalytic concepts such as id, ego, and libido often suffer because the complexity of their assertions and the lack of sufficient knowledge makes exact definition and delimitation impossible. Concepts such as learning, perception, and thinking can be defined more objectively, but they are still too broad to be capable of exact description. Concepts such as intelligence can be approximated with mathematical descriptions in some cases, but only a few such as hunger described as a function of hours of deprivation, or habit strength defined in terms of amount of reinforcement, motivation, stimulation, generalization, and state of the nervous system approach the status of intervening variables (and there is no unanimity among psychologists as to whether these statements include all of the necessary factors). The physical sciences, being far older, are able to specify many of their concepts in the form of intervening variables, but their frontiers are as sparsely populated as those of the younger social sciences.

The function of theory is to knit the available data into some sort of pattern, and it uses constructs, intervening variables, and laws to do this. Although the tools vary in precision and area of applicability, they all serve the same purpose. With their aid, theories can describe phenomena, citing the lesser variables of which they are composed, or showing how the phenomena in question combine with others in broader patterns. The definition of phenomena delimits them in space, specifies their spatial relationships to simultaneous events, and attempts to explain their position in the temporal (cause and effect) sequence of events.

The usefulness of scientific theory depends on the clarity and accuracy of its language (Hemple and Oppenheim, 1953). Language becomes important as soon as a theory seeks to delimit or define a concept, and if a suitable language cannot be found, the concept can never be developed, let alone explained. The vocabulary chosen is specific to a particular field of knowledge, and to the logical procedures involved in creating that theory. Many scientific theories, especially those in the physical sciences, are stated in highly symbolic language. To make this language meaningful, a set of rules has been formulated to govern the content of scientific theory and its mode of presentation. The most basic of these states that in a definition of scientific symbols the referents, i.e., the events and objects they stand for, must be made explicit.

All definitions begin with *primitive terms* which do not require definition. Subsequently others are added which can be defined by reference to the primitive terms; these may be either abstract or concrete. Abstract terms are those which cannot be touched or seen directly—ideas, relationships or qualities; concrete terms refer to entities which can be seen, touched, and measured. The empiricist, or inductive scientist, defines abstract terms by reference to more elementary terms. Theorists point out that no definition of this sort is complete until all the elements which comprise an abstract class can be named, and subsequently, the formalist, or theorist, tends to make abstract terms elementary and to define concrete terms by reference to the abstract classes into which they fit. In other words, empiricists use the nature of its members to define and delimit a class, while theorists use the class to define the nature of its members. A few examples may clarify the difference. An empiricist might define intelligence (an abstract concept) by reducing it to some specific act, such as the ability to achieve a high score on a test of reasoning. The specific act would be the primitive term used to give meaning to the more abstract concept intelligence. However, this definition of intelligence does not extend beyond the limits of the one specific act. For instance, one could not state the status of vocabulary or arithmetic as indices of intelligence. The theorist, on the other hand, might define various specific acts in terms of whether or not they connoted intelligence. Thus, reading is an intellectual act and marble shooting is not. Whatever other acts the scientist might also define as intelligent would have no effect upon his definition of reading. Likewise, the theorist's definition of hallucinations as a symptom of psychosis does not rule out the existence of other symptoms, but the empiricist's definition of psychosis as the presence of hallucinations leaves no means of including as psychotic symptoms delusions, disorientation, or confusion unless the definition is amended.

The practice of defining abstract terms by reference to more concrete events has much in common with Percy Bridgman's concept of *Operational definition* (1927), which he intended as a tool to assist physicists in the development of their concepts. It was of such value as a conceptual tool that it was soon adopted by many other sciences. Operationalism asserts that the meanings and definitions of terms delimit what concepts are admissable in scientific theory and what sorts of questions are legitimate topics for scientific inquiry. Bridgman maintained a concept to be synonymous with the operations or methods used to demonstrate it. For example, if pressed, one would find it difficult to define temperature in terms other than the readings on a thermometer. One can, of course, speak of how hot or cold it is, but hot and cold can only be made sufficiently specific for experiment by indicating some measure of intensity. Concepts which cannot be reduced to operations offer no way of pinning down their meaning, and therefore have no place in science. Likewise, the only meaningful questions for science are those for which an operation can give the answer. It is meaningless to ask what cosmic rays *feel* or *look* or *sound like* because we have no sensory organs to gather such data. It is, however, most useful to ask how cosmic rays *behave* because we have Geiger counters, photographic film, and so forth, with which to record this behavior. By providing a tool for definition and limiting the acceptable concepts and questions, Operationalism does not assure the scientist that his findings will be accurate, or his theories valid, but it does provide that whatever he does will meet a uniform standard. Thus a concept developed by one scientist can be studied by any other who uses similar operations. This is not a guarantee that they will have the same results, but they will look at the data in the same way, and if their findings differ, it will be due to differences in the phenomenon they are studying and not in the techniques. Such variations are likely to be just as revealing to science as the original observation, if not more so.

There is nothing intrinsic to an operational definition that makes every scientist interested in a certain subject employ the same set of operations to test it. He may use whatever measures he feels to be the most significant. While much can be learned by looking at the same thing from different points of view, confusion and controversy can also result if each scientist is convinced of the singular authority of his method. If a definition is in operational terms, its logic is irrefutable and its use acceptable. The operations may seem foolish or inappropriate, and the scientist may be criticized on this ground, of course, but his technique itself is above reproach.

Any area of scientific endeavor may find a proliferation of narrow definitions inconvenient and inefficient. There is no assurance that the concept means the same to all those who set out to study it. The same name may also apply to different things. The differences in research findings may result from different operations or from the fact that different events are being measured. For instance, one psychological concept which seems to suffer from this sort of variety in operational definition is *rigidity*. The rigidity measured on tests such as the Rorschach does not correlate with the rigidity indicated by an inability to change cognitive sets when solving arithmetic problems, and the rigidity indicated by an inability to alter percepts does not correlate with the rigidity indicated by perseverance on simple motor tasks. Such a glut of definitions is not unusual, in certain areas of psychology, and it may actually interfere with the development of a concept. But just as we do not throw away the saw because it makes sawdust, we cannot disregard a conceptual tool because it may lead to a confusion of definitions. If we clean up the sawdust or the confusion, we can be helped by the very tool which made the mess.

The remarks about rigidity noted the presence or absence of correlations among various operational measures. Where relationships do exist, the definitions may be assumed to have something in common, and Operationalism becomes a tool for generalizing the specific concept to a more general set. Where relationships do not exist, it may be assumed that separate phenomena are being called by the same name. If, for example, rigidity measured on the Rorschach is found to correlate with changing percepts, and rigidity measured by shifting approaches to arithmetic problems is found to correlate with the number of careless errors a person makes, we might conclude that there is a class of phenomena we could call perceptual rigidity, and another class we could call inattention to detail. Such observations help to define classes of behavior and also suggest possible explanations for them. (Our examples of correlations are fictions, invented for illustrative purposes only).

The explanatory function of theory introduces problems of logic just as the descriptive function creates complications of language and definition (Hemple and Oppenheim, 1953). The first problem is the temptation to employ *teleological* reasoning, which involves ascribing to some future event the role of cause for some present behavior, that is to suggest that cause follows effect. Defined in this fashion teleology seems to be an absurdity, but the problem is much more subtle than the definition implies. Such commonly heard statements as, "The trees shed their leaves in the fall because they are preparing for the winter," or, "The birds fly south because winter is coming," place the cause, winter, after the effect of shedding leaves or flying south. Among man and the higher animals, there is a possibility that behavior is directed by predictions of future events based on past experience, but this is often overlooked or implied rather than stated. Because they deal with thinking organisms, the social and behavioral sciences are particularly vulnerable to the pitfalls of teleology. Instances of motivated behavior, for instance, are often dismissed with some teleological explanation. Careful study usually reveals that some aspect of the situation provided a stimulus enabling the being to predict or anticipate, or triggered an habitual sequence. Trees, for example, shed their leaves when the temperature falls below a certain level, and the ratio of daylight to darkness produces certain chemical changes in the leaves. Bird migration also appears to be related to the proportion of daylight to darkness. A man works, not for the paper he receives on payday, but because he has learned that if he gives the paper to the grocer, the grocer will give him some food. However elementary these insights may seem to us today, they were not acquired easily. Fortunately the acquisitition of further knowledge is usually the antidote to teleology.

Some of the other logical hazards are not so easily avoided. Anthropomorphic or animistic interpretations which attribute human motives, cognitive behavior, or other human reactions to nonhuman creatures, objects, or organs are sufficiently subtle so that no amount of factual knowledge can belie them. To say that a plant *thirsts* for water, or a howling dog *mourns* his dead master, or that the clenched fist *desires* to strike an offender implies that these events can be equated with thirsting, mourning, and desiring as we experience them. Most scientists would not make statments as naïve as these, but they often fall into the same trap, couching their animism in more sophisticated terms. It is just as anthropomorphic to speak of a sexual impulse *searching* for an outlet, or a brain *sending* a message to a motor nerve, or the ego *forcing* unpleasant memories into the unconscious, as to speak of a river punishing trespassers by drowning them, or a mountain wanting to be beautiful. Impulses have no means of "searching," although they can arouse neural activity which in turn activates muscles; brains cannot send messages, they can only propagate electrical impulses. Ego cannot "force," although some neural activities can behave so as to block or inhibit others.

When these distortions are pointed out, the author of the statements is likely to respond that he obviously did not mean that that was what really happened. He meant his remarks as an analogy, "as if" that were what happened. He is also likely to point out that the analogy has a certain value as an aid to understanding. Of course, he is quite correct, and the fact that his analogy is valuable makes anthropomorphism all the more seductive. Analogy has its place in science; we shall see when we consider models that science can scarcely be without it. But unless the analogy is made explicit, it invites misuse and distortion, because it is too easy to forget the "as if" part of the statement, and remember only the "is." Freudian theory of the id, ego, and superego is a prime example of what can happen when an analogy is applied as if it were a true description. Theorists are tempted to view ids and egos as actual processes, almost as organs, and to treat the metaphysical strife among these processes as actual conflicts. Such treatment is disastrous to any theory which purports to be scientific.

The myth of "group mind" is another example of the disaster of animistic analogy. Many theories of group and crowd behavior propose that groups have an influence on their members which resembles some sort of living mind. People in groups will join in riots, panics, and mobs which they would never do as individuals. To explain this by suggesting a supra-individual entity, however, defeats the explanation because it hypothesizes an influence for which there is no physical parallel and does not explain the appearance and disappearance of the force. Yet the group mind fallacy persists, and tempts social scientists to lean upon it rather than to search for the factors which gave rise to it in the first place.

The use of analogy is another matter, in sharp contrast to anthropomorphism which is part poetic license and part myth. The model is a carefully constructed system of proposals, with realistic suggestions for carrying them out and the results of doing so. Just as a hypothetical construct suggests how to fill the gap between a specific cause and its effect, so the model proposes a system of processes to explain how an organism might function. Constructs may be analogies or they may be concrete hypotheses. Models must, by definition, be analogies, and they usually encompass a number of constructs suggesting how these might be patterned. Like constructs, models are only suggestive. The model builder uses his model to guide his research and modifies it until, instead of a metaphor, it becomes a set of laws, formulated in mathematics or logic. We see the value of models in the theory of atomic structure, the quantum theory of energy and its transmission, and in the cybernetic theory (see Chapter 29) that human behavior may be explained "as if" mechanical principles were involved.

The conventions of theory construction are designed to help the scientist discover and formulate information in a framework of laws. These laws are general statements of scientific truth, and may be either fundamental or statistical (Brunswick, 1951; Carnap, 1953). Fundamental laws state truth in an invariable and universal form. They apply to all things within a particular category. This application is not limited to a specific place or time or individual. For instance, "All apples are green when they are immature" is a fundamental law, while "Some apples are green in June" is not, because it refers only to some things at some times.

Statistical laws differ from fundamental laws in that they state what is probable under what circumstances, rather than what must be under all circumstances. Their subjects are a matter of mathematical probability rather than absolute certainty. Carnap (1953) distinguishes between probability statements about unique events, and probability statements about events as part of a class of events. An accurate prediction concerning the occurrence of a unique event can be formulated only after all of its characteristics have been considered. Each characteristic, in turn, requires knowledge of all the factors influencing it. Such knowledge is not easy to secure, and even if it were, the complexity of computing all the interdependent contingencies would render the task almost insoluble. Science will probably never be able to predict the unique qualities of unique events satisfactorily; it will never, for example, be able to formulate its laws with an accuracy to predict that the next apple I select from the barrel will be green. Predictions about classes of events, however, are another matter. On the basis of empirical data, a scientist can estimate the probability of each of several states and the probabilities of concomitant variations between the characteristics over a series of trials. Statistical laws are probability statements of this sort.

By way of illustration, suppose it has been observed that among mature apples most varieties are red, but one is golden; 90% of all apples are the red variety. The statistical law would state that either there are nine chances in ten of selecting a red apple from a basketful of ripe apples, or that the probability that any one ripe apple will be red is 0.90.

While all laws must state truths, the truths to which they refer may be established by different means. Some laws are based on direct observation, and they ordinarily state facts. Other laws are formulated by inference from facts. They may refer to things which cannot be observed directly (e.g., intervening variables), or they may be causal, deterministic laws, stating cause and effect relationships. Neither type of law should be considered secondary or dependent upon the other; both are equally important to science. Their difference is in function and means of formulation. That one is achieved by microscope and the other by calculator is not important. Laws carry an equal degree of truth no matter what the means of arriving at them.

Aside from convention of language, logic, and laws, theory must satisfy a number of practical requirements. To be of value to any science, a theory must provide comprehensive coverage and integrate all available data concerning that topic without internal conflict. Miniature theories, which deal with some narrow aspect of a large phenomenon, are valuable only if they can be fitted into a larger structure which relates them to other aspects of the same phenomenon.

Theory must be parsimonious. The assertion which can generate accurate predictions with the fewest prior assumptions and the simplest laws is the most useful. Conversely, the theory which is bogged down by weighty qualifications is hardly less complex than the phenomenon it seeks to clarify.

While a theory may be simple and comprehensive, it still has no scientific value unless it is testable. Ideally, it should point up testing procedures in its basic definition of concepts. This provides its author and other scientists the opportunity to manipulate relevant variables objectively.

A good theory must be capable of generating predictions. A theory may be an accurate and valid *post facto* account, but unless it can tell enough about it so that we know whether, when, where, and how to expect it again, the theory is mere description. What a theory predicts should be that which is incapable of being predicted without it. The more novel the predictions and the more diverse the events they include, the greater the unifying power (and the greater the value) of the theory.

Finally, the "good" theory is flexible enough to include new evidence; it can never become closed. When it can no longer accommodate new information, it has outlived its original value and revealed its basic inadequacy. On the other hand, a theory cannot be all things to all data. If it can incorporate any foreseeable event, it lacks sufficient structure.

Such complete theories can be found only in old and well-established fields, and new findings are constantly calling for revisions of these mature formulations. No theory of psychology can yet meet these standards adequately, and probably we should not expect any to do so until much more groundwork has been laid. At this point, however, we can employ the conventions of language, logic, and law, and the practices of theory construction to compare the theories we will now consider.

REFERENCES

Bergman, G., and K. W. Spence, "Operationism and Theory Construction," in M. H. Marx, ed., *Psychological Theories*, New York: Macmillan, 1951, pp. 54–66.

Bridgman, P. W., *The Logic of Modern Physics*. New York: Macmillan, 1927.

Brunswick. E., "The Probability Point of View," in M. H. Marx, ed., *Psychological Theories*, New York: Macmillan, 1951, pp. 188–202.

Carnap, R., "The Two Concepts of Probability," in H. Feigl and M. Brodbeck, eds., *Readings in the Philosophy of Science*, New York: Appleton-Century-Crofts, 1953, pp. 438–455.

Feigl., H., "The Scientific Outlook: Naturalism and Humanism," in H. Feigl and M. Brodbeck, eds., *Readings in the Philosophy of Science*, New York: Appleton-Century-Crofts, 1953, pp. 8–18.

Hemple, C. G., and P. Oppenheim, "The Logic of Explanation," in H. Feigl and M. Brodbeck, eds., *Readings in the Philosophy of Science*, New York: Appleton-Century-Crofts, 1953, pp. 319–352.

Lochman, S. J., *The Foundations of Science*. Detroit: Hamilton, 1956.

MacCorquodale, K., and P. E. Meehl, "The Operational Validity of Intervening Constructs," in M. H. Marx, ed., *Psychological Theories*, New York: Macmillan, 1951, pp. 103–111.

Marx, M. H., "The General Nature of Theory Construction," in M. H. Marx, ed., *Psychological Theories*, New York: Macmillan, 1951, pp. 4–19.

———, "Hypothesis and Construct," in M. H. Marx, ed., *Psychological Theories*, New York: Macmillan, 1951, pp. 112–129.

Spence, K. W., "Types of Constructs in Psychology," in M. H. Marx, ed., *Psychological Theories*, New York: Macmillan, 1951, pp. 68–86.

Stevens, S. S., "Psychology and the Science of Sciences," in M. H. Marx, ed., *Psychological Theories*, New York: Macmillan, 1951, pp. 21–53.

Tolman, E. C., "The Intervening Variable," in M. H. Marx, ed., *Psychological Theories*, New York: Macmillan, 1951, pp. 87–102.

PART II

HISTORICAL FOUNDATIONS AND THE FIRST PSYCHOLOGIES

CHAPTER 3

PHILOSOPHICAL ASSOCIATIONISM AND THE TRANSITION TO PSYCHOLOGY (384 B.C. TO 1911 A.D.)[1]

IT could be said that psychology had its beginnings with man's first self-conscious introspections. Man inquired about himself as he inquired about the meaning of life and death, the world about him, and the objects and events in it. All science has sprung from man's philosophical gropings after the meaning and nature of things. Early psychological theory, therefore, was part and parcel of philosophy. With the passage of time, interest in human experience and mental content grew into a separate field as did man's interest in the stars, in animal species, and in numbers. The theoretical-philosophical speculations which formed the germ from which the body of scientific psychology eventually arose, is known as Associationism.

Associationism was never formally set down as an organized system of thought. It represents, rather, a fairly consistent body of theory, having its origins in the time of the Greeks, and continuing to the present day. Initially, Associationism addressed itself to the mental aspects of human experience from within the general framework of philosophy; it has only recently acquired purely psychological specifications. In its modern form, it is less concerned with thinking and the content of experience, and more with learning—the acquisition of associations.

In the strictest sense, the development of Associationism might be divided into three phases. The first began with Aristotle and retained his influence until the Renaissance, when there was revived activity at the frontiers of philosophy. The ancient theories were considerably refined and expanded by men such as Thomas Hobbes, John Locke, George Berkeley, David Hume, Daniel Hartley, Thomas Brown, James Mill, John Stuart Mill, Alexander Bain, and the concluding investigations of Johann Herbart.

The writings of Hermann Ebbinghaus, Lloyd Morgan, G. E. Müller, and their co-workers belong to an intermediate phase in the development of

[1] Dates cited in chapter titles refer to year of earliest and of latest major publication relevant to that theory.

Associationism. These men were well grounded in the philosophically oriented concepts of their predecessors, but they used an experimental approach to test the validity of earlier speculations. Associationism then entered a third phase, taking on psychological dimensions and becoming identified with learning theory. The theoretical advances which characterized the final period can be attributed to the efforts of Edward L. Thorndike and I. P. Pavlov. The technological discoveries of B. F. Skinner are also relevant to this phase, although his theoretical orientation is more along Behaviorist lines (see Chapter 14).

In this chapter we are concerned only with the first two phases of Associationism, the fetal processes from which psychology was later to be delivered. The more specifically psychological theories will be taken up in Chapter 7 and 8 along with more contemporary trends.

PHILOSOPHICAL ASSOCIATIONISM

Basic Unit

It was the early consensus that mental content could and should be broken down into basic elements, known by a variety of names. In general these elements were meant to connote "ideas," "images," and "sensations." The early Associationists found no reason to make further distinctions among the elements of mental content. From the vantage point of several centuries later, these conceptual tools seem rather crude, but for the Associationists they apparently had sufficient delicacy to account for the mental processes hypothesized. Where more complex processes were observed, they were accounted for as combinations or connections of a set of basic elements.

As the first phase drew to a close, the Associationists were engaged in a bitter controversy over the precise nature of the connection between the sets of basic elements, a controversy precipitated by attempts to trace the construction of complex ideas. That some combination of elements was involved was generally accepted by all the Associationists. But was the combination an amalgamation of simple ideas, created by a sort of additive process which collected them as a sum or group? Or was a complex idea a coalescence, the result of compounding or interaction during which ingredients lost their separate characteristics and melded together into a new entity? On the one hand, James Mill, the leading proponent of connection through summation, maintained that any idea, no matter how complex, was made up of elements each of which retained its own identity even as it fit with the others. To Mill, a complex idea was like a brick wall, built one indivisible unit at a time. On the other hand, Hartley and Brown maintained that each complex idea involved a coalescence of properties of individual elements. The characteristics of the complex idea were different, and unpredictable from the elements out of which it emerged just as chemical compounds possess properties not found in the separate elements. Their classical example of coalescence was the flavor of lemonade, a result thoroughly unexpected from the taste of sugar, lemon, and water taken separately. The analogy to chemical interactions was so striking that Wundt, in his later derivation of Structural Theory (see Chapter 4), referred to this process as "mental chemistry." Ultimately the Associationists rejected the "brick wall" hypothesis in favor of coalescence, but the conflict has never been resolved for the field as a whole. Gestalt and Behavior theorists are currently fighting the same battle in modern terms.

Field of Study

The psychological investigations undertaken by the early Associationists extended only to the study of mental content. During this initial period of theoretical development, the Associationists were "psychologists" only as an aside from their study of philosophy. Nor did they see any need to separate the interest in mental content from their primary concern with the philosophical meaning of life and experience.

Methods of Investigation

To speak of the psychological *methods* used by the early Associationists is as artificial as to speak of their delimiting a field of "psychological study." As philosophers, their method was philosophical—logic and speculation, liberally supported by naturalistic observation and phenomenological introspection. Although currently in disrepute among scientists, these methods enabled the Associationists to derive principles which are still salient. In fact, the basic Laws of Association remain essentially unaltered and are still as vital as they were at the time of their conception by Aristotle.

Principles

Aristotle's first principle stated that ideas were combined or associated because they were similar in some way. For example, one associates bread with rolls because they have similar taste and occupy a similar place on the menu. Likewise, similarity of location associates shoes with socks.

The basis for Aristotle's second principle of association is the contrast between concepts. One associates black with white, yes with no, or up with down, by virtue of their opposition.

Lastly, the principle of contiguity suggests that concepts are associated because they have a relationship in time or space. Thus one associates tables with eating, chairs with sitting, pens with writing, schools with learning, and churches with praying.

The three primary laws account for the process of association but any specific concept may produce several associations. For example, the concept "up" may be associated with height in accordance with the principle of similarity, with "down" by the principle of contrast, or with stairs by the principle of contiguity. In a series of secondary laws, Brown attempted to account for the selection of specific associations. He asserted that concepts which had been associated most frequently in the past were likely to continue to be. If, however, two different associations had been made with almost equal frequency in the past, that which was most recent would take precedence. When there was a conflict between frequency and recency, or if no other determinant existed, then the liveliest and most vivid association, which had the greatest emotional significance, was likely to dominate.

Herbart set forth still another set of principles of combination. Concepts which attract each other and combine he called congruent, while others which repel or inhibit each other were incongruent. The combination of congruent materials made up a body of experience called the *apperceptive mass* which itself became the center for the organization of conscious experience. Congruent experience was accepted into consciousness if it "fit," whereas incongruent or irrelevant experience either was altered to fit or excluded from consciousness.

Consciousness

The philosophers of early Associationism each worked largely in geographical and temporal isolation. Their goal was the same—to understand conscious experience, but their emphasis was on principles which explained the *organization* of experience, rather than upon the nature of *consciousness per se*. They recognized the latter as important, but found it difficult to account for. In addition to the innate complexities of the problem, the culture of the times tended to confuse the issue. Those who approached the problem early in the Renaissance did so gingerly, fearful lest they be accused of trying to dissect the soul. Later writers, somewhat relieved of this anxiety by changes in religious dogma which made inquiry more acceptable, ultimately agreed that consciousness was not a spiritual phenomenon but an appropriate topic for intellectual study. The process whereby consciousness was removed from the realm of the soul and made a topic for scientific inquiry is the proper subject of the history of philosophy, and will not be discussed further in this context.

By the end of their period of influence the early Associationists had made sufficient progress to enable Herbart to evolve a theory describing the organization of consciousness. Utilizing the principle of apperceptive mass, namely that congruent ideas attracted each other and combined, he was able to account for the content of consciousness, and for the means by which experience was recognized, distorted, or overlooked. He ascribed congruence and the creation of the apperceptive mass to two factors. First, consciousness was restricted in scope and could only incorporate a limited number of concepts at a given time. Second, consciousness was an organized process which tended to maintain its organization.

To anticipate a later chapter, there is a striking resemblance between Herbart's concept of apperceptive mass and Freud's formulations regarding the unconscious. One might conclude that even if Herbart did not influence Freud's work directly, he helped to create a climate of thought in which his concept of the unconscious could flourish. In the same indirect fashion the impact of Herbart's concepts seems to have extended to current developments in the theories of perception, perceptual sets, frame of reference, concept formation, and thinking.

Sensation, Perception, and Discrimination

The early Associationists did not distinguish between sensation and perception. They regarded the registration of stimulus meanings as a basic element of mental content, and referred to it as "sensation." As time passed, a distinction grew up between the registration of stimulus events and the interpretation of their meaning. It finally became obvious that perception arose from the large body of previously associated material to which Herbart eventually gave the name "apperceptive mass." That is to say, perception came to be viewed as the relating of elements of present experience to past experience, for the sake of meaning. To put it another way, sensations were the units of which perceptual associations were composed.

In view of their interest in the association of discrete elements, one is surprised at their disinterest in the way these elements became discrete or specific. Indeed, centuries passed before Alexander Bain recognized discrimination as a problem for investigation. Bain pointed out that to acquire knowledge, differentiation, i.e., discrimination, must precede association. Thus, an individual's first task was to *single out* an item from the mass of experience which constantly confronted him. That is, he must discriminate which aspects of experience to perceive as entities or figures, and which aspects to perceive as background. He must further discover the singular characteristics of one experience which distinguish it from similar experiences, and not until he has done this can he have a unit of experience to recognize and associate with other units. While Bain saw the necessity for discrimination, he was unable to explain how it was accomplished. It is a measure of the significance of the problem he discovered that the process of building up discriminations is still being investigated.

Thinking, Cognition, and Memory

The main concern of the early Associationists was to explain the continuity of thought; the principles previously described were designed to elucidate both thought and memory. After the time of Aristotle, the philosopher-Associationists attempted to extend the application, and to refine and clarify the primary Laws of Association. They devised supporting principles where necessary.

To some extent, the Associationists also dealt with problems of thought content. To them, thinking invariably required symbols, and because thinking was a property of human beings, these would be *verbal* symbols. In an attempt to explain what the symbols meant, and how that meaning was acquired, the early Associationists developed the "sign-meaning association" theory which stated that meaning accrued to a symbol because the subject equated it with an object. The symbol stood for, or signified, the object and became a sign to indicate the object because it was contiguously experienced with the object either frequently, recently, or with great salience. This theory, which pointed out that a symbol became a sign for a real event, has received broad acceptance as an explanation of the origin of symbolic connotations.

Emotion and Motivation

Aside from considering contiguity, the early Associationists did not find it necessary to inquire into the reasons why one element of thought combined with another. They never investigated why a thought is initiated, seeming to imply that associations (or thoughts) simply began when one aspect of experience triggered off an association to another aspect. Associations *happened* to the thinker; he was the passive subject upon whom they were imposed. The gap left by this interpretation probably encouraged later theorists to think more positively about the influence of motivation upon thought processes, but this subject was not explored until the more formal psychological inquiries of the last few decades of the 19th century. Among the Associationists themselves, it was not until E. L. Thorndike (see Chapter 7) that the relationship of motivation to association was formally spelled out.

The Nature of the Learning Process

Early Associationism was a study of thought processes, and learning, i.e., the acquisition of association, was subsumed under the same set of principles. It is doubtful if learning was ever thought of as a separate process with its own laws, although there was vague recognition of the fact that more than one bit of experience might be associated with some current event. For instance, Brown was concerned with predicting which association to expect when several had been experienced with equal frequency in the past, and Herbart discussed the organization of experience around the apperceptive mass. The direct recognition of learning as a separate problem represented a distinct departure from earlier theory and initiated a separate stage of development (see Chapters 7 and 8), but we should anticipate this development at this point by remarking that the principles of contiguity, recency, frequency, and saliency have been demonstrated in a large number of studies to be as valid laws of acquisition as they are laws of organization of experience. But according to the large group of theorists who feel that learning presupposes the presence of some reinforcing (pleasurable or tension-reducing) circumstance following the association, the principles do not exhaust the conditions which determine learning.

Behavior and Personality

Behavior of the organism apart from his thought processes was not a human function which concerned the early Associationists. While many of these philosopher-psychologists probably took up some features of behavior as part of a broader interest in the meaning of life, discussion seems to have occurred independently of their formal writings on Associationism. The field itself was confined by definition to the intellectual realm of experience and did not encompass what we call behavior. The concept of personality had yet to be invented, and was not likely to emerge from a group oriented to universal rules of mental combination.

Critique

Principles such as the primary and secondary laws of association, which have endured for centuries, speak for themselves. That they are now accepted, in only slightly modified form, as basic psychological laws testifies to their scientific validity. It has nevertheless been argued that the early Associationists were not sufficiently thorough in their investigations, that is, they did not test their ideas by scientific method. In their defense, if defense is needed, suffice it to say that these early theorists were creating a new field of study and could scarcely be expected to employ methods which did not yet exist. It speaks well enough for their creativity that they formulated principles of crucial significance for the development of psychology with the crude tools available to them.

As one might expect, the concepts used by the early Associationists were very meager. They defined their areas of interest broadly as "experience" and "mental content," and spoke in terms of images, ideas, and sensations as the bits one might use to reconstruct this experience. They felt no need to ask why thought occurred, why and how associations were retained, or what relation mental content had to behavior. For them it was difficult enough to describe what occurred without asking how it related to other events in the present or in the past. The era of Associationism is a good example of the crude but wise kinds of questions man asks in the beginning stages of a science, and how the simple answers he gets help him to make still wiser inquiries. We shall see how these early philosophical inquiries led eventually to a more formal approach to psychology.

Transition to Psychology

The intellectual climate of the last fifty years of the 19th century contained all the ingredients for the growth of a science of psychology. Philosophical inquiry had raised a number of questions about the nature of mental life, and had freed itself from the religious taboos which had earlier prevented seeking these answers. Given, therefore, the desire to know, and the freedom to ask, it did not take man long to discover objective techniques for investigating mental contents. The work of three men—Lloyd Morgan, G. E. Müller, and Hermann Ebbinghaus—represents the final transition from Associationism to psychology. Since they were Associationists, they accepted the established body of theory, but each added to it both method and content after the flavor of his own times and interests.

Lloyd Morgan's contribution was principally methodology. Reports of observed animal activity in nature had comprised an "animal psychology" of sorts. In Morgan's hands these observations became more objective and controlled, for he not only watched his subjects' natural behavior, he observed their reactions to various tasks he imposed on them. Morgan's semi-experimental approach helped both to establish comparative psychology as a science, and also to reveal that animal subjects could be a useful source of psychological data. His concern with method also caused him to raise and answer a question which must have occurred to earlier theorists, though perhaps not with the same impetus, since they were concerned with humans rather than animals. In humans if one is puzzled by some complexity, he can ask another or observe his own reactions. Animals, on the other hand, are simpler creatures,—nonverbal and nonintrospective. In accounting for some bit of behavior it is not uncommon to discover that several hypotheses provide equally logical explanations. The theorist must then select that hypothesis which seems most appropriate. The psychologist can ask his human subjects to explain what is going on, or he can introspectively observe his own reactions. Animal subjects, however, cannot help the uncertain scientist. To guide his choice among alternatives along scientific lines, Morgan developed the *Law of Parsimony*, which has come to be called Morgan's Canon. This law simply asserts that when there are several possible hypotheses concerning a given phenomenon, the one which is likely to make the most scientific good sense is the simplest, the one which requires the fewest *prior assumptions*. This law has since become a general rule of thumb for psychology, human and animal alike.

G. E. Müller was something of a hybrid theorist. He was an early student of Wundt who is often referred to as the first "real" psychologist. Müller is best known for his work on motor set. In brief, motor set is the predisposition to exert effort similar to that associated with like tasks in the past. However important these observations of motor set were to motor behavior and to Structuralism, Müller's re-evaluation of the principle of contiguity had more immediate relevance to Associationism. Prior to Müller's investigations, it had been assumed that the association of two things occurring at the same time or place was the result of some external force which drew the conscious experience of these two things together. Müller asserted that contiguity did not arouse or produce such a force, but rather only *provided the opportunity* for association. The individual learned by perceiving the *relationship* between the several *experiences*. This perception of relationship accounted for association; mere proximity would not be sufficient. Without a feeling of relationship everything that happened to us would be associated with every other thing near it in time or space, no matter how inappropriate such association might be.

Hermann Ebbinghaus began his investigations somewhat before Morgan and Müller, but they spanned the first decades of the 20th century as well as the last decades of the 19th. Whereas the early Associationists inferred cause from effect, Ebbinghaus began with a known cause and studied its effects. That is he isolated the causal variables such as similarity or contiguity, which were involved in the process of association and, controlling all other factors, studied the effect of each of these individual variables on the process. In other words, he was the first to apply the experimental approach to the study of association.

Early in his work it became obvious to Ebbinghaus that if he were going to experiment with association, he required extremely simple materials, something that was easy to learn but had no previously acquired associations. It occurred to him that the use of short words or sound combinations would probably be the easiest way to control all of the factors necessary in this sort of experiment. A contrived series of syllables would not involve previous associations. This idea led him to devise what have since become known as *nonsense syllables*. The syllables could be any length and their supply was unlimited. Using himself as a subject, Ebbinghaus memorized nonsense syllables under various conditions, to study the effects of variables such as fatigue, passage of time, the similarity between lists, etc., on his ability to learn and remember these syllables. His experiments established much basic data on the processes of learning, remembering, and forgetting. The now famous curves, or graphs describing the progress of learning or recall through a series of trials, were developed from Ebbinghaus's pioneer efforts. A brief examination of some of his findings will reveal why his work has become a classic in the psychology of learning (see Figure 1).

The different curves were the result of varying the conditions. One of the most important variables in determining the shape of the curve was the type of material to be learned. Positive acceleration (Figure 1, part A) seemed to occur in learning situations where the basic skills were extremely hard to come by and were therefore mastered slowly. Following mastery, learning became a simple matter of increasing proficiency. Negative acceleration

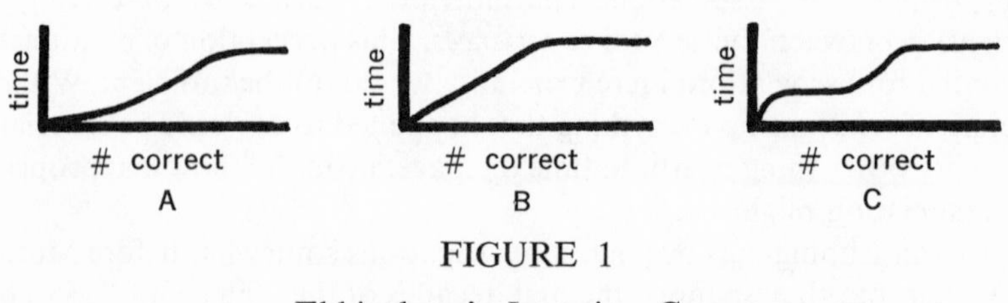

FIGURE 1

Ebbinghaus's Learning Curves

(Figure 1, part B) occurred in learning very simple skills where one could master the whole affair quickly, but then reached a "ceiling." The simplicity of the skills made performance automatic, and further improvement was rendered impossible by the nature of the task. Ebbinghaus came up with S-shaped curves (Figure 1, part C) usually in complex learning problems requiring a number of different skills. Some of these would be easy to learn, some difficult. Some would have a low ceiling and could be mastered quickly, while other aspects called for unlimited proficiency. As the person progressed he would master first one aspect of the problem and then another. Learning the typewriter is a frequent example of complex learning. One begins by learning to type single letters, which is difficult at first, but soon becomes easy. Later, one learns to type words, and still later, phrases of increasing length. One also begins to develop speed. As these skills are mastered, one may learn to compose while typing, or to take dictation on the typewriter.

Consequent research on many kinds of learning has validated Ebbinghaus's findings; his original curves remain unmodified following half a century of experimentation.

The Morgan-Müller-Ebbinghaus phase of Associationism was paralleled by a number of similar developments in other aspects of philosophy. Different problems were approached by different methods, and different interpretations were made, but everywhere the stage was set for the emergence of a science of behavior. The varied contents of the new science are the subject of the chapters which follow.

SUMMARY

Basic Unit. Basic to all the early Associationist theories was the concept of mental elements which in combination produced the observable mental processes. For centuries there was disagreement as to whether this combination was a summation of the elements or a coalescence; eventually the controversy was resolved in favor of the latter.

Field of Study. The early Associationists were philosophers whose interest in mental phenomena grew out of a philosophical concern with the meaning of experience. They did not conceive of their efforts as a field of study separate from philosophy.

Methods of Investigation. As philosophers, the early Associationists employed the methods appropriate to their orientation: logic and speculation, supported by observations and introspection.

Principles. The primary laws of association held that ideas became associated because they were similar, because they contrasted, or because they were contiguous. Several secondary laws asserted that among several equally possible associations of elements, the one most likely to occur would be the one either most frequently, recently, or vividly associated on previous occasions. Ideas combined if they were congruent and fitted with past experience. If they were irrelevant they were distorted or excluded.

Consciousness. Associationism developed no standard theory of consciousness.

Sensation, Perception, and Discrimination. Sensation was one of the basic elements. Perception on the other hand, was the process of fitting sensations into the apperceptive mass. Before association of elements could occur, the idea or sensation had to be differentiated from the apperceptive mass as a distinct experience. How this discrimination took place was a question which the early Associationists could not answer satisfactorily.

Thinking, Cognition, and Memory. Thought, the mental contents, were the early Associationists' primary interest, and the principles they derived were to assist their understanding of thought processes.

Emotion, Motivation, and Purpose. Motivation was not a necessary concept since association was presumed to be a process imposed upon a passive subject.

The Nature of the Learning Process. The Associationists did not consider learning separate from thinking, but their laws did concern the establishment of connections. Retention was a problem they did not consider.

Behavior and Personality. Associationism was a theory of thought, not of action, and it was therefore not concerned with behavior.

The transformation of Philosophical Associationism into Psychological Associationism was effected by the semi-experimental studies conducted by Morgan on animals, the investigations of Müller which demonstrated that perception of a meaningful relationship was necessary to the formation of associations, and Ebbinghaus's famous curves graphing the acquisition of association depending upon the difficulty of the material and upon the number of sub-skills which are involved.

REFERENCES

Philosophical Associationism

Warren, H. C., *A History of the Association Psychology*, New York: Scribners, 1921.

The Transition to Psychology

Boring, E. G., "Bibliography of G. E. Müller," in *History of Experimental Psychology*, New York: Appleton-Century-Crofts, 1950, pp. 382–383.

Ebbinghaus, H., *Über das Gedächtnis: Untersuchungen zur Experimentellen Psychologie*. Leipzig: Duncker & Humblot, 1885. Trans. H. A. Ruger, and C. E. Bussenius, *Memory: a Contribution to Experimental Psychology*, New York: Columbia University Press, 1913.

——, *Grundzüge der Psychologie*. Leipzig: Von Veit, 1897–1911.

Morgan, C. L., *Introduction to Comparative Psychology*. London: Scott, 1894.

CHAPTER 4

STRUCTURALISM (1846–1923)

THE advent of the Structuralist school marked the emergence of psychology as a science in itself, a field apart from philosophy. The new science incorporated the branches of philosophy which were concerned with the mind and with behavior, dating as far back as the work of Aristotle and the Ancients. It also included more recent bodies of data which psychologically oriented philosophers had found it necessary to consider to understand their subject matter. Most significant among the recent data was the work of Weber and of Fechner. The physiologist Ernest Weber investigated sensory processes and discrimination, and Gustav Fechner, who was in addition a philosopher, applied Weber's findings to the objective study of the mind. But the first man to attempt a systematization of the data was the philosopher Wilhelm Wundt. As he became more involved in the field, Wundt devoted more and more of his time to active research, and eventually established the first psychological laboratory, in Leipzig, in 1879. For this and his other activities he has come to be known as the father of psychology. Wundt did not create the new field; rather he insured its status as a science by organizing the earlier studies of psychological problems into the formal theory known as Structuralism.

Another person associated with the beginnings of the science was E. B. Titchener. He was an academician in the strictest sense of the word, and a pure scientist. After training in Wundt's laboratory, he moved to America to continue his work. As a Structuralist, Titchener found himself opposed to most of the trends in American thinking. His controversial opinions provoked so much resistance that they became a focal point around which most of the early American theories developed. When the American Psychological Association was formed, Titchener found this group so foreign to his views that he formed a rival organization in an attempt to keep psychology pure. He would not tolerate alien views, and regarded even the smallest deviation as heresy, a crime sufficient for excommunication. He remained a steadfast and uncompromising Structuralist until his death.

Basic Unit

The Structuralists proposed that the basic units of psychology be what Wundt and Titchener had referred to as *mental elements*. Consciousness (mind) was made up of components which were roughly comparable to chemical elements. These irreducible elements were the building blocks of experience and through them, mental function could be reconstructed and understood. It is from this concern with the *structure* of mental processes that the theory takes its name. Wundt postulated three basic mental elements: sensation, feeling, and apperception, and Titchener hypothesized three different although similar ones: sensation, affection, and image. We will discuss the specific nature of the elements further along in the chapter.

Field of Study

Wundt's apparent hope was to devise the psychological equivalent of the chemists' Periodic Table, employing mental elements in the same manner as chemical ones. To Wundt, the proper concern of psychology was to analyze the conscious process into elements, determine the manner of connection among these elements, and then discover the laws which govern the connection. This could only be done by studying immediate experience as it was taking place. Since experience could only be reported by the experiencing person, it was imperative that experience be treated as an objective phenomenon, even if it be that of the observer himself.

The Structuralists further insisted that psychology be a pure science. No metaphysical concerns were permitted and no armchair philosophy was tolerated. Everything was to be tested or testable. Likewise, no practical concerns were allowable. Knowledge was to be secured for its own sake, since the search for applications was felt to sully the purity of science.

Methods of Investigation

The restrictions which the Structuralists placed on content (immediate experience) and purpose (pure science) led to similar restrictions in their methodology. Only certain methods, for instance, were sufficiently scientific, and they employed only two principal techniques to investigate psychological problems: the psychophysical techniques of Fechner, and the classical method of introspection perfected by Wundt.

Psychophysical Techniques: Fechner developed three varieties of psychophysical measurements, all of which have become classical for the study of sensory thresholds and the dimensions of sensation, and which have also been adopted for the investigation of perception, intellectual and cognitive functions, and social attitudes.

One of Fechner's techniques is known as the *method of just noticeable differences*, the *method of limits*, or the *method of minimal changes*. The subject is exposed to an ascending or descending series of stimuli. Depending on what is being studied, the subject may be asked to indicate at what point he notices the stimulus appear or disappear (the absolute threshold), or he may be asked to indicate at what point he is just able to notice a difference between one stimulus and another (the differential threshold). The subject's ability to *discriminate* changes does not necessarily correspond to the changes in stimulus level. At some intensity levels he may notice change every time it occurs, but at other levels he may not notice it until the stimulus is several physical steps removed from the previous one.

One variation of this method is to ask the subject to indicate the point at which he becomes aware of a difference between a trial stimulus and a standard stimulus.

The second procedure is called the *method of constant stimuli*, or the *method of right and wrong cases*. A graduated set of stimuli is presented in random order and the subject is asked to say whether stimulation is present or absent, thereby determining absolute threshold. If differential threshold is to be studied, the subject is asked to tell whether a randomized test stimulus is the same as, or different from, a standard.

The third psychophysical technique, the *method of average error*, requires the subject to adjust a test stimulus until it appears equal to a standard. The subject's accuracy is the index used to determine the various thresholds and other perceptual qualities. As the name implies, the "score" is the average amount of error in his adjustments.

Several variations on classic methods are now so widely used as to deserve mention. The *method of paired comparisons* presents pairs of stimuli arranged so that every stimulus is eventually compared to every other one. The subject is asked each time which stimulus is bigger, brighter, heavier, or whatever. Here again, the effort is to determine the threshold for a particular type of stimulus or some stimulus quality. The method of *judgment of intervals* requires the subject to separate and order a number of stimuli in some given way. For example, he may be asked to select a stimulus which occurs between two standard stimuli (the judgment of intervals by bisection), or to make a judgment about several stimuli as to which is a quarter of the way, a half of the way, and which three-quarters of the way between two constant or standard stimuli. Another variation requires the subject to arrange a series of stimuli so that the intervals between each of them appear equal.

Classical Introspection: The other principal method employed by the Structuralists, the one with which they are most often identified, was *introspection*. The technique had been used before and has been since, although usually in a different way. Introspection is a form of self-observation. Ordinarily, in introspection one observes the objects and events as he has learned to *interpret* them, rather than the raw materials from which these interpretations were originally derived. The Structuralists, however, wanted to observe the basic ingredients of consciousness, and therefore focused their study on raw sensory data. To observe the final conscious product rather than the raw ingredients introduced what the Structuralist called a *stimulus error*. Thus the subject was instructed not to tell the *meaning* of what he saw but to give his naive impression of what was reaching his sensory organs. Neither the cognitive nor the purposive aspects of his experience was relevant. This is much the same thing that an artist does to reproduce the impression of light and shadow by variations in color. He is not responding to the *meaning* of light and shade, but objectively portraying what is really there. The person who views the finished painting interprets the variation in *color* as variation in *light*, and has thereby, from Wundt's point of view, committed a stimulus error. Likewise, where Wundt's subjects reported in the distance a large red wooden box suffused with blue light, they made a stimulus error. The classical introspective report of an object focused on its dimensions, shape, light qualities, perspective, blurring of details, apparent coloration, and appearance of surface planes. This method contrasts with another type of introspection known as phenomenological introspection which requires the subject to report not only what he sees but also what he *thinks* he sees, i.e., the meaning of his environment. The subject in classical introspection might describe a table as a brown object topped by a flat trapezoidal plane, having four elongated, apparently rectangular extensions resting on the floor. On the other hand, the subject employing phenomenological introspection would describe a table as a wooden object with four legs, at which one might eat or write.

Titchener in particular, and Wundt to a lesser extent, were opposed to the use of phenomenological introspection. Late in his life Titchener did try to use the technique, although he had little faith in it. However, he died before this work had taken form, and what little he did with the technique did not indicate his direction or what he intended to do with the method.

Other Methods. Although psychophysical techniques and introspection were their major tools, the Structuralists used a number of physiological measurements such as breathing and pulse rate, where these were appropriate. They also employed measures of attention span and reaction time, as well as other laboratory procedures, in the analysis of mental elements. These were, however, of secondary importance.

Principles

Weber-Fechner Law. Perhaps the best known of the Structuralists' principles is the Weber-Fechner Law. Although the derivation of the law was not their accomplishment, demonstration and extension of it were among their main concerns.

The law described in mathematical terms the relationship between what we now call sensation and perception. The law held that there was no one-to-one relationship between objective changes in level of stimuli and the perception of those changes; the amount of change which must be made for an observer to report a change was called the *just noticeable difference*, or *JND*. How much change was necessary to produce a JND depended upon the intensity (or some other quality or dimension) of the stimuli. The JND was accordingly stated as a ratio of the amount of change to the previous level of the stimulus. In other words, the bigger, brighter, louder, heavier, more saturated the stimulus, the more it must be changed for the change to be perceived. If there is only one candle in a room, to add one more candle makes a noticeable difference in the amount of light. However, if there are ten candles the addition of one more will rarely make any subjective increase in the intensity of the light. Again, while most people probably could not tell the difference between the weight of one feather and the combined weight of two, they could perceive the difference between a few ounces and a few pounds. By applying the Weber-Fechner formula, it is possible to compute the number of candles, or ounces, or pounds which must be added in order to produce a just noticeable difference in the amount of stimulation.

Thresholds for differences of stimulation were originally investigated by Weber in connection with the discrimination of weights. However, their real meaning and connotations for psychology were not seen until Fechner discovered Weber's work and developed a mathematical formula for the relationship between physical objects and psychical phenomena. Fechner believed that the assumption that mind and body were distinct processes was not valid. Given the body as a physical entity, then any organ which was part of the body must have physical aspects, and these could be measured. He therefore sought evidence that mental processes could be measured, and found that evidence in Weber's experiments. His subsequent work was such an effective demonstration of the possibility of measuring mental processes that it became part of the foundation upon which the Structuralists built.

Theory of Actuality. In addition to the Weber-Fechner law, Wundt formulated a number of principles describing the content and structure of mental life. Basic to all else was his *Theory of Actuality*, which postulated that mind was a dynamic activity, a process rather than a passive substance. This was an important assertion, for at the time most people conceived of mind as indentifiable in much the same way as the soul.

Psychic causality. To support his proposition that mind was a process, Wundt sought principles to describe it. The most elementary of these asserted that the flow of conscious experience was not a random stream. Not only was mind a process, it was a process which followed a definite order.

Creative Synthesis. Among the laws of sequence was the *law of psychic resultants*, or the *principle of creative synthesis*. This principle maintained that when mental elements combined they modified each other, the new product appearing as something different from its original elements. This principle was taken over from the similar mental chemistry of the Associationist philosophers (see Chapter 3), who had used the principle to describe what happened to associated bits of experience. Used by the Structuralists, its purpose was more or less the same, to describe the effect on conscious experience of the interactions among events. In a later section, we will see the same principle: the Gestalt law that the whole is something more than the sum of its parts (see Chapter 23).

Psychic Relations. The law of *psychic relations* also helped describe the sequence of experience. This law maintained that a particular aspect of experience acquired significance from the entire experience of which it was a part. Thus, an experience was determined not only by the interaction among the events which composed it, but also by all other events which were active at the time; experience was relative to the background in which it occurred. Consider, for example, how one might laugh upon seeing a caged tiger roar, but run from the same tiger in another situation differing from the first only in that one of the bars of the cage was broken.

A few years later Gestaltists stressed the same principle, referring to it as the figure-ground relationship (see Chapter 23).

Psychic contrast. Wundt's final law of sequence or conscious organization was the *law of psychic contrast*, which stated that opposites tend to reinforce each other. For instance, a tall girl walking down the street with a short man makes the one seem even taller and the other even shorter. One Negro in an all-white classroom attracts far more attention than he would in a mixed group. It is the contrast which makes the experience outstanding and salient.

Motor set. On the basis of experiments with weight discrimination, another principle which was important to the Structuralist school was developed by Müller, an early student of Wundt's Leipzig group. The *principle of motor set* stated that an individual "set" himself for a given amount of energy exertion on the basis of previous experience. Later experience either validated or invalidated the set, showing the individual whether his anticipation had properly prepared him for the new stimuli.

Insofar as motor set involves anticipation, it bears some kinship to current concepts of frame-of-reference and level of adaptation (see Sensation, Perception, and Discrimination in Chapter 32).

Consciousness

Of primary concern to the psychologist who attempts to understand consciousness is the relationship between mind and body. Several formulations of the nature of this relationship have been advanced, and accepted or rejected according to the scientific orientation of the individual theorist.

One such interpretation, known as *dualism*, was particularly prominent among the early philosophical authors, whose orientation might be described as "religious" in so far as their investigations of consciousness were colored by their concern with the meaning of soul. As might be expected, the "dualists" believed that mind, like soul, was an ethereal essence, distinct from the body, and, in fact, from any physical object known to man. It was an intangible "something," which existed on a metaphysical plane; because of its "spiritual" quality it could not be considered open to scientific investigation.

A second school of thought, known as *parallelism*, asserted that both mind and body were physical entities, but believed them to be dissimilar in nature and function. In brief, despite their basic similarity, mind and body were concerned with two different chains of events which occurred concurrently; perhaps they might be compared to two trains which ran along parallel tracks, each going the same way, but each governed by forces independent of the other. The engineers might take each others' actions into account, but there was no real interaction. Mental functioning might be influenced by somatic phenomena and vice versa, but they were controlled by independent forces.

A third approach to the problem, the identity hypothesis, stated that mind and body were identical. From this point of view, mind was a biological process, the end-product of neurological function in the same way that digestion was the end-product of gastric function. The nervous system was a separate organ within the body, but had no more independence from the other organs than the stomach would have from the liver, or the pancreas, or the large or small intestine. All organs must interact to insure the smooth flow of physiological activity.

Fechner, the "pre-scientific" psychologist, was an advocate of this interpretation of the mind-body problem. This being the basis for his theory, it is not surprising that Fechner was so pleased to find in the Weber-Fechner law a mathematical formulation which showed how the two could be equated.

Both Wundt and Titchener were more or less parallelists, but had not yet completely evaded the dualist aura of soul and mind. Their exact position was never made clear, because it was not important to their theory. For them it was enough that changes in one were usually accompanied by concomitant changes or adjustments in the other, although neither actually caused the other. Because mind and body were different things, it was necessary to seek tools for conceptualizing the essence of consciousness independent of, but similar to, the tools for conceptualizing physical processes.

As pointed out earlier in this chapter, Wundt found tools appropriate to his need in his concept of the formal elements of experience. He conceived of these elements as dynamic processes, and thus consciousness itself became dynamic.

Wundt further postulated that at any given time the components of consciousness were so organized that there was both a *focus* and a *field*. The focus, namely the set of elements in the foreground, was experienced against a backdrop, the field of all other continuing processes. Focus was determined by the aspect of conscious function called attention, itself a dynamic process.

Wundt attempted to explore focus, or at least the range of focus, by studying the differences in stimulus reaction time between simple muscle responses and acts involving sensory experiences such as willing, purpose, and the like. His discovery that reaction time was longer in the case of willed acts proved to him that conscious focusing on (and production of) willed acts was a more complex process than conscious focusing on (and production of) motor responses.

While focus determined the topic of consciousness, the field of other concurrent processes had an important influence on sensory qualities, thresholds, and other aspects of experience by means of the synthesis carried on among all currently active elements. Despite its synthesizing influence, the field was never studied to any extent by Wundt and his followers.

Titchener's theory on the other hand, stated that mind was the sum total of the individual's mental processes. He defined consciousness more narrowly as the sum total of a person's experience at a given time, and like Wundt, described this in terms of its elements, which he saw as dynamic processes patterned by the phenomenon of attention. Despite his dualist inclinations, Titchener stated explicitly that an explanation of consciousness must ultimately be found in the nervous system. However, he did not feel that enough was known at that time about the relationship of consciousness and the nervous system to make explanation possible.

Sensation, Perception, and Discrimination

Fechner pointed out that, while it was not possible to measure sensation directly, it was possible to measure the physical stimulus which produced it. Although not measurable directly, the intensity of sensations could be inferred from responses made to controlled stimuli. Indeed, Fechner was able to perform this sort of measurement with precision sufficient to derive a mathematical relationship between stimulus and sensation. (The reader will note the similarity between Fechner's approach and the concept of intervening variables discussed in Chapter 2.)

Wundt, on the other hand, saw no difference between sensation and stimulus. The stimulus was what the introspecting subject reported when he described his momentary experience. From this point of view, sensory organs were mere channels for the passage of information. But Wundt could not avoid recognizing that there seemed to be something happening to the information beyond mere passage; there seemed to be some processing of the information. He therefore found it necessary to acknowledge the existence of perception as a separate entity. To it he attributed the role of interpretation of meaning, a matter which he had initially felt to be beyond the realm of science. As Wundt continued his work, he found it impossible to avoid dealing with perception. He introduced the term *cognitive signs* to distinguish the objective stimulus from the subjective reaction to it, and eventually came to attach great importance to these signs and how they were integrated into experience as part of what he called apperception. Apparently at this point he was willing to conceive of perception as a fusion of various mental contents active at a particular time. But because only those aspects of perception which fit this limited definition were acceptable as areas of study, for Wundt the status of perceptual processes remained marginal.

Titchener, too, gave reluctant acknowledgement to perception as a psychological process. He asserted that percepts were composed of sensations, which he conceived in a manner similar to Wundt. Moreover, these percepts could be observed to have certain distinctive dimensions; they could vary in quality, intensity, duration, and clarity. Like the other Structuralists, however, Titchener did not deal with perception much beyond this brief assertion. Having described the attributes of perception, he seemed satisfied to forego further exploration of a territory so foreign to the Structuralists' view.

Thinking, Cognition, and Memory

Wundt believed that scientific methods such as introspection and the psychophysical techniques were not applicable to higher mental processes. Indeed, when such studies were attempted by others, he called them "mock experiments." Observation of social phenomena, such as language, could be used to obtain some objective information concerning thought, and reaction-time studies (such as those on the focusing aspects of consciousness) could give some indication of its complexity. But by and large Wundt could find no means of opening the higher processes of the mind to scientific exploration. Undoubtedly, his views were dictated by his conviction that psychology must be a science distinct from the more subjective approach of philosophy. Yet to some extent, his vision was blinded by the same dualist beliefs which determined the philosophical status of mind and soul.

How much this ancient prejudice, and even Wundt's remedial efforts, limited the thinking of Structuralism becomes more apparent when we recall that apperception was one of Wundt's basic elements. One of the basic aspects of human function, one of man's most predominant activities, was therefore a sort of no-man's land, not quite within the pale of science.

Even though he could not study it scientifically to any degree, Wundt did go so far as to say that it differed from association in that it followed some logical sequence, while association did not. Wundt believed that any two events or objects could be associated, regardless of whether such an association made sense. For example, if it happened to rain while an individual was buying a new pair of shoes, these two events were associated even though there was no logical tie between them. In contrast, apperceptive (cognitive or perceptual) connections were based on logical considerations, relevance, and appropriateness.

Titchener, also, assumed that cognition was a basic element of psychological function, but he handled the topic with a greater degree of precision. Cognitive activities were composed, he said, of images, a term which suggests something more of the possible character of cognition, or at least of a vehicle by which it might take place.

Like sensations, these images had the attributes of quality, intensity, duration, and clarity, but they differed from sensations in that they were "transparent." By this Titchener meant that images were less objective, more easily destroyed, and did not seem quite so realistic as sensation. To account for the higher mental processes, Titchener turned first to the problem of attention. By asserting that attention was a patterning of conscious activity, he was able to reduce it to the status of an ingredient of conscious content, which for him was the common denominator of psychology. Any element of conscious content could be explained or described through the patterning of the other elements included in the structure of conscious content. In the case of attention, these elements were images. The constellation of other psychic processes in which a particular image stood gave it its meaning; meaning was determined not only by the salient stimulus of a given time, but by the rest of the present content. In this way Titchener managed to equate thought with variations in conscious content, thereby opening the matter of thought images to introspective study. However, having arrived at this solution, Titchener seems to have retained little interest in the problem.

The Structuralists' handling of cognitive function was not as easily dismissed by other students. Most objections had to do with the general neglect of an important area of investigation. One group of European psychologists raised a more technical criticism. According to their observations, *imageless thought* was possible. While they agreed that images did occur in the thought process, they denied that such images were necessary or even typical of thought. Titchener rejected their argument on the grounds that they had not found images in some cases simply because they had not looked hard enough for them. In addition Titchener felt his concept of thought images was broad enough to include such things as *motor sets* or muscular anticipations of future experiences, based on past motor behavior in relation to an object. Titchener adapted this concept from Müller (see Chapter 3), but in Titchener's theory it seems to have taken on an aura of "motor images," which was not to be found so clearly in the original version. He was also willing to grant the existence of something he called "determining tendencies." Given such variety of image prototypes, it seemed to

Titchener that even in those cases where typical images were lacking, it was still possible to find some sort of image phenomenon. He therefore felt justified in retaining images as a basic element.

The subject of memory was not important to the early Structuralists, and neither Wundt nor Titchener ever devoted much attention to the subject. After Ebbinghaus's famous experiments on learning and retention (see Chapter 3), it captured the interest of a few who initiated studies of their own, but it was never of central concern.

Emotion and Motivation

The Structuralist school did not deal with motivation because it was counted among the higher mental processes which Wundt felt could not be investigated by introspection. However, Wundt and Titchener both had a good deal to say about feeling; each of them gave it the status of a basic element, a somewhat more approachable one than apperception or image.

Initially, Wundt conceived of feeling as part of sensation. Eventually, however, he found that not only could he isolate it as a separate element, but he could also define dimensions for it. Initially, he attempted to cover all the qualities of feeling within the single dimension of pleasantness and unpleasantness. As his thinking progressed, he developed a tri-dimensional theory of feeling which included, besides pleasantness/unpleasantness, the qualities of strain/relaxation and excitement/calm. He felt that combinations of these dimensions could account for the various permutations of feeling. This he attempted to prove by measuring breathing, pulse rate, and other bodily processes which correlated with feeling. He hoped to show that alterations in feeling tone were accompanied by alterations in somatic processes, and his studies met with such success that bodily responses have since been incorporated as standard measures of emotionality, such as the psychogalvanic skin response, or the lie detector.

"Affection" was Titchener's term for the emotional elements. He assigned to them the same attributes of quality, intensity, and duration that he had previously assigned to sensations and images. Affection, however, did not have the clarity of the other two elements. It was vague and undifferentiated, except for its hedonistic qualities of pleasantness and unpleasantness. Titchener did not deal with the other dimensions of emotion proposed by Wundt, although his quality of intensity might well have included some aspects of excitement/calm and strained/relaxed dimensions of feeling.

At the time Titchener was developing his theory of emotion, the James-Lange theory of emotion was popular in the United States, as we will see in Chapter 5. The James-Lange theory held that emotion was the perception of the total pattern of bodily sensation at a particular time; this formulation in effect reduced emotion to sensation. Titchener did not believe such a reduction was possible, and protested that feeling or affection was as basic an element as sensation. He agreed that sensation might play some part in affection, for emotion was the result of highly complex patterns of mental content, but it was hardly sufficient as the sole basis of affection.

The Nature of the Learning Process

The Structuralists did not deal with learning *per se*. They discussed the compounding and interaction among mental contents, attributing these to association. Since associations were assumed to be enduring once they had been set up, the concept of association was somewhat equivalent to a learning theory.

The mental chemistry of association could take several forms. In *fusion* each element contributed to the resultant interaction without any one being dominant. For example, one might recall an embarrassing incident that occurred at a party, yet also recall his pleasure with the rest of the evening. In *assimilation* certain elements or contents would be dominant, although influenced by the other contents. For instance, at the party if one's embarrassment had been more severe, he would recall the whole party as painful for himself but fun for his wife. If one's pain were sufficiently intense it could blot out all other associations. The party under such circumstances would be remembered as a complete fiasco. In this recognition that all aspects of experience are modified by association was a vague acceptance by the Structuralist school of what is now referred to as learning.

Behavior and Personality

It is doubtful that they ever conceived of personality or behavior as proper material to be studied by psychologists. It is even doubtful that they ever conceived of personality at all, except as an influence which contaminated introspection. Yet individual differences which could not be avoided must have been very frustrating to a group of scientists whose goal was to accumulate data about "mind" in the most abstract form. Fortunately, these same differences fascinated and intrigued other psychologists and eventually led to new approaches where variations in behavior were admissible problems, not errors to be avoided by the introspecting subject.

Critique

Structuralism assured itself a place in the history of science by establishing psychology as a field of study. Its adherents organized philosophical speculations and physiological findings into an integrated theory of mental processes and proceeded to use this theory as a guide in research. They established the first psychological laboratory, and made major contributions to methodology. They developed the classical method of introspection, improved upon the existing psychophysical techniques, and evolved measures of reaction time, breathing rate, etc., which have come into general use in psychology. While they did not invent these techniques, they were the first to employ them as tools for laboratory investigation of psychological material, and they gave the early training to many psychologists who went on to have productive careers. Like all theoretical systems, Structuralism had many faults. Many crimes imputed to the Structuralists may well be the result of their efforts to establish psychology as a science. For example, they imposed and enforced very narrow limits on acceptability, both as to content and technique. This rigidity was necessary to set standards, but in the hands of the Structuralists it became so extreme that it hindered further progress. Their approach soon became sterile, because the facts it produced could not be generalized and because it failed to stimulate or support expansive research, confining psychology to one particular area. As a result, research became a matter of repeating what somebody else had done, or studying ever-finer details, and neglected important problems because they were not considered "scientific."

It has also been pointed out that the Structuralists were unrealistic in their demand that experience be studied by one or two methods only. The restriction to pure science and, concomitantly, the prohibition against any practical application of psychological findings were equally unproductive. We now know that knowledge gained can be used for social welfare, and the application of such knowledge will hardly degrade the science. In fact, there is evidence that when great practical demands are made upon a science more progress is made in pure science than when such impetus is lacking and the investigator works completely at the academic level. In any event, Structuralism's narrowness caused it to die an early death, strangled by its own limitations.

SUMMARY

Basic Unit. The elements of conscious experience were taken to be sensation, feeling, and apperception.

Field of Study. The concern of the Structural Psychologists was the analysis of experience into its elements, analysis of the manner of connection among elements, and discovery of the laws governing such connections.

Methods of Investigation. Psychophysical techniques and classical introspection were employed.

Principles. Wundt held that mind was not a substance, but a dynamic lawful sequence of processes. The various elements combined and interacted with each other and with the background of stimulation, possibly complementing each other through contrast. In addition to the principles developed by Wundt, the Weber-Fechner law of the "just noticeable difference," and Müller's law of motor set asserted that past experiences with a given stimulus would result in a set of expectations regarding future experience with similar stimuli.

Consciousness. The question of the relationship between mind and body was closely associated with the theoretical treatment of consciousness. Fechner saw both as aspects of the same organization, but Wundt and Titchener believed that mind and body were separate entities and their research sought to discover the nature of mind in the patterning of the elements of consciousness.

Sensation, Perception, and Discrimination. For Fechner, sensation was an intervening variable between stimulus and reaction, although he did not call it that. To Wundt, stimulus and sensation were one and the same, constituting one of the basic elements of consciousness. Perception was partly included in the process of apperception, which was defined as the appreciation of cognitive signs. The aspects of perception which involved interpretation and meaning, however, were higher mental processes. Awkward as it might be to neglect these, Wundt preferred to leave them beyond the pale so far as Structuralism was concerned. Titchener held that sensation was the element from which perception was built, thereby reducing perception to the role of patterning conscious content.

Thinking, Cognition, and Memory. Thinking was a higher mental process, and not really a matter for psychology from Wundt's point of view, except insofar as the process of apperception was cognitive as well as perceptual. Titchener, on the other hand, believed that thinking involved elements he called images and attempted to reduce it to a matter of conscious content.

Emotion and Motivation. Wundt believed that feeling had three qualitative dimensions: pleasant/unpleasant, strain/relaxation, and excitement/calm. Titchener discussed only one, the dimension of pleasantness, but included attributes of quality, intensity, and duration which seem to subsume Wundt's other dimensions. Motivation was not considered.

The Nature of the Learning Process. Learning *per se* was not explored, but much attention was given to association as the means by which enduring connections between mental elements were established.

Behavior and Personality. These were beyond the scope considered by Structuralism.

REFERENCES

G. T. Fechner

Fechner, G. T., *Elemente der Psychopysik*. Leipzig: Breitkopf & Hartel, 1860.

G. E. Müller

Müller, G. E., "Theorie der Muskelcontraction," *Nachtrichten Gesellsch: Wis. Cöttingen,* 1899, pp. 132–179. Cf., E.C.A. *Amer. J. Psych.*, 2: 490–492 (1889).

E. B. Titchener

Titchener, E. B., *An Outline of Psychology*. New York: Macmillan, 1896.

———, *A Primer of Psychology*. New York: Macmillan, 1898.

———, *Experimental Psychology: A Manual of Laboratory Practice. Qualitative: (i) Students' Manual, (ii) Instructors' Manual*, New York: Macmillan, 1901.

———, *Experimental Psychology: A Manual of Laboratory Practice. Quantitative: (i) Students' Manual, (ii) Instructors' Manual*, New York: Macmillan, 1905.

———, *Lectures on Elementary Psychology of Feeling and Attention.* New York: Macmillan, 1908.

———, *Lectures on Experimental Psychology of the Thought Processes*. New York: Macmillan, 1909. (A)

———, *A Textbook of Psychology*. New York: Macmillan, 1909. (B)

———, *A Beginner's Psychology*. New York: Macmillan, 1915.

———, "Relearning After Forty-Six Years," *Amer. J. Psychol.* 34:468–469 (1923).

———, *Systematic Psychology: Prolegomena*. New York: Macmillan, 1929.

E. H. Weber

Weber, E. H., "Der Tastsinn und das Gemeingefuhl," in R. Wagner, *Handworterbuch der Physiologie* III, ii, 481–588 (1846).

W. Wundt

Wundt, W., *Breitrage zur Theorie der Sinneswahrnehmung*. Leipzig: C. F. Winter'sche, 1862.

———, *Grundzuge der Physiologischen Psychologie*. Leipzig: Engelmann, 1874.

———, "Uber Psychologische Methoden," *Philos. Studien.* 1: 1–38 (1883).

———, *Grundriss der Psychologie.* Leipzig: Engelmann, 1896. Trans. C. H. Judd, 1896.

CHAPTER 5

THE THEORY OF WILLIAM JAMES (1890–1922)

THE principles formulated by William James constitute a major contribution to psychology. Yet, James had no intention of establishing a school, and this may account for the fact that, while he attracted a few ardent followers, his work did not incite the almost religious fervor characteristic of many other schools of thought. In any event, the significance of James's contribution to psychology demonstrates that the scientific importance of a theory does not depend on its ability to attract disciples, or to activate a movement. James's ideas contained the seeds of many theories. More important, viewed in historical perspective, his work seems to have facilitated the transition from Structuralism to other conceptualizations of the nature of behavior and experience. To quote Heidbreder[1], "Whereas Titchener was intent chiefly on making the new psychology a science, James was more concerned that the new science be *psychology*."

James, like Wundt, did not start out as a psychologist. However, unlike Wundt, who had his roots in philosophy, James became interested in psychology while he was teaching biology at Harvard, and set aside space in his laboratory for psychological research several years before Wundt had established the first formal laboratory in Leipzig. Although he provided the laboratory facilities, and inspired others to use them, he himself did little experimental work. Instead, most of his theory was derived from introspection, observation, and cautious speculation.

James did not subscribe to any particular doctrine; his thinking developed side by side with that of other theorists, and he felt free to borrow from them, to include or exclude their concepts, depending upon the scientific appeal a particular suggestion held for him. His flexibility led not only to eclecticism in his own theory, but also to critical evaluation of contemporary theories, and he thereby stimulated the development of other psychological concepts.

[1]Heidbreder, Edna, *Seven Psychologies*. New York: Appleton-Century-Crofts, 1933, p. 152.

Beyond eschewing a dogmatic approach, James wished to broaden the scope of psychology, and advocated investigation of many problems which the Structuralists had considered of doubtful scientific value, such as certain subjective phenomena of experience, mind, spiritualism, and religion. However, as he himself delved deeper into these matters, he became less concerned with their scientific implications and more involved with their philosophical aspects, until he became so occupied with the latter that he removed himself altogether from the field of psychology. This shift in interest was so drastic that by the end of his life he was calling psychology a "nasty little science."[2]

Despite the fact that James's interest in psychology was short-lived, his coverage of the subject matter was thorough. Moreover, almost all of the problems he considered at one time or another are still of current interest. It is unfortunate for the science that his changing emphasis did not allow him much time for the organization or integration of his findings.

Basic Unit

James did not believe psychology could be broken down into elements, and therefore proposed no basic unit. He was convinced, however, that if it were ever to be considered valid, psychological theory would have to take into account certain basic factors. The first of these was the thinker, the experiencing person. It was this individual who made consciousness a personal, idiosyncratic matter. The second more ordinary factor was experiencing, *per se*, and the third was the thought's object, the reality of the external world surrounding the person. James believed that the subject's interpretation of this physical reality, i.e., the relationship between *physical* and *psychological* reality should be the primary concern of any psychological study.

Field of Study

Psychology was therefore, the science of mental life, including the fundamental biological and neurological processes and the individual's personal experience. The proper starting point for psychological investigation was the totality of experience, the *stream of consciousness*, as James called it. By this he meant experience in the phenomenal sense, including events and their meanings, not merely sensations removed from context. James held that the basic elements proposed by the Structuralists were artifacts, the manufactured products of psychological sophistication. "Ideas," "sensations," or "feelings," were abstractions. They were points in the stream of consciousness which the psychologist had isolated to give himself some foothold in the ambiguous territory of the mind; they existed only in the theories formulated by psychologists and not as actual entities.

[2] *Ibid.*, p. 155.

In addition to redefining the subject matter, James expanded the categories of experiencing subjects appropriate for psychological study. While the Structuralists had confined themselves to human adults, he included as appropriate subjects for psychological investigation children, primitive groups, the insane, and animals.

Principles

James established the principle that there must be a physiological substructure underlying all psychological processes, and he formulated a description of the now generally accepted process of neural transmission. A second physiological principle held that the structure of the nervous system was actually modified by psychological experience. He proposed that these modifications took the form of alterations in the connecting pathways, and were manifested ultimately as changes in behavior. James also asserted that psychological processes had biological utility, that is, they produced, guided, and sustained actions which satisfied various biological needs. Given this biological utility, man was not always capable of rational behavior; he was often driven by need rather than reason. He was, however, capable of exercising free will, i.e., he had the capacity to determine his own fate and was not predestined to be the victim of forces or events over which he had no control.

James's contribution to what is now called the James-Lange theory of emotion will be discussed in detail below. Briefly, James conceived of emotion as the perception of physiological changes which were evoked by exciting, frightening, frustrating, or pleasurable experiences.

Methods of Investigation

James either applied introspection to his own experience or collected introspective reports from other persons to work out his theories. However, since he attempted to report a fleeting event in its natural setting, his technique was more interpretive and less objective than the classic introspection method of the Structuralists. Indeed, James recognized that the procedure he employed was often inaccurate and not in itself an adequate methodology. He urged that experimental methods and controls be used when feasible. While he was aware that controlled experiments were difficult and often futile, especially in his own special area of interest, the flow of experience, he felt that such experiments were well worth the effort.

James also believed comparative studies to be a fruitful source of scientific data and for this reason, he was interested in a variety of different human and animal subjects. By contrasting these data with the behavior of normal civilized adults, he felt one could demonstrate how mental life was altered as a function of phylogenetic and developmental variations. He noted at the same time that such material could be misleading unless the investigator made sure that the differences he noted were due to his subject's phylogenetic or developmental status and not to some extraneous condition, such as environment.

In addition to specific methodology, James was concerned with the more general problems involved in psychological studies, and discussed a number of pitfalls which might threaten the accuracy of a theory or an experiment. One of these was the use of language. James anticipated many current writers in recognizing that language can be highly misleading when it is applied to scientific matters, and stressed the need for the precise definition of terms where common sense meanings frequently differed from technical connotations.

James also warned against what he called the *psychologist's fallacy*. The psychologist, he said, tended to forget or overlook the fact that introspection, or observation, in itself, altered the conditions of mental life. The very process of studying mental experience produced a unique and unnatural situation. The psychologist must be aware of this, and allow for such phenomena, otherwise his conclusions might be distorted. For example, just as one behaves differently when he is alone from when he is with others, the subject who participates in psychological research feels and acts differently. Perhaps this is just because he knows he is being watched; perhaps this variation in behavior is the result of his preoccupation with what is being done to him, what his responses mean, and how he can help or hinder the experimenter.

Partly as a comment on Structuralist methods and interpretations, and partly as a general warning, James pointed up still another caveat. The stimulus perceived by an organism might bear no resemblance at all to the real stimulus. Matters of organization, interpretation, and distortion, both mechanical and personal, alter perception. With respect to visual stimulus, for example, a particular stimulus is perceived against a certain background, at a certain distance, from a certain angle, in a certain perspective, and in the framework of past experiences. Each of these factors interacts with the effects of the stimulus *per se* to influence the final percept in some way. The study of these factors was therefore as important as the study of the stimulus itself.

Consciousness

With respect to the mind-body problem, James maintained that there is a complete correspondence between the sequence of states of consciousness and the sequence of states within the brain. Thus, he conceived of both consciousness and brain processes as natural biological phenomena, to be studied on either a biological or a psychological level. Psychology as a natural science should note and accept whatever relationships it found without feeling obliged to account for their existence. In a way, James suggested that there was a difference between mind and body, a difference which need not concern the psychologist. Instead, the science should content itself with the fact that both these phenomena occurred in nature, and that both could be studied.

The relationship between mind and body concerned James more than these statements would indicate, and he turned a great deal of his philosophical interest in this direction. One suspects that in the later investigations James's approach was somewhat metaphysical, but he tried to affect all the objectivity of which he was capable.

By this point it is evident that, to a great extent, his interest in psychology focused on the nature of consciousness. Opposed to the Structuralists' view that it consisted of discrete fragments which had been joined together, James described it as a continuous, flowing current, characterized by a private, personal, dynamic quality. Despite this dynamic, changing quality, consciousness had continuity from one moment to the next, and made smooth gradation, or transition, from one activity to another. It also had the property of choice, because the individual could choose to be conscious of one thing rather than something else. This position probably grew out of his concept of free will and rationality, and was undoubtedly influenced by his religious beliefs. Whatever its origin, James's views on consciousness were reflected in his comments on every aspect of psychological functioning which claimed his interest.

Sensation, Perception, and Discrimination

James felt that each sense organ was selective, that it only responded to a particular variety of stimulation, within a certain range. To him, sensation was the first phase in the biological functioning of the brain, that aspect of the neural process most immediately following appropriate stimulation at the periphery—that is, at the sense organs. An appropriate stimulus contacting a sensory organ initiated a current or impulse in a nerve cell. This impulse then travelled through the sensory nerves to the central nervous system, where it was transmitted along connecting pathways of varying degrees of complexity, until it reached the motor nerves and was carried out to the muscles where it triggered off activity in the muscle cells.

James defined perception as an elaboration of the sensory processes within the central nervous system. As the term "elaboration" implies, he did not conceive of perception as the mere photographic reproduction of images; it involved selections, additions, subtractions, adaptations, constancies, and interpretations, which stemmed from both biological and psychological determinants. Perception as such was not a volitional act; rather, it was influenced by the sum of the subject's conscious experience, past and present. This concept, of course, was not entirely original.

Both the Structuralists and the Associationists had hypothesized interaction among the contents of consciousness. They had not, however, put the same emphasis upon past experience, nor did they describe the interaction in such detail. They only suggested the elements of consciousness which might take part in the interaction and felt that these complex relationships were really the property of unspecified "higher mental processes."

Thinking, Cognition, and Memory

Whereas the Structuralists had contended that thinking and other cognitive phenomena were beyond the scope of psychology, James investigated both their mental and biological aspects, and opened up a new area for scientific study. This achievement seems all the more remarkable because for the most part, James effected this scientific breakthrough without the use of experimental techniques. Briefly, he maintained that believing, reasoning, and other similar processes were the result of further elaboration of sensory processes within the central nervous system, i.e., that thought was a biological process.

To attempt to break down these elaborations into "ideas," "images," "feelings," etc., to facilitate psychological understanding was to impose an artifice. Such a breakdown isolated sections of experience and fixed them with names, so that they became rigid and immutable. Given James's concept of the stream of consciousness, this breakdown constituted a distortion of the higher mental activities which were dynamic in nature, changing from moment to moment.

One of the origins of the dynamic nature of thinking was its biological utility. It could aid the individual in his efforts to adjust to his environment, guide his behavior toward goals which could satisfy his needs, anticipate the difficulties, both physical and emotional, which he might encounter, and produce solutions to these difficulties. To say that thought had utility seemed to many to violate its rational qualities. While we may presently find it possible to view utility at least as a rational direction of impulses toward certain desired goals, neither James nor his immediate contemporaries seem to have been able to solve the apparent opposition of terms. The question of utility can still complicate the prediction of thought processes, even when it is stated to be a rational direction of impulse. For example, depending on the individual's need, he might conceive of paper as a writing material, a fuel, a map, or a hydrocarbon.

Aside from questions of the origin of its dynamic qualities, it was still possible to define many dynamic qualities of thought. Thinking ordinarily involved two separate sequences of events. The first of these James referred to as sagacity or insight, and defined it as a sort of creative ability involving the capacity for perspective and the ability to extract the essential attributes of a given problem from unimportant minutiae. Once the problem was sagaciously structured, the sequence proceeded, beginning with the arousal of previously learned associations, and followed by application of these associations to some decision or choice of solution.

There was a common belief at the time James was developing his ideas that "mental powers" could be built up through exercise (the term mental powers encompassed both memory and problem-solving ability without distinction). Indeed, mental exercise was assumed to have much the same effect on the mind that weight lifting had on the muscles. In one of his few experiments, James disproved this hypothesis. First he measured the amount of time required by a group of subjects to learn a set of verses written by one poet, and then gave them intensive practice in memorizing verses by another. After this training, the subjects were required to learn another set of verses by the original poet, and their speed of learning did not significantly improve. James concluded that mind could not be built up through exercise. Tricks or systems could help one remember, but these had no effect on basic ability.

James's concern with cognitive phenomena was broad enough to include many items which had previously been neglected. Among these was the matter of beliefs. James asserted that beliefs were more closely related to emotions than to thought and reasoning. He saw them as the determinants of psychological reality because they were coercive, forcing the believer to perceive the world according to his belief. The emotional element inherent in a belief arose from its being a function of a need or instinct. Anything that threatened the belief threatened the gratification of the need or instinct, and consequently aroused emotion. The object and the content of a belief were selected in accordance with the individual's past experience with objects in relation to vital needs. This relationship between needs, emotions, and beliefs led James to see the latter as a crucial aspect of the self. Beliefs will be discussed in connection with James's theory of personality.

Emotion and Motivation

We have referred frequently to James's concept of free will. It also has great importance in relation to his theory of motivation. In brief, he rejected the image of man as the helpless victim of the whims of fate or forces over which he had no control. Man, on the contrary, could decide his own goals and determine his own actions. At the same time, James suggested that man's behavior was governed by irrational instinct. This inconsistency may possibly be attributed to the conflict between James's religious and philosophical beliefs and his psychological theory. Moreover, he failed to provide a precise definition of free will which, presumably, would have helped to reduce the incompatibility. Insofar as he meant the term to imply that man's destiny was not predetermined by God or supernatural forces, it was a progressive and scientific concept. But he neglected to delineate the biological and social determinants of free will, suggesting that man could decide his actions at each moment of life, and was therefore morally responsible for *all* his behavior. In this sense it became almost as misleading as the religious doctrine of determinism.

Instincts were not built-in patterns of action, blind and invariable; James used the term to emphasize that man was a biological being, and also to connote certain consistencies in behavior which occurred in most, if not all, normal human beings. For example, the human male prefers female humans to female lions, he likes steak better than hay, he smiles when he is pleased, he cries when hurt, and will strike out automatically to defend himself. While instincts could account for consistencies in behavior, James was unwilling to assume that they were the prime movers. Before we consider the other motivating conditions which concerned him, however, we should first consider his theory of emotion.

James was particularly impressed by the physiological findings regarding the function of emotion, which had been proposed by C. G. Lange, a Danish physiologist. James went so far as to develop a new theory of emotion, using Lange's physiological data. Previous concepts, which had been based on common sense, had postulated that the first phase in an emotion-producing situation was the perception of the situation. The feeling of emotion followed the perception, and the emotion produced action. For example, a person sees a bear (perception), becomes afraid (emotion), and runs (action). James and Lange (1922), however, conceived of this situation somewhat differently and gave a far more behavioristic, less teleological explanation for this phenomenon than did the common sense theory.[3] In brief, they believed that a person would first perceive an emotion producing situation, act, and *then* interpret behavioral and physiological responses to be a particular emotion. The person who saw the bear would run, perceive himself running, and then become aware of the fact that he was afraid. Emotion was identified in terms of alterations in vasomotor sensation, and each emotion was related to its own peculiar pattern of vasomotor change.

These same vasomotor changes probably motivated behavior as well, and like emotions, each motive was correlated with a different pattern. James did not, however, make the next logical step, and assume that emotion and motivation were part and parcel of the same process. He seemed to view motives as separate from both emotions and instincts in some way which he did not specifically state.

The Nature of the Learning Process

James felt learning to be the result of a modification within the nervous

[3]The behavioristic orientation is discussed in detail in Chapter 9; the implications of teleology for the scientific process are discussed in Chapter 2.

system, such that one occurrence of a particular act would facilitate its recurrence. Repetition of experience was sufficient in itself to insure these physiological alterations, because repetition tended to associate a single act, thought, or emotion with others concurrent to it. In the psychological sense, repeated association could be thought of as establishing connections between experiences, and in the physiological sense, between *neural processes*.

The fact that James's theory of learning can be stated so concisely should not imply that it was trivial. On the contrary, it was a highly significant first attempt to give a biological interpretation to learning; the general hypotheses he proposed are still accepted today by most learning theorists.

Behavior and Personality

Perhaps James's greatest contribution in the area of behavior and personality is his theory of self, in which much current work on self-concept has its roots.

To James, man's "self" had three aspects. The first of these, his *material self*, included in addition to the body, the clothes, house, property, and all other material possessions. Normally, when he prospered in material wealth, the individual was elated, and conversely, a decline in his fortunes usually precipitated depression. Thus, the relative status, quantity, and quality of the objects surrounding the individual became an integral part of his personal identity, and played an influential role in its development.

James called the second aspect the *social self*, although the term should have been pluralized, since the individual was said to have many social selves. He felt that the individual presented a different self to each person who knew and reacted to him; he was perceived and in turn treated differently by each of his friends, however slight these differences might be. The individual correspondingly felt and behaved differently toward each person in his "social circle." James further suggested that the people in each individual's social circle fell into groups, and that the social self might therefore more properly be referred to as the "social group self," for instance the family self, the professional self, the religious self, and so forth. The sense of success or failure which pervaded the social self reflected the individual's perception of the way other people behaved toward him. Changes in one's ability to fill a specified role resulted in greater comfort—or discomfort—with one's self. If a particular self-concept became excessively painful or difficult to maintain because it was unrealistic, it had to be eliminated or at the least modified. Almost invariably, such modification would precipitate some degree of emotional disturbance.

James's social self was similar to George Mead's concept (1934) of the *generalized other* and to Cooley's *looking glass self* (1900). All three suggested that the individual's estimate of his own worth was a reflection of what the significant people in his environment thought of him (or what he *believed* they thought of him). All three also suggested that the self presented by the individual was often indistinguishable from the social role which had been assigned to him in that setting. In fact, the individual's perception of what other people thought of him, and expected from him, was often formalized into a prescription for behavior, a role he must adopt. This role defined how he should think and act, and enabled others to react to him in standard, automatic ways.

The third aspect of the self delineated by James was the *spiritual self*. This denoted the individual's intellectual capacities, his sensibilities, his will—all of the faculties of his mind in combination. The spiritual self was what the individual thought of as his true self, as "me."

The three aspects of the self, in some dynamic interaction, combined to form the empirical self. The self-evaluations and self-attitudes originating from these diverse sources might or might not be compatible. Where only minor contradictions were present, the empirical self would be integrated sufficiently to permit adequate social adjustment. Where major inconsistencies were present, problems could be expected. For example, an individual might be quite mediocre physically and mentally (material self), but find himself in a social setting where athletic prowess was expected of or attributed to him (social self), while his own personal needs moved him toward intellectual persuits (spiritual self). Under such conditions, the person could not be what he actually was, what others expected, or what he himself wished to be. In view of the conflict-inducing potential of discrepancies among various aspects of the self, the individual's mental health status provided an accurate index of the degree of unity among his three selves. The greater the unity, the healthier the individual would be; the more disunity, the poorer his adjustment. Conflict could reach proportions severe enough to result in dissociation, or in multiple personalities.

Critique

James's theory was tentative, incomplete, and included many inconsistencies. Although the deficiencies cannot be minimized, it was never James's intention to create a definitive theoretical system. His efforts were restricted to concepts which pertained to areas of psychological function which interested him, or to the reformulation of others' concepts which he believed to be incorrect. At times James tended to neglect scientific pursuits in order to follow his philosophical and religious interests, and this may account for some of the contradictions and inconsistencies. Whatever their cause, one cannot dismiss the contradictions lightly. It is difficult to accept a theory which ascribes many aspects of psychological function to instinct and biological utility on one hand, and yet gives equal emphasis to the significance of free will. It is difficult to conceive of consciousness as an *irreducible* process, composed of associations between various *aspects*. The concept of a spiritual self made up of sensibilities, will and mental faculties also raises a number of questions. James seems to have thought of mind and body as separate entities; yet they were equated in a manner that is left to the imagination. On the one hand, James emphasized the importance of meaning and definition of words, and yet we find vagueness, ambiguity, and a number of undefined concepts in his work.

Nevertheless there is little doubt that James's theory "set the scene" for American psychology. Today, many of his concepts occupy focal positions in the most forward-looking contemporary research. The concept of self has become a tremendously important topic of research. The hypotheses concerning the biological basis of psychological phenomena both supported early efforts to establish psychology as a science, and provided a firm foundation for experimentation in this area. The James-Lange theory of emotion itself has stimulated considerable study of emotion and motivation.

This theory has been the subject of controversy ever since its inception. For one thing, James made emotion part of the pattern of motivation and action. The Structuralists (Titchener in particular) attacked his approach, saying that emotion was an irreducible element. The theory was also opposed by other psychologists sometimes on purely theoretical grounds, sometimes because it was not in keeping with introspective evidence. However, the most effective attempts to disprove the James-Lange theory came from the studies of physiologists. C. G. Sherrington (1906) severed the spinal tracts of dogs, rendering them incapable of any sort of motor response. Under these conditions he still found physiological and behavioral evidence of emotion. This contradicted the James-Lange hypothesis that action takes place prior to the appearance of emotion. In similar experiments, W. B. Cannon (1927; 1929) found fear and rage responses in animals even after he had removed portions of the autonomic nervous system, which James had contended produced the patterns of vasomotor activity interpreted as emotion. In another study, even more damaging to the James-Lange theory, Cannon found that the same pattern of physiological response seemed to characterize every different emotion. Contrary to James's prediction, Cannon was unable to identify a single physiological response specific to its own emotional state.

As evidence continues to mount, it appears more and more likely that the James-Lange theory was in error, or at least that some modification is indicated, if it is to become scientifically acceptable. Yet, despite its questionable accuracy, and precisely because it is so controversial, this theory has probably stimulated more research, and led to more theoretical progress than any other single concept in the area of emotion and motivation.

SUMMARY

Basic Unit. For James personal experiences could not be broken down into elements, but any study of them had to take into account three aspects: the experiencing person, the experience itself, and the physical reality of the situation producing the experience.

Field of Study. Mental life as a biological process and as a dynamic stream of conscious experience was the proper concern of psychology. It could be studied not only in human adults, but also in children, primitives, the insane, and animals.

Principles. All psychological processes had a physiological basis, traceable within the nervous system from sensory organs, through the brain, to motor responses. The physiological substructure *per se* was modified by experience in a way that produced changes in behavior. Psychological processes, since they had biological utility, were therefore irrational, subject to need and not to reason. Emotions were understood as perceptions of the physiological changes which accompanied the experience of emotion. Man did, however, have free will; he could decide his own fate.

Methods of Investigation. Introspection and observation were the methods James ordinarily employed to derive or demonstrate his concepts. He was impressed with the value of experimental procedures although he recognized the difficulties involved in applying such procedures to the complex data of psychology and rarely used them himself. He dealt at length with the problems of methodology, warning of the necessity for careful definition of terms which had both a popular and a technical meaning. He further warned that the very process of observing and experimenting with mental life altered it from its natural state. Still further, he warned of the complexity of sensation and perception, of their multiple determinants which many psychologists had tended to neglect.

Consciousness. Mind and body were both natural phenomena and could therefore be studied by scientific means. Psychologists need not concern themselves with the nature of the correspondence between the two. Consciousness was a continuous, private, dynamic process which could not be analyzed into elements but must be understood as it was. The content of consciousness was a matter of choice; the individual selected which aspect of experience to be aware of. The course of consciousness over time was a gradual transition from one selected focus to the next.

Sensation, Perception, Discrimination. Sensation was the first phase of neural activity induced by stimulation. Perception was an elaboration produced by interaction of central processes leading to recognition and interpretation; it was determined biologically and was not subject to free will, i.e. it was not a matter of choice or selection.

Thinking, Cognition, and Memory. Cognitive processes were further elaborations on sensory events. Thoughts, ideas, etc., were abstractions, man-made conveniences to aid in conceiving of consciousness. These elements did not exist as phenomena. Thinking was a biological process directed by biological need, and as such was irrational. It was a matter of acquiring insight into appropriate relationships within the problem situation, then utilizing relevant associations based on past experience to solve the problem. The capacity for recalling associations could not be built up through exercise as earlier theorists had proposed. Beliefs were emotionally tinged convictions representing psychological reality; they were established on the basis of biological need and resisted refutation, since their continued existence served to gratify the need.

Emotion and Motivation. Man's behavior was directed by his own free will, but was determined by his biological heritage in the form of instincts. Instincts accounted for the consistency of action observed within phylogenetic classes. Motivation and emotion were closely related; the James-Lange theory proposed that emotions were the perception of behavior caused by vasomotor reactions to external events. These same reactions were presumably the basis of motivation. Research concerning this theory has raised serious questions about it, showing that motor activity was not necessary for emotional experience, that emotion could occur when the autonomic nervous system which produced vasomotor reactions was impaired, and that vasomotor reactions were the same no matter what emotion was involved.

The Nature of the Learning Process. Learning was an association of experiences through repetitious exposure. The nervous system was altered by the repetition, so that the occurrence of one experience facilitated its recurrence.

Behavior and Personality. James's greatest contribution to the theory of personality was his concept of self. The self was made up of three aspects: material aspects of identity, social roles, and spiritual-intellectual-personal concerns. These aspects had to be in harmony if the individual were to function. If they were in conflict the person, incapable of playing more than one role at a time, developed some maladjustment.

REFERENCES

William James

James, W., *Principles of Psychology*. Holt: New York, 1890.

———, *Textbook of Psychology: Briefer Course*. New York: Holt, 1892.

———, "Does Consciousness Exist?" in *Essays in Radical Empiricism*, New York: Longmans, Green & Co., 1912, pp. 1–38.

Other Theories of the Self

Cooley, C. H., *Human Nature and the Social Order*. New York: Scribner's, 1900.

Mead, G. H., *Mind, Self, and Society*. Chicago: University of Chicago Press, 1934.

James-Lange Theory

James, W., and C. G. Lange, *The Emotions*. Baltimore: Williams & Wilkins, 1922.

Cannon, W. B., "The James-Lange Theory of Emotions: A Critical Examination and an Alternative Theory," *Amer. J. Psychol.* 39, pp. 106–124 (1927).

———, *Bodily Changes in Pain, Hunger, Fear, and Rage*. New York: Appleton, 1929.

Sherrington, C. G., *The Integrative Action of the Nervous System*. New York: Scribner's, 1906, pp. 255–268.

CHAPTER 6

FUNCTIONALISM (1896–1938)

LIKE James, the Functionalists had no intention of developing a new system of thought. Their theories grew out of their desire to "clear the air" of certain presumed misconceptions fostered by the Structuralists, and thereby to remove the straitjacket which the tenets of that school had imposed upon psychology. The Functionalist movement, which originated at the University of Chicago in the last decade of the nineteenth century, was characterized by a common philosophy and set of values which drew together a group of men with diverse professional interests. No single member of the group can be considered the originator of the system, nor was there a formal codification of theory. The principles which brought the group together were transmitted from generation to generation rather unsystematically by such means as lectures, addresses, and journal articles, and were developed by each successive generation.

Discontent with the theories of Wundt and Titchener was immediately responsible for the organization of the Functionalist movement, and, as we have already noted, this had been expressed some time previously by James and his contemporaries. The latter, however, were less concerned with the restrictions of the Structuralist movement, and were willing to compromise. On the other hand John Dewey, the first spokesman of Functionalism, stated definitively that psychology could no longer exist as a productive science within the narrow bounds of Structuralism. While he did not necessarily want to replace Structuralism, he certainly wished to change it.

Essentially, Dewey was a philosopher and educator, but he had a vital interest in psychology as well, and his journal article of 1896 on the nature of the stimulus-response sequence (the reflex arc, as he called it) marked the birth of the new American psychology. In 1900, shortly after its publication, Dewey was elected president of the American Psychological Association.

Dewey's colleagues at the University of Chicago, James R. Angell, the director of the new Psychology Department, and G. H. Mead and A. W. Moore, both philosophers, were equally important in developing the Functionalist approach. Angell, the second spokesman for the group, emphasized that the principles of Functionalism were not meant to be a *new* psychological approach. Rather, they had always been part of the science, and it was Structuralism which had set itself apart from the main trend. Angell's stated purpose was therefore to direct psychology back to its original orientation.

Mead and Moore had a somewhat different approach, and sought to expand and apply the basic propositions to derive new concepts (Mead, 1903; 1934). These four men and their co-workers were typical of many of the American and European psychologists who wished to extend their study of mental processes beyond the content of the mind. Specifically, they were interested in the mental processes which enabled the organism to adjust to its environment. The Functionalists' concept of mental phenomena as physiological processes with psychological functions bore some resemblance to James's concept of biological utility. However, in contrast to James's policy of passive resistance, the Functionalists became the standard bearers of the growing opposition to Structuralism. Their efforts extended beyond theoretical reform to methodological reform as well, for their new principles required new methods better suited to complexity. Introspection was supplanted by a more catholic methodology.

Partly because of their "radical" views, and partly as a reaction to Titchener's stubborn refusal to recognize the validity of any criticism of Structuralism, Functionalism became a system in spite of efforts to the contrary. The original intent had been merely to counteract the undesirable trends within Structuralism, not to replace the entire system. However, their remedial efforts were so far-reaching that very few of the concepts which the Structuralists considered crucial to their system were left intact. Dewey and Angell soon gained support from American and European psychologists who closed ranks behind them and categorically rejected Structuralism. When it appeared that efforts to resolve the controversy had reached an impasse, Titchener forced the issue.

Possibly in anticipation of the conflict, James had drawn a distinction between a structural psychology which was concerned solely with mental content, and a functional psychology such as he propounded dedicated to the investigation of the nature of mental operations and their biological utility. Titchener returned to this distinction (1898, 1899) and applied it to his differences with the Chicago school. In brief, he contended that while the Structuralist studied "is," the Functionalist studied "is-for." The Functionalist orientation could not be accepted as "part" of psychology under any circumstances since the only subject matter appropriate for psychology was "the world with man left in it."[1] Presumably, by this statement Titchener meant to underscore the contrast between the physical scientist's view of the world and the psychologist's, the former observing

[1] Heidbreder, Edna, *Seven Psychologies*, New York: Appleton-Century-Crofts, 1933, p. 230.

the world directly, the latter observing man's experiences of it. Actually, Titchener's method of introspection revealed a view of the world far removed from human existence. It is largely due to the efforts of the Functionalists that present day American psychology can be said to deal with "man left in the world."[2]

Angell's 1906 presidential address to the American Psychological Association might be called the Declaration of Independence and Constitution of the Functionalist school. He defined the three basic concepts and demonstrated how each of them was intended to correct deficiencies in the Structuralist approach. First, Functionalism was defined as the psychology of mental operations, in contrast to the psychology of elements. Second, it was concerned with the utility of mind, especially consciousness, as a means of mediating between the needs of the organism and its environment. Third, the school addressed itself not only to consciousness, but also to automatic and other unconscious behavior.

Functionalism developed these basic tenets, changing gradually from a resistance movement into a mature theoretical system. The desire to test and expand its principles grew as the need to defend them declined, leaving to the later Functionalists the task of translating abstract principles into research problems for laboratory investigation. Principal among these investigators was Harvey Carr, whose work typifies so-called Current Functionalist theory.

Basic Unit

The reflex arc, or stimulus-response sequence proposed by Dewey, was the basic unit of Functionalist theory. However, the ordinary concept of a reflex as an event involving stimulus and response was too limited to convey Dewey's idea. What he had in mind was a series of such events coordinated into a complex act. The response to one stimulus became stimulus to the next response, and so forth, until the act was complete. In walking, for example, the movement of the right leg creates certain sensations which stimulate the movement of the left leg; the subsequent sensations in the left leg stimulate the right leg to move again. This sequence continues until the activity is terminated. According to this formulation, any single S-R event was an artifice, a part of a complex chain abstracted from it for conceptual convenience. Likewise, activity could not adequately be conceived of as sensation, followed by idea, followed by movement. The entire process was an integrated unit, and the source of its unity lay in its function. The stimulus was the phase of a behavioral event which presented the conditions the organism must meet. The response was that phase which met the conditions and resolved them. The distinction resided not in actual differences between S and R, but in their respective roles in the total

[2] *Ibid.*

process. It was the synthesis of atomic bits into molar acts which constituted the Functionalists basic unit.

Field of Study

The contribution of Angell and Carr was the definition of a field of study appropriate to Dewey's emphasis on stimulus-response sequence, and they attempted to apply psychology within the limits established by his reflex arc concept. Angell contended that psychology should be devoted to the study of mental operations and more particularly to the *utility* of these mental operations in mediating between the needs of the organism and the forces of its environment. Dewey's speculations enabled Angell to spell out how the mental operations occurred and how they produced their functional effect.

Carr defined psychology as the study of mental activity, which for him was the generic term for perception, memory, imagination, feeling, judgment, and will. However, he was more interested in the *sequence* of mental activity, that is, in the acquisition, fixation, retention, organization, and evaluation of experiences, and their use as guides to conduct.

The Functionalist system, then, was concentrated upon behavior which was adaptive or adjustive; that it was consciously directed was of lesser import. Habitual, automatic behaviors were recognized as equally appropriate for psychological study. However, since habit was ordinarily the final stage of a learned adjustive act, the Functionalists were probably oriented more toward conscious activities in their emphasis on adjustment.

Methods of Investigation

The Functionalists employed numerous investigation methods and did not consider one any better or more scientific than any other. In fact, their principal contribution to methodology was the conviction that the procedure used to investigate a particular problem should be determined by the nature of the problem, not the problem by the nature of the procedure which had been the case in the earlier history of psychology. The Structuralists' technique of introspection had limited study to questions of conscious experience. The Functionalists, however, were not above devising techniques fitted to solving the problems which they chose. This commonly accepted conclusion was a major breakthrough at the time and opened many new areas of mind and behavior for investigation.

Dewey and Angell were primarily theorists and spent little time in research. Carr, on the other hand, was more interested in testing and exploring theory. Instead of developing a new technology, he was able to employ existing procedures, for the fruits of several decades of progress were available to him. The first quarter of the 20th century saw the invention of numerous techniques of human and animal experimentation, to a great extent thanks to the methodological philosophy of the early Functionalists.

In spite of a growing sophistication in technique, and in spite of the desirability of experiments, Carr pointed out that experimentalists must encounter profound difficulties in obtaining sufficient control over psychologically intriguing variables. Difficulties were the inevitable result of the complexity of psychological phenomena. Rather than negating experimentation, they merely challenged the experimenter's ingenuity.

In addition to laboratory experiment, Carr made use of literature, art, language, and social and political institutions in his research.

Principles

The principles of Dewey, Angell, and Carr, each in his turn, reflect the maturation of Functionalism. Dewey first defined the basic functional units; Angell followed with postulates describing how these units were coordinated; Carr provided the finishing touches in describing how the units functioned in behavior.

As we have said, Dewey postulated that "stimulus" and "response" had no individual identity. Their meaning accrued from the role played in a sequence of events. Stimulus triggered and therefore determined a specific event; response terminated it, but might well trigger another.

Angell added a set of principles to describe the functional role of consciousness. It appeared, he stated, in adaptive or novel reactions, and its utility was to direct a complex and/or unfamiliar activity. It permitted the individual to discriminate among the meaningful attributes of experience and to focus on those which were appropriate at the time. It selected and organized a course of action, and supervised its outcome. Conscious behavior could thus be identified by its creative, problem-solving, or adaptive function. Habitual behavior did not require conscious intervention, because the sequence of acts was learned to a point where it took place automatically.

Carr felt that more principles were required to describe the functional role of behavior. Accordingly, he proposed, first, that adaptive behavior was the result of a set of motivating factors interacting with a set of external circumstances. The behavior was designed to satisfy the motives insofar as the situation permitted. Second, he recognized another type of activity, namely random behavior, which was unmotivated and goalless; it had no adaptive utility.

All acts, adaptive or random, involved a sequence of S-R events. Sometimes the sequence was directly observable, and at other times some segments of the sequence took place within the nervous system and could not be observed directly.

This last principle provided Carr with a neurological equivalent for behavior and for mental phenomena which had been only implied in earlier theories.

Consciousness

Our earlier discussion approached consciousness from the perspective of the mind-body problem which had plagued philosophers through the ages. Dewey's orientation was not particularly concerned with this ancient problem. While he found it convenient to speak of the mental and physical aspects of experience, this was only a convenience of expression. Thoughts and things were merely different elements of a sequence of roles ascribed to an event as it initiated mental processes. Angell also viewed the mind-body distinction as a pseudo-problem, a matter of convenient usage only. However, he foresaw the danger of arousing the controversy again and warned that contemporary terminology should not delude the psychologist into seeking again for a distinction. Carr's somewhat later view conceived of mental activity as a psycho-physical process. Mind was psychical insofar as the individual had knowledge of his activity, and physical insofar as the activity was that of a physical organism. Although they constituted different levels of the same entity, mind and body were inseparable.

This position on the mind-body problem gave the Functionalist's approach to consciousness a new turn. Angell asserted that a moment of consciousness was fleeting. A particular sensation or idea, when not being experienced, did not exist, and having once taken place, the identical sensation or idea could not recur. Because of this amorphous, momentary quality, it was not a proper matter for scientific concern. Feeling and thinking, on the other hand, being processes of sensory and cognitive *function*, were constant, invariable, and reproducible. Therefore the process, or more precisely the function, rather than its content, should be the focus of psychological study.

Angell also pointed out the contradictions in the Structuralists' assertion that consciousness could not be understood apart from the conditions under which it occurred. In considering these conditions, one became involved in how consciousness worked, in other words, in an investigation of function. The very subject matter of psychology therefore dictated a Functionalist view point. Having proved to his satisfaction that what he felt was worthwhile in Structuralism was really Functionalism, Angell proceeded to elaborate on the theme.

Consciousness, he stated, was synonymous with adaptation, since it mediated between the environment and the organism's needs. It was a companion process to habit-formation and problem-solving, an agent for understanding and mastery. Once learning was well established, the necessity for such an understanding guide decreased and conscious supervision of the activity gradually ceased, leaving it to take place automatically. Consciousness was manifested as variations of behavior in response to changes in surrounding conditions. The behavior variations could be seen, for example, in reaction to slight changes of stimulus level during trial-and-error behavior, and in spontaneous alterations of perception which redefined problem situations and alerted the organism to unsuspected new relationships. Angell's conceptualization of consciousness is similar to that of the later writer, Tolman, whom we will consider in detail in Chapter 13. For the moment, we will simply note that Tolman felt that consciousness appeared at this point of choice or decision.

Sensation, Perception, and Discrimination

For Dewey, "sensation" and "stimulus" were only semantic devices to denote roles in a sequence of activities. These roles could be subject to re-assignment as the sequence progressed. For example, the visual sensation of a traffic light might be a response to a policeman's whistle, but it is also a stimulus to put on the brake. The distinction is useful only to give a clue to a phase in the S-R sequence of activity.

It is a further oversimplification to refer to segments or sequences as if one event were followed by another. In spite of order in time, the "sensation" and "responses" overlap, and may even be simultaneous, each interacting with the other and leading to other events which follow them in time. For example, seeing cannot be separated from looking. The head must move and the eyes focus for accurate vision; thus action and sensation interact. Similarly, reaching for an object does not follow seeing it; the visual sensation of the object precedes reaching, but the act of reaching is observed and guided by the eye. The extension of the arm alters the visual field and the visual image allows the person to correct his reach.

Because this interpretation of the sensation-action cycle is similar to the "feedback" concept of importance to Cybernetics (see Chapter 29) and Group Dynamics (see Chapter 24), some preliminary discussion of feedback may help to clarify Dewey's ideas. The term feedback was introduced by scientists employing electronic equipment in the automation of industry, warfare, communication, etc. Computing machines were used, for example, in the aiming of anti-aircraft guns, to process target data such as position, rate, and direction of movement. The computer enabled the gun to track the plane, aim itself, and fire, but to do this, the computer had to be fed information about the original course, speed, and altitude of its target. Further, as the gun was aimed, the computer required a feedback of information as to the location of the gun in relation to the plane in order to verify or correct its aim. Even though he lacked the analogy of the electronic device, Dewey's concept of the concurrence of sensation and response involved this same feeding-in-and-adjusting-to-information about a continuing process.

Angell did not treat the matter beyond what Dewey formulated. In the years intervening between the early Functionalists and Carr, Gestalt theories sprang into prominence, with their emphasis on the total stimulus situation, including both figure and ground. Carr reacted to their influence by pointing out that not only the central stimulus event, but the whole sensory situation acted as a determinant of behavior.

The Functionalists did not concern themselves to any significant degree with perception. Their treatment of sensation implies that it connoted more to them than raw data, and they employed the term, but without defining or enlarging upon it. On the whole, Dewey and Carr seemed to be far more impressed with the *function* of a stimulus than with the *means* by which the organism received, recorded, and interpreted that stimulus. It may be that the Functionalists were more interested in the general nature of behavior than in its mechanics. However, we suspect that in turning from the contents of consciousness to its utility they over-reached and threw the baby out with the bath, because it was many years after the work of Dewey and Angell that it became acceptable once more for psychology to study product as well as process.

Thinking, Cognition, and Memory

The Functionalists made their greatest contributions in areas where they felt there was the greatest need for improvement of Structuralist views. Thus, they had relatively little to say about thinking, cognition, and memory, because the Structuralists had given these topics sparse attention. Angell implied that thought was the vehicle for the mediating and adaptive qualities of the organism, but he had no major interest in developing a theory of thinking. He was apparently satisfied to ascribe it some status in the larger process of adaptation.

Emotion and Motivation

The Functionalists believed that organisms were active because of their inherent sensitivity to stimuli. Activity became adaptive only when a motivating stimulus determined the direction of the act. Carr, who was most prominent in formulating the Functionalist theory of motivation, maintained (1925, pp. 72–73) that a motive was "a relatively persistent stimulus that dominates the behavior of an individual until he reacts in such a manner that he is no longer affected by it." However, Carr also pointed out that motives were not an essential prerequisite for activity; they simply determined the direction it would take. Human beings were capable of unmotivated action, which he described as random "mere activity."

Although Carr's hypothesis derived from his observations of the spontaneous behavior of infants, he believed that adults demonstrated the same kind of purposeless activity. He rejected random, unmotivated behavior as proper subject matter for psychology, and in so doing, unfortunately ruled out many areas such as emotional reactions, "play," day-dreaming, psychopathological states, and the trial-and-error, random activity of the initial stages of child development, which have since become valuable sources of scientific data.

In addition to motives, Carr underscored the importance of what he called the incentive in directing adaptive behavior. By incentive he meant both the external sensory situation at the end of a sequence of acts, and the anticipation of goal achievement upon completing ongoing sequence.

Such a theory inevitably involved Carr in a teleological tangle. To presuppose the existence of motives and goals appeared to violate the concept of causality. For, superficially at least, the premise that incentive was prerequisite to behavior implied that future consequences determined present acts, i.e. that the cause occurred after the effect. He therefore postulated that an adaptive act had two sets of consequences. The first satisfied an immediate motive, and the second an implicit, long-range one. For example, eating relieved an immediate hunger and also provided long-term nourishment. These eventual consequences were not to be considered the goals. To ascribe such functions to them opens the way to the teleological problem. Behavior must be explained on the basis of the conditions nearest to the act, not those distant from it. This apparently fine distinction is not so delicate as it appears, and variations of it are still employed to account for "what is reduced" in drive-reduction explanations of behavior and learning. Certain immediate gratifications must be found to reinforce the responses since the ultimate consequences act too slowly to have a reinforcing effect. Otherwise we shall have to seek an alternative to drive-reduction-type explanations.

The Nature of the Learning Process

The Functionalists had little to say about learning. Their theory of behavior assumed it to be the process which eventually enabled behavior to pass from conscious control to automatic habit. They did not, however, describe the mechanisms of this transition.

Behavior and Personality

The two-stage theory of adaptive behavior proposed by Dewey suggested a phase of disorganization, followed by a phase of habitual action. In the first phase there was no fixed order of events, no stable stimulus, and no set response. In the second, confusion gave way to the completed act, and took place automatically. At this point one could no longer distinguish stimulus as stimulus or response as response, just as there is no pause between the flip of a switch and the lighting of a bulb. Both had been coordinated into an irreducible sequence. The concepts of "coordination" and "interaction" did not, however, explain behavior satisfactorily any more than the simple stimulus-response reflex did. These were descriptive terms abstracted from a sequence, artificial concepts to aid understanding. The total coordinated act must, of course, be related to the past (cause or stimulus), to the future (effects or responses), and to the total situation, just as stimulus and response were related in the reflex arc concept. But to isolate these different kinds of relationship, and treat them as distinct entities, was to overlook the fact of relationship.

Dewey suggested the following principles of the stimulus-response sequence which might be applied to behavior in general. First, all stimuli exerted some effect on the activity of the organism. Second, all activity, ideational or motor, was initiated by stimuli. Third, there was a continuous interaction between sensory stimuli (both initiating stimuli and concomitant stimuli), and motor responses (i.e., feedback).

According to Dewey's theory, every event, whether internal or external, called for a response. All behavior was the result of some event; it was, in turn, guided by anticipation of consequences and by other, intervening events. Finally, it was itself a determinant of the events which followed it. Dewey, however, did not account explicitly for utilitarian or adaptive behavior. While his principles implied an explanation, it was not until Carr's concept of motivation that Functionalist theory could predict *what activity* would occur in response to a stimulus.

For Carr, adaptive behavior was generated against the background of environmental conditions, by motivating stimuli. The behavior continued until the motive had been satisfied by an alteration in the conditions. This had the effect of removing from the situation both the stimulus to which the adaptive behavior was a response, and the external goal.

On the other hand, behavior itself could act as a motive for other acts. In the course of a motivated activity, fatigue might set in, for example, or the activity in itself might satisfy the organism. The hungry gourmet might be sated with a particular dish long before his hunger disappeared. The person who had just finished an entertaining book was not likely to re-read it immediately, even though he still wished to read something.

Along with motivation and initiating stimuli, the total sensory situation was involved in any act. The individual, of course, was not always equally aware of all aspects of it, and not all aspects were equally relevant. Among those which were appropriate, he could only focus on one aspect at a time, since his cognitive and motor apparatus would not permit him to do everything at once.

The intensity of one aspect of a stimulus could intrude upon the entire situation as a distraction, arousing new responses incompatible with the dominant behavior pattern. New stimuli could supply some reason for changing the original behavior to a new, perhaps more appropriate form, thereby altering the old response. This interpretation, of course, cast the stimulus itself as another source of motivation.

Critique

As might be expected, the Structuralists reacted violently. They naturally objected to the fact that the Functionalists did not use introspection, and pointed out that since pragmatic concerns were beyond the pale of psychology, the Functionalists were not psychologists. The Structuralists also pointed to confusing and inconsistent definitions; thus, for example, "function" sometimes meant *what* a thing does, and sometimes *how or why* the thing was done.

The Functionalists of course replied that they were justified in calling themselves psychologists, but were certainly not Structural psychologists. Although they rejected most of the Structuralists' theories, they still felt that the growing field of psychology could accommodate both camps. In response to the Structuralists' charge that applications were "unscientific," Carr pointed out that if concern over the eventual applicability of one's findings negated science, then the Structuralists were more unscientific than he, since they were concerned and he was not. The Functionalists conceded that they had given the term "function" a dual meaning, but pointed out that the double definition had existed for some time in biology with no demoralizing effect. It had, in fact, contributed to certain theoretical advances.

The evaluation of Functionalism as a school of psychology is complicated by its status as a resistance movement to Structuralism. It was criticized for being primarily an abstract statement of principles rather than a comprehensive, well-articulated theory. Many areas not touched upon by the Structuralists had been neglected and others covered only partially. But the Functionalists had no real intention of establishing a school or a systematized theory with precise definitions. The founders of the movement, Dewey and Angell, wanted merely to serve as critics. It was left to Carr to organize their principles, and he dealt only with the areas which he felt were important.

Functionalism has also been criticized for its teleological approach, its emphasis on biological utility and motivation. We have described Carr's attempt to solve this problem earlier in the chapter. This attempt produced a somewhat awkward set of hypotheses, but it did serve the purpose of showing how to circumvent teleology. Whether or not motivation fits certain logical preconceptions, psychology must find some acceptable technique for incorporating its phenomena into science. Carr's approach was a good beginning. Aside from its theoretical benefits, it also encouraged the search for physiological equivalents of psychological constructs. Subsequent research on the existence and nature of neural traces and the physiological elements of consummatory acts have their roots in Carr's suggestions.

Another aspect of Functionalism which is open to criticism is the account of adaptive behavior. Because they failed to devote serious thought to learning, their description of how adaptive behavior appears is incomplete. Behavior which is disorganized at its inception does not suddenly become automatic. There is an intervening period of increasing integration, and unfortunately, neither Dewey, Angell, nor Carr gave it sufficient attention.

In general, Functionalism was a rather vague, intellectualized theory, too difficult to be broken down into catch phrases. It was therefore not a popular theory among either psychologists or the general public. Newer, more aggressive theories such as Gestalt psychology, Behaviorism, and Freudian psychoanalysis soon took the limelight, and left Functionalism to mature and mellow gracefully without outside intervention.

We have already discussed how Functionalist theory has become one of the cornerstones of American psychology. This was obviously not accomplished by proselytizing, but rather by the universal recognition and acceptance of the value of the concepts. These have been so completely absorbed into psychology that while they can still be identified, it is no longer possible to identify individual psychologists as Functionalists *per se*. For a time in the 1940's and perhaps the early 1950's it was fashionable to refer to McGeoch (1942), Hilgard (1948; Hilgard and Marquis, 1940), and Woodworth (1954) as *Current Functionalists*, since they manifested a Functionalist orientation. Over the years this orientation has broadened to the point where it seems more appropriate to refer to them as eclectic, and to their concepts as "functional" without the capital letter, to emphasize their concern with the utility of the concepts rather than with their theoretical origin.

SUMMARY

Basic Unit. Functionalism's basic unit was the chain of stimulus-response events composing an activity, but this did not mean that the activity was a simple stimulus-response sequence. "Stimulus" and "response" were abstractions referring to the function of an event in a behavior sequence. What was the final (response) stage of one act might well be the initiating (stimulus) phase of another.

Field of Study. Psychology was a study of the origin and function of consciousness, mental activity, and behavior.

Methods of Investigation. Functionalists dealt only with the philosophy of methods, not with the technology. Their greatest insight was the assertion that the problem at hand, rather than the psychologists' theoretical orientation, should determine the method of solution.

Principles (*Dewey*). Stimulus, idea, and response had no existence except as abstractions describing their roles in a behavior sequence. Their role was determined by their function.

(Angell). Consciousness appeared in adaptive reactions and was useful as a

means of directing and organizing behavior. Habitual acts, on the other hand, were automatic and unconscious.

(Carr). All acts involved a stimulus-response chain, although some or all of this chain might be covert. Adaptive behavior was directed by internal motives and the external setting in which it occurred. Mere activity (such as the random movements of an infant) was unmotivated and had no utility.

Consciousness. The distinction between mind and body was an artificiality but could be useful for communication. Mental activity was psychophysical, i.e., a biological process which the individual could experience and appreciate. The *contents* of consciousness were amorphous, dependent on the conditions surrounding the conscious state. The process of consciousness itself was invariable, however, and of interest to psychology. Consciousness mediated between the organism's needs and its environment, and therefore appeared during novel situations which the organism had to learn to understand and master. It showed itself in behavior only as it effected changes in activity. Once the novel situation was over mediated behavior took place automatically, with no more conscious intervention.

Sensation, Perception, and Discrimination. Like stimulus, sensation was an abstraction, referring to an event which initiated an act. It was not separate from perception and action, but concurrent with them as a mechanism for feeding back information which enabled the organism to direct the progress of its behavior.

Thinking, Cognition, and Memory. These matters were not considered in detail because it was not necessary to reinterpret an area more or less untouched by earlier theorists. Thought was conceived of as the vehicle of consciousness which allowed the organism to mediate between internal and external events. The mechanics of how this happened were not spelled out.

Emotion, Motivation, and Purpose. Adaptive behavior had biological utility; it was directed by persistent stimuli which dominated activity until the organism altered behavior and was no longer to be affected by the stimuli. That is, the organism was motivated, whereas in so-called random behavior it was not. Goals also directed the course of behavior, and the very *process* of action could affect future action. The Functionalists' concepts of motivation and goals can be seen as non-teleological if one considers that the eventual adaptive act had some immediate consequences which were not displaced into the future, as the biological context of thought seemed to imply. The occurrence of immediate results made goal-oriented behavior a proper cause followed by a proper effect, rather than a teleological misfortune.

The Nature and Process of Learning. Functionalist theory saw learning as the process whereby an act became habit. They did not deal with it further, probably because it was not an area of theory in which there were earlier misconceptions to correct.

Behavior and Personality. Adaptive behavior in its initial stage was disorganized and unstable, but in its later stages became habitual and automatic. All stimuli were assumed to have some effect on the organism. Activity of any kind was thought to be stimulated, and there was felt to be continuous interaction between sensory and motor activity. Adaptive activity was both stimulated and motivated, continuing until the motive was satisfied, unless the very process of behaving altered the motivational conditions or some new element arose to distract the process. Adaptive behavior required adjustment, initiation, and maintenance of motor and sensory sets until action was appropriate. In this process, what has come to be known as feedback guided the activity by informing the organism of its progress and enabling it to correct its errors.

REFERENCES

E. B. Titchener on Functionalism

Titchener, E. B., "The Postulates of a Structural Psychology," *Phil. Rev.* 7: 449–456 (1898). Reprinted in W. Dennis, ed., *Readings in the History of Psychology*, New York: Appleton-Century-Crofts, 1948, pp. 366–376.

———, "Structural and Functional Psychology," *Phil. Rev.* 8: 290–299 (1899).

John Dewey

Dewey, J., "The Reflex Arc Concept in Psychology," *Psychol. Rev.* 3: 357–370 (1896). Reprinted in W. Dennis, ed., *Readings in the History of Psychology*, New York: Appleton-Century-Crofts, 1948, pp. 355–365.

———, "Psychology and Social Practice," *Psychol. Rev.* 7: 105–124 (1900).

———, *Human Nature and Conduct*, New York: Holt, 1922.

———, "Conduct and Experience," in C. Murcheson, ed., *Psychologies of 1930*, Worcester: Clark University Press, 1930, pp. 409–422.

J. R. Angell

Angell, J. R., "The Relations of Structural and Functional Psychology to Philosophy," *University of Chicago Decennial Publication*, 1903, Ser. I, Vol. 3, Pt. 2, 55–73. Reprinted in *Phil. Rev.* 12: 243–271 (1903).

———, *Psychology: An Introductory Study of the Structure and the Function of the Human Consciousness*, New York: Holt, 1904.

———, "The Province of Functional Psychology," *Psychol. Rev.* 14: 61–91 (1907). Reprinted in W. Dennis, ed., *Readings in the History of Psychology*, New York: Appleton-Century-Crofts, 1948, pp. 439–456.

———, *Introduction to Psychology*, New York: Holt, 1918.

G. H. Mead

Mead, G. H., *Mind, Self and Society*, Chicago: University of Chicago Press, 1934.

——, "The Definition of the Psychical," *University of Chicago Decennial Publ.*, 1903, Ser. I, Vol. 3, Pt. 2, pp. 77–112.

H. A. Carr

Carr, H. A., *Psychology: A Study of Mental Activity*, New York: Longmans, Green, 1925.

——, "Functionalism," in C. Murchison, ed., *Psychologies of 1930*, Worcester: Clark University Press, 1930, pp. 59–78. (A)

——, "Teaching and Learning," *J. Genet. Psych.* 37: 189–218 (1930). (B)

——, "The Quest for Constants," *Psych. Rev.* 40: 514–532 (1933).

——, *An Introduction to Space Perception*, New York: Longmans, Green, 1935.

——, "The Law of Effect: A Round Table Discussion: I," *Psych. Rev.* 45: 191–199 (1938).

——, and J. B. Watson, "Orientation in the White Rat," *J. Comp. Nerv. Psychol.* 18: 27–44 (1908).

Hicks, V. C., and H. A. Carr, "Human Reactions in a Maze," *J. Animal Beh.* 2: 98–125 (1912).

Current Functionalists

Hilgard, E. R., *Theories of Learning*, New York: Appleton-Century-Crofts, 1948.

——, and D. G. Marquis, *Conditioning and Learning*, New York: Appleton-Century-Crofts, 1940.

McGeoch, J. A., *The Psychology of Human Learning*, New York: Longmans, Green, 1942.

Woodworth, R. L., and H. Schlosberg, *Experimental Psychology*, 2nd edit., New York: Holt, 1954.

PART III

PSYCHOLOGICAL ASSOCIATIONISM: BEGINNINGS OF LEARNING THEORY

CHAPTER 7

EDWARD L. THORNDIKE: LAW OF EFFECT (1898–1938)

EDWARD THORNDIKE, a student of William James and James Cattell, taught and carried on his research at Columbia during the period when that institution was establishing itself in the new science of psychology. Thorndike's first interest was animal psychology, specifically learning and intelligence, and before he was 25, Thorndike had published what has become a classical monograph: *Animal Intelligence* (1898). It set forth the basic observations and interpretations upon which his theory of learning and behavior was to be built over the years. Whether as a reflection of his times, or out of personal preference, Thorndike presented a specific, concrete, objective psychology and his emphasis on the *measurement* has been immensely influential in the value system of American psychology. Thorndike's work with animals and his objective approach to his data was the beginning of true animal experimentation. These studies led him to do further pioneer work in human intelligence and learning. He became prominent in educational research, particularly evaluation of achievement and ability (intelligence), and later was involved in industrial assessment. Yet for all of his contributions to education and industry, his stature as a basic scientist and learning theorist overshadows everything else.

Basic Unit

The behavior processes which Thorndike wished to study could be broken down into simple stimulus-response units. So far as he was concerned, to isolate a single, concrete, initiating event, and the organism's single, concrete reaction to it was to discover the building blocks from which all behavior could be reconstructed. Regardless of its apparent complexity, any behavior was reducible to a stimulus-response bond, and the key to psychological understanding lay in discovering the means by which these bonds were established.

Field of Study

Contrary to the earlier emphasis on mental contents, experience, and associations, Thorndike believed that psychology's area of concern should be the study of behavior. In part, this probably grew from the general clamor in America for a more objective approach, but the greater source of his interest in behavior was his stimulus-response approach, and the conviction that animal function was of as much concern to science as human function.

Methods of Investigation

Thorndike's new focus naturally required alterations in methodology. He agreed with the other critics of Structuralism that psychology could not be limited to one method, but whereas the others had contented themselves with criticisms, Thorndike developed new methods.

His reforms were based on the Functionalists' assertion that research methods should be appropriate to, and determined by, the subject matter. His own emphasis on animal behavior and stimulus-response bonds precluded the use of introspection. His apparatus and procedures had to be fashioned to fit the idiosyncracies of the subjects he used and the problems he studied. For example, to investigate learning in baby chicks, he constructed problems similar to elementary mazes, a technique which helped to introduce the maze into the psychological laboratory. An equally important invention was his puzzle box, devised to study the learning behavior of cats and dogs. As with all experimental devices, the puzzle box produced data unique to itself, just as introspection had produced data pertaining to the contents of consciousness and nonsense syllables data concerning the formations of associations.

The puzzle box was a simple enclosure, constructed of some transparent material so that the subject, a hungry cat or dog, could see the food placed in plain view outside the cage. The strongly motivated animal had to discover how to free himself to obtain the reward. The door to the cage was fastened with a complex arrangement of latches which could be released by tugging at a chain or ring hanging where the animal must eventually manipulate it by accidental contact. To escape from the box required a series of random exploratory activities (which often bordered on panic in the naive animal), and encouraged the growth of a simple, mechanical habit. Similar simple problems were employed with human subjects, and the behavior observed was the basis for Thorndike's theory of learning.The method was therefore unique to the problem to be investigated, and the theory was also unique to the data on which it was based.

Principles

Law of Effect. Thorndike's major contribution to theory was his Law of Effect, which held that any act which produced satisfaction in a situation became associated with that situation, so that when it recurred the act became increasingly likely to recur as well. Conversely, any act which produced discomforts became dissociated from the situation, so that when it recurred the act became less likely to appear. In other words, pleasurable effects "stamped in" associations; punishment "stamped out" associations. Some thirty years later when Thorndike observed that the statement regarding punishment was not applicable to human beings, he revised the law to some extent. He eliminated the proposition that punishment stamped out or negated some association of stimulus and response, and stated instead that punishment caused the learner to vary his behavior until some act was discovered which was rewarded. This gave punishment an indirect rather than a formative role in learning, since it led to the substitution of given responses rather than their suppression.

Law of Exercise. Thorndike's second principle of learning, the Law of Exercise, stated that repetition of an experience led to a stronger connection or association. This was a restatement of the temporal congruence part of the Associationistic principle of Contiguity, but went one step further, including the secondary law of frequency, namely that repeated experience of the congruence is required for learning to occur. The factor of contiguity itself, regardless of its frequency, was not enough to account for learning. It could strengthen a connection by deepening the impress of the stamping-in process, but it could not provide the impetus for this process. Only the effect of the activity could do that.

Law of Spread of Effect. When an act had pleasurable consequences, this pleasure became associated not only with that act and the stimulus leading to it, but also with other acts which occurred at approximately the same time. Thorndike believed this phenomenon, which he called *spread of effect*, was due to some underlying physiological process, although he could not specify its nature. The proof of this phenomenon has occupied many experimenters since Thorndike's discovery of it, and its existence is still open to controversy. Why psychologists find spread of effect from one physical location to a near neighbor more questionable than generalization from one tonal stimulus to its neighbor on the scale is not clear. Long accepted concepts of anticipation and/or expectation seem to be implied in the concept of spread of effect, and should make possible a broader acceptance of it.

Because Thorndike considered consciousness, sensation, perception, and discrimination only in a perfunctory way, we will focus on his major contributions to thinking, cognition and memory, emotion and motivation, the nature of the learning process, and behavior and personality.

Thinking, Cognition, and Memory

Thorndike was interested in problem-solving, but not in cognition *per se*. The seeming paradox of a noncognitive theory of cognition disappears upon a closer look at his approach. Thorndike was, first of all, an animal psychologist. When he sought universal laws of behavior he saw no reason to assume that human behavior was qualitatively different from animal behavior. Man must differ only in degree. So far as Thorndike could see, animals did not evidence a capacity for inference or reasoning. They learned by chance associations, by trial-and-error. If, despite the inability to reason, animals could solve problems, then problem-solving must be mechanical. The Law of Effect described how this mechanical solution came about.

As he studied problem-solving, Thorndike was exposed to differences in learning ability, and eventually took up the question of intelligence. Here again, he saw no reason to depart from his simple stimulus-response explanation. Differences in ability, that is, intelligence, seemed to him to be differences in the ease with which S-R bonds could be set up. The greater the individual's capacity for forming bonds, the greater his intelligence. This concept of intelligence applied equally to man and to animals; man merely had the greater potential for forming S-R bonds.

The problem of bond-formation included a number of areas. There were varying *degrees* of intelligence, varying *dimensions* of intelligence from narrowly specialized to widely inclusive, and varying *speeds* in bond-formation. Finally, there were different *kinds* of intelligence; some bond-formations contributed to abstract intelligence, some to concrete intelligence, and some to social intelligence. An individual could have one kind without the other kinds. For example, a person could possess a high degree of abstract intelligence, yet be completely inept in social situations.

Thorndike's ability to reduce higher mental activities to simple S-R bonds tended to have a stultifying effect on studies of cognition and thought among American psychologists. This was only gradually overcome by the Gestaltists' studies of insight (see Chapter 23), and by the theories of the psychoanalysts (see Part V).

Emotion and Motivation

Motivation was crucial to Thorndike's theory of learning. It was what made the organism responsive to begin with, determined what he would respond, and what effects would be reinforcing. Thorndike saw motives as "overhead controls" that determined which of the organism's "confirming reactions" (i.e., responses), were most likely to occur. Some motives were narrow, resulting in specific responses to specific objects. For example, thirst led to the specific act, drinking. Other motives were broad, nonspecific, satisfied by any number of varied responses to any number of different goals. For instance, the need for companionship could be satisfied in a number of different ways with a number of different persons. Whatever their nature, motives might act singly or in combination, several determining the outcome of a given activity.

Reward and punishment themselves, apart from their reinforcing effects, also motivated behavior. There seemed to be an upper limit beyond which reward only added to excitement and did not produce any changes in consummatory response; there was also a lower limit below which reward was not actively sought, although it was accepted if given. Likewise, punishment could motivate escape only within certain ranges of intensity. Above this range it disorganized the organism, and below the range it produced no observable effect. The motivating effects of reward and punishment we now take for granted and call *incentives*; the prediction and control of incentive effects is still a matter of contemporary research.

The Nature of the Learning Process

A hungry cat placed in a puzzle box for the first time with a bowl of fish in plain view just outside the cage struggled to get the food. She bit, jumped, rubbed, patted, pushed, and scratched until, by accident, she somehow pulled the chain, unfastened the latches, and opened the door. The cat's performance was the same for many subsequent trials. Gradually, she became more efficient and found her way out more quickly. The behavior was still clumsy, however, and there was no indication that she understood the relationship between manipulating the latch and release from the cage; she might back into the latch, rub against it, or repeat whatever other act she may have found most consistently associated with the accidental opening of the door. As learning progressed, after a long series of approximations, the cat would use more efficient methods to lift the latch; many more trials were required before she was able to effect a polished performance. Once perfected, the act became a simple, automatic, stimulus-response sequence.

Thorndike considered this pattern typical of animals and humans alike, and referred to it as trial-and-error learning. The experimental subject would normally try many types of response. Those which proved effective in achieving the reward were added to the subject's repertoire, and those which were ineffective were eliminated. In addition, reactions which were similar to the rewarded act, or closely contiguous to it in time, were likely to become fixed, while those responses which were similar to a punished or unrewarded act were gradually omitted.

These observations of trial-and-error behavior were Thorndike's bases for the Laws of Effect, Exercise, and Spread of Effect, as well as for his assertion that learning was a simple mechanistic process, quite unrelated to "ability to reason." Seen from Thorndike's perspective, learned behavior lost its frightening complexity, but tended to become somewhat oversimplified.

Behavior and Personality

Thorndike's entire theory focused on behavior at the level of simple stimulus-response events, but it is our intent in this section to consider behavior on a larger scale as an organized system. Since this definition is not the same as Thorndike's, it becomes evident that he did not address himself to those facets of behavior appropriate to our present inquiry.

His study of learning and intelligence led Thorndike to the study of individual differences through the back door, so to speak, as he attempted to find ways of measuring intellect and achievement. Once on the subject he found challenging questions to pursue, and approached personality theory more directly. These contributions were, however, secondary to his theory of learning, and were mostly generalizations about learning. While this material was valuable, it was not of the same significance as his experimental work.

Critique

Thorndike contributed the first coherent theory of learning, which in itself would make him historically noteworthy. But his laws have far more than mere historical significance, because they have remained focal points for research and theory. One of the basic issues among present-day learning theorists is the relationship of the Law of Effect and the Law of Contiguity. (The reader will recall this as the principle derived by Aristotle to describe the evolution of association). One group holds to one or another of the modifications of the Effect interpretation. This group is commonly referred to as reinforcement theorists, and generally has a Behaviorist orientation (see Part IV). The other position is held, for the most part, by field theorists and by ultra-empiricists, to whom contiguity seems to be more compatible, although not for the same reason.

The Law of Effect has been criticized most strongly on the grounds that it is essentially teleological. To presume that pleasure stamps in an association or response is to presume that a future event, pleasure, is causing a prior event, the association of stimulus and response. As we have already observed, any theory of motivation or tension release must answer this criticism. The teleological aspects can be avoided by realizing that the "pleasure" is not really future to the response but more or less contemporary. Furthermore, the organism, having experienced pleasurable consequences of an action, can anticipate that repeating the response would also bring pleasurable consequences.

The proponents of the Law of Effect have also found it difficult to demonstrate a physiological counterpart of reinforcement. Consider the apparently simple problem of food as a reinforcer. Given a certain stimulus, the hungry organism acts in some way to secure the food, which it eats. The stimulus and the acts it initiates are far removed in time from the chemical changes which constitute the physiological end results of food consumption. In other words, perception of food and physical relief of hunger do not take place simultaneously; they may be separated by a period of an hour or more. It is unlikely that the physiological effects of the food could reinforce a stimulus-response sequence which preceded it by such a long period. Reinforcement theorists seeking some more immediate connection between stimulus-response and reinforcement have hypothesized that an event or action might leave traces in the nervous system which become connected with neural impulses produced by the physiological reinforcement. Such traces have been demonstrated experimentally, but we know that the trace within the neuron is maintained at full strength for only a fraction of a second, and diminishes completely within a few seconds. It therefore seems unlikely that the electrical trace within the nerve cell can be instrumental in establishing any connection between an event and its reinforcing consequences.

The physiological laboratory has demonstrated another type of mechanism which can hold a trace for longer periods. Among sets of neurons, there are interconnections which provide a reverberating circuit. When one neuron is activated, it activates its neighbor, which activates another in turn, until eventually the impulse is transmitted back to the place it started from, only to go around the circuit again and again.

A trace may also be maintained if there is a structural change within the neuron as it passes an impulse along. Thus Hebb (1949) suggested that neurons grow bumps or amoeboid projections which extend in the direction of the cells to which they transmit an impulse. To begin with, these projections are temporary, but under at least some circumstances they become permanent. Another potential vehicle for the maintenance of permanent traces is alteration in the chemical construction of the neuron. One proposal, described by Landauer (1964), suggests that nuclear proteins alter from moment to moment according to the electrical forces acting upon them. An event impinging upon a set of neurons will alter their chemistry, making them all resonant to and triggered by certain wave frequencies, thereby coordinating their future firing patterns.

While such mechanisms may account for the way traces are maintained, and thereby permanently dispel the stigma of teleology, the reinforcement theorist must still explain how the circuit gets started, or how the events which alter the chemistry take place, and how these occurrences are related to the reinforcing event. Moreover, even before he can deal with such technical details, he must face the issue of the ultimate reinforcers. For example, in the case of eating, just what *is* the reinforcing event? Is it the change in the blood sugar level, or the changes in the metabolism of nerve and muscle cells? What effect does the cessation of hunger pangs, or the ingestion of food have? Clearly the latter phenomena are not the ultimate reinforcers, but they may be secondary ones, secondary in the sense that in early life the cessation of hunger pangs may become connected with the ultimate reinforcer, and thereby become capable in itself of reinforcing. Appeal to the possibility of secondary reinforcers, however, cannot dismiss the question of the nature of the ultimate one.

The recent work of Olds (1956, 1958**A**; 1958**B**; 1959; Olds and Milner, 1954; Olds and Olds, 1958) may provide the answers to these questions. Olds began with the experimental finding that electrical stimulation in certain parts of the brain could be substituted for 'natural' reinforcers. Other areas of the brain were found to have negative reinforcing value. It was subsequently observed that some chemicals had similar effects. Having proved to his satisfaction that the effects of these direct brain stimuli were comparable to other reinforcers acting through sensory channels, Olds proposed the existence of a central hedonistic mechanism. Since animals will learn and/or perform various acts to receive stimulation in certain parts of their brain, and will learn and/or perform various acts to stop it in other parts, there must be a neural pleasure system and a neural displeasure system. So far, Olds has confined his investigations to the pleasure system, obtaining evidence that it is divided into separate areas which deal differently with different motives (such as sex and hunger), and that it is so constructed as to be self-perpetuating. That is to say that once an act triggers it off, the pleasure center initiates behavior which will maintain or enhance its activity. Pleasurable activities then will continue until halted by some external event.

Combining this theory with the trace hypothesis, one might propose the following explanation of the physiological basis for reinforcement. Contact with an event which arouses a pleasure center brings about an immediate reinforcement, such that stimuli present and acts in process become associated with pleasure experiences, and the traces of the stimulus-response sequence are augmented by these reinforcing consequences.

Whatever the eventual solution, the contiguity theorist cannot profit from the physiological dilemma of the reinforcement theorist for he, too, must rely on something like traces to explain his concepts. For example, a fork, a chair, and the clothes on one's back are equally contemporaneous with the act of eating; something must account for the salience of one association over the others. If contiguity and reinforcement both require a similar neurological correlate, then perhaps neither is the basis for learning. Instead, each may be a distinctive aspect of the shared neurological underlay.

The critics of reinforcement theory have also questioned the role of punishment. At times, punishment seems to weaken bonds, while at other times it merely causes variation in behavior without affecting underlying response strength. It can result in the suppression (withholding) of response, and it may even have cue value. For example, Honzik and Tolman (1938) studied the effect of punishment on the ability of human subjects to learn a stylus maze. The subject, blindfolded, was required to learn the path to the goal box by tracing it with a stylus which had been inserted in a track running the length of the maze. A mild electric shock for a correct turn actually increased the speed of learning. Honzik and Tolman concluded that the shock served as a cue for the subject. Other investigators have demonstrated the same phenomenon. Presumably there must be changes in the effectiveness of punishment as it becomes more intense, for it is generally observed that strong shock disorganizes the subject to the point of disrupting behavior. What the varying functions of punishment and the conditions which make it influential might be are problems the reinforcement theorist has yet to answer in the future.

The observed cue value of punishment has led the advocates of contiguity to propose that reinforcing agents serve only as a source of information, so that their effect on the stimulus-response bond is indirect rather than basic. More specifically, reinforcement provides the organism with information it needs to select from a number of learned responses, any of which could take place, the one that it needs in the present situation. The actual learning of responses (and consequences) is the result of contiguity. In this interpretation, the Law of Effect becomes a law of performance rather than a law of learning. Reinforcement theorists respond to this view by pointing out that the consequences are the same thing as reinforcement value. If reinforcement can account for such learning, why presuppose another kind of process as well?

The opponents of reinforcement theory have other criticisms, too. There is a large and telling body of experiments on latent learning which demonstrate weaknesses in the Law of Effect. In the classical latent learning experiments an unmotivated animal is placed in a maze or puzzle box. Typically the animal will wander around aimlessly, and make no particular effort to get out of the enclosure or to reach its reward. However, if this same animal is later placed in the maze or puzzle box in a strongly motivated condition, he learns the solution much more rapidly than animals naive to the situation. It appears that the animal must have learned something about the maze in his first experience, but he was unmotivated and therefore could not have learned by reward. Thus the Law of Effect does not seem to apply.

The problem of latent learning has been difficult for all Law of Effect theorists to handle. The most common solution is to suggest that the unmotivated animal was not really unmotivated. He was instead subject to some exploratory drive or curiosity; exploration was therefore reinforcing and learning did occur. To a certain extent, this is an acceptable explanation. However, it does not have the generality desirable in an explanation of a large class of learning phenomena.

In an effort to resolve the reinforcement-contiguity controversy, several theorists have suggested that there may be several kinds of learning. Tolman (1947) hypothesized six kinds, including variants of contiguity and reinforcement, and mixed types as well. O. H. Mowrer (1947) at one time proposed that emotional reactions were learned by contiguity while motor behavior was learned through reinforcement. Despite these efforts, no mutually satisfactory agreement has yet been reached.

SUMMARY

Basic Unit. Thorndike's basic unit was the simple stimulus-response mechanism.

Field of Study. Psychology should be the study of behavior, including the means by which behavior is learned.

Methods of Investigation. The problem determined the method. Lacking appropriate methods for studying his problems in animal behavior, Thorndike devised many new techniques and apparatuses. Most important of these were the puzzle box and the maze.

Principles. Thorndike's principles have become classical. Reward, he found, "stamped in" associations, while punishment stamped them out, or at least caused the organism to vary its behavior until some new act appeared which was rewarded (Law of Effect). The repeated occurrence of a connection between stimulus and response aided learning, but did not cause it (Law of Exercise). Responses close in sequence to the rewarded one were strengthened to some degree through the generalization of the effect of the reward (Law of Spread of Effect).

Consciousness, Sensation, Perception and Discrimination. Not dealt with.

Thinking, Cognition, and Memory. In considering association, Thorndike was concerned with learning, not thinking. He believed that animal behavior, even in problem-solving tasks, was the result of simple mechanical S-R learning. Explanations of human learning demanded no new concepts beyond those dealing with animal learning. He thereby reduced intelligence to the capacity to form stimulus-response bonds.

Emotion and Motivation. Motives were the overhead controls determining behavior. They could be specific or general, could act singly or in combinations. Amount and quality of reward and punishment also had motivating effects.

The Nature of the Learning Process. Motivation was essential to learning. A properly motivated organism learned through trial and error, fixing upon those actions which were rewarded, dropping those which were not rewarded or were punished. It was from observations of this random behavior that Thorndike derived the laws of Effect, Exercise, and Spread of Effect.

Behavior and Personality. The concepts developed in these areas grew, for the most part, out of generalizations based on Thorndike's theory of learning.

REFERENCES

Edward L. Thorndike

Thorndike, E. L., "Animal Intelligence: An Experimental Study of the Associative Processes in Animals," *Psychol. Monogr.* 2: No. 8 (1898).

———, "The Law of Effect," *Amer. J. Psych.* 39: 212–222 (1927).

———, *Human Learning*, New York: Appleton-Century-Crofts, 1931.

———, *Fundamentals of Learning*, New York: Columbia University Press, 1932. (A)

———, "Reward and Punishment in Animal Learning," *Comp. Psych. Monogr.*, No, 39, 1932. (B)

———, *An Experimental Study of Rewards*, Teach. Coll. Contr. Educ., No. 580, 1933. (A)

———, "The Influence of Irrelevant Rewards," *J. Educ. Psych.* 24: 1–15 (1933). (B)

———, "A Proof of the Law of Effect," *Science*: 173–175 (1933). (C)

———, "A Theory of the Action of the After-Effects of a Connection upon It," *Psych. Rev.* 40: 434–439 (1933). (D)

———, "The Spread of Influence of Reward to Corrections Irrelevant to the Learner's Purposes," *J. Genet. Psych.* 44: 428–435 (1934).

———, and R. T. Rock, Jr. "A Further Note on Learning Without Awareness of What is Being Learned," *J. Exp. Psych.* 18: 388–389 (1935).

Reinforcement—Contiguity Controversy

Hebb, D. O., *Organization of Behavior*, New York: Wiley, 1949.

Honzik, C. H., and E. C. Tolman, "The Action of Punishment in Accelerating Learning," *J. Comp. Psych.* 26: 187–200 (1938).

Landauer, T. K., "Two Hypotheses Concerning the Biochemical Basis of Memory," *Psych. Rev.* 71: 167–179 (1964).

Mowrer, O. H., "On the Dual Nature of Learning: A Reinterpretation of 'Conditioning' and 'Problem Solving,'" *Harvard Rev.* 17: 102–148 (1947).

———, *Learning Theory and Behavior*, New York: Wiley, 1960.

Olds, J:, "A Preliminary Mapping of Electrical Reinforcing Effects in the Rat Brain," *J. Comp. Physiol. Psych.* 49: 281–285 (1956).

———,"Effects of Hunger and Male Sex Hormone on Self Stimulation on the Brain," *J. Comp. Physiol. Psych.* 51: 320–324 (1958). (A)

———, "Self Stimulation of the Brain: Its Use to Study Local Effects of Hunger, Sex, and Drugs," *Science* 127: 315–324 (1958). (B)

———, "High Functions of the Nervous System," *Ann. Rev. Physiol.*, Palo Alto: Annual Review 21: 381–402 (1959).

———, and P. Milner, "Positive Reinforcement Produced by Electrical Stimulation of Septal Area and Other Regions of the Rat Brain," *J. Comp. Physiol. Psychol.* 47: 419–427 (1954).
———, and M. E. Olds, "Positive Reinforcement Produced by Stimulating Hypothalamus with Iproniazid and Other Compounds," *Science* 127, 1175–1176 (1958).
Tolman, E. C., "There is More Than One Kind of Learning," *Psych. Rev.* 56: 144–155 (1947).

CHAPTER 8

I. P. PAVLOV: CONDITIONING (1903–1928)

PAVLOV, a contemporary of Thorndike, was a physiologist whose chief interest was the various processes and secretions of the gastro-intestinal system. He began a series of experiments with the salivary gland using techniques which eventually led to the accidental discovery of conditioning. He soon became aware that his work had a much wider significance, that it might be possible to use the technique as a way of studying the physiology of behavior. Like Fechner (see Chapter 4), he was convinced that mind and body were only different aspects of the same process, and felt that conditioning could provide him the means of testing this conviction. To Pavlov, his technique was the window through which he might view the functions of the nervous system, but his was a purely neurological interest. Even though he rejected the psychological relevance of his work as beneath his concern, he was occasionally criticized or tormented by his purist colleagues in physiology for being a psychologist. These criticisms so increased his vehemence that what we shall refer to as Pavlov's theory of psychology was not only an unwanted outgrowth of his physiological investigations, it was a roundly rejected one, completely disowned by its author.

Basic Unit

Pavlov saw all mental events as simple, reflex units of behavior. The similarity to Thorndike derives from the fact that both used animal subjects in simple, mechanical types of experiments. Since all larger units of activity were thought to be multiplications of simple stimulus-response connections, it was possible by means of conditioning (puzzle boxes in Thorndike's case) to study the very process by which behavior was initiated or discouraged.

Field of Study

Pavlov was interested in behavior and mental events only as correlates of physiological processes. For him, psychology, insofar as it could be scientific at all, was actually nothing but physiology.

Methods of Investigation

The conditioning process required the substitution of a new stimulus for one with a well-established connection to some response. Pavlov's famous work with salivation in dogs illustrates the technique. The salivary reflex, as it occurs involuntarily, may be diagrammed as follows:

presence of food⟶ salivation.

Pavlov referred to food as the *unconditioned stimulus*, and to salivation as the *unconditioned response*. Unconditioned stimulus-response bonds were presumed to be native to the organism. In conditioning, on the other hand, an artificial stimulus was presented in combination with the natural stimulus over a series of trials. After a sufficient number of trials, the artificial stimulus became connected with the response in such a way as to replace the original stimulus. Thus

bell⟶ food⟶ salivation

became

bell⟶ salivation.

Pavlov referred to the bell as the *conditioned stimulus*, and the salivation which occurred in response to it as the *conditioned response*.

Pavlov felt that the conditioning method had a number of advantages. First, it made the objective analysis of behavior a great deal easier. More important, it provided a physiological means of studying what had previously appeared to be psychological problems, which reinforced his conviction that psychology was really physiology. Finally, it provided a valuable technique for investigating intact brain function.

From the time of its introduction the method appealed to psychologists, and it assumed a major importance in studies of the acquisition of behavior as well as in numerous other contexts. The process of developing conditioned responses, and the responses themselves, demonstrated properties which were most illuminating to behavioral scientists. Originally developed as laws of stimulus substitution, they were equally applicable to brain excitation and inhibition, and were later adapted to learning.

Principles

Reinforcement. To establish a conditioned response to a substitute stimulus, both the conditioned and the unconditioned stimulus were presented at approximately the same time. The unconditioned stimulus tended to act as a reinforcing agent; i.e., the presence of food reinforced the tendency to salivate. Moreover, to maintain the strength of the conditioned response after it was established it was occasionally necessary to accompany the conditioned stimulus with the unconditioned, that is to reinforce the act.

Inhibition. A well-established conditioned response might be inhibited even under favorable circumstances if one of the two following conditions prevailed: First, if a new or distracting stimulus were added to a familiar one, the distraction sometimes led to inhibition. More specifically, it appeared that the distracting stimulus changed the context of the stimulus, transforming it into something strange and therefore incapable of eliciting the conditioned response.

Second, inhibition could be induced by *extinction*, the pairing of conditioned stimulus and conditioned response over a long period with no presentation of the unconditioned stimulus. After a sufficient number of unreinforced trials, the conditioned response ceased to occur. For example, a dog once well-trained to salivate to a bell would gradually cease to respond when the bell was no longer accompanied by food. It appeared that the conditioned response was unlearned because the conditioned stimulus was no longer followed by reinforcement. Covert responses were found to continue long after overt acts disappeared, but these, too, were eventually extinguished.

Disinhibition. Just as a distracting stimulus would inhibit a conditioned response, a new or distracting stimulus occurring during the process of extinction might re-arouse a conditioned response long after it had ceased to occur. Like distraction, this seemed to be due to a subtle alteration in the state of the stimulus, an alteration which inhibited the inhibition, so to speak. In fact, the phenomenon was called *disinhibition.* Its occurrence suggested to Pavlov and others that the conditioned response had not necessarily disappeared from the organism's repertoire in the process of extinction; it was merely suppressed because a new stimulus context carried no reinforcement. In the place of the conditioned response a habit of no-response was established, but the conditioned response would occur once again whenever this inhibition was not triggered off.

Delayed Conditioning. Under certain circumstances it was possible to introduce a conditioned stimulus relatively far in advance of the unconditioned stimulus and produce a normal response. The original conditioned response was established in the usual way and the conditioned stimulus was gradually removed further and further in time from the response. Eventually the stimulus could be presented several minutes before food was presented. After a few such trials, Pavlov's subject would begin to salivate after the established period of delay. The ability to maintain a state of readiness and to delay response varied with the species of subject. The higher the status in phylogenetic order, the greater the capacity to delay.

The behavior of the organism during the period of delay was rather interesting. If the delay was not too long, the animal showed signs of preparation and expectation. If, however, a longer period of delay was required, the animal became drowsy and indifferent, and sometimes even fell asleep. As the appropriate time for the conditioned response approached, the animal became more active. From this evidence it was assumed that delayed conditioning required some type of inhibitory mechanism which might be similar to the inhibition involved in extinction, except that it was temporary.

Delayed conditioning is important in the organization of complex behavior where a set to act in a certain way must be maintained over a period of time until action is appropriate. The application of the principle presents certain technical problems. Delayed conditioning is unstable; it is susceptible to the unexpected occurrence of anticipatory responses and subject to disinhibition when distracting stimuli appear.

Generalization. Once Pavlov had established a conditioned response to a particular conditioned stimulus, he found that similar stimuli evoked the same response. When the new stimulus was very similar to the original one, there was little difference in the intensity and the quality of the response. As the stimulus became less and less like the original, however, the response became weaker until finally it ceased altogether, leaving only slight covert evidences of it. For example, an animal conditioned to respond to a tone set at a certain pitch, also responded to tones close to this pitch without further learning. Tones much lower or higher than the original pitch produced a weaker response, and with very dissimilar pitches there was no response at all.

This explained why an organism could perform a learned reflex under stimulus conditions not exactly identical to those which obtained at the time of learning. In fact, since a particular set of conditions could never be duplicated exactly, Pavlov concluded that even the simplest learning situation involved generalization. An organism which could not generalize and had to learn a response to each new situation would be completely ineffectual.

Differentiation. Pavlov's concept of stimulus discrimination or *differentiation* complemented his principle of generalization. He found that if generalized responses to stimuli similar to the conditioned response were not reinforced, they would disappear over a series of trials. The original conditioned stimulus remained effective so long as it was reinforced, that is accompanied by the unconditioned stimulus. In other words, it was possible to discourage generalization. Stimulus discrimination seemed to involve inhibition, for if there was some distraction, the generalized response reappeared.

Experimental Neurosis. Organisms found it fairly easy to discriminate between widely differing stimuli, but when stimuli were almost identical, discrimination became difficult if not impossible. If the animal were forced to make too fine a discrimination, he displayed what Pavlov called an *experimental neurosis.* To demonstrate this reaction he used an experiment in which he conditioned a dog to respond to a circle and not to respond to an ellipse. Once the responses had been well established, the figures were gradually changed over a period of trials until they were almost identical. Differential reinforcement was continued, but the animal was unable to tell the difference between what was and what was not reinforced. At this point, the dog began to display signs of emotional disturbance resembling the symptoms of human neurosis. He became angry, snapped, barked, trembled, put his tail between his legs, and crouched on the floor.

Because of its meaning for human pathology, we take note of the work of several psychologists who followed up Pavlov's observations. Liddell (Liddell, Sutherland, Parmentez, and Bayne, 1936) worked on the problem of experimental neurosis some years later, using sheep as well as dogs for subjects. He found that the neurotic reaction might be retained over a period of years. An animal constantly kept in the experimental situation after the neurosis had developed tended to become worse. His behavior was displayed not only in the laboratory but elsewhere. If the experimental procedure were terminated, the animal's general disruption disappeared, and outside the laboratory it behaved quite normally. The minute it was brought into the laboratory, however, the neurotic behavior reappeared. Many of the animals rendered neurotic also became extremely antagonistic toward the experimenter who produced the neurosis. One dog was so hostile toward him that when Liddell appeared in the animal yard the dog attacked or urinated on him. Norman Maier's rats (1939), which were rendered neurotic by a slightly different procedure with similar results, also showed aggressive responses toward anyone attempting to open their cage door. There has been some success with reversing the experimental neurosis by putting the animal in the original situation, under conditions which make discrimination possible, and retraining it. It has therefore been proposed that experimental neurosis is a prototype for the various human disorders and that psychotherapy, shorn of its magical couches, might well be a process of reconditioning, or reestablishing essential discriminations.

As we have said, Pavlov had no interest in psychology *per se*; he was not concerned with psychological function. The concepts of consciousness, as well as sensation, perception and thinking were too abstract to interest him. He seemed to be unaware that his principles were laws of learning, although he did realize that they applied to the establishment of "reflexes." He did not treat motivation, but he did believe reinforcement was necessary for behavior, and reinforcement in his terms implied motivation. Individual behavior and personality were of no interest to him. Yet, since Pavlov's time, his principles have been applied to all these areas, as we will see when we take up Hull (see Chapter 10) and the Neo-Hullian theorists (see Chapter 11).

Critique

Pavlov's discovery of conditioning ranks among the most important contributions to the psychology of learning. Not only as a method of studying the learning process, but also as a concept, it merits study in its own right.

Nevertheless, it is difficult to assess the status of conditioning in current learning theory. It has formed the basis for a wide range of learning theories such as those of Hull, Guthrie, Skinner, and Tolman. Yet despite its important role, and probably because of it, psychologists cannot agree on the nature of the process. It is now universally agreed that conditioning is not a matter of substituting one stimulus for another, as Pavlov believed. Not only is the conditioned stimulus different from the unconditioned stimulus, but the conditioned response is different from the unconditioned response. In Pavlov's dogs, for example, while the unconditioned response was eight or ten drops of saliva, the conditioned response was only two or three. In other types of conditioning, for example avoidance of electric shock, the unconditioned response is a violent and emotional withdrawal of the shocked member, whereas the conditioned response is a calm, efficient removal. While this may seem a rather petty consideration in some cases (such as the amount of salivation), it can make a great difference in the interpretation of conditioning as a learning process. If this variation of behavior is taken into account, one sees conditioning not as a new stimulus producing an old response, but rather as the acquisition of an entirely new stimulus–response pattern. Many contemporary learning theorists built their principles on the stimulus substitution concept, and have yet to restate their ideas. Moreover, the contiguity-reinforcement controversy adds further uncertainty to this question, and the practical significance of conditioning has therefore long been vague. What relevance, for example, has conditioning for class room teaching? Such questions may presently raise doubt about the validity of current theories of conditioning, but they assure an active future for the field of study.

Instrumental Act Conditioning

In the type of conditioning process used by Pavlov, the experimental subject was a passive participant; he did not have to do anything for the unconditioned stimulus to appear. The reinforcement was provided by the experimenter. For a long time psychologists believed that there was an unbridgeable gap between the active learning behavior studied by Thorndike and the passive conditioning of Pavlov, and were baffled by the fact that the studies involved two different phenomena which generated similar but isolated sets of principles.

A Russian contemporary of Pavlov's, V. M. Bechterev (1932), worked on the conditioning of motor responses. His work differed from Pavlov's in that he studied voluntary activities in human beings. His findings have remained obscure because very little of his work has been translated and that which has is not generally available. There is historical importance in the fact that the work was done, but the bulk of its content was never made available, except within Russia.

Therefore, so far as Western psychology is concerned, it was left to B. F. Skinner (1932, 1935, 1938) to demonstrate the similarities between the two types of learning. As is so often the case, his discovery, which established a rapprochment between Pavlov and Thorndike, was the result of what Skinner called a fortunate accident. In his work with animals, he found that he frequently encountered problems which could not be investigated with existing techniques. Consequently, he developed a new technique known as *instrumental act conditioning*. This method was based on a puzzle situation similar in some ways to Thorndike's. The animal was placed in an apparatus, or "Skinner box," and required to manipulate a bar or lever which would release food or water into a trough inside the box. However, the problem posed to the animal was more complex than learning the use of the lever, as in the Thorndike box; he also had to master the timing of the response by learning to wait for a signal which indicated when lever-pressing would be effective. The signal was therefore a conditioned stimulus.

A brief review of the details basic to the experiments of Thorndike, Pavlov, and Skinner will help to show how the latter integrated the contributions of his predecessors. For Thorndike, the learning situation can be diagramed:

experimental situation⟶ action⟶ food.

For Pavlov, a conditioned response took place in two steps. The first, experimental situation⟶ signal⟶ food⟶ salivation, after learning, became

experimental situation⟶ signal⟶ salivation. Lastly, for Skinner, the steps of learning were as follows:

experimental situation⟶ action⟶ no food
experimental situation⟶ signal⟶ action⟶ food.[1]

Insofar as they both included the *action⟶food* sequence, Skinner's chain of behavior resembled Thorndike's. However, since Skinner's animal was also called upon to learn the *signal⟶food* sequence of classical conditioning, his technique was a combination of conditioning and puzzle box. It appeared to offer a medium for bringing together the disparate theories of Thorndike and Pavlov, showing how each was involved in learning.

[1] As a result of Skinner's later work, it became apparent that no actual auditory or visual signal was required to produce instrumental conditioning. Subjects put on a reinforcement schedule so that they were reinforced every few minutes or every so few responses would demonstrate conditioning. Of course, there was still a signal in the form of passage of time or number of responses.

Aspects of both could be manipulated within the same experiment and observed for similarities or differences of results.

Finally, Skinner's work suggested that there were both stimulus learning and response learning. It has been theorized that stimulus learning or conditioning takes place by contiguity, while response learning is based on reinforcement. Future work may give Skinner's techniques the lead role in clarifying the relationships between Thorndike's response learning and Pavlov's stimulus learning.

SUMMARY

Basic Unit. All activity was the result of integration of simple stimulus response units.

Field of Study. Psychology could be reduced to the study of physiological processes.

Methods of Investigation. Pavlov developed the technique of conditioning, which to his mind was a simple matter of substituting a new stimulus for an old one.

Principles. Pavlov's formulations, based on his observations of the conditioning process, were intended as principles of brain excitation and inhibition, but have come to be seen by psychologists as laws of learning. According to these principles, reinforcement was necessary to establish a conditioned response. Distraction or nonreinforcement (extinction) inhibited the conditioned response. Once conditioned, an organism could learn to delay the appearance of a response to a stimulus until the response was appropriate. A response could be generalized to a stimulus similar to the conditioned stimulus, unless the organism had been taught to discriminate between the two stimuli by means of nonreinforcement. If discrimination became too difficult the organism would become upset and display what was referred to as experimental neurosis.

Pavlov did not consider the other concepts with which we are concerned.

Skinner's technique of conditioning a voluntary (instrumental) act created a new way of studying the similarities and differences between Thorndike's trial-and-error learning and Pavlov's conditioning.

REFERENCES

I. P. Pavlov

Pavlov, I. P., *Conditioned Reflexes: An Investigation of the Physiological Activity of the Cerebral Cortex*, G. V. Anvep, ed. and trans. London: Oxford University Press, 1927.

———, *Lectures on Conditioned Reflexes: Twenty-Five Years of Objective Study of the Higher Nervous Activity (Behavior) of Animals*, trans. W. H. Gantt. New York: International, 1928.

Experimental Neuroses

Liddell, H. S., G. F. Sutherland, R. Parmentez, and T. Bayne, "A Study of the Conditioned Reflex Method for Producing Experimental Neurosis," *Am. J. Physiol.* 116: 95–96 (1936).
Maier, N. R. F., *Studies of Abnormal Behavior in the Rat*. New York: Harper, 1939.

V. M. Bekhterev

Bekhterev, V. M., *General Principles of Human Reflexology*. New York: International, 1932.

B. F. Skinner

Skinner, B. F., "On the Rate of Formation of a Conditioned Reflex," *J. Gen. Psych.* 7: 274–285 (1932).
———, "Two Types of Conditioned Reflex and a Pseudo-type," *J. Gen. Psych.* 12: 66–77 (1935).
———, *The Behavior of Organisms: An Experimental Analysis*. New York: Appleton-Century-Crofts, 1938.

PART IV

BEHAVIORIST THEORIES

CHAPTER 9

JOHN B. WATSON: BEHAVIORISM (1907–1925)

TO many students of psychology, Behaviorism is synonymous with the work of John Watson. Certainly Watson was the guiding light of this movement, and the fact that he attracted so many converts that his theory became almost a fad undoubtedly encouraged the tendency to view this school of thought as his personal possession.

Like Dewey and Angell, and many of his own co-workers, Watson was disturbed by the scientific blinders which Structuralism had imposed upon the study of psychology. Unlike Dewey and Angell, however, Watson did not consider himself just a reformer; he emerged on the scene as an outright rebel. His prescribed cure for the ills he saw was to form a new school to replace the old one. Those who preceded him had merely tried to improve upon existing concepts, and had their reform movement not gotten "out of hand," it would have stopped there. In any event, his fervor and the glamor which surrounded his work soon made Watson popular among scientists and nonscientists alike; and this popularity gave further impetus to his theory.

At the start, Watson felt that the only accomplishment of psychology to date had been to substitute the concept of mind for that of soul. To his way of thinking, more than a mere revision of terminology would be necessary to make the field of study a science. He was not a prophet, however, but a spokesman, since many of his goals and opinions were shared by his contemporaries. Cattell (1904) had long been convinced that psychology should not be limited to the study of experience; McDougall (1905, 1908) had urged that it become a science of behavior; Pillsbury (1911) had contended that investigations of consciousness were valuable only if they widened the understanding of behavior.

Watson did not ally himself with these men, or with others who shared their views. Because he was unable to alter Structuralism, or to compromise with the Structuralists' orientation, he was forced to strike out for new territory on his own. In the process he won the backing of many of the discontented members of the profession, and for a while was regarded as a sort of new Messiah. The violent opposition voiced by the Structuralists, mostly in the person of Titchener (1914), only hastened his progress.

Watson's theory was founded on his early experimental work which had led him to believe that there could be a completely objective formulation of all psychological processes, including mind. During his doctoral work and for some time thereafter, his research aimed to discover how learning took place, and how the various sensory activities contributed to it. To explore the utility of each sense, Watson worked, so to speak, backward. By depriving a rat of a particular sense and then testing its ability to perform tasks, he discovered what that sense had contributed to the original learning process, and what and how well the rat could learn without it. In the course of his experiments, he discovered that rats could learn new mazes and be re-trained in old ones, although they had been deprived of vision, hearing, touch, or smell. Apparently, the only crucial sensory modality was the kinesthetic sense.

It seemed that there was nothing more destructive to the status of the concept of mind than this discovery that a rat stricken of all senses except kinesthesia could still adapt by muscle sense alone. Mind seemed relatively unimportant. This reduction of learning and action to the crudest muscular reflexes became the basis of Watson's theory. Behaviorism has even been called a "psychology of muscle twitches."[1]

Basic Unit

Watson felt that behavior could be broken down into simple stimulus-response units or reflexes. Actually, he conceived of the organism as a stimulus-response machine. He believed there was a physiological basis for these simple units, but he left the physiological analysis of behavior to persons trained in that science. Instead, he focused on what the individual would *do* in a given situation, on how a certain stimulus produced a certain response.

At first, he concentrated on explicit, observable activity, ruling out all else as beyond the realm of psychology. He rejected such concepts as sensations, feelings, and images. He soon found, however, that single overt stimulus-response behaviors were not entirely satisfactory as a means of accounting for complex acts. To resolve this problem, and to expand the scope of his theory, he evolved the concept of *implicit response*, which he said was a minute muscular contraction, nerve impulse, or glandular secretion occurring as a result of stimulation and apparently an

[1] The effectiveness of kinesthesia was later sorely questioned in the study by C. H. Honzik, "The Sensory Basis of Maze Learning in Rats," *Comp. Psychol. Monog.* 13; No. 6, p. 4 (1936). In this study, Honzik found that kinesthesia was the least effective of all senses in producing maze learning.

unobservable part of the chain of behavior. They were responses, and as such were scientifically acceptable. Even though presently unobservable and unmeasurable, Watson argued, they were potentially so, given the right circumstances. This concept made it possible for him to preserve what was useful and necessary from older concepts. Instead of sensations, he spoke of various sorts of sensory responses, classifying them according to the specific sense organ which received the stimulus, for instance, "visual response," "auditory response," and the like. Watson classified non-sensory implicit responses according to the muscle group from which he believed they originated. While he employed the concept of implicit response in a number of ways, his hypothesis that thought could be equated with implicit verbal response is probably the best known, as well as the most controversial, example. We discuss this matter at greater length in the section on Thinking and Cognition.

In sum, he stressed the objective and potentially tangible processes, rather than the subjective, intangible ones which had been described by his predecessors. He limited Behaviorism to the study of behavior, *per se*. If this occurred within the epidermis and was therefore covert, he nevertheless considered it within the prescribed area of study.

Field of Study

We have said that Watson's goal was to free psychology from leanings he believed to be unscientific. He pointed out that mentalistic concepts of any sort were unnecessary, whether they used terms such as mind and consciousness, or focused on processes such as thinking and feeling. Watson defined psychology as the study of behavior, animal or human, and the environment in which that behavior occurred. He felt accordingly that investigation should result in prediction and control of behavior by means of environmental manipulation.

He saw behavior as a function of the whole organism, its neurological as well as its physiological systems. This perspective gave the psychologist three sets of variables to use in studying an organism's behavior: the organism's receptors, its nervous system, and its effectors. The first option was not given much attention in Watson's theory, not out of an opinion regarding its relative importance, but as a matter of personal preference. He placed great emphasis on the nervous system, and was distressed that other theorists all too often transformed the nervous system into a mystery box filled with mentalistic concepts. Too many investigators begged off explaining a phenomenon by referring it to a brain function, thereby implying a neurological basis. They assumed this to be a sufficient explanation, calling for no further study.

To avoid this pitfall, Watson at first limited his investigations to overt behavior. Eventually, as we have seen, he was forced to include covert reactions, but he tried to set them forth as responses to given stimuli, not as unseeable phenomena. He left the attempt to spell out the nature of neurological function to scientists trained in that field. It was the effectors, the muscles and glands, which Watson viewed as the direct agents of behavior, and these attracted the greatest amount of his research effort. He did not, however, reduce psychology to physiology as Pavlov had done before him. Psychology was the study of the total individual; physiology was the study of organic function. Both were concerned with the same data, but physiology viewed it on a less abstract level.

Watson's penchant for studying behavior in its simplest form turned his scientific interest toward infants and children, as well as animals. He wanted to observe behavior shorn of its adult complexities, to gain insight into activity in its most primitive form. As we will show he was interested in using environmental manipulation to control behavior. Once his laboratory efforts proved successful, he turned to the effects of environment on the everyday life of humans. For the first time, investigations in applied psychology were not only condoned, but viewed as a scientific obligation.

Methods of Investigation

The Behaviorists relied upon controlled observation. Introspection was rejected as nonscientific because the data could not be observed by anyone except the subject. They could not be controlled, and were also highly inaccurate and misleading. But many experimental problems were difficult to deal with unless they allowed some sort of verbal communication from the subject. For example, in a color discrimination study it would be essential to have the subject report the color of light he saw. Although this could be thought of as introspection, Watson pointed out that "verbal reports" of such a nature were still in the class of behavior. As responses, they were open to scientific investigation. Watson was never really comfortable with this solution, however, and although he did use verbal reports when necessary, he did so with reluctance. Despite his own discomfort in such an awkward position, his sympathy was never roused for others who might have been forced to use a technique for lack of a better, even as he had been.

Most psychological methods were only partially acceptable to Watson. He recognized the growing body of psychological tests, but pointed out that they elicited behavior rather than intelligence, personality, or the like. Watson used measures of reaction time, the various psychophysical methods, and the memory and learning techniques of Ebbinghaus, but with caution and controls applied.

The major research tool of Behaviorism was actually adopted after the theory was well established. As soon as Watson discovered Pavlov's technique of conditioning, he recognized it as appropriate for his own studies, because it, too, employed the simple S-R bond, and explained complex actions by showing how they were built up from simpler ones. There was one problem. The conditioned reflex was a little too unstable; it necessitated constant reinforcement to be maintained over any period of time. Even then the response occasionally changed and was subject to interference from outside influences. These faults did not render conditioning a useless technique, but they did create difficulties in research. Despite the difficulties, conditioning studies became the preferred research method of Behaviorism.

Principles

The principles of Watsonian Behaviorism were never set down systematically, but they may be inferred from his writings. First and foremost, every object or phenomenon studied must be observable. Watson later changed this to "potentially" observable, when he included implicit responses as admissible data. All behavior, including thinking and feeling, could be studied as sensorimotor phenomena. While the nervous system was admittedly involved, a complete understanding of thinking and feeling must include the activities of the muscles and glands.

Watson granted that certain mechanical aspects of the body were given at birth, but most traits and talents were developed as the result of environmental influences. He thus reduced all learning to conditioning. Behavior was established as a result of repetition. Personality Watson saw as a combination of manual, visceral, and verbal habits.

Consciousness

Watson discussed the mind-body problem only to dismiss it as nonexistent because there was no such thing as "mind." Mind he reduced to behavior, and behavior to body; hence there was no problem. Everything mental was actually physical. It followed from this that there could be no such thing as consciousness. The term was merely a mentalistic invention applied to behavioral phenomena. As we shall see, many other traditional concepts were dismissed on similar grounds.

Sensation, Perception, and Discrimination

Sensation and perception, for example, were terms too unscientific for Watson. He preferred to study "visual response," "auditory response," or "kinesthetic response," but exactly what these concepts implied we cannot say, for Watson himself was not much concerned with them, and the theoretical climate he created did not encourage his followers in this direction.

Whatever the merit of the new vocabulary, it soon created problems. To deal with all the areas he wished to cover and yet remain acceptably objective, the concepts of stimulus and response soon took on meanings which Watson did not originally intend. They were often substituted for taboo expressions, all of the prior connotations remaining with the new word. For example, "visual response" was used to refer to "visual perception." This technique apparently explained a process by naming it. Actually the terminology specified nothing and allowed the terms to become so all-inclusive that they lost their original objectivity and precision.[2]

Thinking, Cognition, and Memory

Watson's early studies with rats, depriving them of the various senses, convinced him that images, presumably the basic material of thought, could be understood simply as sensorimotor events. It is not surprising that, for Watson, thinking came to be implicit speech. Just as there were visceral and motor habits which comprised other aspects of behavior, thinking was a "laryngeal habit." Watson hypothesized that an investigator should be able to discover minute movements in the vocal cords of someone who was thinking. These movements, he said, were speech which was subvocal. Watson arrived at this equivalence of thought and speech because thought employed verbal symbols—words. If thought took place in the form of words, then the response processes to which it could be reduced must also be verbal in nature, and take place in the larynx.

Tests of this hypotheses produced equivocal results (Max, 1934). There were laryngeal movements during *some* thoughts in *some* people *some*times. However, it was soon pointed out that people without a larynx could think, and Watson was forced to agree that thought was not necessarily a laryngeal habit. But he persisted in the belief that it could be reduced to motor behavior, and, to test his theory, hypothesized that deaf mutes using sign language should show implicit movements in the muscles of their arms. He managed to show (Max, 1935; 1937) that such movements did appear in some deaf mutes, although not necessarily all.

To say that thinking was implicit speech or motor behavior was not really to start at the beginning. If thinking were implicit *speech*, then words were the basis of thinking. To explain how words came about, Watson turned to his assertion that learning was a matter of conditioning. From the earliest moments in an infant's life visual stimuli were accompanied by auditory stimuli—the words spoken in response to certain events. Over a series of repetitions, the child came to connect the auditory and visual stimuli and to substitute one for the other. Out of such connections a vocabulary was born.

If one could not make substitutions of this sort, he could not think about a thing. Watson defined two behavior situations in which speech, and consequently thinking, were impossible. One of these was the emotional

[2] This problem is well discussed by E. G. Boring, *A History of Experimental Psychology*, New York: Appleton-Century-Crofts, 1st ed. 1929, p. 586.

response, the other the experiences of early infancy. A system of unverbalized reactions, ordinarily infantile and primitive visceral responses, developed and influenced behavior in a manner beyond the individual's control since without words for the responses he could not even think about them. This concept was quite closely akin to Freud's idea of the unconscious and may have been an effort to substitute an objective interpretation for Freud's more mentalistic one.

Emotion and Motivation

In Watson's day there was a good deal of controversy over the existence of instincts. Instincts had come to be a concept very widely used to explain behavior. Watson felt that they were another mentalistic artifice, and doubted that they could actually be demonstrated. He felt that patterns of behavior called instinctive were really the result of environment and training. In developing his theory of instincts, Watson relied heavily on the pioneer work of Z. Y. Kuo, who held the view that instinctual behavior was actually *learned* in utero. Kuo demonstrated this hypothesis in several studies (1921; 1922), among them his classic investigation of pecking behavior in baby chicks (1932A; 1932B; 1932C; 1932D; 1932E).

Since most chicks are able to peck from the moment they are hatched, pecking had been assumed to be instinctual. Kuo doubted this, and made a careful study of the chick's development within the egg. He observed that as the chick grew, its head and beak rested directly over its heart, so that each time the heart beat the head would be raised and lowered. Gradually, in what seemed to be a matter of simple mechanical leverage, the chick's bill began to open and shut, accompanying the up and down movement of the heartbeat. Kuo proposed that after many repetitions the movement of the head and the opening of the beak became independent of the heart beat, innervation being supplied by developing neurons which grew (by neurobiotaxis) in the direction of the continued stimulation. In a like manner, Kuo demonstrated how pecking at a particular spot was determined by the location of the head in the egg, and that, as the chick grew, the head came closer and closer to the shell until the animal pecked at something as a result of the movement of the head. At the time of hatching, the pecking movement was sufficiently vigorous to break the shell, a rewarding activity which reinforced a bond established through contiguity. Such a combination of factors strengthening the bond rendered the action habitual, so that the chick pecked at things in its environment even as it had pecked at its egg shell. This study, and others like it (Watson, 1925), satisfied Kuo and Watson that other apparently instinctual behavior was also learned, although they granted that demonstration of this fact might be difficult.

Watson sought to objectify emotion in a similar fashion. For him there was no such thing as a feeling; there were merely sensorimotor events. For example, he saw as pleasure sensory impulses coming from slightly tumescent sex organs or other erogenous areas, and from the beginnings of implicit motor responses to these. All other emotions as well could be reduced to implicit behavior. Each emotion was related to a specific visceral change.

In many ways this theory resembles the James-Lange theory, but the differences between them originate with the starting assumptions of each. The James-Lange theory postulated the origin of emotion as:

Situation⟶ perception⟶ bodily changes⟶ overt behavior⟶ conscious emotion.

For Watson, however, the order was slightly different:

Situation⟶ overt behavior⟶ visceral change (emotion).

Both theories suggested that behavior precedes emotion, but Watson rejected the possibility of perception and "conscious" emotion, saying that each emotion came from a specific visceral change.

Under this assumption, emotional states were concomitants of motivational states, since a situation which motivated a certain overt behavior also produced certain visceral changes. Sensory events first affected the muscles, producing behavior, and then affected the glands, producing emotion. Emotion and action were therefore inseparable.

Watson believed he could best study the development of emotions by observing infants whose actions were not yet subject to environmental contamination. His studies convinced him that three emotional reactions were present from birth: fear which was produced by falling and loud sounds; rage which was stimulated by restriction of movement; and love which appeared in response to patting and stroking. All other emotions were amalgamations of these basic reactions, or the result of conditioning various visceral states to new stimuli. Emotions, except for the most primitive, were learned, and could be altered through further learning. To demonstrate this, Watson (Watson & Rayner, 1920) performed the famous experiment with Albert and the white rat.

Basically, Watson saw no reason to expect a child to be afraid of animals, since this was not one of the natural fear stimuli. However, all children are basically afraid of loud noises. Watson introduced Albert, a young child, into his laboratory and showed him white rats and other furry objects. Albert enjoyed the experience. Then he was put through a series of conditioning trials. A loud noise would be followed by the exposure of a rat close to Albert. After several trials the boy began to manifest fear of the rat even without the loud noise. Albert developed not only a fear of rats but also of other furry objects and animals. Watson then demonstrated (Jones, 1924) that emotional reactions, once learned, could be changed. Having established the fear response, Watson then sought to extinguish it. He did this by feeding the child his favorite dishes while he gradually introduced a rat into the child's field of vision. At first the animal was kept at some distance. As soon as he could tolerate this, the rat was moved closer until finally it sat beside him while he ate. After a number of trials the boy lost his fear of rats and other furry objects.

This experiment in the learning of emotion proved Watson's point. But no matter how supportive this demonstration appeared to be, the final form of Watson's theory of emotion depended on developments in his theory of learning.

The Nature of the Learning Process

Although learning was undoubtedly reducible to processes in the brain, Watson preferred to approach it in terms of events and connections in muscle groups rather than cells, since the muscles were more easily understood and gave more objective data.

Watson had much to say about the basis of learning. If pleasure could be reduced to a physiological state, then the Law of Effect was a mentalistic assumption and had no place in psychology. Learning became the establishment of connections between physiological events; since the things that one was exposed to most frequently and most recently were the things that one learned, the Law of Exercise was sufficient to explain all learning phenomena. Watson came into conflict with Thorndike over his views about the Law of Effect. In the heat of the controversy, Watson proposed that a rat in a maze learned because, in order to get out of the maze, he had to take the right path more often than the blind alley. This did not involve reinforcement; it was a simple matter of frequency. Thorndike replied that the statement was true as far as it went, but pointed out that in any one trial the rat might enter the same blind alley several times. How could Watson explain that this most frequent act was not the one which the rat eventually learned? Defeated by this logic, Watson withdrew from the controversy, without, however, modifying his theory.

Watson's learning theory was developed before conditioning phenomena were well known. Once he became aware of Pavlov's work, he adopted it as a basic part of his theory. He found that conditioning concepts fit all of his preconceptions about objectivity, focus on motor response, the role of frequency in learning, and so forth, and it also provided an elementary process on which to base all acquired behavior from the simplest habit to complex personality patterns.

Behavior and Personality

Watson did not propose an organized theory of personality, but had a good deal to say about its evolution. In contrast to the prevalent instinct theories, Watson believed that heredity gave a person only a body and its mechanics; everything else was acquired. Mental traits were not inherited, there was no such thing as general intelligence, no talents, and no instincts. Instead Watson said that environment and experience filled all these roles. This is clear from his famous statement, "Give me a dozen healthy infants and I'll guarantee to take any one at random and train him to become any type of specialist I might select" (1925, p. 82). For him, personality was a combination of verbal, visceral, and manual reactions established and then altered by conditioning, that is, traits were habits. Being subject to conditioning, personality, therefore, could not be constant. However, certain habit patterns were all-pervasive and could not be changed easily because so many separate responses were involved.

Watson's emphasis on acquired behavior focused interest on the study of infant development. To discover what was basically given, what was acquired, and under what circumstances, would be to explain human nature and to be able to predict and control it.

Critique

Watson's work has been called "a crusade against the enemies of science," in psychology and in other fields as well. He was most influential in encouraging studies of behavior and its physiological basis. He gave life to certain new trends and also freed psychology from traditions which had been crippling it.

The difficulties with his theory arose from his conventional effort to treat feeling, thinking, and images which could not fit into his system. He extended the scope of his theory at the cost of its purity, which defeated his own purpose.

Watson has also been criticized for his views on consciousness. By insisting that all mental phenomena were behavior, Watson turned mind into matter. While trying to escape dualism, he actually built it into his own system. He simply placed matter above mind, whereas the philosophers and early psychologists had reversed the relation.

Although he could not admit that there was such a thing as consciousness, he did have to admit that there were things of which people were aware and things of which they were not aware. He finally rejected the concept of awareness of any stimuli from introceptors, but accepted awareness through exteroceptors. That is, he would not admit that anybody was "aware" of anything going on within his own body, but he could be "aware" of external stimuli. This same sort of inconsistency also appeared in his handling of introspection and in the concept of implicit response.

Watson translated phenomena from one level to another; for example, he equated association with conditioned response, believing this to be an explanation. The new words carried new connotations and suggested new hypotheses, but in themselves brought no greater understanding of cause-and-effect relationships.

Perhaps it is because Watson aimed so high that he opened himself to so much criticism. In any event, he failed in many ways to meet his own standards of adequacy for a theory. The emphasis he placed upon his environment, behavior, objectivity and scientific procedure permanently affected the outlook of psychologists, but in most respects his theory is no longer influential; his philosophy of psychology seems to have outlived it. This is not surprising, since he often took extreme positions to activate a progressive movement. But that extremism, while invigorating, was also a distortion, and in time was itself replaced.

SUMMARY

Basic Unit. Behavior was made up of simple stimulus-response units which could be studied either in their own right, or as part of a pattern of reactions. The latter approach was Watson's preference.

Field of Study. Psychology was the study of observable behavior and the conditions under which it occurred. Its goals should be to predict and control activity.

Methods of Investigation. Introspection was rejected as unscientific, although verbal responses were accepted as a valid source of data. Studies involving conditioning were the preferred method, but others were used as required.

Principles. All proper psychological data must be observable. Behavior was understood as a sensorimotor phenomenon which took place in the whole organism, not just in the nervous system. Traits, abilities, talents, aptitudes, and so forth, were learned, not innate. Learning was made equivalent to conditioning—brought about solely by repetition. Personality was the sum total of response habits built up in the organism.

Consciousness. Mind and consciousness were said to be mentalistic concepts. As entities they were nonexistent, referring to events which were in reality physiological.

Sensation, Perception, and Discrimination. While Watson emphasized that sensory receptors were a variable worthy of psychological study, he was not personally interested, and felt that any data regarding anything beyond the sense organs themselves was too subjective to be used in psychology. As a result, neither sensation nor perception were considered in Watson's writing.

Thinking, Cognition, and Memory. He equated thinking with implicit speech. He hypothesized that minute responses of the vocal apparatus were the vehicle of thought. Anything which could not be verbalized could not be thought about. Emotional reactions and infantile experiences were not connected to verbal symbols; they did not involve thought. Experimental tests of the implicit speech hypothesis have produced ambiguous results.

Emotion and Motivation. Instincts did not exist. Behavior which appeared to be instinctual could be shown to be the result of very early, perhaps prenatal, learning. Emotions were the product of implicit behaviors preparatory to certain courses of action and therefore indivisible from motivation. The infant manifested behaviors suggestive of fear, rage, and love. Since infants had no opportunity to acquire experience with the world, their reactions must be determined by their nature as infants. The emotional responses they showed were assumed to be primary. All other reactions were the result of conditioning these basic responses, alone or in combination, to new stimuli.

The Nature of the Learning Process. Learning was not the result of the pleasurable, but rather of the mentalistic consequences of an act, as the Law of Effect proposed. Repetition of an S-R unit was sufficient to establish it.

Behavior and Personality. Personality was entirely the result of the person's environment and could be understood as the sum total of an individual's verbal, visceral, and motor habits.

REFERENCES

Pre-Behaviorist Formulations

Cattel, J. McK., "The Conceptions and Methods of Psychology," *Pop. Sci. Mo.* 66: 176 (1904).

McDougall, W., *Physiological Psychology*, London: Dent & Sons, 1905.

———, *Introduction to Social Psychology*, London: Methuen, 1908.

Pillsbury, W. B., *Essentials of Psychology*, New York: Macmillan, 1911.

E. B. Titchener on Behaviorism

Titchener, E. B., "On Psychology as the Behaviorist Sees It," *Proc. Amer. Philos. Soc.* 53: 1 (1914).

J. B. Watson

Watson, J. B., "Kinesthetic and Organic Sensations: Their Role in the Reaction of the White Rat to the Maze," *Psychol. Monogr. No.* 33 (1907).

———, "Psychology as the Behaviorist Views It," *Psychol. Rev.* 20: 158 (1913).

———, *Behavior: An Introduction to Comparative Psychology*, New York: Holt, 1914.

———, "The Place of the Conditioned Reflex in Psychology," *Psychol. Rev.* 23: 89 (1916).

———, *Psychology From the Standpoint of a Behaviorist*, Philadelphia: Lippincott, 1919.

———, *Behaviorism*, New York: Norton, 1925.

Thought and Implicit Speech

Max, L. W., "An Experimental Study of the Motor Theory of Consciousness: I. Critique of Earlier Studies," *J. Genl. Psychol.* 11: 112 (1934).

———, "An Experimental Study of the Motor Theory of Consciousness: III. Action Current Responses in Deaf-Mutes During Sleep," *J. Comp. Psychol.* 19: 469 (1935).

———, "Experimental Study of the Motor Theory of Consciousness: IV. Action Current Responses of the Deaf During Awakening, Kinesthetic Imagery and Abstract Thinking," *J. Comp. Psychol.* 24: 301 (1937).

J. B. Watson and Z. Y. Kuo on Instincts

Kuo, Z. Y., "Giving Up Instincts in Psychology," *J. Phil.* 18: 645 (1921).

———, "How Are Our Instincts Acquired?" *Psychol. Rev.* 29: 344 (1922).

———, "Ontogeny of Embryonic Behavior in Aves: I. The Chronology and General Nature of the Behavior of the Chick Embryo," *J. Exp. Zool.* 61 (A): 395 (1932).

———, "Ontogeny of Embryonic Behavior in Aves: II. The Mechanical Factors in the Various Stages Leading to Hatching," *J. Exp. Zool.* 62 (B): 453 (1932).

———, "Ontogeny of Embryonic Behavior in Aves: III. The Structure and Environmental Factors in Embryonic Behavior," *J. Comp. Psychol.* 13 (C): 245 (1932).

———, "Ontogeny of Embryonic Behavior in Aves: IV. The Influence of Embryonic Movements Upon the Behavior After Hatching," *J. Comp. Psychol.* 14 (D): 109 (1932).

———, "Ontogeny of Embryonic Behavior in Aves: V. The Reflex Concept in the Light of Embryonic Behavior in Birds," *Psychol. Rev.* 39 (E): 499 (1932).

Watson, J. B., "What the Nursery Has to Say About Instincts," in C. Murchison, ed., *Psychologies of 1925*, Worcester: Clark University Press, 1925, pp. 1–35.

Conditioned Fears

Jones, M. C., "Elimination of Children's Fears," *J. Exp. Psychol.* 7: 382 (1924).

Watson, J. B., and R. Rayner, "Conditioned Emotional Reactions," *J. Exp. Psychol.* 3: 1 (1920).

CHAPTER 10

CLARK HULL (1929–1951)

CLARK HULL and all of the other scientists we will consider in this section, namely Guthrie, Tolman, Skinner, and the Neo-Hullians, were strongly influenced by Watson's Behaviorist philosophy. That is, they emphasized the need for an approach which stressed objective, manipulable variables and carefully avoided mentalistic concerns (although many of them sought to demonstrate how mental phenomena could be reduced to Behavioristic variables). These scientists were also influenced in the same direction by developments in philosophy which resulted in the appearance of the specialized philosophy of science. Since this group has probably been more sensitive than any other to the current philosophical evolution, we include a brief discussion to provide perspective on the theories of psychology which follow.

OPERATIONALISM AND LOGICAL BEHAVIORISM

Some forty years ago, at the time that Bridgman (1928) was developing his concept of Operationalism, a group of scholars in Vienna were becoming interested in the philosophy of science. They felt that the metaphysical nature of philosophy was sidetracking attention from the proper field of investigation, namely the systematic study of the logic of science. They felt that such a study would broaden the base of science at the same time it purged philosophy of the obscure and often nonsensical subjects with which it had been dealing. In a manner reminiscent of Bridgman's work on the problem of definition, the movement turned its attention to scientific language.

Two Americans, Blumberg and Feigl (1931), incorporated this movement into a new approach to philosophy which they called Logical Positivism. They said that a scientist should investigate the empirical relations among his variables, representing them in some sort of symbolic language, by which they meant qualitative or quantitative mathematics. This was to be accompanied by a study of the nature and grammar of the language that the scientist employed. Rather than laying down laws for scientists to follow, philosophy was to be an aid for developing conceptual tools. First, the Logical Positivists wanted to clarify the language of science, and, second, to investigate the conditions under which empirical propositions (statements of fact) were meaningful. They used Operationalism as a means toward both of these ends. The emphasis on factual propositions led to a movement to abandon theoretical constructs altogether. Although such strict empiricism was not the goal of Logical Positivism, it became a side effect of their approach.

Since all scientific statements must be derived from experience, they were reducible to observable phenomena of one sort or another. Therefore, all concepts could, and should, be translated into physical language, that is, the form of expression used by contemporary physics—abstract mathematical formulas. Out of this approach grew what came to be known as Physicalism. This was not a metaphysical doctrine asserting the ultimate physical nature of things, for this could have no meaning, but was rather a thesis relating to language. Any meaningful language must have physical correlates. Addressed to the mind-body problem, for example, this approach eliminated the use of different languages to refer to mind and body, since the words used were, in the final analysis, part of the same vocabulary. The necessity for terms with physical referents tended to make the language of the Positivists operational. For instance, in psychology this meant that studies could be reduced to descriptions of actions. The result was necessarily a psychology of behavior and has even been called Logical Behaviorism. While no organized system of psychology was built around this philosophy, it appealed to many who had a Behavioristic orientation, especially learning theorists and experimentalists who saw in the purity of language a tool with which to establish the purity of science (although this stringently operational approach turned out to be too neglectful of important subjective sources of data in psychoanalytic studies, personality theories, or Gestalt psychology, as we will see later).

Physicalism, however, was a philosophical point of view extending beyond any single scientific application. If the data of all sciences could be expressed in physical terms, then all sciences were simply aspects of the same whole, a view which asserted the potential unity of all science. No matter what the specific focus of a science, it should be possible to demonstrate certain basic operative principles; for instance, chemistry, biology, and sociology might be mere manifestations of the same principles, made individual by the frame of reference within which they were observed. The discovery of universals has since become a challenging preoccupation to scientists in many fields.

CLARK HULL

The theory of Clark Hull gained the name *hypothetico-deductive* or *mathematico-deductive* because it stated a series of general laws and then deduced hypotheses which it proceeded to test. If the hypotheses were affirmed, Hull assumed the validity of his law. If the hypotheses failed, he altered either them, the experiment, or the theory, whichever seemed to be indicated by the results. After the manner of physics and chemistry, Hull presented laws, postulates, and axioms so systematized and defined that each could be related to all others by means of mathematical formulae. In the process of testing, the laws and postulates were modified, sometimes very thoroughly and sometimes only a little.

As this testing process continued, and he grew older, Hull feared that his work might not be carried on after his death, and for this reason he prepared and distributed numerous revisions within the last few years of his life. These alterations are of importance to learning theorists but not as much so to those of us interested in a general overview of Hull's theory. The principles we will discuss are from mimeographed notes circulated by Hull in 1949; they are among the latest versions, recent enough for our purposes, but they are technically not in final form.

Basic Unit, Field, Methods of Investigation

Hull's theory did not differ much in basic unit, field, or method from the traditional Behaviorist position. The basic unit was the familiar conditioned response or stimulus-response unit; the field of psychology was the study of human and animal behavior. The methods of conditioning and maze behavior were used because they were best suited to the animal subjects and to the content of his theory.

Since we are already familiar with the specific concepts, we will discuss Hull's treatment of them in terms of his method of handling them. This will necessitate treating the postulates out of their logical order, but should do no harm to the presentation of the theory.

Consciousness

While Hull undoubtedly recognized the problem of defining consciousness, a matter which still concerns psychologists, he did not wish to handle the concept within his theory and therefore derived no principles dealing with it.

Sensation, Perception, and Discrimination

Sensory Processes. Hull called the initial phase of the sensory process *stimulus reception.* He suggested that when an external stimulus impinged on a receptor, an afferent neural impulse was activated. It is this neural activity which we suggest that Hull would consider to be sensation. He provided a mathematical statement of the relationship between the intensity of the stimulus and the intensity of this neural activity.

He suggested further that if the external stimulus continued to act over a period of time, the neural activity initiated by it gradually dropped off to a fairly low, but unspecified, level. This dropping off represented sensory adaptation, wherein the subject ceased to perceive a constant stimulus acting over a long period of time.

Trace. Hull further stated that after the termination of external stimulus, the neural activity initiated continued for some time, that is, it left a trace, which gradually decreased as a mathematical function of the intensity of the original stimulus and the neural activity aroused.

Hull was probably thinking of a trace as being located within the neuron, since in the 1940's when he wrote, psychologists were apparently convinced that traces, if they existed, were to be found in the individual nerve cell. This presupposition caused a good deal of trouble for all reinforcement theorists, as we have seen in Chapter 7. Traces within the nerve cell could be demonstrated, but the properties of these traces were somewhat alien to Hull and others because the traces were too short-lived. More recent investigations have provided evidence for another type of trace, called the reverberating circuit, whose characteristics are more satisfactory. In view of the complex nature of the circuit, however, it is doubtful that it fits Hull's mathematical formulations exactly.

In any event, the trace construct allowed Hull and his colleagues to make predictions about learning since it provided a link between sensory events and responses.

Perception. Hull did not concern himself with what intervened between sensory events and the responses to them, perception being too far afield from his study of learning. He dealt with discrimination, but in a manner which made it so much a part of learning that we will take it up with that topic.

Thinking, Cognition, and Memory

Hull did not deal directly with thinking, but several of his postulates, for instance the concepts of afferent neural interaction, the temporal gradient of reinforcement, and the phenomena of secondary reinforcement and generalization, have relevance to cognitive processes.

Afferent Neural Interaction. One of the greatest challenges to an S-R theory has been the phenomenon of insight, the sudden solution of a problem by cognitive manipulation. The Gestaltists, who introduced the concept, suggested that, on a physiological level, insight must involve interconnections among neurons. Hull's afferent neural interaction implied something similar among nerve cells. The postulate stated that all incoming impulses active at any given instant interacted with all other impulses presently active in the nervous system. The response was therefore the product of the interaction of *all* these impulses. Insight, the sudden emergence of new connections, Hull accounted for by such interaction.

Generalization. What might appear to be thinking in one situation, Hull thought might really be generalization from behavior learned in some like situation. The principle of generalization was one of Hull's laws of learning, and we will abstract it here. In brief, the law stated that if a subject responded in a certain way to one stimulus, he was quite likely to respond in a similar way to a similar stimulus. If a simple conditioning phenomenon could account for an unlearned act by virtue of the similarity of the situation which produced it, it would not be necessary to introduce a cognitive process.

Temporal Gradient. Certain aspects of thinking have much in common with the temporal gradient of reinforcement, the "goal gradient," as it had previously been called. Although the process was important to Hull's theory, it was not one of his primary laws because its existence had not yet been thoroughly established, nor was its nature completely known. According to Hull, when reinforcement followed a complex act made up of a chain of simple S-R units, it came to be associated not only with the last act in the chain but also with the acts just preceding it. The reinforcement was, of course, weaker the further removed the effect. The similarity to Thorndike's spread of effect concept is evident.

Hull first used his concept of temporal gradients to explain anticipatory errors, asserting that errors of anticipation were the result of "short circuiting." He said that a distant stimulus indirectly conditioned to the goal response might cause the organism mistakenly to omit all intervening responses, reacting as if the goal had been achieved before it actually had been. Random oscillation in the neural processes underlying behavior (a matter which we will discuss later) somehow reduced the strength of all responses save this erroneous one, making it temporarily dominant. The same process could account for dropping out unnecessary responses which had intervened previously; if it were rewarded for the omission, one experience might reinforce a more efficient act. What would look like thinking in such a case would really be a neural short-cut.

To demonstrate dropping out of unnecessary responses, Tolman initiated studies in which animals were forced to take a round-about path to the goal box of a maze; although not previously exposed to a shorter path, they selected it when once offered a choice. This study was part of Tolman's larger effort to negate the importance of reinforcement. To meet Tolman's challenge, Hull and his followers came forth with the goal gradient hypothesis, using temporal gradients as substitutes for all the various anticipatory responses proposed by Tolman (see Chapter 13). Retrospective association of a reward to an earlier stimulus and response should lead to expectation of a reward later in the behavior sequence. As a result of such anticipations, the organism would come to appreciate future consequences of present courses of action. There is actually little difference between "anticipation" and "goal gradient" so far as their predictive power and explanatory value. Hull's concept is molecular, Tolman's more molar. They appear, however, to describe the same process at different levels.

The construct, once evolved, was found to be enormously useful in many other contexts.

Secondary Reinforcement. Hull saw some additional explanations of cognitive behavior in the fact that stimuli closely connected with a rewarding situation came to have reinforcing effects of their own. This is known as *secondary reinforcement*. Erstwhile neutral stimuli become cues for goal-oriented activity; this has often been mistaken for actual reasoning. For instance, monkeys who work for poker chips which can later be used to buy food seem to be thinking. They are actually showing secondary motivation since they have been conditioned to the value of the chips.

In sum, Hull's theory dealt with thinking by making it something else. An act appearing to a casual observer to involve thought was reduced to an aspect of conditioning by diligent application of the appropriate postulates.

Emotion, Motivation, and Purpose

Innate S-R Bonds. Hull stated a number of laws dealing with motivation. The most basic stated that organisms possessed certain innate receptor-effector connections, which produced appropriate behavior and led to either cessation or enhancement of the stimulus which initiated it. This was an indirect way of saying that S-R bonds were structurally determined. Hull probably meant the statement to refer primarily to simple reflex acts, but it seemed to imply that more complex behaviors were also structurally determined. Hull did not describe the identifying characteristics of these built-in behaviors. He simply stated their existence and then turned his attention to other aspects of motivation, especially to the nature of drives.

Growth and Inhibition. Hull saw drives as a function of physiological deprivation. With an increase of deprivation over time the drive strength also increased. Once again, Hull expressed this relationship in mathematical formulae. But in addition to the positive "growth" of drive strength, Hull also felt that there was a negative element involved. For instance, after a certain time the organism might become unmotivated even though it was more deprived. A person who hadn't eaten for 48 hours might act less hungry than someone without food for 10 hours; someone "smothered" by his scarf in a windstorm might experience a panic unknown to the anoxic airplane pilot. Deprivation apparently had effects in addition to initiating drive states, and these other effects eventually became intense enough to interfere with or reduce the drive stimuli. Hull felt the "other effects" might be fatigue, inhibition, or damage or weakening due to severe deprivation.

Drive Stimulus. Each drive created its own characteristic drive stimulus, which increased in intensity with the drive up to the point where the *negative component* set in. After that the drive stimulus grew weaker. The person hungry for 48 hours *feels* as well as acts less hungry. He does not experience the same intense hunger pangs or stomach contractions.

Interaction of Drives. Hull proposed that some drives were able to motivate habits which had been learned as responses to other drives. For example, the human adult eats in an orderly manner, a habit previously acquired through need for social approval but also motivated by the hunger drive (that is, unless this drive is too strong). Drives were capable of interacting or fusing; more than one drive could be involved in a certain act.

Intensity. According to Hull, any strong stimulus had the capacity to arouse or initiate a state of motivation. The more intense the stimulus the stronger the tendency to act, up to the point where the intensity of the stimulus becomes disorganizing. In a like manner, the intensity of the incentive had motivating qualities. Up to a certain point, the greater the incentive, the more concerted the behavior. Beyond this point, an increase of incentive might either have a negative effect, becoming a hindrance rather than a help, or cease to have any appreciable influence at all. For instance, a child will do many things for ice cream, up to the point where he has eaten enough to make himself sick. The same child may strive for a ten-dollar prize, but would strive equally hard for a nine-dollar one. In both cases, increasing incentive will have no positive effect; it may create negative reactions as in the first example, or produce no effect at all, as in the second.

Motivational states not based on physiological needs appeared to possess the same positive and negative growth functions as physical drives. Their graphs showed the same curves of growth and decay.

Inhibitory Potential. Another process, not involving drives, which could become motivating was behavior itself. Any response whatever made by an organism, Hull said, produced a certain amount of negative drive, a certain inhibition of the tendency to act. This he called *inhibitory potential.* The inhibition would dissipate with the passage of time, unless increased by continuing behavior. But if a number of responses were made in close succession without reinforcement, the negative drive produced could culminate in the development of a real inhibition. The stimuli and physiological traces associated with the activity could become conditioned to the negative drive, cueing off inhibition to act at the same time they produced the action tendency. In such a state of affairs, behavior at best would become disorganized by the conflicting motives, and might cease altogether if the inhibition were great enough.

Hull gave much thought to the nature of this inhibitory process. To him it seemed that the organism must become tired after a long series of responses, and if it became tired enough, behavior was impaired. He called this *work inhibition* or fatigue. But fatigue alone did not seem sufficient to explain inhibition. Hull sensed that some other factor must be involved, a desire not to do something, a *negative* counterpart of the *positive* impulse to act. Hull stated the relationship between amounts of positive motivation and inhibition mathematically, predicting the appearance, disappearance, and intensity of response at various times during a given period of activity. Insofar as his predictions were accurate, he could offer at least indirect proof for his theories of inhibition.

Secondary Reward and Secondary Motivation. In addition to discussing drives and other motivational states not involving drives, Hull considered how the primary physiological impulses were altered by experience so that new motives were actually acquired. Not only were the main stimuli preceding a response conditioned to it by reinforcement, but any other neutral or background stimuli consistently associated with the main stimuli tended themselves to become conditioned to the response. These stimuli, presented by themselves, could eventually produce the same response as the main ones. For instance a dog being conditioned to salivate in a room which has gray walls might eventually salivate not only to the stimulus of food or a bell, but also to the sight of something gray. The response would be weaker than that made to the main stimulus, but nevertheless, it would occur. To Hull this meant that a previously neutral stimulus had come to have some motivating quality or to evoke a response. He felt that the learning of motives and this phenomenon of *secondary motivation* were one and the same thing.

Just as stimuli secondarily associated with responses could come to initiate the response themselves, so stimuli associated with reward or reinforcement might themselves acquire the ability of reinforcers. Suppose the dog is fed always in a round bowl, but never in a square one; he may eventually come to possess a marked preference for round bowls. He may be interested in them, like them even when empty, perhaps fight another dog who comes too close to one. He is now demonstrating the process of *secondary reinforcement.* Conceivably, we could induce salivation (and perhaps other acts preparatory to eating) by flashing a gray card (secondary motivation), and then reinforce this new motive by giving him an empty round bowl (secondary reinforcement). Neither of these provides any direct physical reinforcement, but both have a secondary, psychological value.

Any act produced or sustained by secondary processes is highly unstable, at least in laboratory examples. Yet Hullians, and many other psychologists as well, see them as the prototype of much of man's socialized behavior. Perhaps the best known example of secondary motivation and secondary reinforcement is man's use of money. Money in and of itself has no innate value, yet it has so often been associated with the reduction of drives that people come to work for it alone (secondary motivation). Not only is man motivated to work for it, but a hungry man will accept money in lieu of food (secondary reward). Another example of secondary reinforcement occurs in child development. An infant being fed has no apparent interest or awareness of anything but eating, but a number of pairings of bottle or breast with the presence of mother makes mother herself a rewarding experience to the child, although she was at first a neutral object.

The Nature of the Learning Process

Reinforcement. Hull's theory of learning was reinforcement-oriented. He stated that whenever a response was closely associated with a particular stimulus trace and the conjunction was closely associated with diminution of a need, there was an increment in the tendency for the same stimulus to evoke the same response in the future. In other words, when a particular stimulus produced a response and the response reduced the strength of a drive, the response was reinforced and tended to recur.

Frequency. Another postulate stated that habit strength increased in proportion to the number of trials involved in the learning situation. Stated another way, habit strength increased with the number of reinforcements a particular stimulus-response bond had received. This postulate was simply a restatement of the Associationist's Law of Frequency, but in a more advanced, mathematical formulation.

Delay. Reinforcement does not always follow immediately upon an act. Hull stated that the greater the delay between the time of the act and the time of its reinforcement, the weaker would be the connection.

The importance of this postulate can not be seen best in laboratory situations, where it is merely another variable in the learning process, another quantity in an equation. Delayed reinforcement is most applicable to real life, where we do not always meet the consequences of our actions immediately. This delay tends to blunt the effects of the natural reinforcement process and makes it difficult to predict real-life reactions. The effects of delay suggested by Hull can be helpful in predicting real-life learning.

Inhibition. We have already discussed the potential for inhibition or the appearance of fatigue and negative drive in a person over a series of responses. It will be recalled that Hull believed that stimuli and stimulus traces closely associated with an activity also became conditioned to inhibition, becoming cues for it as they had previously been cues for activity. Thus, while a person learned to respond, he learned at the same time *not* to respond. The final outcome was determined by the relationship of fatigue or inhibition to the presence or absence of reinforcement. If the individual were tired from a long series of responses, or if the drive state had acted long enough to build up some distracting influences, inactivity was likely to be reinforced. If the negative motivation were strong enough, response might cease even in the presence of reinforcement. Where a balance of positive and negative tendencies was involved in the response, the absence of reinforcement would tip the scales in the direction of inhibition and the response would be withheld. If negative forces predominated over a period of trials, they would become conditioned to the initiating stimulus, forming a habit of no response.

Generalization. Hull gave a good deal of attention to the generalization of stimuli. Among the factors involved in its appearance he noted first the basic habit strength of the original S-R bond. Second, the presence or absence of generalization at a particular time depended upon many aspects of the organism's physiological status which we have yet to consider. The final factor affecting whether or not a generalization occurred was the amount of inhibition which had become connected with all or part of the act.

Generalization would occur if the original habit strength could overcome any inhibition which might have developed, and the physiological status of the organism was adequate to the task. For Hull, the amount of generalization was a specific mathematical function representing the balance among these factors. But before the formula could predict the amount of generalization in a particular situation, two other situations had to be evaluated. One was the degree of similarity between the present stimulus and the original stimulus, and the other the intensity of the present stimulus. Predictions, even with the aid of a formula, were complex indeed.

Discrimination. The opposite of generalization, discrimination, was nothing more to Hull that the conditioning of inhibition toward a particular stimulus. Inhibitory conditioning affected a response which might ordinarily generalize to a similar stimulus in such a way that the response would not appear.

Behavior and Personality

Reaction Potential. Although Hull is usually assumed to be a pure learning theorist, many of his postulates dealt with learned responses and consequently presupposed a theory of behavior. In dealing with learning we have so far discussed *habit strength.* In his statements pertaining to behavior, Hull developed the concept of *reaction potential.*

Reaction potential was the probability that a particular learned behavior would appear at a particular time. It was a function not only of the habit strength of the act, but also of the strength of the immediate drive, the intensity of the stimulus, the intensity of the reinforcement or incentive, and the amount of delay previously experienced in receiving a reward. Learning *per se* was only one factor in the reaction potential which in turn was only one factor in the production of behavior. The psychological state of the organism and the state of his environment were also important determinants.

Summation. Hull felt that if several stimuli could evoke the same response and they all occurred together, the reaction potential would be the algebraic sum of the separate S-R connections. For example, a response conditioned to occur to both a light and a bell would be stronger for both together than for either occurring separately, other variables being equal. If, however, one reaction potential were extremely weak and the other extremely strong, the response would be less intense than the strong potential but stronger than the weak potential. Hull also postulated the algebraic summation of the variables composing the reaction potential, such as habit strength, incentive, stimulus intensity, and so forth. The amalgamations occurred by means of afferent neural interaction, Hull's hypothetical process of neural interaction.

Inhibition and Generalization. In addition to reaction potential and summation, the actual appearance of learned behavior depended upon inhibition generated by previous trials, and upon the amount of generalization which was possible in the situation at hand.

Behavioral Oscillation. In spite of his widespread mathematical efforts, there was still a small amount of behavioral variation for which Hull could not account with his postulates of reaction potential, inhibition, generalization, and afferent neural interaction. In part, this behavior seemed to result from physiological variation from moment to moment. He felt it could also be due in part to some factors not left to chance but of which he was not yet aware. He combined the two possibilities in what he called *behavioral oscillation*, suggesting that the physical potentiality for any behavior varied from moment to moment. The oscillation appeared to occur at random, so that when there was a low probability of occurrence for one act, there was not necessarily a low probability for all acts.

Individual Differences. Besides these determining factors for the probability of a particular act, Hull also considered the matter of individual differences. Again he left himself a means to account for errors in predictions. His postulates regarding behavioral oscillation and individual differences acknowledged that there were aspects of behavior for which Hull's other postulates could not account. Hull assumed that these laws of variation within and between persons were sufficient to dispose of what he could not otherwise explain.

Critique

Hull's Neo-Behaviorism has been much criticised, in many cases justly so, but even his strongest critics are willing to admit that his work has inspired more experimentation than any other theory of psychology. It is not that the content is new, for shorn of his special vocabulary and his mathematics, Hull is very much like Thorndike and Pavlov. However, the rigor of formulation and definition, and the carefully worked out quantitative statements are milestones in the development of psychological theory. Regardless of what Hull said, his theory would be important because of the way he said it.

As a reinforcement theory, Hull's formulation is open to the usual controversy and shares the weaknesses common to other theories which we have discussed. Like most theorists who focus on the importance of reward, Hull made the reduction of needs central to his theory. The actual equivalence of need reduction and reinforcement is still hypothetical, indeed controversial. Need reduction is usually equated with lessening of tensions, with the removal or lowered intensity of stimulation, with quiescence and with homeostasis. If this were true, psychologists would have trouble explaining the prosperity of amusement parks, good attendance at sports events, or the amount of time spent in courtship and dating. Accordingly, many psychologists now propose that reinforcement is not necessarily equivalent to tension reduction. They suggest, rather, that reinforcement simply enhances the functions of the organism. Some proponents of this view stress hedonic tone, saying that reinforcement means an increase in pleasurable emotions. The concept of enhancement, however, can involve more than just pleasure; it can even encompass the learning which seems to take place when unpleasant consequences are the cues to build up to some stimulus-response connection. Seen in this light, enhancement is anything which maintains smooth functioning in the organism. The enhancement theory of reinforcement avoids some of the problems of the tension reduction point of view, provided it stays on a molar level. However, a molecular account of enhancement, just like any other reinforcement theory, finds itself in difficulty when it tries to explain the physiological basis of the events it hypothesizes.

Another problem area of reinforcement theories is the status which they attribute to punishment. Hull sought to avoid the problem by equating punishment simply with lack of reward. As such it did not fall into special class and did not require further attention. While this may seem to dodge the issue, we should point out that the concept of punishment has caused even greater controversy than that of reinforcement. Few psychologists dare venture onto such unsteady ground; those who have usually retreat after the first tentative step and thereafter treat the matter in generalities.

At other important points Hull's theory was not really equipped to handle latent learning. While many assert that latent learning is only apparently latent, that it is really motivated by an exploratory drive, the argument is not necessarily convincing.

Just as Hull is subject to the same criticisms as Thorndike for the concepts he borrowed from the Law of Effect, he was also an appropriate target for the objections raised to the theories of Watson and Pavlov. Hull, confronted with mental phenomena, answered the question like his predecessors by denying their existence or by reducing them to his own terminology and explaining them away. To deal with Tolman's concepts of expectancies he incorporated his postulate of temporal gradients, and to compete with Gestalt theories of perception, thinking, and insight, he employed his principles of afferent neural interaction, secondary reinforcement, and generalization. Once these matters were brought within the grasp of the conditioned response, Hull considered them to be explained and no longer a problem; both here and elsewhere he reduced mountains to molehills by simply looking at them through the wrong end of a telescope.

All criticisms, however, seem rather inconsequential when considered in the light of the impact this theory has had and will continue to have on American psychology. In the next chapter we will see some of its broader implications.

SUMMARY

Basic Unit, Field of Study, Methods of Investigation. The basic aspects of Hull's theory are the same as those of Behaviorism in general.

Principles. Hull's postulates dealt with most of the salient concepts selected as reference points for this text.

Consciousness. This was not a point of concern to Hull.

Sensation, Perception, and Discrimination. Sensation was described as the action of a stimulus on a receptor. The intensity of the activity initiated in the sensory centers of the nervous system was described as a mathematical function of the intensity of the stimulus. After stimulation ceased, traces of the earlier activity could still be found in the nervous system. Hull did not deal with perception, and he subsumed discrimination under learning.

Thinking, Cognition, and Memory. Hull himself did not deal with thinking, but those who have extrapolated from his theory have reduced cognitive processes to various phenomena of conditioning. Insight could be explained as the result of interaction among afferent (incoming) neural impulses. Generalizations from past experience and secondary reinforcement were made to account for much which might appear to be thoughtful behavior. Anticipation was really only the retroactive effect of reinforcement, which Hull called the temporal gradient of reinforcement.

Emotion and Motivation. Hull included a postulate dealing with innate S-R bonds. While he probably meant to refer primarily to reflexes, it suggests that he was prepared to accept the possibility of instinctual S-R connections. Drives and acquired motives, however, were much more important to his theory. Drives were the result of some physiological deprivation, and increased in strength as deprivation increased. But another effect of drive eventually came into play, a negative effect which reduced motivation and activity, apparently as a result of inhibition. Each drive had its own pattern of internal stimuli; some could even be partially satisfied by actions which had other goals or drives for their motivating force. Motives could arise from a number of sources besides physiological deprivation. The intensity of a stimulus or an incentive could be drive-inducing. The process of behavior itself produced a motivational state of fatigue and inhibition, i.e., a desire *not* to behave. New motives were acquired through the phenomenon of secondary motivation, whereby neutral stimuli associated with a motive state became able to arouse that state by themselves. Similarly, neutral stimuli associated with reinforcing situations could come to have an induced reward value—a secondary reinforcement.

The Nature of the Learning Process. Hull's was a reinforcement theory of learning, which suggested repetition to provide for the strengthening of associations. The strength of a habit was a function not only of reinforcement and repetition, but also of the length of delay in reinforcement and the amount of inhibition. Inhibition could become conditioned to a stimulus as easily as a positive response could. The presence and amount of generalization of learning to new situations was determined not only by habit strength, but also by the physiological state and the amount of inhibition present, the intensity of the existing stimulus, and its similarity to the original one. Inhibition of the tendency to generalize to a particular stimulus produced "discrimination."

Behavior and Personality. In addition to describing how a response was acquired, Hull was interested in how behavior was evoked, i.e., what accounted for the appearance of an action at a particular time. The reaction potential of a response was a function of its habit strength, the intensity of the stimuli which initiated it, the amount of reinforcement present, and the immediacy of reinforcement. Even given a high potential for occurrence, an act would not occur if other conflicting stimulus-response units were also initiated. On the other hand stimuli which complement the one in question could strengthen a response potential by summation through neural interaction. Generalization from past experience could also influence the nature of behavior, as could inhibition. Random oscillation in the functioning of the nervous system, and individual differences in responding were uncontrolled sources of variation necessary to consider to insure accuracy of prediction.

REFERENCES

Operationalism

Bergman, G., and K. W. Spence, "Operationism and Theory in Psychology," *Psychol. Rev.* 48: 1 (1941). Reprinted in M. H. Marx, ed., *Psychological Theories*, New York: Macmillan, 1951, pp. 54–66.

Blumberg, A. E., and H. Feigl, "Logical Positivism," *J. Phil.* 28: 281 (1931).
Boring, E. G., "The Use of Operational Definitions in Science," *Psychol. Rev.* 52: 243, 278 (1945).
Bridgman, P. W., *The Logic of Modern Physics*, New York: Macmillan, 1928.
———, "Some General Principles of Operational Analysis," *Psychol. Rev.* 52: 246, 281 (1945).
Feigl H., "Operationism and Scientific Method," *Psychol. Rev.* 52: 250, 284 (1945).
Isreal, H. E., "Two Difficulties in Operational Thinking," *Psychol. Rev.*, 52: 260 (1945).
Pratt, C. C., *The Logic of Modern Psychology*, New York: Macmillan, 1939.
———, "Operationism in Psychology," *Psychol. Rev.* 52: 262, 288 (1945).
Skinner, B. F., "The Operational Analysis of Psychological Terms," *Psychol. Rev.* 52: 270, 291 (1945).
Stevens, S. S., "Psychology and the Science of Science," *Psychol. Bull.* 36: 221 (1939). Reprinted in M. H. Marx, ed., *Psychological Theories,* New York: Macmillan, 1951, pp. 21–54.

Clark L. Hull

Hull, C. L., "A Functional Interpretation of the Conditioned Reflex," *Psychol. Rev.* 36: 498 (1929). Reprinted in M. H. Marx, ed., *Psychological Theories*, New York: Macmillan, 1951, pp. 399–410.
———, "Mind, Mechanism, and Adaptive Behavior," *Psychol. Rev.* 44: 1 (1937).
———, "Conditioning: Outline of a Systematic Theory of Learning," *Natl. Soc. Stud. Educ.*, 41st Yearbook, Part II, 1942, pp. 61–95.
———, "Principles of Behavior," New York: Appleton-Century, 1943. (A)
———, "The Problem of Intervening Variables in Molar Behavior Theory," *Psychol. Rev.* 50: 273 (1943. (B) Reprinted in M. H. Marx, ed., *Psychological Theory*, New York: Macmillan, 1951, pp. 203–215.
———, "Behavior Postulates and Corollaries," mimeographed notes, Yale University, November, 1949.
———. "Behavior Postulates and Corollaries–1949," *Psychol. Rev.* 57: 173 (1950).
———, C. I. Hovland, R. T. Ross, M. Hall, D. T. Perkins, and F. B. Fitch, *Mathematico-Deductive Theory of Rote Learning: A Study in Scientific Methodology*, New Haven: Yale University Press, 1940, pp. 1–13. Reprinted in M. H. Marx, ed., *Psychological Theory*, New York: Macmillan, 1951, pp. 217–233.

CHAPTER 11

THE NEO-HULLIANS (1937 TO PRESENT)

O. H. MOWRER

THE additions made to Hull's theory by O. H. Mowrer had a double aspect: first, he expanded the theory to include more than one type of learning, and second, he extended its scope to deal with behavioral abnormalities and psychotherapy. We shall discuss only those of our categories where he made significant additions to existing theory.

The Nature of the Learning Process

Mowrer's research led him to believe that the reinforcement learning described by Hull pertained only to motor activities, and he suggested, in addition, that there was a variety of learning involved in emotions and motives. He felt that emotions and expectancies were the result of learning stimuli rather than responses. With regard to emotions and motives, not only was the content of learning different, but the process by which it was established was not the traditional reinforcement of Hull and Thorndike. Rather, stimuli were learned by contiguity.

Mowrer derived his theory of emotional learning from observations of animals faced with the problem of avoiding noxious or traumatic situations. He used this technique for convenience to create emotion-producing situations, but a by-product of it became an interest in avoidance learning as a special variety of behavior, worthy of study on its own merit.

In recent years Mowrer (1960) has revised his ideas considerably; indeed, the original Hullian influence has so thoroughly disappeared that these revisions have been treated in Chapter 32 with other current developments. His earlier position has much more than historical importance, however, for the position which he introduced, and then abandoned, has become popular.

Behavior and Personality

Mowrer's second contribution was the development of concepts dealing with abnormal behavior. It seemed ridiculous to him to speak of acts as adjustive or maladjustive. He felt that any act the organism performed was of necessity an attempt to adjust to the environment. In some cases it was performed for immediate gratification only, regardless of eventual consequences, while in others the long-term effects were considered before the act was performed. He called the first category *nonintegrative* acts and considered them primitive or childish, while the second category, *integrative* acts, were characteristic of mature, adult behavior.

In neurotic, psychotic, or otherwise disturbed behavior, the person was unable or unwilling to view his actions in long-range perspective. He responded to maximize immediate gratification without regard to ultimate consequences, either because of the intensity of his motives or from lack of a more adequate way to deal with the world. Most symptoms and defense mechanisms were of this nonintegrative variety; for example, a hysteric might develop a functional paralysis of his arm which kept him from hitting his boss, but also could cause him to lose his job, limit his activities, and anger his wife. Mowrer called this combination of immediate benefits and long-term hazards the *neurotic paradox*. There is much similarity between Mowrer's views on neurotic behavior and Freud's remarks on the developing appreciation of reality. Nonintegrative acts would correspond to acts governed by the primary process or pleasure principle (see Chapter 15), maximizing momentary pleasure; integrative behavior would correspond to behavior oriented to the reality principle, focusing on the ultimate results.

In his further speculations about neurosis, however, Mowrer's views were diametrically opposed to analytic concepts. Freud and his successors believed that neurotics and psychotics were troubled because their desires for social conformity were too intense. Their moral consciences were too strong to permit accepting themselves as human animals. Mowrer, on the other hand, felt that the troubles of a neurotic or psychotic arose from an insufficient understanding of social demands and moral values, and his psychotherapy accordingly involved helping the person to acquire an understanding of social values. Like other Hullians, Mowrer viewed psychotherapy as a learning process and attempted to apply learning principles to it. His work has been voluminous, but the findings so far demonstrate mainly that learning theory can have practical applications.

Critique

Mowrer's concepts of emotional learning (particularly avoidance learning) and his discussions of integrative and nonintegrative acts have become well enough absorbed into the literature of psychology that they are no longer identified with any particular theoretical orientation. Others of his concepts, however, particularly the social nature of mental illness, are viewed as peculiarly his own and are not so widely accepted.

While it is valuable to realize that lack of proper socialization may lead to mental illness, the belief that all neurotics and psychotics are simply unsocialized or amoral places them in a context which seems more Victorian than scientific. Yet there is little doubt that Mowrer's prodigious work has contributed greatly to the behavioral applications of learning theory.

THE YALE GROUP

Since its inception the Yale Group has been held together by an allegiance to Hull's principles and a desire to broaden their application. The most prominent members of the group are Neal Miller, John Dollard, and Leonard Doob. Mowrer was associated with the group for a while, and his published works reflect that association. Robert R. Sears participated in some of the early work, but is perhaps better known for his more recent studies of children (1947; Sears and Davis, 1948; Sears, Maccoby, and Levin, 1957; Sears, Rau, and Alpert, 1965), and his efforts to apply experimental evidence to Freudian theory (1943, 1944). Sometimes *en masse*, sometimes in pairs, sometimes individually, the group have been at work for fifteen years, embroidering on certain aspects of Hull's theory, and pioneering new areas. We shall discuss only the areas which they have touched upon directly.

Emotion and Motivation

Origin of Drives. Departing from the concept of biologically determined drives, Miller and Dollard hypothesized that any strong stimulus could produce a drive. Cessation of this stimulus reduced the drive and was consequently reinforcing. Drive and reinforcement could therefore be equated with level of stimulation.

This approach gave the concept of drive greater simplicity at the same time it gave it greater generality. Drive in this sense included both biological and socially acquired motives without much concern for distinctions between them. It avoided the problem of tension reduction, and supplied a definition for reinforcement which was not contingent upon physiological effects; it resolved some of the perennial issues of reinforcement that is, theory.

To equate drive with level of stimulation, however, still left the problem of explaining how stimulation became motivating in the first place. Some strong internal stimuli were drive-inducing by their very nature,[1] but other kinds of motives had to be learned. Miller and Dollard called such acquired motives *response-produced drives*, referring to their suggested origin. The original occurrence of a response, they said, could have consequences which

[1] Miller has also studied these, but from a point of view that has nothing to do with this Hullian-Behavioristic orientation. We will discuss this aspect of his work in Chapter 32 when we consider current theory and research.

called forth emotions, or the consequences themselves could be the result of the original stimulus situation, which was just as effective. Such responses gradually became conditioned to the strong internal stimuli, which were the physiological correlates of emotion, so that the recurrence of the responses would induce the emotional reactions. These emotional reactions were strong enough to arouse drives, and response-produced drives could therefore be learned. For example, if a person were punished for an act, it would become conditioned to pain, and to the emotion of fear. Repetition of the act, or of the stimuli which produced it, would come to arouse the fear drive. Reduction of this new drive would be reinforcing, so that any act which reduced fear was learned and likely to appear as a substitute for the old response. The appearance of fear, or any other learned drive, was the cue to the organism to initiate a set of internal and external reactions which had previously been learned and were now generalized to the new situation. Not only fear, but anxiety, anger, sex, and various other appetities could be learned in this manner.

Characteristics of Motivated Behavior. Whatever the origin of a drive, whether biological or acquired, it had certain properties as a function of the general class into which it fell. The discovery of these properties, their behavioral correlates, and the effects of change in intensity of motivation were problems to which Miller gave a good deal of study.

He divided drives into two categories: those which led an organism to approach certain situations, and those which led it to avoid them. The manner in which the approach or avoidance motivation manifested itself depended upon the proximity to the goal object. Since behavior was altered depending on proximity of the goal, Miller assumed that the intensity of the underlying motive was also altered; the nearer the goal the more intense the motive. The rate and pattern of change varied according to whether approach or avoidance motivation was involved. The rate of increase, or gradient, of approach motivation seemed to be fairly smooth and gradual; not so the avoidance gradient. When an organism, whether white rat or college sophomore, was far away from something he feared or disliked, he showed relatively little reaction to it. As he came closer, providing he was still not in the area of danger, he became somewhat anxious, but not really uncomfortable. Only upon coming into direct contact with the object did he begin to show any strong motivation to get away from it. At this point avoidance motivation increased sharply.

For example, an eager teenage girl (approach motivation) grows progressively more giggly from dinner until 8:00 when her first date is to arrive. Meanwhile the reluctant boy, whose mother made him ask the girl, is fairly apathetic until he suddenly panics at the girl's front door (avoidance motivation). This situation is presented graphically in Figure 2, in the fashion which Miller used to demonstrate his hypotheses.

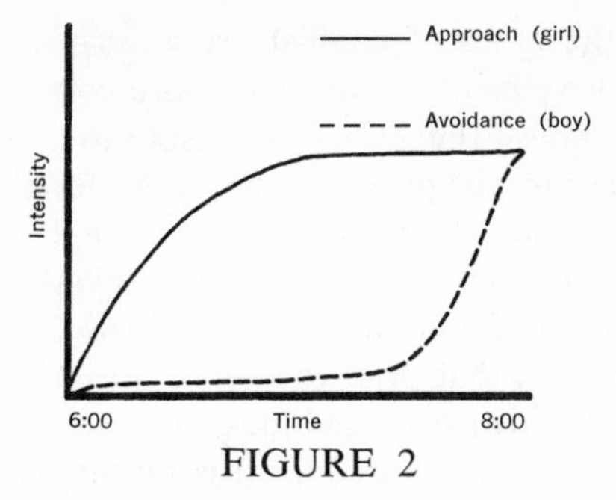

FIGURE 2

Differential in Approach and Avoidance Gradients

Conflict. Miller was also interested to see what would happen when the person was influenced by more than one motive at a time. Hull had already described the summation of complementary motives, so Miller took up the question of conflicting motives. He could conceive of three kinds of conflict in an approach-avoidance context. One of these, the so-called *approach-approach conflict*, occurred when there was an equal desire for two positive but irreconcilable goals, as exemplified by the proverbial donkey between the two stacks of hay. There might be a period of indecision, but once a move was made toward either goal the motive to approach it grew stronger as that goal came nearer, while the conflicting motive became weaker as its goal grew farther away. One move, in either direction, solved the conflict and broke the impasse.

Miller referred to a second type of conflict as an *avoidance-avoidance* conflict. This can be illustrated by the well-known dilemma of being "between the devil and the deep blue sea." This type of conflict was much more difficult to cope with, since no matter what the individual did, it would be unpleasant. If the motives were of equal intensity, the individual would vacillate back and forth, tentatively approaching one goal, and then quickly withdrawing from it in fear until he reached the danger area of the opposing goal. Theoretically, it would be possible to vacillate back and forth forever. The more ordinary response, however, was complete withdrawal and avoidance of both goals if possible. Miller predicted vacillation only when withdrawal was impossible.

The third, and most common, type of conflict was the *approach-avoidance* conflict. In such a situation a goal invited approach, but either the goal itself or the circumstances of approach to it were somehow unpleasant, and ambivalent feelings resulted. As long as the subject was fairly far from the goal, the difference in the two motive gradients would lead to some sort of preparatory approach movements. However, when a subject came close enough to the goal area to feel danger he would stop, freeze in this position, start withdrawing, or engage in a number of defensive maneuvers.

In everyday life the types of conflict are most often found in complex combinations, only very rarely alone. The more complex the conflicts become, the more complex the efforts at resolution, but no matter how complicated the situation, the principles which Miller observed in the study of simple conflict behavior can be observed in an individual's actions.

Frustration-Aggression. The Yale group also investigated frustrated behavior, its antecedents and consequences. Dollard, Doob, Miller, Mowrer, and Sears (1939), showed that prior to any manifestations of aggression by an organism, there was always some block or frustration of drive-induced activities. This observation suggested the frustration-aggression hypothesis; frustration was the cause of aggression. Direct aggression against the perceived source of frustration was the natural consequence. However, most human and many animal subjects learned from experience that it was unwise to attack the frustrating object directly lest pain or punishment follow. Under these circumstances the aggression was likely to be displaced against something else in the surroundings. Displacement was less satisfying as a means of overcoming the frustration, but was safer than direct aggression. If displacement was impossible or incompatible with either the personality or situation, a number of other indirect means might be used to surmount the frustration and achieve some measure of release, depending upon the goal, the person, the severity of frustration, and so forth.[2]

Behavior and Personality

Instrumental and Cue-Producing Responses. Hull's speculations about behavior were highly abstract, and the Yale group, principally Dollard and Miller, set out to make them more concrete and explicit. To objectify the science of personality, they substituted the principle of reinforcement in the role previously played by hedonism, the Law of Effect and the pleasure principle. Behavior was induced, they said, by the presence of strong stimuli; it was reinforced if it reduced the intensity of the stimuli, and was learned if it was so reinforced.

The group divided behavior into two broad types: *instrumental responses* reduced drive by bringing the organism to the goal object; *cue-producing responses* became stimuli for yet other responses because of the meaning perceived. Cue-producing responses included the so-called implicit behaviors of Watson and others—emotion, drive, and purpose—which directed subsequent patterns of activity. Verbal behavior, thinking, and other symbolic acts could also have cue value to the person and/or to his associates. Cue-producing responses could be generalized, so that similar meanings

[2] This description of substitute behavior has much in common with the Freudian concept of defenses, as we will see in Chapter 15.

could be perceived in distinctive situations and appropriate response could be made to variations in external conditions.

Since cue-producing responses determined behavior, external agents were therefore capable of controlling behavior by manipulating the cue-producing responses. To Dollard and Miller, the socialization of a child could be reduced to a simple matter of reinforcing the cue-producing responses—thoughts, words, or emotions—which led to accepted responses, and inhibiting those which led to unacceptable ones. Inhibiting cue-producing responses was the equivalent of Freudian repression, since without the appropriate internal cues, the person could not think about, talk about, or even recognize events. Although such inhibition was a normal outcome of development in children, it could also become the basis of abnormal behavior. In fact, to Dollard and Miller, behavior, normal or abnormal, was a matter of establishing or controlling these instrumental and cue-producing responses.

Neuroses and Psychoses. They felt that neuroses and psychoses were learned. Behavior which reduced conflicts was reinforced, and neurotic and psychotic symptoms were among such types of behavior. Seen from this vantage point, symptoms were habits. The symptom often took the form of a compromise among conflicting motives; the compromise was the algebraic sum of all the drives and habit-strengths acting in the particular situation.

Symptom-producing conflicts were felt to be the inevitable result of the human condition. Children, helpless to cope with their environment, were therefore prone to conflict, most frequently in connection with feeding, toilet training, and the mastering of sexual and aggressive impulses. Neurotic habits or symptoms could easily be formed in the process of solving these conflicts.

Dollard and Miller attempted to show specifically how neurotic and psychotic disorders came about. They presumed phobias to be conditioned fears and compulsions to be either learned tension-reducing habits or a means of distraction from a painful experience. Hysterical conversions originated in organic compliants, but were gradually conditioned so that they remained even after the physical cause disappeared. Displacement, they said, was the result of generalizing a response from the original stimulus to another, safer, one. Paranoid projection was also generalization, but of a more complex sort; the victim assumed that his peers perceived him as he perceived them. In hallucinations, another distorted form of generalization, cue-producing responses were carried over to inappropriate stimuli, usually as a result of a high degree of drive arousal. Hallucinations, in other words, were misperceptions resulting from need. Finally, they said alcoholism was a means of reducing fear.

As these examples show, Dollard and Miller equated the etiology and content of mental illness with that of simple behavior observed in the laboratory. Such illnesses were merely the occasional unfortunate outcomes of normal processes and were brought about by strong drives, emotional arousal, and/or situations which blocked normal reactions.

Psychotherapy. With the assumption that illness was assumed to be learned, treatment could be reduced to the principles of Pavlov, Thorndike, and Hull. Even if new laws were discovered in any treatment situation, there was no reason to expect them to apply only to the special class of phenomena found in psychotherapy. As a teacher, the therapist simply created a permissive milieu conducive to the acquisition of new behavior patterns and the extinction of fear or other negative emotional reactions. The therapeutic climate motivated and rewarded free expression, rendering repression unnecessary. Under these circumstances, a person could come to face aspects of himself which he had previously avoided. There were cases in which the person could not have faced the problems even had he wished to, because repression had deleted the cue-producing responses and with them the tools for thinking or talking about the experiences involved. The therapist had literally to teach the patient the symbols he required so that he could conceptualize his threatening experiences and deal with them. The symbols helped the patient further to discriminate what was dangerous from what was safe, and to classify and understand what was going on inside himself and between himself and others.

The patient also had to learn how to discriminate between reality and distortion in his perception of other people. Too often he perceived in terms of his own past experience rather than experience the person as they were at the time. Freud had also noted this tendency to distort perception, especially in transference phenomena (the patient's misjudgement of the therapist's behavior resulting from childhood experiences with parents and other authority figures). Miller and Dollard asserted that transference misperceptions were not unique to psychotherapy, but occurred every day in a nonpathological form. They were merely misdirected generalizations of past experience. Psychotherapy could help the patient discriminate when generalization was appropriate and when it was not.

Still further, therapy helped to cure symptoms by eliciting responses incompatible with them. For instance, how could a person continue to feel frightened about his anger when his therapist accepted it as natural? How could a child continue to avoid classroom achievement when relieved of his anticipation of failure and aware of his true curiosity about arithmetic, reading, or science? In short, psychotherapy provided an atmosphere for new learning, and the conceptual tools, and the motivation for new behavior.

Thus, some of the most complex human experiences yielded their obscurity in the face of the theoretical simplicity of the Yale group. (We shall postpone, for the moment, the question of whether this simplification was a gain, a loss, or of mixed consequences.) It seemed to Miller, Dollard, and their colleagues that interpersonal or social phenomena might also lie within the structure of Hullian reinforcement theory.

Social Learning and Imitation. Miller and Dollard began their inquiry into social psychology with an attempt to discover the origin of social learning. They noted that an infant's behavior was dominated by primary drives such as hunger or thirst, but although the ordinary child grew up in an environment which met these primary needs without undue difficulty, the environment did seem to create social insecurities. The primary drives were gradually displaced in importance by social motivations toward acceptance, security, and status. Miller and Dollard suggested that among these secondary social motives was a need to imitate others. A person imitated because he wanted to achieve conformity, make his behavior fit what was expected, and enhance his own personal security. When imitation was so reinforced, the imitated act tended to be preserved.

Miller and Dollard suggested three classes of imitative behavior. Two of these were true imitation, while the third was actually parallel behavior, where two or more people performed the same act in response to the same cue, but each on his own initiative. To the casual observer, it might appear that one was really imitating the other. True imitation, they asserted, was either copying or matched-dependent behavior.

The person who was *copying* went through the process of gradually adjusting his responses to match those of his guide. He might not know what the guide was doing or why; he needed only to be able to gauge when his behavior was the same as that of his standard. His stimulus to action was really the action of another person, usually someone with status in the eyes of the copier. Miller and Dollard felt that this was imitation in the true sense of the word and that the so-called herd instinct was based on this sort of imitative process. What had looked to early sociologists like an inborn tendency to follow the group they said was really a learned preference for copying.

In the other type of imitation, *matched-dependent behavior*, the leader was able to read relevant environmental cues which the follower could not decipher. The follower was therefore dependent on the leader for a signal as to when he should do something, what he should do, and where. But the leader was only a stimulus, the follower fashioned the act himself, and although it might seem superficially that imitation was involved, there was no actual intent to ape the leader. This phenomenon, said Miller and Dollard, played a considerable role in crowd behavior and suggestibility; it also accounted for fads, fashions, and many social trends.

They felt that society designated which people were leaders, the models for other individuals. Children modeled themselves after older children and adults, particularly parents. In larger social groups, the relationships between leader-follower or model-copier were defined by the culture to facilitate contacts and preserve society. The importance of imitation to the culture was the reason for the high status of the model in his area of influence. Prestige was the effective tool for getting people to copy him.

Many abnormal social phenomena could also be understood within the context of the same theory. The behavior of mobs or crowds was the topic of greatest interest to Miller and Dollard. Each individual, they said, came to the crowd with a number of needs common to all other members. The crowd itself might activate the needs, or they might have been aroused in the individual's previous experience. The crowd also afforded additional stimuli. The individual's observation that his peers shared his feelings intensified his own motives, and stimuli from the group introduced feelings and opinions which he had not held before his association with it. The more people entertained common feelings, the more likely it was that similar feelings would be induced or intensified in all other members of the group. Soon a leader or model appeared, concentrating attention upon himself, and the members generalized to him the obedience they had learned to display toward models in general. Obedience to the leader aroused expectations of reward, and disobedience, expectations of punishment. The leader suggested the responses which would be rewarded by his own approval and that of the crowd, and established patterns of group rejection for nonconformity. In a crowd which might be moving in an anti-social direction, the fact that an action had been suggested to him relieved the follower of his anxiety and guilt. Through mutual stimulation and reinforcement, leaders and followers could build to a crescendo of mob action and riot.

Crowd phenomena could be the result of either copying or matched dependent behavior. The form which they took in each individual case was a function of the personalities in the crowd and the leader, and of the problems to which the crowd was responding. Whatever their form, however, Miller and Dollard sought to reduce the events to functions of the postulates of Hullian theory.

Critique

The work of Hull's followers generalized his theory from the rat laboratory and the conditioning apparatus, to the broader areas of psychology and speculative fields of psychotherapy and sociology. Whether this approach produced a great contribution or a travesty depends upon the individual point of view. While the scientist finds these writings impressive in their simplicity and objective outlook, those with a phenomenological orientation are likely to feel that much of the richness and complexity of human nature and society have been ignored. But they have nevertheless succeeded in demonstrating that a theory derived in the laboratory can be applied to clinical and social data.

SUMMARY (Mowrer)

The Nature of the Learning Process. Mowrer hypothesized two kinds of learning: response learning based on reinforcement, and stimulus (or emotional) learning based on contiguity.

Behavior and Personality. Behavior was an effort to adjust to biological or environmental situations, some acts being more effective than others. Neurotic behavior resulted from ineffective learning which was nonintegrative, which did not take the long-range consequences into account. Normal integrative behavior maximized eventual gratification even though some temporary discomfort might be involved. Mowrer also believed that neurotic behavior resulted from insufficient appreciation and acceptance of moral values, and could be remedied through the new learning process of psychotherapy which clarified moral requirements.

SUMMARY (Yale Group)

Emotion and Motivation. Miller and Dollard suggested that drives were the result of strong stimuli, biological or social. Social drives were acquired by a conditioning process. Response-produced drives were conditioned when a response became associated with its own consequences in such a way that the original stimulus aroused emotions and drives which would result in the appropriate consequences. All drives could be classed according to their approach to or avoidance of the goal object. Approach drives had the tendency to increase slowly in strength as the goal was approached. Avoidance drives were usually quiescent until the negative goal became "too close for comfort," at which point they became very strong. Two or more drives aroused at the same time came into conflict. Approach conflicts were easily resolved once action was initiated and the person was caught up in the inertia of motion toward one goal. In an avoidance conflict, however, both goals were equally distasteful; the problem was therefore without solution, and the only course was withdrawal.

Conflicts between approach and avoidance motives generally led to vacillating, ambivalent behavior. Frustration was the source of aggression, although it might not be expressed directly toward the frustrating object, but toward some appropriate substitute.

Behavior and Personality. Behavior was either instrumental (result-producing) or information seeking (cue-producing). The cue-producing responses determined all behavior since reinforcing a thought, word, or emotion in a child led to socialized behavior and to the inhibition of undesirable acts. Neurotic and psychotic behaviors were learned, like any other behavior, but had unfortunate results because they were elicited by pathologically strong drives or emotions, or by situations which blocked more adequate action. Psychotherapy was effective because it produced an opportunity to learn new behavior patterns, to extinguish negative emotional responses, and to correct misperceptions based on inappropriate generalization. It also elicited responses incompatible with the continuation of neurotic symptoms such as anxiety. In the ordinary human being, social problems were more a matter of concern than biological ones. Early in life children learned the reinforcement value of conforming to social mores. They also learned to imitate adults and receive the rewards of conformity. True imitation involved either copying the model or matching behavior with the model because the model understood the proper stimulus, while the follower only knew how to respond to it. Often behavior could look like imitation but not be; the individuals involved were merely doing the same thing at the same time, but independently of each other. Adult behavior in crowds was often a matter of imitating a leader who was able to dispense rewards for conformity and punishment for lack of it, in much the same manner as a parent.

REFERENCES

O. H. Mowrer

Mowrer, O. H., "A Stimulus-Response Analysis of Anxiety and Its Role as a Reinforcing Agent," *Psychol. Rev.* 46: 553 (1939). Reprinted in M. H. Marx, ed., *Psychological Theories*, New York: Macmillan, 1951, pp. 487–497.

———, "An Experimental Analogue of 'Regression' with Incidental Observations on 'Reaction Formation,'" *J. Abnorm. Soc. Psychol.* 35 (A): 56 (1940).

———, "Anxiety-Reduction and Learning," *J. Exp. Psychol.* 27 (B): 497 (1940).

———, "The Law of Effect and Ego Psychology," *Psychol. Rev.* 53: 321 (1946).

———, "On the Dual Nature of Learning—A Reinterpretation of 'Conditioning' and 'Problem Solving,'" *Harvard Educ. Rev.* 17: 102 (1947).

———, "Learning Theory and the Neurotic Paradox," *Am. J. Orthopsychiat.* 18: 571 (1948).

———, "A Stimulus-Response Analysis of Anxiety and Its Role as a Reinforcing Agent," *Psychol. Rev.* 46: 553 (1949).

———, *Learning Theory and Personality Dynamics*, New York: Ronald Press, 1950.

———, "Two-Factor Learning Theory: Summary and Comment," *Psychol. Rev.* 58: 350 (1951).

———, ed., *Psychotherapy, Theory and Research*, New York: Ronald Press, 1953. (A)

———, "Neurosis: A Disorder of Conditioning or Problem Solving?" in E. J. Kempf, ed., *Comparative Conditioned Neuroses*, New York: New York Academy of Science, 1953. (B)

———, *Learning Theory and Behavior*, New York: Wiley, 1960.

———, and R. R. Lamoreaux, "Avoidance Conditioning and Signal Duration—A Study of Secondary Motivation and Reward," *Psychol. Monogr.* 54: No. 247 (1942).

———, and A. D. Ullman, "Time as a Determinant in Integrative Learning," *Psychol. Rev.* 52: 61 (1945).

———, and P. Viek, "An Experimental Analogue of Fear from a Sense of Helplessness," *J. Abnorm. Soc. Psychol.* 43: 193 (1948).

John Dollard

Dollard, J., *Caste and Class in a Southern Town*, New York: Yale University Press, 1937.

———, "Hostility and Fear in Social Life," in T. M. Newcomb and E. H. Hartly, eds., *Readings in Social Psychology*, New York: Holt, 1947, pp. 269–281.

———, L. W. Doob, N. E. Miller, O. H. Mowrer, R. R. Sears, *Frustration and Aggression*, New Haven: Yale University Press, 1939.

———, Miller, N. E., *Personality and Psychotherapy*, New York: McGraw-Hill, 1950.

Neal E. Miller

Miller, N. E., "An Experimental Investigation of Acquired Drives," *Psychol. Bull.* 38 (A): 534 (1941).

———, "The Frustration-Aggression Hypothesis," *Psychol. Rev.* (B) 48: 337 (1941). Reprinted in M. H. Marx, ed., *Psychological Theories*, New York: Macmillan, 1951, pp. 482–486.

———, "Experimental Studies of Conflict," in J. McV. Hunt, ed., *Personality and the Behavior Disorders*, New York: Ronald Press, 1944, pp. 431–465.

———, "Studies of Fear as an Acquirable Drive: I. Fear as Motivation and Fear Reduction as Reinforcement in the Learning of New Responses," *J. Exp. Psychol.* 38 (A): 89 (1948).

———, "Theory and Experiment Relating Psychoanalytic Displacement to Stimulus response Generalization," *J. Abnorm. Soc. Psychol.* 43 (B): 155 (1948).

———, "Experiments on Motivation," *Science* 126: 1271 (1951).

———, and J. Dollard, *Social Learning and Imitation*, New Haven: Yale University Press, 1941, pp. 91–97. Reprinted in M. H. Marx, ed., *Psychological Theories*, New York: Macmillan, 1951, pp. 543–549.

Robert R. Sears

Sears, R. R., "Survey of Objective Studies of Psychoanalytic Concepts," *Soc. Sci. Res. Council Bull.* No. 51 (1943).

———, "Experimental Analysis of Psychoanalytic Phenomena," in J. Mc. V. Hunt, ed., *Personality and the Behavior Disorders*, New York: Ronald, 1944, pp. 306–332.

———, "A Systematic Child Psychology," in W. Dennis, ed., *Current Trends in Psychology*, Pittsburg: University of Pittsburg Press, 1947, pp. 50–74.

———, H. C. Davis, *et. al.*, "Effects of Cup, Bottle, and Breast Feeding on Oral Activities of Newborn Infants, *Pediatrics* 2: 549 (1948).

———, Eleanor Maccoby, and H. Levin, *Patterns of Child-Rearing*, New York: Harper and Row, 1957.

———, Rau, Lucy, and Alpert, R. *Identification and Child Rearing*. Stanford: Stanford University Press, 1965.

CHAPTER 12

EDWIN R. GUTHRIE (1930–1944)

E. R. GUTHRIE'S theory was an outgrowth of the behaviorist orientation because he found no theory of learning and behavior sufficiently objective to suit his taste. In Guthrie's case, objective meant almost, but not quite, purely empirical. He had nothing to add to the behaviorist definition of basic unit, field of study, or method. His principles dealt mostly with the conditions under which learning took place and its ramifications in later behavior. He did not deal with perceptual or cognitive processes, and mentioned consciousness only to render it malleable to his purpose.

Principles

Guthrie did not spell out a specific set of postulates, but three principles are at the base of all aspects of his theory:

1) Loss of homeostasis motivated the organism to initiate a series of acts which continued until homeostasis was restored.

2) In all subsequent activity, restoration of homeostasis was associated with the environmental events which had previously been concurrent with it.

3) All behavior, no matter how complex, could be understood as simple habit based on the sequence described in the first two principles.

Consciousness

Guthrie never really considered consciousness. He did, however, assume that awareness of an event was brought about by implicit or explicit verbalization concerning it. Consciousness, then, was merely applying a word to an act or stimulus.

Emotion and Motivation

Guthrie conceived of organisms as being understandable in terms of the physiological concept of homeostasis. The purpose of the organism was to maintain a state of constant balance, i.e., an equilibrium. Motives were persistent stimuli, either internal or external, which created and maintained a high level of neural excitement. The excitement produced activity, which eventually removed the disturbance and restored the equilibrium. Emotions were conceived of as the psychological concomitants of the varying intensities of physiological excitement. Emotions could range from extreme excitement to extreme depression. Responses at either extreme were sufficient distortions of normal processes to be considered emotional disorders; emotional health and emotional illness, then, were based on the same processes — they differed only in intensity. Likewise, an act might be labeled an adaptive response to an emotion-arousing (motivating) situation, or labeled a symptom of some disorder, depending upon the severity of disruption of the normal chain of events. In either case, the behavior was aimed at restoring homeostasis. It had been learned as a means of adjustment and could be unlearned or altered by appropriate later experiences.

The Nature of the Learning Process

Guthrie treated learning on both the molecular and the molar level; before we discuss Guthrie's learning theory, we must define the terms, molecular and molar. A *molecular* approach is just what the name implies, a specific, detailed analysis which concerns itself with the parts of experience, the individual incident, or the specific reflex; its goal is to isolate enough components to reconstruct a whole phenomenon. A molecular study of the eyeblink would, for example, examine the nature of stimuli producing this reflex, its innervation, and its muscular instrumentation. A *molar* approach attempts to cover the whole problem at one time: it does not deal with the parts of things, the individual phenomena of which a general class of events is made up, but concerns itself with the broader case or with the entire class. In contrast to the specificity of the molecular investigation of the eyeblink, a molar study might approach it as one of a number of physiological defenses, concentrating on its variations in response to different environmental and physical states.

On a molecular level, according to Guthrie, learning involved the establishment of connections in the central nervous system. Each time an event occurred, a new connection was established. Therefore, on this level learning occurred in one trial. If something appeared contiguously with something else one time, a connection was established in the central nervous system, and this endured from that time on.

On the molar level, learning involved an association of a stimulus pattern with a kinesthetic pattern of responding muscles. Here the problem was much broader than the establishment of a connection between neurons; it was a matter of the association of two general patterns of activity. At this level of complexity, therefore, one-trial learning was impossible. Although a stimulus and response pattern might be associated a number of times, each occasion would be characterized by minute differences. Even though all learning was established in one trial, the complex and variable environment in which learning took place required the acquisition of numerous highly similar S-R connections, each one specific to some variation in the situation, before a particular stimulus-response pattern could be observed.

Guthrie's theory was an S-R theory, but on a highly involved level. Behavior was an S-R chain. There was an observable initiating stimulus and an observable final response. Intervening was a series of connecting stimulus-response units. While Guthrie recognized that all aspects of these connecting units might not be directly observable, he concentrated his attention upon explicit behavior. He sought a strictly Behaviorist interpretation of activity and avoided any emphasis on covert, implicit processes.

This belief was most manifest in the roles he ascribed to motives and to reinforcement. Motives were important in Guthrie's theory because they determined the occurrence and vigor of movements which might become associated. Motives produced action; the nature of the action was unimportant, for in the course of the action the organism would eventually stumble onto the appropriate response. Then the motive and the action would cease. The stronger the motive, the more vigorous the resultant action and the more impressive were the associations between stimulus and response. Guthrie did not attribute any importance to purpose or goal-direction.

Reward and reinforcement were equally secondary. Reward influenced the outcome of the particular chain of behavior, but it added nothing new to associative learning. Once behavior was initiated, an individual continued to respond until the activating stimuli were removed. Rewards, coming at the end of a sequence of acts, had the function of terminating a motivational state, and consequently of terminating behavior.

What was learned under these conditions was the association of a stimulus situation with the response which stopped the chain of behavior. When a stimulus recurred, the association previously set up made it more likely that the same act which had terminated the previous chain would recur. Moreover, the similarity of situations made similar behavior more probable on a simple, mechanical basis, regardless of learning. Both learning and the recurrence of certain situations worked together to bring about the reappearance of a certain act. If the act was successful in terminating behavior, it was maintained. If it was not, action was continued until the initiating stimulus was altered. Seen in this manner, reward aided in the establishment of an association by removing the necessity for further response. Once the association was established, it prevented weakening the S-R bond, again by making further response unnecessary.

Just as reward prevented further behavior and thereby averted a weakening of the bond, punishment encouraged variation in response. It stimulated different behavior, negating learning either by changing the stimulus or by increasing the stimulus level.

Viewed in this manner, learning became a simple process, regulated by the law of contiguity. To explain learning required few assumptions. In fact, Guthrie's theory was more a description of how learning looked to an observer than a set hypothesis concerning the phenomena which produce it. The nature of the theory imposed one crucial requirement on the learning process, however: that it must involve activity contiguous with the stimulus. By definition, learning could not take place if S and R were not present simultaneously. Most attempts to test Guthrie's theory have focused on this requirement, since it is one of the few assumptions made, and is certainly the most vulnerable. Much human learning does not require motor responses at the time of learning; people can figure out how to repair a car or climb a mountain without actually doing so. This fact by itself is not compelling, but it did force Guthrie to fall back on implicit responses, which he preferred to avoid. More to the point were a number of studies demonstrating that even in motor learning itself, responses need not take place for learning to occur. In studies by Lauer (1951), by Black, Carlson, and Solomon (1962), and by Solomon and Turner (1962), dogs were forcibly prevented from responding during avoidance conditioning by administering curare, which paralyzed their muscles. When the curare wore off, a conditioned avoidance consistently appeared. These findings sorely challenged Guthrie's postulate that all learning required an S-R bond to be established.

Behavior and Personality

Guthrie maintained, along with most psychologists, that man's behavior was adaptive, and that the normal goal of any human activity was to restore equilibrium which had been destroyed by physical or chemical disturbances. Mental activity was no exception to this general rule. It, too, was adaptive. In fact, the brain was the most sensitive and flexible organ of adjustment available. The adequacy of adaptation within the brain was correlated with the capacity to learn, and consequently with intelligence. Learning was not identical with adaptation, but it was the means by which adjustment, once achieved, was maintained.

Within an individual there was a high degree of consistency of adaptive behavior from one occasion to another. Despite the fact that discrete acts were involved, a common background of interests and motives guaranteed that in time, a general mode of behavior would come into existence. This consistent and relatively immutable pattern of adaption was the most outstanding characteristic of the individual, and it led Guthrie to define personality as a persistent patterning of the acquired modes of adjustment.

All personality traits were social in nature; they derived from and pertained to interpersonal relationships. Most fundamental of the social habits was the person's role in life. Role was composed of the actual social status the person occupied in society and the ideal goal he sought to achieve. By association with others, especially the family, the infant acquired a repertoire of response habits and assumed a certain role and a certain ideal. Since it was from this repertoire that personality was developed, the family constituted the most important part of the environment for the majority of children. The way the family trained the child to react, and the way it reacted to him, developed the habit patterns which determined his entire personality.

In addition to the direct influence of society, we must also consider the indirect influence of physiology and the physical traits of the person, for these would dictate the family's response to a child. A fat child and a thin child will acquire different social habits, even in a similar environment. Their basic skills differ, and their family reacts differently to them, thereby magnifying their differences. Aside from the individual's nature, the family's response to a youngster's material needs was of prime importance in determining personality. Whenever the family's needs were incompatible with the needs of a specific member, conflict was created. Common areas of difficulty included jealousy among siblings or parents, too much or too little discipline, and barriers to the normal exchange of affection. These family problems could, of course, lead to personal maladjustment. A few examples will serve to clarify this point. Children must be dependent on their parents, yet some parents cannot tolerate "babying" their offspring. Others over-protect their children, actually shielding them from life. Some parents are so concerned with toilet habits that they begin to train their babies within the first few months of life. Others overlook training until their children are kindergarteners. Some parents become alarmed at any sign of anger in their child. Others punish their children for not "standing up for themselves."

Aside from environmental influence, intra-personal conflicts and emotional states were seen to be of great importance in personality formation. Conflict, for Guthrie, was a failure to inhibit incompatible responses. Most conflict could be resolved by introducing inhibition on the molecular level. Implicit inhibiting responses of speech or motor apparatus restored the dominance of one response over another, and the conflict was gone. (Other psychologists might say "cognitive activity" or "thinking it over" instead of implicit responses.) If not resolved, the conflict produced generalized excitement by stimulating kinesthetic receptors which aroused incompatible sets of gross muscles. The stimuli from this muscular arousal could become so intense as to overwhelm stimuli from all other sense organs. Rigid preservation of activity resulted since no other stimuli were available to arouse responses which could resolve the situation. Eventually the excitement induced by the conflict itself produced the emotional impetus to resolve the conflict by spilling over into some activity. However, chronic conflict states produced fatigue which in turn reduced the potentiality for action. This sort of fatigue was the cause of such abnormal conditions as neurasthenia and psychasthenia.

Emotional disturbances in general were the end result of a prolonged failure to establish a habit which could remove exciting, upsetting stimuli. As a matter of fact, although Guthrie did not say it quite so simply, all mental disturbances and personality disorders were the consequence of bad or ineffective habits. Habits were bad when they were unrealistic or did not provide adequate relief from some activating stimulus. They were bad in that they impaired the adaptive ability of the organism. A nervous breakdown was seen primarily as a social breakdown, and came about because of physical defects, emotional conflicts, or, most commonly, by some combination of the two.

If faulty learning was the cause of maladjustment, then cures had to be some kind of remedial learning. A habit could be broken by establishing another habit; it was this tendency to substitute habits which afforded Guthrie his theory of therapy. To cure a bad habit, Guthrie stated, one simply presented the stimuli for this undesirable action and prevented that action from being performed. This broke the contiguity between the stimulus and the response and led to the establishment of some new response habit. This could be done by presenting the initial stimuli at sub-threshold level so that the response did not occur, or by presenting the stimuli when the subject was too fatigued to respond, or by presenting the stimuli during the absolute refractory phase of the neuron involved, or by sidetracking the response through the presentation of stimuli which evoked incompatible responses. Under any of these circumstances, new habits could be learned.

New habits could also, however, be erected in defense of old habits. This made the cures very difficult. In trying to break up a bad habit, clumsy maneuvering could lead to the establishment of more bad habits. Quinine on the finger nails may prevent nail biting, but if the child then begins to show fear of all medicine bottles as well as starting to chew his knuckles, the cure can become as bad as the disease. Recognition of this possibility seems to go beyond the simple S-R contiguity which Guthrie espoused, and it implies a purposive element in defensive behavior which is alien to Guthrie's general belief. It must be noted, however, that he is neither the first nor the last theorist to find the phenomena of psychotherapy resistant to simple explanation.

Critique

The virtue of Guthrie's theory lies in its parsimony. It involves few assumptions and accounts for the phenomena of learning in as simple a way as possible. Its weakness grows from the fact that even simple behavior is not that simple, and more complex acts of cognition seem to have no place in Guthrie's theory.

Despite Guthrie's attempts to be objective, he has developed a theory which cannot be verified insofar as it deals with the establishment of molecular neural connections not currently open to experimental demonstration. Moreover, he hypothesized such a multiplicity of neural connections that, even were it possible to study them, one would not know how or where to go about looking for a particular bit of learning.

His handling of reward and punishment has been questioned because it is difficult to explain how termination of motivating stimuli differs from a decrease of tension or drive reduction, or why reward terminates behavior, but does not effect it. What began as objectivity and parsimony ends by presupposing many necessary but insufficient variables. In contrast, a theory which attributes to motives and reinforcement the role of sufficient causes does not have to hypothesize still other factors.

Guthrie further detracted from his position by hypothesizing kinesthetic stimulation as important in learning and personality. Experiments by Honzik (1936) and others have shown that kinesthesia is actually the least useful of the senses in the process of learning.

Whatever its faults, Guthrie's zeal for scientific purity is an illustration of what can be done with a strictly Behaviorist-Empiricist approach.

SUMMARY

Principles. Loss of homeostasis led to behavior which persisted until equilibrium was restored. All behavior could be accounted for on the basis of the associations established between various stimuli and responses as a result of restoration of the homeostatic state.

Consciousness. The simple ability to name a stimuli or an act was sufficient to explain conscious awareness of the event.

Emotion and Motivation. The ultimate purpose of the organism was to maintain a state of homeostasis. Motives were persistent stimuli which created neural excitement disrupting homeostasis, so that activity was required to restore it. Excitement or its absence were considered to be the physiological basis of emotion and, at its extremes, the basis of emotional illness.

The Nature of the Learning Process. On a molecular level learning was the establishment of neural connections. Bonds were established each time a stimulus and response occurred contiguously. This meant that learning of a simple S-R connection occurred in one trial. On a molar level, however, learning was the creation of an S-R chain instigated by an arousing stimulus, and continuing until some act removed the disturbance. Learning was the association of this act with the cessation of the arousing stimulus. Because complex situations were so variable, molar learning required a number of trials. Each trial was a separate learning experience, forming a molecular S-R bond. Numerous minute S-R bonds had to be formed before learning was overtly manifested. Neither motivation nor reinforcement caused associations; their function was mechanical. Motivation aroused activity, and rewards terminated the chain of behavior. The contiguity of a stimulus with cessation of activity was the basis of learning.

Behavior and Personality. Personality was composed of an individual's habits of adaptation to his environment. It was a social phenomena since the conditions to which a person had to adapt were social. Childhood experiences were of prime importance, since they formed a foundation of learned habits for all experience that followed. Personality disorders, mental disturbances, etc., were either bad habits, or the result of conflict. Cure, or psychotherapy, was a process of blocking the occurrence of a bad habit, forcing the person to substitute a new action.

REFERENCES

E. R. Guthrie

Guthrie, E. R., "Conditioning as a Principle of Learning," *Psychol. Rev.* 37: 412–428. (1930). Reprinted in M. H. Marx, ed., *Psychological Theory*, New York: Macmillan, 1951, pp. 428–438.

———, *The Psychology of Learning*. New York: Harper, 1935.

———, *The Psychology of Human Conflict*. New York: Harper, 1938.

———, "Personality in Terms of Associative Learning," in J. McV. Hunt, ed., *Personality and the Behavior Disorders*, New York: Ronald, 1944.

Experimental Negations of Guthrie's Theory

Black, A. H., N. J. Carlson, and R. L. Solomon, "Exploratory Studies of the Conditioning of Autonomic Responses in Curarized Dogs," *Psychol. Monogr.* 76 (29): 31 (1962).

Honzik, C. H., "The Sensory Basis of Maze Learning in Rats," *Comp. Psychol. Monogr.*, 13, No. 64 (1936).

Lauer, D. W., unpublished Ph. D. dissertation, Univ. of Michigan: 1951.

Solomon, R. L., and L. H. Turner, "Discriminative Classical Conditioning in Dogs Paralyzed by Curare Can Later Control Discriminative Avoidance Responses in the Normal State," *Psychol. Bull.* 69: 202–219 (1962).

CHAPTER 13

EDWARD C. TOLMAN: PURPOSIVE BEHAVIORISM (1932–1959)

TOLMAN sought to create an ideal psychology, selecting the best of Behaviorism and adding to it cognitive and purposive aspects based on Gestalt theory. The result was a hybrid, something of each, and something more than either. His goal was not to inspire followers, and his approach was perhaps a little too studied to arouse ardent partisanism. His desire was to erect a firm bulwark of ideas and experimental evidence, and the respect atributed to him is ample evidence of his success in meeting his goal.

Basic Unit

Tolman's theory was molar. He approached behavior in terms of its general properties rather than its molecular or physiological details. As a consequence, it is awkward to speak of a basic unit within his theory. It is much easier to write in terms of a set of basic concepts.

In Tolman's theory a number of factors were involved in any act. The environmental stimuli were the *ultimate* or initiating causes of behavior. Intervening between ultimate cause and final act were mental processes. Tolman's "mental processes" were not "mentalistic processes," however. He derived the concept of the intervening variable to avoid this epistemological trap. Mental processes were inferred determinants of behavior, tied objectively to the ultimate causes or stimuli on one hand and to the final act on the other.

Among the inferred mental determinants, those most significant for Tolman were purpose and cognition. These neural activities he referred to as *immanent* causes of behavior, in contrast to the *ultimate* causation of the external stimuli. They were immanent in the sense that they were the last or most immediate causes of a particular act. One might compare the environmental stimuli to a trigger and the immanent processes of purpose and cognition to the firing pin which actually explodes the shell. An act was, in this view, the result of a chain of causal events, some closer in time to the act, some further away.

Other mental determinants of behavior were the organism's abilities and capacities. These determined what type of act it could produce. Still other neural events intervened: certain implicit behaviors produced by the stimuli might be substituted for overt acts. Such was Tolman's definition of thought; it was a response just as the motor response was, but it took place in the nervous system rather than in the environmental field, and it was covert rather than overt.

Tolman's intervening variables appear to be a modification of Watson's implicit behaviors, rendered in a style more acceptable to scientific circles by a careful specificity.

Field of Study

For Tolman, as for most present-day psychologists, the field of study to which psychology should address itself was behavior. Tolman did not mean behavior in the narrow sense of Watson's definition of it as something one could merely see. He was interested in the act in its totality from beginning to end, including everything that went on within the organism inside and outside, in brain and body. To study behavior at this level obviously required a methodology different than simple conditioning.

Methods of Investigation

Tolman adhered to no one methodology, but used whatever technique was appropriate for the problem he was studying at the moment. While much of his theory was developed by observation of rats in mazes, this was not the sole source of his data. The more or less chance selection of this tool led him to concentrate upon place learning in his theories, which emphasis may explain certain discrepancies between Tolman and theorists who studied other varieties of learning.

Principles

Unlike Hull, but like most other psychologists, Tolman did not set down explicit principles. He made some statements which can be considered in the general category of laws, but for the most part the principles on which his work was based must be inferred from the general framework of his writing. The majority of these can most easily be discussed when we turn to his handling of specific concepts. However, there are several general principles which it is appropriate to consider here.

Tolman held that all behavior was purposive. There was some reason, some motive, for its occurrence. In human beings, at least, there was conscious recognition of these directive forces, until such time as the sequence initiated by them became automatic. Then habit took over, and behavior proceeded without conscious intervention.

Behavior was governed by expectancies about the environment. These expectancies were founded either upon observations of the current stimulus situations, or upon past experience which gave the individual some idea of which means to take to what end. To use Tolman's term, the organism anticipated which path among a number of paths would lead to its goal and how it must conduct itself to follow this path. In like manner, the organism could appreciate the meaning or sign value of the stimuli with which it was confronted. The manner in which this appreciation took place gave consciousness a peculiar position in Tolman's theory.

Consciousness

Consciousness was simply a special wrinkle imposed upon behavior. It appeared primarily in moments of change, especially during learning or when decisions were necessary, providing a medium in which thinking could occur. While the cognitive aspects will be considered in greater detail when we take up the thinking process, at this time we can consider certain aspects relating to consciousness.

When an individual was faced with a new situation, he had to comprehend and evaluate it. He also had constantly to be aware of what he was doing and what he was accomplishing. If his course of action was not effective, he had to figure out how to change it. Consciousness, or awareness, served first to aid the organism in discovering what was required to meet a certain situation and then guided the ongoing activity, taking into account the results of actions as they occurred, and continuing or altering the activity as it took form.

To Tolman, consciousness was a sampling process. It was analogous to a rat running back and forth at a choice point in an unlearned maze. The behavioral vacillation of the rat clarified the field. Consciousness had the same function, but it proceeded vicariously. The person didn't run back and forth physically; he did it mentally. As a result of these mental excursions, the person could predict the outcomes of various possible actions. This procedure was invaluable in new situations and was efficient in that it made overt trial and error unnecessary. But it was really a rather impractical luxury, requiring time and energy which disrupted the smooth flow of familiar behaviors without adding to them. Therefore, in order to enhance action, awareness dropped out as soon as the newness had worn off, allowing automatic processes and well-formed habits to take over.

Although Tolman called consciousness a mental process, he applied it to a strictly behavioral referent. His treatment of other cognitive processes was equally behavioristic.

Sensation, Perception and Discrimination

Tolman claimed that the content or raw feel of sensation which concerned the introspectionist was private data. As such, it could only be observed by the experiencing person. Being unobservable and subjective, it could be ignored by science. The objective process of sensation was something else again. Sensation was defined as a readiness to discriminate and translate stimuli in a relatively enduring fashion. This definition equated sensation with perception, for sensation came to involve a sensory input plus anticipations or expectations about the meaning of this input and what could be done with it. This sensation-perception process was a preparatory phase in which the organism interpreted what was going on in its environment and began to organize action in terms of this interpretation.

The expectations correlated with sensory input were of two general types. Some were *means-end expectations*, ideas of how effective certain acts would be in reaching a particular goal, and an understanding of how to go about these acts. Others were what Tolman called *sign-Gestalt expectations*, i.e., anticipations as to the meaning or import of a particular stimulus. In other words, Tolman typed expectancies according to whether they concerned responses (means-end) or stimuli (sign-Gestalt). These expectancies were the part-processes of which thought was composed.

Thinking, Cognition, and Memory

Cognition, or thinking, was a particularly important aspect of Tolman's theory. When we took up consciousness, we discussed how in higher animals the running-back-and-forth or the sampling activity of the rat in a maze did not actually take place, since it became, through the medium of consciousness, a *behavioral feint*. There was no overt action, but implicitly, within the organism, the acts were performed symbolically as the animal considered what would be the outcome of a particular series of acts. One might say that the animal was engaging in implicit testing behavior, or *vicarious trial-and-error*, *VTE*, as Tolman later called it.

Tolman accepted the concept of subvocal speech, proposed by Watson, as a potential characteristic of thinking. He ascribed to it a different function, however. In his theory subvocal speech was not a kinesthetic basis for behavior. It was rather a substitute for behavior, a tool used to represent the field symbolically.

These mental efforts brought the organism into contact with consequences, as if it had actually done something. But thinking did not stop there. It also adjusted the course of action to these projected results and guided and evaluated the ongoing activity. All of this was a further application of VTE.

Consciousness and thinking occurred in situations where behavior was blocked by the fact that the animal or human being did not know what to anticipate. If any predictions were possible, they were conflicting, inconsistent, and confusing. The absence of knowledge or the arousal of conflicting expectations did not cause consciousness or thought; they merely provided the opportunity for the organism to employ them. Tolman suggested that such moments of conscious awareness or thinking, though not observable, could be recognized by sudden and unpredictable changes in behavior. He cited as an example the abrupt changes in learning curves, which indicate the sudden acquisition of some new skill. This criterion for the presence of thought was taken from Gestalt theories of insight.

When such sudden changes involved doing something entirely new, untried and different, they seemed to indicate an especially creative process which Tolman called *inventive ideation*. Such productive thought was characterized by the appreciation of novel relationships not previously suspected. These aroused new anticipations, followed by preparations to respond in new and different ways. Thus cognitive innovations led to behavioral innovations.

In thinking about anything, creatively or not, the organism employed what Tolman called a *cognitive map*. The concept of cognitive maps was first developed in connection with maze learning in animals, and perhaps if the first examples are derived from this area, it will be easier to understand their application to thinking in general. Observing rats in a maze convinced Tolman that they learned about it as a place, not as a series of responses. This conviction was strengthened when rats showed themselves so appreciative of the geography of the maze that they could select the shortest path to the goal if given the opportunity, even though this path was one which they had never traversed and which took them through unfamiliar areas. To Tolman it seemed almost as if the rats had formed a map in their heads in which they represented the various choice points of the maze, the entrance, the goal box, and the spatial relations among these. It was from these observations that the concept of cognitive maps was developed. Tolman assumed that the map included not only an appreciation of relationships among stimuli, but also expectancies about their meaning and readinesses to respond in appropriate ways. That such maps exist can be demonstrated to the reader if he tries to visualize the route he would take to get to a particular store in a familiar city.

The cognitive map was not limited to one's location in space, especially in human beings. In the sphere of interpersonal relations there were maps or expectancies about how people would or should act in a number of different situations. There were also maps or expectancies as to what the person himself would or should do. All sorts of acts could be visualized, as could the means of carrying them out and their consequences. Tolman did not mean to imply that pictorial images were involved. He merely suggested that the person carried with him a symbolic representation of all the physical, physiological, psychological and social aspects of his environment, and his potential reactions to them.

These anticipations, maps, and vicarious trials-and-errors had no meaning to the organism in and of themselves, however. They derived from, and pertained to, whatever purpose was presently influencing behavior.

Emotion, Motivation, and Purpose

Emotions. Emotions had the power of an immanent or immediate cause of behavior. Tolman defined emotion as the arousal of rather generalized expectations about the environment and the consequent occurrence of preparatory sets in the form of incipient visceral and muscular reactions. When the organism anticipated eventual quiescence and prepared itself to achieve it, the emotional tone was pleasant. When the organism anticipated physiological or psychological disturbances and sought to prepare itself for them or to find a means of avoiding them, the emotional tone was unpleasant. The behavior of the organism was purposive, governed by a need to achieve quiescence and avoid disturbance. Emotions were aroused as one or the other state seemed immanent, and were therefore the inseparable companions to drives and motives.

Fundamental Drives. Another immanent cause of behavior was drives. The organism was provided innately with a number of readinesses or expectations as to how to get to, or away from, certain goals. These readinesses, and the physiological states they accompany, Tolman called *fundamental drives*.

Drives arose out of the biological nature of the organism. They were activated when physiological equilibrium was disrupted, and manifested themselves in a peculiar constellation of internal and/or external stimuli. Once a drive was aroused, the organism had to seek some object or activity which would relieve it. The goal itself was determined by the nature of the drive, but the consummatory responses to the goal as well as the means for achieving it were more elastic and could be modified by experience, i.e., they could be learned. The fundamental drives were the basis of all behavior, including the elaborate social motives of adults.

Tolman divided drives into two categories: *appetites* and *aversions*. Appetites occurred in a cyclical fashion, brought about by recurring physiological events. Once the stimulating condition was removed, there was a period of quiescence until changes in bodily function again produced stimuli. Hunger, thirst, and similar drives were appetites. Aversions were ordinarily produced by external stimuli. They were aroused whenever appropriate stimuli appeared and were therefore not subject to cyclical variation. They were continuously active, enduring until the aversive stimulus was removed. Fear and anger were aversions. Although the term aversion had a negative or avoidance connotation, not all aversive drives were avoidance-oriented, as we shall see when we turn to secondary drives. The situational determination seemed to be the identifying characteristic.

Secondary Drives. In addition to primary drives, all organisms possessed a great many characteristics such as curiosity, gregariousness, etc. These characteristics were of such a nature as to be more salient in interpersonal affairs than fundamental drives, but did not have the same biological importance. These *second-order drives* were probably brought about by some physiological stress and had some loosely prescribed goal. However, the goals and responses necessary to satisfy them were far less specifically defined than in the primary drives, where only certain goals were appropriate, and where there was a much greater possibility of modification of goal and response through learning. For example, one could satisfy thirst only by drinking, but one could be curious about many things and in many ways, according to one's past experiences.

The second order drives appeared to have arisen as a way of enhancing primary drives. If they ceased to be useful in this regard, they tended to disappear. Generally secondary drives were aversions. They were situational, being produced by external stimuli and enduring until the stimuli were removed. Both fundamental and secondary drives seemed to have the same origin.

Instincts. For Tolman, instinct referred to those varieties of response produced by the interaction of the maturing fetus with some normal standardized environment such as the womb, the shell, or the like. Since these conditions were common to a species, all members, irrespective of training, should exhibit the response.

This definition avoided the usual problems contained in the instinct concept, while it maintained the feature which the concept was derived to contain: the commonality of behavior among members of a species. Tolman appeared to be using the Watsonian interpretation, framing it in broader terms.

Tolman's first and second order drives seem to meet the criteria of commonality of behavior possibly produced by prenatal environment. He implied that both types of drive had a biological basis. Therefore, it seems safe to assume that to him drives could be called instinctual within certain broad limits. However, he emphasized that consummatory responses and goals were subject to learning and were therefore highly variable. In this fashion, he imposed learning upon instinctual activity.

Need for Specific Goals. The goal object itself had motivating properties. Certain goal objects were more preferred. When a preferred goal object was present, performance was usually superior to that when less desirable objects were present. The phenomenon assumed the nature of a demand, having a motivating force apart from the drive it satisfied. This demand effect was the result of expectations that the organism had about the goal object. Either the organism remembered past encounters or it perceived certain relationships in the existing field. This treatment of goal had much in common with Hull's concepts of incentive and secondary reward.

Within Tolman's theory there was no specific concept of acquired motives. Actually such a concept was unnecessary, since it was incorporated in the assumption that consummatory responses are acquired by training, and that the fundamental and secondary drives underlie social motives. Further, the matter of acquisition was implied in his concept of means-end expectancies.

Means-End Expectancies. The presence of drive roused the organism and potentiated some broad class of behaviors. Among the several possible acts so potentiated, the one which finally appeared was the result of the *means-end expectancies* produced by the drive and the situation. These expectancies contained beliefs concerning which of several procedures would be most effective in reaching the goal under the existing circumstances. These expectancies were acquired in previous congress with goal objects in similar situations, and could be confirmed and retained, or infirmed and eliminated by later experiences.

The fact that expectancies were learned and could be confirmed or infirmed suggests that still another factor must enter into motivation. Behavior required not only a stimulus to instigate it and expectancies to guide it, but an environment in which it could take place, an environment which supported the behavior and verified or negated it. A rat could not run a maze without a floor. First, the floor supported him physically and provided a medium for him to work on and with to achieve his goal. These aspects of the environment which provide the opportunities for motor responses, like walking, turning, running, swimming, handling, and maneuvering, Tolman called *manipulanda*. In addition, the environment provided cues which direct behavior. Contact with the floors, walls, alleys, and goal boxes of a maze aroused expectations and at the same time validated or invalidated previous anticipations. These Tolman labeled *discriminanda*.

Both manipulanda and discriminanda were *environmental supports* to behavior. They were the tools which made behavior possible and the guideposts which directed it. They were what the organism had to learn about.

The Nature of the Learning Process

Learning, to Tolman, was the acquisition of expectancies. To understand the nature of expectancies one must first understand Tolman's concept of the environment. He conceived of the world and the experiencing organism as a *psychological field*.[1] The organism was immersed in this field and was himself part of it. Objects in this field had meaning, or sign value, as things to be approached or avoided. Objects were arranged in various spatial, temporal, and causal configurations with other objects. Expectancies were predictions of the sign or meaning of an object or of its relationships to

[1] The field concept was originally applied to psychology by the Gestaltists and will be discussed when we take up Field Theories in Part VI.

other objects (means-end expectations). They were based on past experience with similar fields. Tolman gave much attention to how these expectations were acquired.

From the first he suggested that there might be several different kinds of learning. His earlier theories discussed conditioning as a learning process distinct from acquisition through trial-and-error procedures. Neither conditioning nor trial-and-error required reference to the Law of Effect in order to explain learning. Learning was the establishment of expectations about the contiguity of events based on repeated past experiences with their sequential appearance. To support this stand, Tolman performed a number of studies on latent learning. These studies demonstrated that learning could occur without reward, provided there was sufficient repetition of the contiguity of stimuli. He also performed an experiment which indicated to his satisfaction that punishment, at least mild punishment, had results incompatible with the Law of Effect. In this experiment, Tolman had blindfolded human subjects learn a finger maze by propelling a stylus along a track in the floor. Each time a subject made a correct response, that is, entered a correct alley with the point of the stylus, he would receive a mild electric shock. Under these conditions the human subjects actually learned more quickly than when they were not shocked. Tolman felt punishment must have functioned as a cue or sign, altering expectancies despite the slight unpleasantness it wrought.

In addition, Tolman proposed a learning process similar to insight, which he called *inventive ideation*. It was characterized by the sudden appearance of new and different behaviors as the organism became aware of hitherto unsuspected field relationships. While this process was largely cognitive and perceptual in its origin, it was also related to learning, for once a new idea was established, it tended to endure without repetition. Since it did not require frequent exposures, but could be accomplished in one trial, and since it involved perception, not motor behavior, it was viewed as a separate kind of learning. As in conditioning and trial-and-error learning, reinforcement was unnecessary.

The response of Hull and his followers to Tolman's theory of learning, and Tolman's response to Hull's, led to the reinforcement-contiguity controversy. This controversy, as well as further research, eventually caused Tolman to reconsider the nature of learning. In 1949 he revised his theory, concluding that there were at least six different types of learning. In describing these types an attempt will be made to distinguish stimulus learning from response learning and reinforcement from contiguity. Tolman did not formulate his concepts in this fashion, but for present purposes these differentiations are important enough to justify inferring them from Tolman's presentation.

The first of these types was what he called *cathexis*, that is, learning which goal objects were effective, and which ones were less desirable. Tolman implied that this was stimulus learning based primarily on the concept of reinforcement.

The second type of learning which Tolman proposed was called *equivalence beliefs*. This was the type of learning in which the organism came to connect previously neutral stimuli with the appearance of a positive or negative goal object, and thus to react to these previously neutral stimuli as he would ordinarily react to the goal object itself. Hence it seems to be a matter of stimulus learning. The concept of equivalence beliefs resembles secondary reinforcement, and as such can be interpreted as the result of either reinforcement or contiguity, depending on whether one follows Hull or Tolman.

Tolman's third type of learning was *field expectancies*, anticipations about the physical and social environment in which one functions. It was the appearance of such expectancies that made it possible for the organism to take short cuts, or to exhibit round-about detouring behavior which temporarily moved it further from the goal in order to bypass some barrier. This was perceptual learning. It could involve some sort of physical contiguity or understanding of the psychological field. It required repeated experience in a situation.

The fourth type of learning was what Tolman referred to as *field-cognition modes*. It involved inferences and perceptions of relationships among various aspects of the field, that is, an insight type of learning: the discovery of principles or generalities, and the altering of frames of reference. It might be the result of contiguity in the sense of realizing some previously overlooked relationship.

The fifth type of learning which Tolman described was *drive discrimination*. This was a type of learning in which the organism became able to distinguish one type of internal drive stimulus from another, as hunger from thirst. We would infer that this was a type of stimulus learning, i.e., learning to differentiate between stimuli rather than learning to connect them. This type of learning could result from reinforcement.

The last type of learning was the *acquisition of motor patterns*. It was the only one of the six types which involved S-R connections. This kind of learning seems very similar to Guthrie's. Cessation of a chain of activity was correlated with a particular act and led to the learning of the act. Viewed in this manner, one would infer that motor learning is a result of contiguity.

In conclusion, Tolman's later theory would distinguish learning about goal objects from learning about the secondary cues, which also determine behavior. He would further distinguish between establishing expectancies about the field and developing new insights about the field. He would distinguish discriminating between internal drives from all of these as a type of learning, and would propose a special variety of learning to account for motor behavior.

Behavior and Personality

Although Tolman aimed for a theory of behavior, his final product was more a theory of the learning or acquisition of behavior than the elicitation of it. This is in contrast to Hull, who claimed to be a learning theorist, but who dealt as much with prediction of action as with how connections are established. In attempting any sort of explanation of behavioral phenomena, it is probable that Tolman would appeal to the expectations that the person has set up as a result of past experiences with the situation. He would assume that the behavior had purpose and was guided by the relationships existing in the environment or field of behavior. So far as elicitation is concerned, one would infer that an act would be selected which the organism anticipated as most likely to be appropriate to the situation and most likely to lead to the return of some physiological quiescence.

Personality was not considered. Indeed, it would be difficult to fit this problem into Tolman's theory at all.

Critique

Much of Tolman's work was an effort to expand the theories of the Behaviorists, particularly Hull. Since Tolman often built his theory specifically to improve on Hull's interpretations, and since these two offer the major learning theories of the day, it may be well to compare them.

The major points of difference between Tolman and Hull were the questions of how many kinds of learning there were and what the basis of this learning was. Hull was a reinforcement theorist, Tolman was primarily a proponent of contiguity, although he recognized the efficacy of rewards in certain minor roles.

Tolman was much more likely than Hull to say that learning was a *discontinuous* process, that is, one not built up by gradual strengthening of neural connections; rather, it was uneven and could even occur on a one-trial basis. For evidence, he pointed to sudden changes in the learning curve as the result of inventive ideation or insight. Hull, on the other hand, was of the opinion that learning is a process of gradual strengthening of associative bonds as a result of repetition. He found the sudden changes in the learning curve very difficult to explain.

For the most part, since Tolman's data was based on maze learning experiments, he dealt with a theory appropriate to learning places, or stimuli, whereas Hull dealt mostly with conditioned responses and talked more about response learning. Each of them attempted to explain the type of material the other one concentrated upon in terms of the concepts developed in his own area.

Leaving the area of learning to consider other conflicts between these two men, Tolman stressed the existence of purposiveness and cognitive processes which were unacceptable to Hullian objectivity. Hull lost out to Tolman here, for the latter was able to establish the significance of purpose and of anticipatory reactions.

Tolman's efforts to broaden and enrich psychology came at the cost of some of the rigor and objectivity of Behaviorist theories. It would seem at the present that those areas within psychology which are most easily quantifiable are not necessarily those areas which are most meaningful to the understanding and prediction of behavior. Such phenomena as Tolman's concept of expectancies fit in with the introspective evidence all of us can report. Yet these things are hard to define objectively and cannot be observed or easily related to any physiological process. This makes research difficult. It is not surprising, therefore, that Tolman should have had problems of definition, but often he was guilty of not defining at all, even when this was feasible. He invented a number of terms, and sometimes substituted his own words for someone else's, assuming that this was explanation enough.

Despite its necessary looseness and the additional ambiguity contributed by neglect of definition, Tolman's theory is capable of growth, and was so constructed as to be easily altered when necessary. The theory seems to represent a coalescence of all modern theories, taking something from each. At the same time it is a compromise of various extremes. In any controversy it was likely to be Tolman who came to the rescue suggesting some crucial experiment or proposing some compromise, and combining the opposing ideas without damaging either. Thus Tolman's theory is a product of the present state of psychological theory, and at the same time has been most influential in determining that state.

SUMMARY

Basic Unit. The molar or generalized aspects of behavior were Tolman's basic unit. He included a consideration of stimuli as the ultimate or final cause of reactions, but inferred the existence of many mental processes (intervening variables) which acted as the immanent or immediate cause.

Field of Study. Any behavior, explicit or implicit, of which an organism was capable was the legitimate concern of psychology.

Methods of Investigation. Tolman did not prescribe any particular method. His most pervasive tool was the maze, which resulted in a heavy concentration upon place learning in his theory, and may have contributed to certain differences between Tolman and other theorists.

Principles. All behavior was purposive, being directed by anticipations of its consequences based on past experience. These anticipations included both the nature of goals to be sought and the means to these goals.

Consciousness. The human being was aware of his behavior only when it was unique or when decisions were required. The more commonplace, habitual actions occurred automatically. Consciousness involved a sampling or vicarious trial-and-error process which allowed the person to anticipate, through the use of symbolic representations, the possible consequences of various acts without actually carrying them out.

Sensation, Perception, and Discrimination. Tolman did not really distinguish between sensation and perception, but discussed a preparatory phase to action, during which various readinesses to discriminate between stimuli and translate them into meaningful information were roused to form expectancies and implicit anticipatory reactions.

Thinking, Cognition, and Memory. Thinking was equivalent to the behavioral feints or vicarious trials which characterized consciousness. It involved the use of a cognitive map, some sort of symbolic representation of the field which the person might mentally traverse in considering a problem or a decision. These maps also included expectations about the field as it would exist in the future before and after the person had acted.

Emotion and Motivation. Emotions were expectancies regarding the future state of the organism and the preparatory responses resulting from these. Pleasurable feelings accompanied quiescent states. Unpleasant feelings were aroused by disturbance, either physical or psychological. Behavior occurred when psychological equilibrium was destroyed and had as its purpose the restoration of a state of balance or quiescence. The organism was equipped with a number of innate readinesses to respond to particular disturbances in an appropriate manner and could develop these further through learning. These drive states with physically defined solutions were fundamental, the basis of all behavior. They might be either appetites (cyclical increases in demand for certain materials), or aversions (continuous states of disturbance enduring until the organism could escape the stimuli producing them). In addition, there were certain second order drives such as curiosity and gregariousness which were less well defined by nature, so that experience had a significant influence in establishing the means and goals which could satisfy them. These secondary drives served to enhance the fundamental ones and to promote their gratification. The goal object itself and the means for securing it also had motivating properties, as did emotional states. Means-end expectancies guided motivated behavior while the environment supported it by providing a place where it could occur, and by giving it the tools for action and the means for validating expectancies.

The Nature of Learning Process. Learning was the acquisition of expectancies about means-end relationships or stimulus meaning. Originally Tolman recognized three general kinds of learning: conditioning, trial-and-error learning (both established by repetitive exposures to a contiguous relationship of some sort), and inventive ideation (wherein thoughtful consideration led to permanent changes in perception in one trial). Reinforcement was not necessary to any of these three kinds of learning. Later Tolman changed his theory to include learning of goal objects, conditioning of previously neutral stimuli, learning of expectancies, insight, drive discrimination and motor learning. At least one of these, learning goal objects, was established through reinforcement.

Behavior and Personality. Tolman's theory discussed in detail the bases of behavior in purpose and expectancies, but it did not deal with how specific acts were organized.

REFERENCES

Edward C. Tolman

Carr, H. A., E. C. Tolman, E. L. Thorndike, E. A. Culler, J. F. Dashiell, and K. F. Muenzinger, "The Law of Effect," *Psychol. Rev.* 45: 191–218 (1938).

Honzik, C. H., and E. C. Tolman, "The Perception of Spatial Relations by the Rat: A Type of Response Not Easily Explained by Conditioning," *J. Comp. Psychol.* 22: 287–318 (1936).

———, "The Action of Punishment in Accelerating Learning," *J. Comp. Psychol.* 26: 187–200 (1938).

Tolman, E. C., *Purposive Behavior in Animals and Men*. New York: Appleton-Century, 1932. A section is reprinted as "Molar and Purposive Behaviorism" in M. H. Marx, ed., *Psychological Theories*, New York: Macmillan, 1951, pp. 410–458.

———, "Operational Behaviorism and Current Trends in Psychology," *Proc. 25th Anniv. Celebr. Inaug. Grad. Stud.*, Los Angeles: Univ. S. Calif. Press, 1936, pp. 89–103., Reprinted in part as "The Intervening Variable" in M. H. Marx, ed., *Psychological Theories*, New York: Macmillan, 1951, pp. 87–102.

———, "There is More Than One Kind of Learning," *Psychol. Rev.* 56: 144–155 (1949).

———, *Collected Papers*. Berkeley: Univ. Calif. Press, 1951.

———, "Performance Vectors: A Theoretical and Experimental Attack Upon Emphasis, Effect, and Repression," *Amer. Psychol.* 14: 1–7 (1959).

———, and C. H. Honzik, "'Insight' in Rats," *Univ. Calif. Publ. Psychol.* 4 (A): 215–232 (1930).

———, "Degrees of Hunger, Reward, and Non-Reward, the Maze Learning in Rats," *Univ. Calif. Publ. Psychol.* 4 (B): 241–256 (1930).

———, "Introduction and Removal of Reward, and Maze Performance in Rats," *Univ. Calif. Publ. Psychol.* 4 (C): 257–275 (1930).

CHAPTER 14

B. F. SKINNER (1932 TO PRESENT)

SKINNER is a Behaviorist par excellence, an adherent of the ultra-objective school, and a radical empiricist. He denied the necessity for any sort of formal theorizing, believing that knowledge is obtained by observation alone. Once enough facts are known in a given situation, cause and effect become obvious. "In representing and managing relevant variables, a conceptual model is useless: we come to grips with behavior itself. When behavior shows order and consistency we are much less likely to be concerned with physiological or mentalistic causes. A datum emerges which takes the place of theoretical fantasy" (1960, 231). Hopefully, it is not unfair to include Skinner in a text on psychological theory, having pointed out in advance that his work is a descriptive exercise, not an explanatory one.

Skinner employed the general theory of Behaviorism to define what should be studied and how. He reduced behavior to the reflex, intending to show the correlation between stimulus and response. By studying this reflex he hoped to uderstand behavior and the contingencies which produce it.

Methods of Investigation

The Skinner box has already been mentioned in connection with instrumental act conditioning (see Chapter 8) as the technique which enabled psychology to relate Pavlovian conditioning and Thorndike trial-and-error behavior. As Skinner continued his work, the box became a highly complex arrangement of bars to be pressed by the subject, with electrical mechanisms governing the rate and amount of reinforcement, timing the presentation of stimuli, controlling other variables, and recording all sorts of data. What started out as a fairly simple puzzle box has become an expensive machine requiring considerable electronic gadgetry. With such a tool, records can be kept of the moment-by-moment variations in behavior under numerous conditions. The studies which use it in its current form often present conclusions based on millions of responses.

The introduction of such a controlled testing situation and the mass of recording of information led to an innovation in experimental procedure. Skinner found himself able to use "single-organism designs," investigations which required only one subject. The large amount of data and the cautious control could, he felt, rule out the influence of experimental errors. Moreover, Skinner came to see his cumulative records (which plot some dependent variable against some independent variable) as sufficient to demonstrate laws of behavior. No statistical procedures or theories were necessary; his data was complete and valid enough to speak for itself.

Principles

Most of Skinner's laws of behavior are restatements of the principles of neural transmission and the laws of learning formulated by Thorndike and Pavlov. As Skinner originally put forth his laws in *The Behavior of Organisms* (1938), there were three general types: static laws, dynamic laws, and laws of interaction.

According to the static laws, a stimulus must reach a certain threshold before a response would occur. Given an adequate stimulus, a latent interval would still intervene before response occurred. The strength of the eventual response was a result of the intensity of the stimulus, although prolonging or repeating the stimulus would have the same effect as increased intensity.

The dynamic laws described the refractory phase of response elicitation, during which recurrence of an act was quite unlikely. In addition, fatigue built up as response continued, and dissipated when the organism was at rest. Stimuli could interact to facilitate or inhibit each other. The phenomena of classical Pavlovian conditioning and extinction, and of operant conditioning (reinforcement learning) and extinction were also described in the dynamic laws.

The laws of interaction discussed the summation and interference of concurrent responses. Acts leading to reinforcement had different amounts of strength depending on the amount of reinforcement each had received. Compatible responses could occur simultaneously, and would summate algebraically, while in the case of incompatible responses, the prepotent response would block the other one unless they were of equal strength, in which case they would blend. A response could become a stimulus for another response (this was called *chaining*), but if extinction occurred only those chained responses which actually took place would be extinguished. Change in one response could induce a change in related responses (*generalization*); induced change could be extinguished without affecting the original conditioned response (*discrimination*).

Consciousness, sensations, perception, discrimination, thinking, cognition, and memory were not covered by Skinner in any specific fashion. He concentrated on matters of motivation, learning, and behavior.

Emotion and Motivation

Skinner warned against indiscriminate use of terms like "drive" and "need" and preferred to specify in more operational terms what other psychologists might call "motivational states." In the case of hunger, for example, Skinner found it sufficient to state the number of hours the organism had been deprived of food. Deprivation, in turn, rendered certain things reinforcing, e.g., so long as the hungry organism was unsatiated, it could be reinforced with food.

As this account implies, Skinner's empiricist approach led him to describe the course of behavior in terms of the external stimuli which elicited it and the events which followed it. As a further precaution against subjective and non-operational concepts, Skinner introduced new terms to assist him in his description of behavior. In dealing with stimulus phenomena, Skinner distinguished between two different kinds of behavior, respondent and operant. *Respondent behavior* referred to responses for which there were known eliciting stimuli, such as the eye-blink or the knee-jerk reflex. *Operant behavior* referred to responses which were emitted by the organism in the absence of any *overt* eliciting stimulus. The consequences of these operant or instrumental acts were important in determining the future course of events.

The Nature of the Learning Process

Reinforcement was crucial to Skinner's formulation of the learning process, for those responses which were reinforced were strengthened and tended to be emitted more frequently. A hungry animal new to a Skinner box might accidentally come near the bar and be rewarded with a pellet of food. As this happened several times, it would be noted that the animal began to approach the bar more frequently, and perhaps began to touch it. If rewarded for the touching, the animal soon developed a bar-touching habit which, with continued reinforcement, could shape into an efficient bar-pressing habit. If reinforcement were withheld, the response would eventually cease. This learning process Skinner called *operant conditioning* or *instrumental act conditioning*.

Those stimuli which were present just prior to reinforcement became associated with the response, becoming what Skinner called *discriminative stimuli*; they served to set the occasion for the response. If, for example, an animal was reinforced for pressing a bar in the presence of a red light and not a green one, the red light became a discriminative stimulus signaling a condition under which reinforcement could be obtained.

Just as concomitant responses were reinforced, stimulus conditions present at the time of reinforcement but incidental to it took on reinforcing properties through continued pairing with the reinforcer. The sound of the food magazine rising may acquire reinforcing properties through its association with food, for example, and could be used to condition new behavior. The reader may recognize this as the phenomenon commonly called secondary reinforcement.

While reinforcement shaped and preserved behavior and established discriminative stimuli, punishment was a means of getting the organism to vary its behavior. It did not eliminate or weaken learned response; it merely suppressed it. A punished animal still emitted as many responses before final extinction of a response tendency as one which had not been punished. The only difference was that immediately following punishment the responses were emitted less rapidly. A series of experiments performed by Estes (1944) resulted in data which generally supported Skinner's position on punishment.

Behavior and Personality

Reward and punishment were not merely narrow independent variables influencing learning; they were broad behavioral determinants. Skinner studied the behavioral effects of reinforcement in great detail and his work here is a major contribution. His investigations have shown that the timing and the probability of reward influenced how, when, where, and if action would occur, as well as whether or not it would be learned. Reinforcement *shaped* behavior. In trying to establish a new act, reinforcing any response which bore the slightest resemblance to what the trainer wanted soon served to produce a polished performance. For example, Skinner succeeded in teaching pigeons to "bowl" by reinforcing any motions which happened to resemble the proper response. Now, obviously pigeons have little natural propensity for bowling, but they are responsive to stimuli. They will look, approach, peck. First, whenever the pigeon looked at the ball, he was reinforced. If the pigeon approached the ball, he was reinforced. When the pigeon was thus seduced into approaching the ball, he was likely to peck at it, and when he did, he was reinforced. A ball which is pecked at may roll. When this happened, the pigeon was reinforced again. In an amazingly short time, the pigeon learned to roll the ball down a miniature alley. This exercise is a demonstration of how reinforcement can be used to select responses and to establish complex acts, or *chains of reflexes* to use Skinner's term. The dancing hens and other performing animals currently seen in zoos, parks, and fairs are further examples of Skinnerian shaping.

In addition to selecting and establishing a response, reinforcement has still another effect. Putting pigeons on *schedules of reinforcement*, Skinner found wide variation in response according to the way reward was given. If the bird was rewarded for a certain act every five minutes, he would be relatively inactive, perhaps even go to sleep for four minutes, and then come frantically to life, responding vigorously as the rewarding moment approached. Birds rewarded every fifty or sixty responses acted much differently. They performed as quickly as possible, not pausing to rest for periods as long as several days. Pigeons on schedules of very long periods between rewards, or where rewards were given at random, also responded violently and persistently.

The whole matter of scheduling rewards is related to *partial reinforcement*. In partial reinforcement procedures, rewards are not given each time the organism responds, but less frequently according to some pattern, schedule, or purely by chance. Partial reinforcement at least within broad limits has been found to make responses more resistive to extinction. Not only the presence and amount of reward, but sometimes its very absence make the response grow stronger.

The scheduling of reinforcement, including what was reinforced and how often, was the one instrument Skinner felt a psychologist needed to study behavior. The most complex act could be built up through proper scheduling. It might, of course, be necessary to put the subject through numerous simple schedules in order to construct the final scheduling. It was the lack of adequate build-up which had prevented psychologists from discovering that all learning and problem-solving tasks were based on reinforcement. Careful analysis and study showed that any act, human or animal, could be understood as a matter of reinforcement contingencies. Skinner demonstrated that even complicated Freudian dynamics and the involved problems of social psychology would yield to reinforcement. Reinforcement and its application, then, were the keys to Skinner's psychology.

Critique

The major criticism of Skinner concerns his stand on theory. To the student brought up on a rich diet of hypotheses, axioms, laws, and principles, Skinner's factual approach is likely to appear as rather watered-down brew. Are facts sufficient, or must they be interpreted and organized? Can science depend upon the lucky accident, or must it engage in an active search based on predictions?

Skinner's ultra-empirical formulation was important as a demonstration of the assets and liabilities of such an approach. The assets lay in the simplicity of his formulation, the lack of assumptions, the avoidance of fruitless debate over which hypothesis is best. He reported what he saw; he did not have to guess at why he saw it.

The liabilities of the empirical approach are equally obvious. Skinner's major contributions were to technology (the Skinner box) and to the body of fact surrounding the shaping of behavior and the effects of reinforcement schedule. To neither of these was the empirist orientation fundamental. Any experimental psychologist, providing he had Skinner's ability to devise and interpret research, could have conducted such studies. The experimenter's beliefs about theory would not determine his findings. Skinner seems to have demonstrated that it is possible to be empirical, but he has not been able to show that empiricism is more profitable than speculation. He has not been able to do anything better than the theorists, but he can do many things at least equally well.

Skinner has become more and more ambitious in his claims, to the point where he now feels he can explain almost everything. To believe that a beginning student can learn all about psychology, given a rat and a Skinner box, or that psychoses, group behavior, anthropology, psychoanalysis and Utopia are reducible to the same rat in the same box is viewed by many psychologists as gross overgeneralization and oversimplification.

SUMMARY

Basic Unit and Field of Study. Skinner followed Behaviorist tradition in defining his field.

Methods of Investigation. In ever finer improvements on the Skinner box, its inventor eventually established a controlled setting in which all variables could be set and manipulated electrically, all data recorded automatically. Given such masses of data, it no longer seemed necessary to use more than one subject, and statistical analysis gave way to frequency counts based on large numbers of responses.

Principles. Skinner's laws were re-statements of empirical propositions concerning spinal reflexes. He dealt with the laws of threshold, latency, strength, of response, summation, refractory phase, fatigue, facilitation, inhibition, Pavlovian conditioning and extinction, law of effect learning and extinction, interaction of compatible and incompatible responses, blending and chaining of responses, generalization, discrimination, and building up of reflex reserve (strength).

Emotion and Motivation. Although Skinner did not talk about motivation *per se*, he stressed the importance of reinforcement in shaping behavior. Operant responses (those for which there was no known stimulus) were emitted by the organism and, is reinforced, were strengthened. Stimuli present at the time of reinforcement acquired reinforcing properties and served as secondary reinforcers.

The Nature of the Learning Process. Skinner described learning as the establishment, by means of reinforcement, of conditioned connections between operant behavior and reinforcement. The strength of a learned response depended on the amount of reinforcement it had received and the current motivational state of the organism. Punishment led to the suppression of a particular act.

Behavior and Personality. Reinforcement and punishment were not only factors in learning, but also were behavioral determinants. Skinner concentrated primarily on the effects of reward. He found that the schedule of presentation of reinforcement, as to both timing and consistency, could alter performance and could even produce new patterns by a process of experimental shaping. Even the most complex acts became a matter of reinforcement contingencies.

REFERENCES

B.F. Skinner

Ferster, C. B., and B. F. Skinner, *Schedules of Reinforcement*. New York: Appleton-Century-Crofts, 1957.

Heron, W. T., and B. F. Skinner, "An Apparatus for the Study of Behavior," *Psychol. Rec.* 3: 166–176 (1939).

Skinner, B. F., *The Behavior of Organisms: An Experimental Analysis.* New York: Appleton-Century-Crofts, 1938.

———, "The Operational Analysis of Psychological Terms," *Psychol. Rev.* 52: 270–277 (1945). Reprinted in H. Feigl and M. Brodbeck, eds., *Readings in the Philosophy of Science*, New York: Appleton-Century-Crofts, 1953, pp. 585–595.

———, "Are Theories of Learning Necessary?", *Psychol. Rev.* 57: 193–216 (1950).

———, *Science and Human Behavior*. New York: Macmillan, 1953.

———, "A Case History in Scientific Method," *Amer. Psychol.* 11: 221–233 (1956).

———, "Reinforcement Today," *Amer. Psychol.* 13: 94–99 (1958).

Estes on Punishment

Estes, W. K., "An Experimental Study of Punishment," *Psychol. Monogr.* 57, No. 263, iii (1944).

PART V

ANALYTIC THEORIES

CHAPTER 15

SIGMUND FREUD: PSYCHOANALYSIS (1893–1936)

IN a science whose theories originate from diverse and paradoxical situations, it should not surprise the reader that one of the most important and influential theories is not technically a theory of psychology at all. Psychoanalysis is a field of study in its own right. While psychology borrows heavily from it, it does so to supplement and complement its own theories, and does not use psychoanalysis as if it were the natural province of the psychologist. Indeed, the orthodox analyst is most typically a medical person whose interest in the science of behavior is confined to Freudian theory.

Freud's theory was the product of the intellectual climate in which he lived, on one hand, and of the social climate in which he grew up on the other. During the latter part of the 19th century and the early years of the 20th century, tremendous theoretical advances were made in physics and biology which had ramifications for all of science. Many social scientists, including Freud, were particularly attracted to the concepts of force and energy dynamics. Employing these concepts, Freud set about trying to understand the behavior of his patients. Many of these patients had come to maturity in a paternalistic family typical of the Jewish culture of that time. Their lives were spent in the highly autocratic and intensely Catholic society of the Austrian Empire. In this rigidly moral Victorian era a number of people suffered from some form of sexual difficulty, since sex was one of the major areas of social taboo and therefore of intra-personal conflict. This mid-Victorian Austrian-Jewish culture formed not only the personalities of Freud's patients, but also his own. The ideas which he derived, then, had to do with the problems of his time as seen through the eyes of a scientist who was a product of his time.

Freud's theory came as a great shock to his professional colleagues, as well as to the general public. Breuer, his collaborator in his classical studies of hysteria, broke with him because of the direction his theories were taking;

and in psychiatric circles Freud was long considered a dirty-minded heretic, to be mentioned in hushed whispers and ostracized from the scientific community. Gradually, however, the real weight and potential of his theories were realized, and the impact of his work was so great that it has come to form the basis of most current theories of personality. Even the strictest empiricists have been forced to take cognizance of Freud's concepts, if only in an attempt to refute them.

Freud began his career as a medical doctor specializing in physiology and neurology. As part of his training, he studied in France, where he came into contact with a group of French psychiatrists, including Charcot and Janet, who used various hypnotic techniques in the treatment of mental illness. Freud became interested in their work and experimented with these procedures, first in France and later in Germany and Austria. He discovered that under hypnosis it was often possible for the patient to recall incidents and feelings which had apparently been instrumental in producing a symptom. Freud concluded that the recovery of such memories and the emotional experiences which had accompanied them were therapeutic, for almost invariably the patients' symptoms disappeared once recall was possible. With Breuer, Freud worked to perfect this new method. But as they worked, they discovered that hypnosis itself was of value only insofar as it helped the patient to remember and re-live some traumatic experience. Eventually they recognized that the re-living of the experience (catharsis) was the true therapeutic agent. By trial-and-error Breuer learned that it was possible to supplement the hypnotic treatment with what one of his patients called the "talking cure," wherein emotional topics were discussed directly without hypnosis. However, Breuer soon lost interest in the cathartic method. He found that the intimate and sexual details his patients discussed, and their emotional involvement with him, were too disconcerting. Freud encountered the same difficulties with his patients, but he eventually realized that their overtures toward him were part of the pathology, and that his patients' emotional reactions to him as therapist were a lever he might employ in treatment. This observation eventually led to the concept of *transference*, a major tool of psychoanalysis.

After Breuer withdrew, Freud continued work by himself, combining hypnosis with Breuer's talking cure, and becoming more and more dissatisfied with the efficacy of hypnosis. For one thing, many people could not be hypnotized. Secondly, those who were hypnotized and did experience *some* alteration of their initial symptoms as a result of hypnotic suggestion were likely to return later with other symptoms, the result of pathology not touched in the original treatment. Consequently, Freud leaned more and more heavily on the talking technique, and less and less on hypnosis, until finally all that remained of the latter method was the requirement that the patient recline on a couch, relax, and allow his mind free range. These conditions were conducive to the production of a running account of the patient's mental processes, for as the patient thought aloud about his problems a chain of associations occurred which eventually led back to the original area of difficulty. However, it was often hard for the patient to let his mind roam so freely and to report its wanderings without censorship. Freud soon found that an analysis of the patient's dreams was a useful means of getting around this censorship. Gradually Freud's technique took form as a new method of studying experience, *free association.*

At the same time, Freud learned more about the nature and origin of mental disorders. We have already seen that he tended to regard the sexual material reported by his patients as indicative of something about the pathology of their illness. Concomitantly, he began to realize that many of the patients' problems involved a strong sexual conflict of some sort. Initially, he believed that these sexual problems arose as a result of a childhood trauma; later, he learned that the patient need not have actually been exposed to such traumatic experiences. Rather, his infantile wishes and desires created conflicts which led to his initial emotional disruption, and this disruption in turn led to distortion and confusion of perception of experiences and/or of the memory of them.

Throughout his life Freud continued to organize, polish, reorganize, and revise his theory. Because he constantly sought to perfect it, his theory appeared in numerous versions, each different from the last. The material discussed in this chapter will include all the better-known revisions of the theory, with emphasis on the version currently most widely accepted by orthodox psychoanalysts.

Basic Unit

Freud did not feel that it was possible to break personality down into elements. It was necessary, in treating patients, to understand the entire problem. There were, of course, such distinctions as the types of conflict the patient experienced or the defenses he employed, or the kinds of traumatic experience that he went through, but there was no one basic unit for all human behavior. There were numerous different parts or aspects of personality, but none was more elementary than any other.

Field of Study

Freud felt that the appropriate concern for psychologists and psychiatrists was the nature of a person's life experiences, how each of these experiences occurred, and how they interacted with previous experience and general psychological structure to form personality. He assumed that the early life experiences were most influential in setting up the basic personality and that very little that happened to a person after adolescence changed this pattern. Later experiences could, however, *redintegrate* (rearouse) earlier difficulties if they involved similar problems or trauma. Freud assumed a biological basis for behavior, but he himself did no more than speculate about it, being much more interested in content and function than in physiological structure.

Most of the data from which Freudian theory was developed came from patients. Freud felt that neurotic symptoms represented exaggerations of normal behavior. Studying neurotics, he believed, helped him to understand both the normal and abnormal personality. Later case material, coming from the training analyses of potential Freudian therapists, has seemed to orthodox practitioners to substantiate this belief. Aside from such rather indirect and admittedly subjective validation, however, Freud's conclusions have never been tested on normal groups. For the most part analysts are clinicians, too busy treating people to be able to test their theories, even where they see a need for it.

Methods of Investigation

The free association technique developed by Freud, combined with the observations and interpretations of the analyst, comprised the classical method of *psychoanalysis*, a tool Freud found equally well suited to treating patients and to collecting data to build or test theory; indeed, both purposes were ordinarily served at the same time. The patient was instructed to report to the analyst anything which came to mind, regardless of how illogical, insignificant, foolish, or anti-social it might be. This requirement was based on the assumption that the train of thought was actually a series of associations, each one related in some way to the one which preceded it. Under ordinary conditions distasteful ideas, including the nature and source of a person's problems, were censored by his fears, his moral values and his general culture. Given practice in following the analyst's instructions, the patient could learn to by-pass these controls. The resultant chain of associations led eventually to the feelings, ideas, and impulses which had caused the difficulties, and finally beyond these to the original experiences which gave rise to the maladjustment. As the process continued, the therapist analyzed and interpreted the material until both he and the patient discovered the relationship between various past experiences and the patient's current situation. For example, a patient might begin a series of interviews by talking of his symptoms, gradually move on to tell of his difficulties with his boss and finally speak of how his father treated him. The patient's free associations during such a course of treatment might well reveal that his current symptoms were a function of his irritation at his boss. He might feel guilty about this irritation since his earlier relations with male authorities, especially his father, taught him that one should not have such reactions to superiors. The research value of the technique lay in exposing such relationships; the treatment value lay in the patient's coming to understand the relationship with the aid of the therapist's interpretations.

Principles

Freud never made an explicit statement of principles, but a number of them were implied. What follows has been extracted from various parts of Freud's writings and seems to represent his basic premises.

The basic intent which Freud saw in any act was to maximize pleasure and minimize pain. Behavior, according to Freud, was oriented toward hedonism. Pleasure was equivalent to gratification of some need or to sensual experiences.

At first the infant sought pleasure regardless of the consequences. At this point his behavior was guided by the *pleasure principle* and had its origin in the *Id*, the seat of all desire.

As the child grew older he learned to govern his behavior by the realities he faced. In such a manner he was able to achieve maximal gratification with minimal ill effects. This orientation was called the *reality principle*, and was the result of a maturing capacity for self-control. The process of control, planning, and conforming to reality was known as the *Ego*.

In addition, the activities of the older child and adult were modified by moral values, or *Superego*, acquired in the course of the child's modeling himself on the pattern of his parents.

Inasmuch as it was regulated to maximize pleasure and achieve satisfaction within moral limits, all behavior became purposive, having meaning for some need existing in the person. The need or motive might be conscious or unconscious. In the latter case, a person might engage in distinctive, perhaps peculiar responses for which he could give no reason. The casual observer might find the action no more reasonable than the person himself, but detailed study would reveal an underlying motive.

Behavior was ordinarily induced by more than one drive. A person could often report the presence of several conscious determinants to an act, and one or more unconscious motives could usually be found as well. The multiplicity of motives has become known as *overdetermination.*

Just as several motives might influence behavior, so also was there the possibility that more than one stimulus was involved in initiating a response. Memories, too, could be involved. Life experiences both present and past combined to determine the mode of reaction at any particular time. Every act was the result of the situation in which the person found himself at the time, his basic physiological structure, and his past experiences.

Action involved the expenditure of energy. This energy was carefully channeled and economized so that no more was used than absolutely necessary to achieve the desired end. Energy apportioned to a certain act could be shunted from its original goal to similar goals without difficulty, but conflict among various means of energy-expenditure might lead to trouble.

Conflicts arose when the economics of energy consumption were interfered with by opposing motives or by social prohibitions against a certain form of energy release. The energy remained available even if blocked, and the person experienced constant pressure until some satisfactory outlet was found. If direct expression was impossible, the person would eventually engage in an indirect kind of behavior known as a *defense mechanism*, a maneuver produced by unconscious processes which avoided activating the conflict and yet afforded some degree of satisfaction.

The drives, the life experiences, the current situation, the moral values, the modes of energy-expenditure and defenses all interacted to form the personality.

The pattern of this interaction was established in childhood as a product of physical and social maturation. The biological nature of the man was believed to be such that there were certain common problems which the child must meet and solve in the course of socialization. Among these problems were the experiences of feeding and weaning, toilet training and other aspects of self-control, the handling of sexual and aggressive impulses, and relationship to parents. At certain ages in life these problems became salient to the individual, and his success in solving them determined his ability to deal with all later problems. If a person was unsuccessful in mastering the conflicts involved in one of the formative stages of his personality, his ability to handle later problems was weakened. On the other hand, a successful resolution usually enabled the person to meet later developmental problems with less difficulty.

For the most part, Freud's principles described events which took place outside of the awareness of the individual, i.e., they were unconscious processes.

Consciousness

As this last principle implies, Freud found it necessary to consider not only what was conscious, but also what was unconscious. Awareness was the distinguishing feature of conscious activity. Absence of awareness was the criterion of unconscious forces. Before one can appreciate Freud's theory of consciousness, however, it is necessary to know how he conceived of the psychic structure.

Freud recognized three regions within the personality. The first of these he called the Id. The *Id* was composed of the various biological urges and drives, all in their primitive, unsocialized state. One might refer to this as the animal part of man. The second aspect of any human personality Freud called the Ego. *Ego* was that part of the personality which sought to find realistic outlets for the Id impulses, at the same time keeping the person out of trouble with his environment and avoiding painful experiences. The Ego was the source of self-control, the means for maintaining contact. It was a decision-maker and judge. There was a third region, known as the *Superego*, which included the person's moral values and ethics, i.e., his conscience.

Each of these structural aspects of personality had a specific relationship to consciousness. The Ego's task of collating the demands of the Id and the Superego with reality was necessarily conscious, as was its function of dealing with the external world. In like manner, some of a person's moral values were conscious, although Freud felt that the Superego often influenced the person without his being aware of it. This occurred because many social values were learned before the child could understand and verbalize about them. The consequences of trespassing upon these values must have seemed so monstrous that the child blinded himself to the existence of the mores, yet continued to conform to them. The Id, with its wildly striving impulses, was also unconscious. This unconscious material constantly sought expression and often came out in some indirect fashion. For example, dreams and slips of the tongue were really disguised manifestations of unconscious content which somehow escaped the ego and became overt. In the case of dreams, the indirect release of impulsive materials drained off material which might otherwise disturb sleep and other activities.

In addition to the conscious and the unconscious, there was a phenomenon which Freud called the *preconscious*. This was the material a person could recall at will, but which was not in his awareness all the time. The material was not pushed out to censor or control the organism, but rather to foster its efficient functioning. To be constantly aware of every cue and connotation, every intention and memory, would interfere with activity; yet all this information must be available when the organism needs it.

In summary, Freud conceived of mind as being influenced by primitive animal drives, censored by moral values, and modulated by an appreciation of the requirements of reality. The individual was necessarily aware of reality demands, and might be partially aware of the moral edicts which modified his acts; but he went through life forever unaware of the true nature and extent of his primitive animal urges, apparently because awareness would be too frightening and distasteful. (Figure 3 illustrates their relationship.)

Sensation, Perception, and Discrimination

Freud made frequent mention of sensation, perception, and discrimination. These processes were not, however, important in and of themselves. They were significant only as parts of the broader personality. Freud did not investigate them directly, but he did describe something of their origin and function.

FIGURE 3

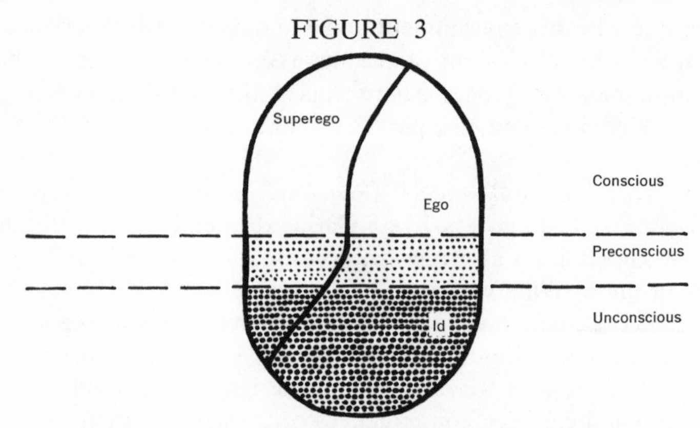

Freud's Structural Relationships of Personality

For Freud the newborn infant was not a perceptive being in the ordinary sense. That is to say, he did not appreciate the meaning of events in his environment. The world was a mass of confused, disorganized stimuli. Gradually, as a result of the frequent exposure to breast or bottle during feeding, these objects were separated out from the meaningless mass. The mother, too, because of her close connection with the feeding process, came to be sorted out as a significant object. Other persons and new objects were gradually noticed as their importance was recognized. The perceptual process, then, was built up as the life experiences made the infant aware of the meaning and significance of the various details of his surroundings.

Freud hypothesized certain symbolic meanings and expressions which were generally appreciated only on an unconscious level, being the special property of the Id. They were built into the organism through its genetic structure and represented a sort of social inheritance. Freud never spelled out the mechanism involved in this heritage, but it was based on the belief that personality characteristics could be inherited, so that experiences throughout mankind's history were preserved in his germ plasm and handed down through the succeeding generations. This meant that perception was partly determined by biological factors, although one would assume that these percepts were not available until the infant had enough experience to know how to perceive. Symbolic percepts of this sort were universal. For example, Freud believed all children perceive girls as inferior to boys because they lack a penis. In like manner, all boys were thought to perceive their fathers as dangerous rivals for their mother's affections, capable of injuring (castrating) their sons to protect their own rights.

In discussing the therapeutic problem of transference, Freud again introduced the problem of perception. He noted early in his work with mentally disturbed patients that they often behaved toward him in an irrational fashion. They assumed that he was angry and tried to placate him, or became enormously fond of him without particular reason, or attributed great powers and skills to him. It gradually occurred to Freud that these people were acting toward him as they had learned to behave toward other significant figures in their lives, especially their parents. He concluded that the ways in which the individual had learned to deal with significant persons during childhood were the ways in which he attempted to deal with authority figures such as therapists and doctors during his adult life. In the case of therapists this reaction was irrational and inappropriate, since the therapist did nothing to elicit the perception; the individual merely perceived this new figure as similar to his parent figures due to the similarity of role or status, and he tended to expect from them all the things which he had perceived in, and expected from, his parents. (In passing, one might wonder why Freud limited this concept to therapy; if the way one perceived his analyst was influenced by his earlier interpersonal experiences, there was reason to assume that his perception of other people was similarly influenced.)

The foregoing discussion indicates that Freud viewed perception as an evolutionary process between universal (hereditarily determined) symbols and social experiences inside and outside the family. Thinking evolved and was patterned by the same set of forces; but while perception was a primary interpretation of events, thinking was the attempt to solve problems introduced to the person through his perception of himself and the world about him.

Thinking, Cognition, and Memory

In Freud's view the infant could neither perceive nor think. He merely responded to stimuli automatically and impulsively, guided by what Freud called the *pleasure principle*. This principle referred to the tendency to act so as to maximize the pleasure of the moment, regardless of what the eventual consequences might be. This type of behavior was typical throughout infancy, but gradually the child became aware of the necessity of fitting his behavior to the reality of the situation. Sometimes momentary pleasure had painful results such as injury, punishment, or rejection. The child had to learn to postpone gratification until a time when he would not be hurt and to carry out his eventual action in a socially acceptable form. To consider society's demands and how to meet them, and to evaluate the possible consequences of an act, required thought. Thoughtful behavior reached beyond those processes described by the pleasure principle; it represented a more mature stage of cognitive development described by the *reality principle*. Once a person matured sufficiently to maintain a realistic orientation, he might still revert to the pleasure principle in dreams and fantasies and in various neurotic and psychotic symptoms. However, this regression could only occur if the ego were rendered inactive by sleep, extreme stress, or incomplete maturation.

While the reality principle accounted for the origin and outcome of thought, it did not define the nature of thought processes or their content. Freud emphasized that all thought was a symbolic representation of something rather than of the thing itself. The symbols, words, and images used to represent things had to be learned, and the infant could not think until he had learned them.

Most thought was symbolic in another fashion as well; it was a symbolic expression of unconscious material, a means of satisfying repressed urges. Unconscious symbolism was most prominent in fantasy, daydreaming, and aimless thinking, but it could influence problem-solving as well. The nature of this kind of symbolism, according to Freud, was often determined by racial or cultural heritage, as we have already seen in discussing inherited percepts. Thus, in dreams and other fantasy material, snakes, sticks, guns or any other elongated objects could be interpretated universally as phallic symbols. Objects which involved an enclosure surrounding vacant space, such as houses, shoes, or purses, were universally interpreted as female symbols. Freud described numerous symbols standing for parents, sexual intercourse, and various other objects and activities which a person might find too threatening to deal with consciously.

Although Freud was interested in all symbolic processes, dreams held special significance since they were almost entirely symbolic and represented a means of tapping the unconscious forces at the base of personal problems. Freud pointed out that the manifest content of the dream, i.e., what it appeared to be about, was very different from its latent content, what it really meant when one interpreted the symbols. Freud believed that dreams occurred in order to preserve the state of sleep. During sleep, he said, the Ego relaxed its guard, and unconscious elements could be more easily expressed. Any direct gratification of the Id impulses, however, would be so traumatic as to waken the person instantly. Therefore, a process that Freud called *dream work* was set in motion. In dream work the unconscious strivings were transformed into symbols, which were acceptable forms since they were indirect expressions of impulses which did not threaten the Ego. As a result of this disguise, forbidden wishes could find fulfillment in dreams without upsetting the delicate intra-psychic balance. Indeed, only minute analysis could reveal the true content of the dream.

What has been said of dreams was equally true of any sort of symbolic expression, whether it be poetry, art, literature, or psychotic hallucinations. Something in the Id became strong enough to need an escape from the unconscious. By some unknown process, the undesirable material was transposed into the more acceptable symbolic form and thereby given expression.

Emotion and Motivation

One of the principal questions to which Freud addressed himself was that of motivation. Motives or instincts were seen as having three dimensions:

source, aim, and object. The *source* was biologically determined and therefore immutable. *Aim*, the behavior one must perform as a means of achieving satisfaction, was broadly limited by nature, but within these bounds the life experiences of an individual molded his actions. For example, one must eat with one's mouth, but whether one uses a fork or chopsticks, and whether one chews or gulps, is a result of training and background. The *object* or goal which one sought as gratification was likewise subject to individual variation within the broad confines dictated by physiology. Returning to the previous example, it is necessary for persons to consume digestible materials to satisfy hunger, but within these limits what is eaten is a matter of choice, taste and opportunity.

The aim and the object were more matters of behavior than of drive in the Freudian approach, and will be considered in the section on Behavior and Personality. The various concepts dealing with the source of impulses were motivational concepts, as were the economy of energy expenditure and the inter-relationships of the various biological forces.

Freud proposed that impulses were subject to the physical laws which described energy consumption and the interaction of forces. Motivation was a matter of releasing, transforming, and directing energy. Freud assumed that the human being was born with a large amount of free floating energy, a reservoir not attached to any particular function. This large mass of energy Freud called *libido*. When any biological drive was aroused, libidinal energy was available for the performance of any act which might satisfy it. Since animal impulses were the property of the Id, it was this aspect of personality which was most closely indentified with the libido.

The energy triggered off by a need was the source of purposive behavior. In infants there was no direction to energy discharge; it occurred at random. As the child grew older and came to have experience with the modes appropriate to the satisfaction of various needs, the release of energy was channeled, so that certain habit patterns were set up and certain objects came to be seen as goals or means. Energy so directed was said to be *cathected*, positively or negatively depending on whether it was utilized to approach or avoid an object.

In addition to the energy channeled into certain activities and attached to satisfaction-giving objects, there remained, even in adults, a large body of nonspecific energy. Some of this energy was utilized by the Ego and Superego in carrying out their functions. Some of it was available for use in emergency situations, or when particularly strong needs called for extra exertion. Some of it was probably never consumed in any way.

Although there were numerous impulses and desires, they could be classified into two general groups. The first typology Freud employed divided drives into *sexual instincts* and *self-preservative instincts*. Sex had a different connotation to Freud than that prevalent in our culture. Perhaps the term "sensual" would better cover his meaning, for he assumed that any pleasurable activity is "sexual" in nature. Sex included feelings, desires, and activities directly referable to the genital parts of the body, such as masturbation, fondling, and intercourse, but it also included eating, excretion, and looking at or examining things.

The self-preservative instincts, or ego instincts as they were also called, included those activities which kept the person from hurting himself or getting into trouble. Freud did not have nearly so much to say about these. For one thing, they were already recognized. For another, they were "drives to health," and Freud was concerned with illness.

Freud soon found a weakness in his first typology. Neither type of instinct could supply a motive for a person purposely doing something which he knew would induce displeasure. This became a problem to Freud when he began to work with "shell shocked" soldiers during World War I. Many of these men seemed to demonstrate an intense need to dwell on their war experiences, particularly those which preceded the appearance of their neurotic symptoms. They would dream, talk, and think of nothing else, yet manifest at the same time signs of extreme discomfort and anxiety aroused by what they were going through. Freud's theory could not explain the recurrent battle dreams or the constant preoccupation with traumatic incidents.

At about the same time Freud noticed that many young children seemed to place themselves voluntarily in unpleasant situations time and again. Close observation of these children convinced Freud that they were attempting to gain some control over their feelings about the situation by forcing themselves to experience it. For example, Freud noted that one child of his acquaintance reacted to his mother's brief absences by throwing his favorite toy out of his crib, retrieving it, throwing it again, etc. Tossing the toy away appeared to be very painful for the child. In contrast he would gurgle and laugh when the toy came back to him. Freud interpreted this as an effort on the part of the child to control the unhappiness he felt over his mother's absence by proving to himself that good things do come back and that he could master the feeling of discomfort and anxiety he experienced in the meantime. Freud referred to this type of behavior in children as a *repetition compulsion.* He assumed that the traumatic neuroses were examples of the same phenomenon, namely, that the person was intentionally suffering temporary hurt to overcome the pain and regain mastery of his environment and his reactions.

This hypothesis led Freud to revise his theory of instincts. Besides the *sexual instincts*, now referred to as *life instincts* or *Eros*, he proposed a *death instinct* which he called *Thanatos*. The life instincts encompassed the sexual motives as well as the tendencies to self-preservation. They were activated by a desire to achieve gratification through discharge of energy in the form of behavior. Restoration of equilibrium was the final result, but not the principal goal. The death instinct, on the other hand, was the need for complete quiescence. The goal was elimination of all stimulation, the establishment of a state of Nirvana. Freud could think of no state of inactivity more lasting than death. He therefore assumed that death would be the ultimate goal of this instinct. Such a goal involved self-destruction, an end which was highly incompatible with erotic instincts. Therefore, Freud hypothesized that the nature of the death instinct would be modified to some degree during development. Part of the energy of the instinct was channeled to new aims, toward new goals. In this way there came to be a need to master one's surroundings in order to preserve the biological equilibrium, as manifested in the repetition compulsion. The rest of the energy allotted to the death instinct was changed only insofar as the goal was concerned. The aim remained the same; there was still the need to destroy, but it was directed toward others rather than the self. In this manner, Freud accounted for the origin of aggression.

In addition to life and death instincts Freud recognized a number of what he called *partial instincts*. These were behaviors which everybody seemed to manifest, but which were secondary insofar as survival was concerned. They did not have to be satisfied in order for the person to exist. Curiosity, and the need to look at and examine things, was such a partial instinct. Freud felt this instinct originated from sexual drives in the form of voyeurism. As the person matured, however, this desire became independent from the sexual drive and became a motive in its own right. There were a number of other partial instincts, but none of them were of great importance to Freud's theory.

The Nature of the Learning Process

Motivation was a key aspect in Freud's handling of learning; in fact the establishment of cathexsis appeared to be the Freudian equivalent of learning. According to Freud, the energy available to a drive became channeled, or positively cathected, to those goals which supplied pleasure or gratification. The greater the pleasure, the more intense the cathexsis. Negative cathexsis, or avoidance, appeared when an act or goal resulted in punishment. As a result of punishment, a certain behavior might cease but the potential for it would be retained in the unconscious and continue to influence the person's reactions. Punishment caused the person to censor or repress the impulse, removing it from consciousness (but not from existence).

Cathexsis was a reinforcement-based phenomena, pleasure and pain being the forces which forged associations. Learning, or association, was a matter of energy transmission; as a result of pleasurable or painful consequences of an action or an experience a connection was made. This connection, in turn, caused energy to attach to some object or experience and achieve the ability to rouse actions appropriate to its consequences.

While Freud undoubtedly gave great weight to repetition as a factor in establishing cathexsis, it was not a matter of greatest importance since traumatic experiences could lead to one-trial learning. Pleasure or pain were the necessary and sufficient conditions; learning was predicated upon them. Indeed, behavior in general was predicated on reinforcement and punishment.

Behavior and Personality

Freud assumed that human development from infancy to adulthood took place in a number of stages. Each stage called for a special kind of interaction between the existing psychological structure, the biological instincts (especially the sexual ones), and the environment. This interaction led Freud to refer to the various stages as *psychosexual levels*. The developmental process was biologically determined, and therefore invariable within certain limits. Each new phase brought forth new aspects of the basic animal nature which had to be dealt with and made fit for society. The family and the society in which the person grew up could make these greater or lesser problems, depending upon what was emphasized during the socialization process and the means used to achieve conformity.

Birth Trauma. Development began before birth, for the fetus first had to pass through the trauma of birth. Freud himself did not attribute any psychological importance to birth until Otto Rank (1929) developed a theory of *birth trauma*, suggesting that being born was such an anxiety-inducing experience for the infant that it was a *prototype* of all later anxiety. Rank believed that from the birth process grew a fear of separation from the mother which generalized to other people and to a more encompassing fear of independence. Eventually Freud adopted Rank's theory of birth trauma, but did not make it so important as Rank did. Freud could not believe, like Rank, that birth trauma was the sole determinant of the amount of anxiety a person would have throughout life, nor did he feel that it was a pattern of all later anxiety experiences.

Oral Period. Freud referred to the first stage of post partum life as the *oral stage*. He observed that infants first interacted with other people mostly through the process of feeding. Being fed was, of course, necessary for survival, but Freud felt it had other biological significance aside from its import for sustaining life. He held that in infancy the mouth was the most sensitive zone of the body. He attributed to this sensitivity a sexual aspect, speaking of the mouth as an erogenous zone, that is, a part of the body which was a source of pleasurable or sensual sensations. Through life the mouth remained erogenous, but never again achieved the same salience it had at first.

The newborn infant dealt with the world through activities involving his mouth. He was fed by sucking on nipples, and later from spoons. Sucking was, indeed, his first coordinated motor skill. But what began as a motor response necessary to the act of feeding soon became a social skill as well. It was the only way the infant had of dealing with any object, whether it be mother, father, nurse, bottle, teething ring or nipple. The infant explored the world literally by mouthing it, and his first knowledge of the world was in terms of what objects could provide oral satisfaction, and what ones could not. Objects were first distinguished by their value as oral reinforcers, an observation which led Freud to refer to this period as the *oral sucking stage.*

At this early age, the infant had no means of coping with or understanding problems which arose. Even the simplest biological processes could become terrifying; the intense stimuli which accompanied hunger and excretion, for example, combined with the infant's ignorance of their significance or of their duration, could be agonizing. The infant could not know that the adults about him could appreciate his needs and would supply food and minister to his other discomforts when he cried. Indeed, he was not even aware that other beings existed. Freud speculated that it must therefore seem to the baby that relief appeared magically, simply because he desired it. Not knowing of the external intervention in his affairs, the infant must come to think of himself as an omnipotent organism who could command satisfaction as he required it. In the infant's mind, the wish became equivalent to the act, and thinking of something made it real. These wishful, magical qualities were the dominant characteristics of infantile thought.

As the infant reached the second six months of life, the parents found it unnecessary to be so extremely solicitous of him. Consequently, when he cried, gratification was somewhat delayed. The child, having learned that wishing for something meant getting it, responded to these delays by wishfully conjuring up the desired object, imagining or hallucinating that he had what he wanted. If hungry, for example, he fantasied he was being fed, and, unable to tell fantasy from reality, expected to achieve the same satisfaction from this fantasy that he would receive from reality. However, it inevitably became obvious that fantasy was an inadequate substitute when no material results were experienced.

The results of these disappointments were the initiation of a new phase of development, brought about in part by changes in the mother's behavior, and in part by the appearance of new skills in the child's repertoire as he approached the second six months of life. Turning first to the mother's contribution, not only did she delay gratification, but when she did come she was likely to do some unpleasant thing such as clean him, or take away some interesting object, or correct some misbehavior. Of course the mother had always done many of these things, but earlier the child did not connect them with her. Also, she had expected less of him and allowed him to be completely dependent. As a result, the mother became a source of security and satisfaction to the very young infant, but that source seemed, for the time being at least, less reliable as the child passed out of the age of complete protection. The delay in satisfaction and the mother's new expectations aroused the child's anger toward her, leading to a very uncomfortable state. The child now hated and wished to destroy the person he also needed and loved; he was, for the first time, *ambivalent*. The infant sought some way out of his new dilemma and found the answer in the new skills and capacities he was developing. Having grown teeth, he could use them to bite. This propensity led Freud to call the second stage of development the *oral biting stage*.

The act of biting had two functions. Just as the reinforcement provided by sucking generalized from eating to other sorts of gratification, so with biting. By biting something off and consuming it, Freud said, the infant could take this object into himself, making it a part of him. This process was referred to as *incorporation*, or *introjection*. In the child's mind, if he incorporated mother as he incorporated food, then she would become a part of him just as his food did, and he would no longer have to fear that she might leave him. She would always be near. Although the literal desire to consume a loved one to possess him ordinarily disappeared after this period, symbolic consumption of love objects could be observed in many adult activities, such as feasting at funerals, and weddings.

The second function of biting was aggressive; it hurt and destroyed. Mother winced and cried out if the child bit her, and the child was angry over her apparent desertion of him. Biting, therefore, provided a solution to both love and anger.

The solution was only temporary, however. The parent, being pained by this latest development, punished the child for such direct aggression. Added to the child's uncomfortable ambivalence was a fear of punishment and rejection for his feelings and actions. The fears roused in the infant were the rudiments of guilt. They were also signs of further maturation. The anticipation that impulse release might lead to trouble was the first step away from the pleasure principle toward a reality orientation and the acquisition of an Ego. At this point the child began to control and regulate his impulses, although his skills were still primitive.

Anal Period. By the end of the first year of life eating problems had been worked out, and parental attention had shifted away from oral activities to toilet training. Accompanying the parent's new focus was an alteration in erogenous sensitivity, dictated, said Freud, by physiological factors. The oral zone receded in importance while the anal zone became the major erogenous area and the seat of a new series of problems in biological and interpersonal adjustment. There was a potentiality in the *anal phase* which was not present in the oral stage of development. As soon as the child realized what was wanted of him by way of toilet behavior, he was, for the first time, able to choose whether or not he would conform. He could act as an individual on his own initiative and exercise his will without the parent becoming suspicious, although too intense a rebellion led to trouble.

Freud stated that the demands the parents made in terms of toilet training must seem completely illogical and inappropriate to the child, who could see no reason why he should be asked to perform in this manner. However, the child was already aware that he must obey parental demands or be punished. Required to do something for which he could see no good reason, and punished if he did not do so, the child came to perceive the world as rigid and arbitrary. Punishment could descend upon him for unknown reasons when he behaved in a presumably natural manner. Under these circumstances, Freud believed, new activities came to be perceived as requiring caution. They seemed dangerous because one could not know their consequences. The yearling child became extremely conservative, preferring old and tried means of doing things and avoiding new ones that might get him into trouble.

The period of toilet training produced other traits as well. As the parents lectured, pleaded, nagged, and explained, the child came to perceive adults as talking endlessly about meaningless matters. The child was just learning to talk himself and found his own sounds equally meaningless, but in view of their magical results, he too, came to prize empty verbiage, debate, and argument.

The interest the parents showed in the excretory products, and the value they seemed to place on them, led the child to value these things. Because of the induced value, the child might feel that in excreting as his parents wished, he was giving them pleasing gifts, and that by withholding, he was punishing them for what they had done to him. Because the parents showed so much interest in collecting this material, the child could come to see worth in the very act of collecting. The child was therefore likely to collect all sorts of things. He was also likely to value material objects because his parents seemed to do so.

These habits and interests were characteristics of the anal period in general. Like the oral period, however, the anal period could be divided into an earlier and later phase, each presenting its individual problems to the child. The child just past a year of age had little ability to retain his bowel movements, but was able to exert some voluntary control over expulsion. He could not prevent a bowel movement, but he could cause one. He soon learned that having a bowel movement at an inappropriate time displeased his parents and could be used as a means of expressing aggression. Expulsion of feces became a means of getting back at the parents for their illogical demands, a habit which led Freud to refer to this as the *anal expulsive stage*. Later, the child came to see the fecal material as something of value, and as he gained more muscular control, he began to withhold his bowel movements, giving only as he saw fit. The *anal retentive stage* lasted until the child was between three and four, by which time parents and child had reached some sort of compromise over toilet behavior, and biological sensitivity began to shift from the anal to the genital area.

Phallic Period. As these biological changes progressed, the child entered what Freud called the *phallic stage*. Socially the child of three or four was much freer than he had been in infancy. He was now quite independent of his parents and could roam around, exploring the world and experimenting with it. He was likely to engage in daring and dangerous enterprises because he did not realize their potential consequences beyond the fact that they were interesting and fun. The child reacted to the growing sensitivity in the genital area by exploring and experimenting with it as he did with any other fascinating discovery. Consequently, there was a good deal of masturbation, and a good deal of interest and questions about sex, particularly the differences between boys and girls.

Boys were often threatened with the possibility of having their penis cut off when parents observed their masturbation or their other mischief. This tended to rouse in the boy anxiety over possible castration. When the boy observed the physical differences between boys and girls, he often concluded, Freud said, that girls had once had a penis, too, but had been castrated because they were naughty. This further aroused the boy's anxiety over the possible loss of his own penis. Freud speculated that the little girl believed she had already lost her penis and felt deprived of this valued object as a result of some unknown misdeed. In the world of a five-year old a penis had social significance, being an item of interest, entertainment and amusement. It also had importance as a mark of status. The apparent or potential loss of such an object was, from Freud's viewpoint, such a vital threat that it took the form of an anxiety ridden *castration complex*. Whatever the child's experience with castration threats, he or she would develop some fears concerning it, for the castration complex was biologically determined and therefore present in everyone to some degree.

Against the background of this anxiety appeared the *Oedipal conflict*, another instinctual phenomenon. It is simplest to discuss the Oedipal situation of the boy first. The boy's mother was his first and most important love object. She cared for him, nursed him, pampered and loved him. In the ordinary household the father was out of the home a good deal of the day. The child consequently leaned on the mother and was closer to her. Now, in the phallic stage this love acquired sexual overtones. The boy did not wish to share his mother with his father, resented his father's presence, and in his jealousy wished to do away with his father so that he could possess his mother completely. Since his father was much larger than he and was likely to be angry at the child's desires if he knew of them, the boy feared destruction, particularly castration, if the father learned of his newly aroused desires, and therefore he tried to smother his aggressions toward the father. Since he did not wish to give up his mother, and yet feared his father's reactions, the child found himself in severe emotional conflict. Eventually, sometime between age five and six, he finally realized that by assuming his father's identity he could achieve vicariously the desired relationship with his mother, and yet avoid the danger inherent in direct expression of his desires. As the child had sought to incorporate the mother in the oral stage for security, he now sought to incorporate the father so that he could take the father's role. At this point he *identified* with the father to the point where he unconsciously believed he was the father. He acted like his father, talked like him, and did all the things he did. In the process of identifying, the child acquired not only the various privileges which he could now imagine, but he also took unto himself the social and moral values of the father.

Up to this time, the prohibitions of the culture had been something external to the child. But in identifying with the father and the father's moral values, he acquired a conscience; morality now became a matter of personal conviction. Already in his life the boy had acquired a series of personal aspirations known as the *ego ideal.* The moral convictions and the ideals together formed the *Superego.*

The Oedipal conflict was resolved by unconscious fantasy, but in order to retain this new-found adjustment, and to satisfy his new *Superego,* the child found it necessary to smother his sexual feelings completely and to avoid sexually stimulating objects. Concomitant with this, the biological sensitivity of the genital zone decreased, leading the child into the *latency stage.*

The Oedipus (*Electra*) complex in the girl had the same form, but it was much more complex in nature. The girl, too, had her mother as her first love object, but somehow transferred her early sexual feelings to her father. In order to resolve her conflict, she eventually identified with her mother, and once the identification was accomplished, the girl likewise entered the latency period. Freud really did not understand what happened in the Oedipal complex of the girl. In fact, he seriously feared that it might never be possible to understand women.

The Latency Period. The *latency stage* was correlated, in the Western cultures at least, with the fact that the child left home more and more often (usually to go to school) and began to center his interests on peers rather than on parents. During the latency period the child was very much afraid of sex and avoided any expression of it. He did not even like children of the opposite sex and preferred to stick to his own kind. He might have violent "crushes" on other children in which there were homosexual qualities, but for the most part the child congregated in groups and sought to isolate himself from adults, becoming a little scornful of them, although still respectful.

Adolescent Period. By the time the child was twelve or thirteen, biology again interfered with his adjustment. Somewhere in this age range the child reached puberty and suffered a resurgence of sexual problems. He was subject to adult sexual urges but was still a child under the thumb of his parents and could not express or gratify his desires. Complicating the situation was the rearousal of many of the conflicts which arose originally during the Oedipal period. In addition, the adolescent was of an age when he was desirous of more independence from his parents, yet was too immature for adult life. He rebelled against his parents but was dependent on them. As a consequence, he was intensely ambivalent. He could be neither child nor adult; he was something in between. As the teen age years passed, independence was gradually achieved, and the individual became a biological adult, but not necessarily a psychological adult in the Freudian sense. Psychological adulthood required that the individual achieve the genital stage.

Genital Period. Only if the individual successfully resolved all the conflicts of the earlier psychosexual stages was he able to reach genitality, the Utopia of Freudian theory. The person achieving this state was mature sexually, socially, and psychologically. He had a strong Ego and was able to sublimate all his impulses so that he experienced no conflicts and manifested no defenses. He was perfectly adjusted. The occurrence of perfect adjustment was quite rare, and therefore very few people were truly genital personalities.

Abnormal Patterns. So far we have discussed the ideal development and sequence, but ordinarily the progression from one phase to the next was not so smooth. The person, because of his parents' personalities and his own biology, found solutions to some problems more difficult than others. If the parents were too demanding, or did not give enough love, or if they placed the child in some extreme or unusual situation, he was unable to master the biological and interpersonal skills he must learn to solve the riddle of adjustment. Most Freudians believed that overgratification was as pathological as undergratification. However, an examination by Whiting and Child (1953) of the personality patterns growing out of various cultures where the developmental stages are over- or undergratified could show no pathological effects as a result of indulgence. When they found evidence of emotional disorders, they found them only in conjunction with deprivation.

A person who could not solve the problems of a particular stage was more or less "stuck" there, *fixated* as Freud called it. His energy became tied up in maintaining himself at this crippled, inefficient level, so that none was available for other kinds of behavior or for maturation to more advanced stages. Even if some energy was left for further development, the person was penalized by lack of basic tools and skills. If the difficulty was severe, or if traumatic events occurred, the person might not be able to progress at all. Freud compared the developmental process to an army advancing into hostile territory. If too much energy was expended in holding territory once captured, the army became smaller and weaker until all forward progress was halted by decimation of the ranks.

Fixation at any stage led to deviation in personality. The description of character traits correlated with fixation at various periods was begun by Freud and developed further by Abraham (1927). According to the Freud-Abraham theory, persons fixated at the oral period were extremely dependent, expecting others to care for them, to provide "emotional supplies" for them to consume. The *oral personality* demanded, but could not give in return. Cognitively, such persons were likely to be unrealistic and to spend much time in fantasy. They were prone to make bitingly hostile remarks. They were likely to manifest mannerisms involving mouth gestures, and they might display peculiar modes of speech because of their fixation on the mouth. Oral activities took up much of the person's time and attention. Eating or drinking was likely to be so excessive as to be a "symptom" of such a fixation. Other activities like smoking or gum chewing were also present to an inordinate degree.

The personality correlated with anal fixation was superficially conforming, but passively hostile and resistant to external intervention. The individual could be expected to display numerous compulsions about cleanliness and other respects of daily life. He was likely to be obsessively preoccupied and indecisive. He displayed a tendency to value some or all objects to an excessive degree and to collect (retain) things. His speech was pedantic, wandering, full of irrelevant detail and meaningless terms.

The phallic personality was a daring, impulsive individual who was actually fearful and who yet engaged in that which he feared in order to prove his courage and hide his fear. This was called a *counter-phobic* activity, or in lay vernacular, a daredevil. Just as he was fearless about driving, fighting, drinking, so he behaved sexually as a Don Juan (or a "fast woman", as the case may be) to hide his fear. Remnants of an unresolved Oedipal conflict colored and confused his reaction to peers and parent figures alike. If he did not identify with the parent of the same sex, confusion of sex role and homosexuality resulted. Likewise, if the opposite sex parent was not an acceptable Oedipal love object, the same sex parent might become the primary love object and homosexuality was again the result.

Fixation implied a failure to develop beyond a certain stage. Some people had much difficulty with a particular phase but mastered it sufficiently to move into the next and so avoid fixation. Any additional stress, however, made adjustment difficult. The superficial adequacy broke down, tenuously based as it was, and the person *regressed*, i.e., he reverted back to earlier, more immature, but better established habits. Character disorders were the result of complete fixations. Neuroses and psychoses were regressions to stages of minor fixation following severe conflicts. For example, hysteria and anxiety reactions were regressions to the phallic stage, compulsions and obsessions involved regressions to the anal stage. Paranoids regressed to early anal and late oral stage. Depressives represented a regression to late oral stage, schizophrenics to the early oral period. In later developments of the theory, psychosomatic symptoms were also considered to be evidence of fixation and/or regression. It was believed that persons with similar symptoms had similar behavior patterns determined by fixation. Their symptoms appeared in a part of the body relevant to the point of fixation.

Defense Mechanisms. The pressure which led to neurosis and psychosis was usually an intra-personal one. The person was faced with Id impulses which his Superego and Ego could not tolerate. The impulses were a threat to the Superego when moral values were involved. The puritanical taboos perceived by a puzzled and often terrified three- to five-year old were the misunderstood standards of his parents. Rigidly enforced, they could not be questioned; therefore they were not exposed to the rational evaluation which might shape them into mature and realistic guides. The Id impulses threatened the Ego when they posed a realistic threat of unfortunate consequences, or when those impulses might, if given free rein, inundate the Ego, or when the Ego was so weak that it could not cope with the impulses and/or integrate them with the demands of the Superego. Given such a three-way conflict, anxiety was the result.

At first Freud believed that anxiety was due to sexual frustration, i.e., to insufficient opportunity for release and gratification of impulses. As he considered the matter further, he observed that gratification was blocked from within the personality, and that any release of impulses would only create more anxiety as long as the personality remained the same. In light of this observation, anxiety could be interpreted as a danger signal, an emotional reaction produced when something threatened the delicate balance the Ego sought to maintain within the personality.

Upon the appearance of this danger signal, the personality rallied to protect itself by removing the source of threat, the errant impulse. This was accomplished at first by *repression*, forcing the Id impulses back into the unconscious and not allowing them access to cognitive or motor outlets. Since the impulses were still activated, however, they were only driven from awareness and continued to exert pressure on the Ego from underground, so to speak. To control the impulse and maintain the repression, the Ego had to exercise energy equal to that of the impulse in order to keep it subdued. The expenditure of energy was costly, particularly if a number of impulses had to be repressed simultaneously. The laws of energy conservation, which Freud believed applied equally to the psychological and the physical phenomena, required some sort of resolution, some compromise which would preserve the integrity of the Ego, bypass the Superego, and allow some release of the impulse. This compromise was found in the *defense mechanisms*.

Defenses were habits of dealing with situations which originally developed during childhood as solutions to various psychosexual problems. They represented skills and techniques available to the child at that level of maturity. If the difficulties at this stage were acute, the person might never have been able to learn other defenses and might therefore be forced to use the same procedure in all situations.

If there were numerous minor conflicts during the first years, a series of specific defenses might be set up to cope with specific experiences. In each defense there were to be found precipitates, or *derivatives*, of the conflict. That is, examination of defensive behavior would reveal elements of the impulse, as well as elements of the Ego and Superego forces which were set against it.

Certain crude defenses, *denial*, *withdrawal* and *fantasy*, originated from skills in the oral period. Since they were the first means the infantile Ego had for defending itself, they were primitive and inefficient. The infant, unable to prevent threatening situations from occurring, relieved his anxiety by denying they were going on, or by withdrawing or by engaging in fantasies that whatever he wished was true. More workable defenses, which did less damage to reality, could not be established until after the child developed the ability to repress, since true defenses all required repression as a preliminary step in meeting conflict before defensive resolution could occur. *Repression* differed from denial in that it occurred when an impulse was about to become conscious or stimulate behavior and led to the prevention of any awareness of it or any overt expression of it. Repression could be lifted so that a person could, under special circumstances such as psychotherapy, recognize and express repressed material consciously. In contrast, denial rendered the person totally ignorant of some event, but would not prevent expression of impulses or feelings. It could not be removed.

Repression developed during the phallic period as part of the resolution of the Oedipus complex. Following its development, the crude defensive systems of the infant were built up into the more adaptively defensive mechanisms of the older child and the adult, which derived from the problem solving skills of the various psychosexual stages.

Projection involved attributing one's own undesirable characteristics to others. It began when the infant learned he could eject ill-tasting objects by spitting out, and was reinforced as a behavior pattern during the anal phase when the child gave off distasteful objects to others.

Reaction formation developed during the late anal and early phallic stages when the child learned to do the opposite of what he really wished in order to retain his parent's affection. The more he wished something undesirable, the harder he must try to undo the wish. Therefore, he developed the habit of acting in contradiction to his feelings, appearing, for example, to love when he hated, appearing brave when he was fearful, etc.

In addition to defense mechanisms so far discussed, there were some important ones which were not referrable to a particular point of origin, but which were generally found in more mature personalities. These included rationalization, isolation, displacement, and intellectualization. In *rationalization* the person attempted to supply a number of good reasons for an impulsive act or thought in order to hide from himself the real determinant. In *isolation* and *intellectualization*, defenses closely related to each other, recognition of the possible existence of some impulse was permitted by the Ego, although the person never consciously experienced the full effect of the motivating force of the impulse itself. Isolation cut off congnitive recognition of the affective impact so that the person realized some impulse was aroused, but he could not feel it. Intellectualization surrounded the cognitive recognition with so many intellectual explanations that the image or percept of the impulse was altered or smothered. *Displacement* involved releasing the impulse against some object to whom it was more acceptable, e.g., kicking the dog when you're mad at your wife, or marrying some girl who is "just like mother."

Persons fixated at a particular stage utilized the predominant defenses of that stage. Schizophrenics denied reality, withdrew and lived in fantasy. Paranoids projected, hysterics repressed. The syndromes we identify with certain neuroses, psychoses, or character disorders were consistently predictable patterns of defenses, conflicts, attitudes, with consistently predictable historical antecedents.

As we have already seen, instincts were attributed three dimensions in Freudian theory–source, aim and object. The source was innately determined and could not be changed, but the aim and object were subject to modifications and were therefore the focus of defensive maneuvers. Some of Freud's followers have attempted to categorize defenses according to what dimension of the instinct was affected. If one tries to take into consideration all of the detail which the analyst includes, the task becomes complex and open to some controversy. For this reason the following formulations concerning instincts and defenses and merely illustrative and might not be accepted by the analytic group.

Among defensive maneuvers which seem to involve alterations in the aim, or means of achieving a goal, but which leave the goal and the impulse intact, might be identification, fantasy, reaction formation and, most likely, rationalization. Defenses which seem to be effective by virtue of changing goal objects are displacement and projection. Some defenses seem to change all aspects of motivation, apparently attempting to do away with the impulse entirely either before, during, or after the fact. Denial and repression function in this manner. Isolation and intellectualization do not really appear to affect the impulse, aim, or goal, but rather the person's perception of it. The individual is aware of each aspect, but does not realize that each is related to the other. He experiences each one as a separate entity, thereby cutting off the emotion involved from the behavior, and placing the behavior in an intellectual Gestalt.

Because they represented indirect outlets for drives and prevented full gratification, defenses were originally considered unhealthy. No matter how effective they might be in the current situation, they eventually got the person into trouble. For example, a person who defended himself by continual withdrawal could never live a very satisfying life, and the person who projected his anger towards others could not maintain smooth interpersonal relationships. The healthy person was one who did not have to use defenses, but was able to find a socially acceptable aim and object for his forbidden impulses which gave him direct satisfaction. This was known as *sublimation.* The best-known example of sublimation is the sculptor who sublimates his anal impulses by means of his work in clay. The prize fighter may use his profession as a means of sublimating aggression, and the ordinary citizen can find ballroom dancing a sublimation of sexual urges. Freud believed that these acts were not defensive since there was no attempt to disguise aim or object, and no substitution. Society smiled on such behavior and so did psychoanalysis.

Over the years, however, analysis has come to accept the possibility that the normal individual may employ defenses other than sublimation and still be healthy, as long as the defense does not produce great distortion in his life, and as long as he can achieve a balance between Id, Ego and Superego without excessive use of defenses. The presence of defenses, therefore, is no longer regarded as a sign of illness, but Freudians still maintain that the perfectly adjusted (genital) personality would not require them; such an individual would be able to sublimate all of his unacceptable impulses.

Critique

It would be difficult to find an area of psychology or psychiatry which has not been influenced by Freud's thinking. Thousands of fruitful hypotheses and exciting experiments have been stimulated by his theories. His influence in sociology and anthropology is similarly immeasurable. At the same time, the very greatness of this theory tends to make others, especially those who adhere strongly to it, overlook its weaknesses.

Freud believed his theory was as much biological as psychological. He never attempted to explore the biological basis himself. Perhaps at the time of his writing much of what he said could not be checked against biological fact. In the light of present knowledge, however, many of his concepts are impossible or highly improbably biologically. His theory of energy or libido is one example. Another is his concept of a racial inheritance of symbolic expression. No such genetic mechanism can be discovered. Actually his concept of instinct as a whole has been discredited by modern psychology. His death instinct is in so much disfavor that even many of his closest disciples have disclaimed it.

His theory also provokes problems of definition and specification. Just what is Id or Ego? Whether or not Freud viewed Id, Ego, and Superego as physical entities, they have certainly been interpreted as such, and as a result have become so anthropomorphic as to sound more like folklore than science. They suggest an analogy for which there is no physical counterpart. So many of Freud's concepts are vague and undefinable that it is often impossible to prove or disprove the theory. In other places the theory contains such a series of interlocking hypotheses that no crucial test can be devised. How can one test a theory which predicts that a child must hate his father and, if the child gives no evidence of hate, concludes that the affection the child shows is really a reaction formation? How can a scientist tell whether the child is defending himself by turning his hate into love or whether he simply loves in the first place? If a theory is so loose that everything can be made to fit it, then it may be too general to explain anything satisfactorily. It proves itself, yet nothing is proven.

Freud assumed that what he had to say was true for all human beings because it was biologically determined. Anthropological studies have shown that this is not so. A different culture with different patterns of child-rearing produces different reactions. For example, Malinowski (1929) has shown that in cultures where children are not raised by their natural parents, but by some group or individual serving as a parent substitute, there is no such thing as classical Oedipal conflict. Instead, there is some other type of relationship between child and adult which is determined by the particular customs of that culture.

Even within Western culture, Freud's hypotheses are often too broad and all-inclusive. It is possible to find many European or American children who do not have castration fears, who do not manifest a latency period, and so on. The orthodox Freudian theorist may be able to explain this or point to some evidence that such a phenomenon is merely masked, but to the neutral bystander this is not necessarily impressive. The limits of the theory need to be worked out, and some acceptable formulation of apparent exceptions must be provided.

Freud ordinarily would not tolerate questioning of his ideas. Those who criticized were ignored or cast out of his good graces. Dogmatic acceptance is still a requirement of the Freudian School, and individual attempts to evaluate and alter the theory are discouraged. People who violate this rule are often assumed by the classical analyst to be disturbed by some aspect of the theory which has a personal reference and consequently to be defending themselves by destroying the theory. Such an orientation is not compatible with science, where constant testing, retesting, and alteration are assumed necessary in the process of approximating the truth. The Freudian is likely to see no need for this to the extent that he feels he already possesses the only real truth.

SUMMARY

Basic Unit. Freud wished to understand the entire personality as a functioning unit and felt that such sub-processes as the conflicts and defenses a person manifested could be useful as tools in comprehension.

Field of Study. The area to which Freud addressed himself was the interaction of physiology and life experiences, and the consequent psychological structure created by these influences. Freud was primarily interested in mentally ill persons but felt his theory could generalize to all human behavior.

Methods of Investigation. Freud gradually developed a technique for aiding the patient in recovering "forgotten" experiences (free association). This technique plus the analyst's observations and interpretations of the patient's productions provided the method of psychoanalysis.

Principles. All behavior was purposive, and its purpose was to maximize pleasure and minimize pain, although mature behavior considered the consequences of an act more readily than immature behavior. Normally more than one drive was involved in directing a particular act, and both present stimuli and past experiences determined its final form. Conflicts occurred when one of these determinants was incompatible with the rest. In the process of biological maturation a number of difficulties were encountered. Development involved finding some means of adjusting to these difficulties. Since the developmental problems were biological in origin, they had to be met and solved independently by every child.

Consciousness. Consciousness involved a state of awareness of events occurring inside and outside the individual. There were many additional occurrences of which a person was unconscious. The basic animal nature of the person, his Id, was entirely unconscious, being suppressed or repressed for social and moral reasons. The conscience, or Superego, was partially conscious, but the primitive prohibitions learned in infancy often influenced the person without his awareness. The Ego part of the personality, which comprehended and dealt with the external world and directed and controlled internal events and behavior, was necessarily conscious. In addition, the person was aware of the number of stimuli, impulses, and memories only as they were salient to his efficient performance. Such resources constituted the preconscious.

Sensation, Perception, and Discrimination. Infants did not really perceive the world. Probably their only awareness was a mass of meaningless feelings. Gradually as a result of feeding experiences, certain stimuli (breast or bottle) became distinct and assumed a simple meaning (relief). With more experience these stimuli became associated with a person, and along with many other sensations, formed the percept of mother. Other percepts emerged as a result of significant emotional experiences with objects. In addition to the learned percepts there were a number of symbolic meanings and expressions perceived primarily on an unconscious level and utilized by the Id. These were genetically determined, a racial heritage. Perception was also determined by unrealistic generalization from past experience. The term transference referred to misperception of the analyst as a result of such a distorting process.

Thinking, Cognition, and Memory. At first the infant did not think, but reacted impulsively and sought out immediate pleasures. Such behavior was said to accord to the pleasure principle. Within a year or two, however, the child learned that he must consider the future consequences of an act in order to prevent some immediate pleasure from causing eventual pain (the reality principle). To consider consequences in this fashion was to think. Thinking was a symbolic representation of objects, events and feelings. Most of these symbols were learned, but some of them utilized unconscious connotations which were part of the person's genetic inheritance. Dreams were rich in such symbolism, and since they were determined mainly by unconscious forces they were quite revealing of covert conflicts and impulses.

Emotion and Motivation. Freudian theory recognized three dimensions of motivation: source, aim and object. The source was given biologically. The aim and object were determined by experience within certain broad limits, and were actually more matters of behavior than of drive. The infant was born with a reservoir of free-floating energy which was available for use by any drive as a means for activating behavior. As an infant moved from random activity to the stage of definite aims and objects for each impulse, energy was permanently attached or cathected to the activity and the goal. Energy was also available to the Ego and the Superego for carrying out their functions. Still other energy was unassigned but could be used in emergencies. Freud first proposed that all motives could be divided into sexual (pleasure seeking) and self-preservative instincts. Later, he came to believe there must be an instinctual need for complete quiescence. Since the most completely quiescent state is death, he hypothesized a death instinct, or Thanatos, as well as a life or sexual instinct, Eros. The self-destruction that death would involve was unacceptable to the Ego and to the erotic drives, and therefore the destructive tendencies were transformed and directed away from the self and towards others in the form of aggression.

The Nature of the Learning Process. The Freudian theory of cathexsis was equivalent to a learning theory. The person learned (positively cathected) behaviors or goals which were pleasant and avoided (negatively cathected) those which were painful.

Behavior and Personality. The development of personality took place in a number of stages. Each of these stages involved the interaction of the existing psychological structure, the biological needs (especially the sexual ones), and the environment. Because of this interaction they were called psychosexual stages. Development was biologically determined and each phase brought forth new impulses to be socialized. The environment could influence the intensity of developmental problems, but no matter what the situation the problems would appear to some degree. Beginning with the trauma of birth, the first stage of development was one of helpless dependency characterized by a concentration of attention on oral activities and eating (oral stage). This was followed by a period of socialization of bowel and bladder habits, and a resultant emphasis on anal activities (anal stage). The next phase, the phallic, was marked by attempts to resolve infantile love relationship with the parent (Oedipal conflicts), during which process the fear of retaliation (castration) for his rivalry with the same sex parent eventually led the child to take on the identity of this parent, including his or her moral values. Thus a conscience or Superego was established, and the child entered the latency period wherein all sexual striving were suppressed until the onset of adolescence. If adolescence was passed without difficulties, the individual approached the genital stage, although the achievement of a fully genital personality was rare because so few individuals were able to pass through all the earlier stages unscathed. If the child had serious problems in passing through any stage, the social skills he should have developed were learned poorly or not at all. He might become fixated at this point and not be able to continue development, or he might limp along through other stages and fall back or regress to better established skills when under pressure. Fixation resulted in a particular kind of pathological adjustment, such as dependency in oral fixations, or pseudo-sexuality, Don Juanism, and daredevil activities in phallic fixations. Neuroses and psychoses were regressions in times of stress to earlier stages of development which had been more successfully resolved. The pressure leading to regression came from intra-personal conflicts over the repression of forbidden impulses. When an impulse was unacceptable it was pushed back into the unconscious and expressed only indirectly through some compromise behavior which allowed some disguised form of gratification while it also satisfied social and moral prohibitions (defenses). Each developmental phase brought with it skills which could be used as defenses, e.g., the fantasies of the oral period, the projections of the anal, or the repressions and reaction formations of the phallic.

REFERENCES

General References

Fenichel, O., *The Psychoanalytic Theory of Neurosis*. New York: Norton, 1945.
Mullahy, P., *Oedipus: Myth and Complex*. New York: Hermitage, 1948.
Munroe, Ruth, *Schools of Psychoanalytic Thought*. New York: Dryden, 1955.
Thompson, Clara, *Psychoanalysis: Evolution and Development*. New York: Hermitage, 1950.

Sigmund Freud

Brill, A. A., ed., *The Basic Writings of Sigmund Freud*. New York: Random House, 1938.
Freud, S., *Introductory Lectures to Psychoanalysis*. New York: Boni & Liveright, 1920.
———, *Beyond the Pleasure Principle*. London: International Psychoanalytic Press, 1922. (A)
———, *Group Psychology and the Analysis of the Ego*. London: International Psychoanalytic Press, 1922. (B)
———, *The Ego and the Id*. London: Hogarth & Institute for Psychoanalysis, 1927.
———, *Civilization and Its Discontents*. New York: Norton, 1930.
———, *New Introductory Lectures on Psychoanalysis*. New York: Garden City Pub. Co., 1933.
———, *The Problem of Anxiety*. New York: Norton, 1936.
———, *The Standard Edition of the Complete Psychological Works*, I. Starchey, ed., London: Hogarth, 1953.

Other References

Abraham, K., Selected papers on Psychoanalysis. London: Hogarth & Institute for Psychoanalysis, 1927.
Malinowski, B., *The Sexual Life of Savages*. London: Routledge, 1929.
Rank, O., *The Trauma of Birth*. New York: Harcourt Brace. London: Routledge & Kegan Paul, 1929.
Whiting, J. W. M., and I. L. Child, *Child Training and Personality: A Cross Cultural Study*. New Haven: Yale Univ. Press, 1953.

CHAPTER 16

THE NEO-FREUDIAN THEORIES (1928 TO PRESENT)

NEO-FREUDIAN is a term used to refer to a number of writers whose theories take on psychoanalytic shadings, but who developed Freud's original propositions within or beyond his system. Some of these authors merely expanded on one aspect of the master theory and were more or less orthodox in all other regards. Others proceeded to make modifications so far-reaching that their works are Neo-Freudian only in the sense that they employed the technique of free association and included the basic concepts of unconscious motivation, conflicts between impulses and society, and defense mechanisms. Each of these major revampings became a school of thought unto itself, and each differed not only from Freud's interpretations, but also from all newer suggestions, occasionally to the point of active opposition. The growth of new systems was encouraged by the intolerance of each new theorist for all ideas but his own, and by the fact that Freud and his loyal followers were not prone to accept alterations in his ideas. Only those developments which were logical outgrowths of his work were permitted within orthodox circles; all else was rejected.

We will begin our discussion of Neo-Freudian theories by taking up three analysts whose works are well within the orthodox limits. Indeed, the first two, Anna Freud and Melanie Klein, need only be mentioned briefly because their contributions are not significant departures from Freud's views. The third, Erik Homberger Erikson, will be discussed in somewhat more detail. These authors are taken up out of chronological sequence because their ideas were directly descended from Freud's, not influenced by other theories, and probably did not influence other theories outside the orthodox realm.

ANNA FREUD (1928 to present)

Freud's daughter, Anna, practiced psychoanalysis with children, first in Austria and later in England. Although she rarely saw patients beyond the adolescent age, her formulations of her father's theory have determined the recent trend of analytic practice.

Anna Freud stressed the functions of the Ego in controlling impulses, adjusting to the outside world, solving problems, and, above all, setting up defenses. It was her emphasis which led psychoanalysis away from its earlier concern with the Id and sexual material. She established in their stead an interest in the behavior of the individual as well as his unconscious. This orientation became known as Ego Psychology. Following Anna Freud, psychoanalysis has turned more to the consideration of defensive processes. It does not neglect the Id or the sexual impulses, but it is now concerned with what the person actually does, as well as with what he wishes and fears. The fine details of Ego Psychology are of great importance to psychoanalytic theory and practice, but they represent technicalities which are beyond our present purpose.

MELANIE KLEIN (1932–1960)

Another child analyst, also working in England, Melanie Klein, took a tack directly opposed to Anna Freud. She came to stress the sexual significance of all behavior to a much greater extent than Freud had ever done. Her published work is primarily an account of how this orientation has been put into practice in her work with children. Actually, beyond her application of Freudian theory to children's behavior and fantasies, her work presents no developments which are not predictable from the father system.

ERIK HOMBURGER ERIKSON (1950 to present)

Erikson practiced and taught an extremely orthodox variety of psychoanalysis, but felt free to make certain "improvements," adding detail to various concepts of symbolism, pathology, etc. His most important contribution, and the reason for his being included here when many other prominent analysts are not, is his handling of behavior and personality in the form of an altered view of psychosexual stages.

Behavior and Personality

Erikson followed Freud in suggesting that at different times in a child's life different body areas or *zones* are the focus of personal and social attention. These zones, the oral, anal, phallic, and genital, were determined partly by biology and partly by parental emphasis on certain physical processes. The activation of these zones corresponded to the several psychosexual levels. Within the zone in which he operated, even the tiny infant was capable of various general *modes* of response. He could be passively or actively receptive, he could hold everything to himself (retain), or reject and throw away (expel), and he could force himself into a situation. These modes were respectively referred to as *passive incorporation*, *biting incorporation*, *retention*, *elimination*, and *intrusion*. Among the possible modes, some were more common in some stages of maturation, some in others. Infants during the oral period were most often passively or actively incorporative, children in the anal period most often employed retentive or eliminative modes, children in phallic and later periods were more likely to be intrusive. If a person engaged in some extraordinary mode, he was likely to have difficulties in adjustment. But ordinary or extraordinary, a person could be characterized by the bodily zone of central importance to him and the predominant mode of response he utilized. Erikson felt he could give a somewhat better account of the maturation process by converting Freud's stages into mode-zone terminology.

Each period of the child's life brought with it new types of problems to be solved and new orientations toward life and one's fellow man, as well as the possibility of new modes and zones of activity. During early infancy a basic attitude of trust or distrust was established. As the infant matured, the problems of toilet training and parental discipline brought him to the point where he could achieve autonomous control over self and environment. If the child was unable to become autonomous, either through personal weakness or environmental blocks, he lived his life in doubt of his own integrity, haunted with shame and dominated by others. If the child passed this hurdle, he reached a stage in which it was possible for him to take initiative in directing his own activities, going out "on his own." The inability to solve the problems of this age and fulfill one's birth right as an individual led to intense guilt. By the time the child started school, another type of problem arose. He must either develop habits of industry which enabled him to master the demands of the educational and training agencies which shaped his future skills, or suffer feelings of inferiority if he failed. In adolescence the problem of identity returned, no longer in the form of becoming an individual, but now in the form of crystalizing one's personality and assuming a stable image to one's self and others. The alternative was to develop a series of role-playing facades which changed chameleon-like as one sort of personality or another was in vogue. The problem of identity was hardly solved before the individual, in late adolescence, had also to establish a pattern of heterosexual adjustment. If this adjustment was successful it led to a capacity for emotional intimacy with others. If the person could not achieve such intimacy, he lived his life in emotional isolation from others and found any sort of close union impossible. As the person advanced into maturity, his life became focused around adult responsibilities. The person might respond to these with a productive orientation vitally concerned with his children, his family, and his job. Lacking the capacity for this *generativity*, as Erikson called it, the person stagnated and produced nothing. The phase of social and sexual productivity continued into old age where the final dilemma of adjustment was posed. Faced with growing evidences of physiological decline, the person might be able to maintain his integrity, but if he was a less stable being he could fall into despair over his current condition and what he had made of his life.

These life problems were fashioned from an interaction of cultural and psychological forces, and the solutions were likewise determined. Fixation on a particular body zone or particular mode of response to stress colored choices of, and hampered, success in later adjustment.

Critique

Erikson sought to clarify Freudian theory, to remove its instinctual bias, and to make it account for more deviant types of adjustment. The concept of mode and zone was useful in this regard. The stages which Erikson proposed seem to be much more appropriate to contemporary American behavior. They were not, of course, intended to replace Freud's phases, but to lend more perspective to them. They provide for more flexibility than the Freudian stages because they take cultural and social factors into account as well as biological influences. They cover the entire life span, whereas Freudian theory stops with adolescence and never really deals with adult problems. They concentrate on behavior and supply a more objective set of criteria for assessing developmental level. As a result, Erikson's stages have found wide favor among clinicians and have become a popular research tool. As such, they serve not only as a scheme for selection and classification of research subjects, but also as a rich source of hypotheses.

SUMMARY

Behavior and Personality. Among the orthodox group of Neo-Freudians, Anna Freud was influential in developing Ego Psychology, while Melanie Klein worked primarily in spelling out the sexual significance of various aspects of child behavior. Erik Homburger Erikson added detail to the description of psychosexual stages: first, he suggested that in addition to biological modes of sensitivity the child had the biological potential for various modes of response—passive or active incorporation, retention, elimination or intrusion; second, he added social considerations to Freud's biological stages, spelling out a socio-biological theory of development. According to Erikson, as the infant matured, he must first establish an orientation to the world, learning to trust or distrust others. Then he must develop an ability to deal with it autonomously, and, as he reached school age, a capacity for assuming initiative and applying himself industriously. As he reached adolescence he was faced with the problem of establishing his identity. In adulthood he must first learn how to deal constructively with heterosexual situations, and once these were resolved, must go on to fulfill a productive role in society. In old age the person had to face what he had accomplished in life and the fact that death was approaching. Any failure in resolving these problems distorted the person's ability to meet subsequent difficulties.

REFERENCES

Anna Freud

Freud, Anna, *Introduction to the Technique of Child Analysis*. New York: Nerv. Ment. Dis. Pub. Co., 1928.

———, *The Ego and the Mechanisms of Defense*. London: Hogarth, 1937.

Melanie Klein

Klein, Melanie, *The Psychoanalysis of Children*. London: Hogarth Institute of Psychoanalysis, 1932.

Erik Homburger Erikson

Erikson, E. H., *Childhood and Society*. New York: Norton, 1950.

CHAPTER 17

CARL JUNG: ANALYTIC PSYCHOLOGY (1923–1962)

CARL JUNG was trained by Freud and worked closely with him until a disagreement over some of Jung's theoretical innovations led to a break between them. As his theory took more distinct form, Jung adopted the name Analytic Psychology to distinguish his approach from that of Freud and Adler. Jung accepted the basic tenets and methods of psychoanalysis, but added an intricate embroidery to the superstructure. The additions grew out of his religious and philosophical convictions and his emphasis on the differences among individuals. Where Freud described how all men came to adapt their biological nature to their social circumstances, Jung described how each man came to find his place in the cosmos. In its final form, Jung's theory was quite complex and exceedingly mystical, involving mythology, philosophy, alchemy, and various Oriental and Occidental religions. We cannot hope to do justice to all of these components within the limits of a textbook of this sort. We have therefore selected what seems most relevant to our purpose.

Basic Unit, Field of Study

Jung had nothing to contribute to Freud's views of basic unit and field of study.

Methods of Investigation

Jung described four methods for studying human behavior, and all four were equally applicable as research tools and treatment techniques. Indeed, research was conducted even as treatment progressed, the two being more or less synonymous. Jung's methods were not his singular invention, but their application and the atmosphere in which they were applied was a great departure from classical analysis. The first tool was the Association Method, or a word association task which required the patient to respond to each of a list of words with the first word that came into his mind. The second method was Symptom Analysis, wherein the meaning of the symptom for the patient's psychic economy was assessed by means of the patient's associations to it and the analyst's observations and interpretations. This method was developed by Freud, but employed only in work with traumatic neuroses and dropped rather quickly. The third method was Anamnestic Analysis, an extensive collection and examination of the incidents and coincidences in the patient's life history. While it was mainly a data-gathering device, it could be useful in aiding the patient to see patterns and relationships in his actions. Freudian analysis did not involve such a formal history-taking, and the discovery of its value as a means of developing insight was apparently made by Jung. The final and most extensively used Jungian method was the Analysis of the Unconscious as it appeared in dreams, fantasies, and general behavior. Jung took such phenomena at their face value, i.e., as overt manifestations of unconscious forces, not as symbolic disguises. Much of what Freud interpreted Jung took literally and criticized Freud for looking too far when what he should have seen was right before him. When repression seemed to be involved, Jung sought to recognize what had been repressed, but when he dealt with unconscious material he did not assume it meant something else than what it appeared to be on the surface. What Freud unmasked, Jung viewed as primal longings.

These methods were employed in a much less formal climate than classic analysis. While the Jungian analyst was careful not to affect the direction of the patient's thoughts, he entered into the situation actively in the role of friend and companion on a journey into unknown territory, not as an expert and not-to-be questioned guide. He was more democratic and less aloof, lending not just his knowledge, but his personality as a foil for the patient. To prepare himself for such usage, and to assure that he not act out his own neurosis on the patient, Jung introduced the idea that the analyst-in-training undergo analysis himself. Even then, the intimacy of the treatment was bound to have some effect upon him, for treatment consisted in great part of a mutual interplay between the patient's unconscious and the analyst's unconscious. The resultant emotional impact must necessarily be tremendous. Jung, in describing the intimacy of the transference, makes an analogy to the alchemist's allegorical search for the philosopher's stone, in which the production of the stone is depicted in terms of sexual congress between two god-like figures. However, this valuable fetus can only endure to be born if the soul is reconstructed to heal all the opposing forces into one (hermaphroditic) body. As the allegory implies, Jung's goal was to join all the disparate and incompatible forces of the individual into some union strong enough to allow the existence of all aspects in harmony; hence the hermaphroditic reference. The reunion of the personality called for reliving with the patient the formative experiences in his life and reconstructing with him the historic struggles of man as these were preserved in his collective unconscious (Jung assumed that these were inherited in the germ plasma). These classic events tended to unfold themselves in a predictable course, so that the content of treatment and its sequence in persons of common racial heritage tended to be similar. For example, in addition to experiences with his parents, the patient could be expected to suggest material pertaining to the primordial Father and the magical Magna Mater at predictable times. While the form of the dream or symbol varied from person to person, its referents did not. The details of this process are rather far afield from our concern, so that with the flavor of Jungian technique, if not its letter, we shall move on.

Principles

Those traits which were dominant in the personality patterned themselves into a few set types. These traits determined the conscious content, the perceptions, the thinking, the motives—the total behavior of the individual and what and how he learned.

Consciousness

Jung concerned himself less with the nature of consciousness than with what was conscious and what was unconscious. Consciousness included the dominant orientation of a personality and those things upon which this orientation focused. The unconscious was the resting place for all that was in opposition to the conscious orientation. Since the two were incompatible, the normal, healthy forces were pushed into a limbo from which they later departed in exaggerated form, shaped by the dominant structure, distorted by the rest of the unconscious, and deprived of the opportunity to develop beyond a primitive level, until they were caricatures of what they might have been.

The contents of the unconscious were not all bad, evil things as Freud would have us believe; nor were they all sexually colored. There were, of course, animal vestiges in human nature, but the evil attributed to the unconscious by Freud was not to be found except as the primitive and malformed remnants of repressed facets of personality. The unconscious could create good or evil equally well, depending upon what parts of it had access to behavior, how these parts were molded as they passed into consciousness, and how flexible or rigid the conscious personality was.

Aside from the cast-off bits of personality and experience, the unconscious was the storage house for all the past experiences and conflicts that man had undergone, all his folk wisdom, his yearnings, his misalliances, his struggles with nature. Jung spoke of these as the *collective unconscious* or *racial unconscious*, and referred to the various inherited memories as *archetypes*. These archetypes were carried in the genes and were represented in the adult mind by universal symbols which could be observed in dreams, myths, religion, mystical works, and philosophical essays.

Sensation, Perception, and Discrimination; Thinking, Cognition, and Memory; Emotion and Motivation

These processes were discussed at length by Jung, but not as cognitive or affective phenomena so much as behavioral traits. We will therefore consider them under Behavior and Personality.

The Nature of the Learning Process

Jung, like Freud, emphasized reinforcement as the basis of learning. He was, however, more inclined to view behavior as genetically determined than most other psychological theorists.

Behavior and Personality

Personalities could be characterized according to whether they were centered on the objective or subjective aspects of living. To the former, whom Jung called *extroverts*, the outer world was a theater of operations. They were interested in the objects (including people) around them and open to external stimulation, but not concerned with their own inner workings; indeed, they were closed off from their own emotions. The subjectively oriented, whom Jung called *introverts*, were preoccupied with their inner experiences and shrank from the world beyond their skin. Whether extrovert or introvert, the individual was also either *masculine* or *feminine*. The individual's position in regard to these two sets of characteristics served as anchoring points for his personality. Around them developed a constellation of complimentary traits which stressed either rational or irrational functions. The rational functions, thinking and feeling, required suspension of perception, the taking in of new information in order to make judgments or decisions. Thinking was aimed at some logical conclusion; feeling was aimed at appreciating and evaluating events for their worth or propriety. Irrational functions, sensation and intuition, called for the exposure of the self to perceptual experience without rendering judgment. Sensation required that one give over his attention to the appreciation of sensing for its own sake. Intuition required focusing upon the conscious products of unconscious events, and was likely to be manifest in hunches, whims, and speculations without adequate external stimuli.

A personality, anchored in either extroversion or introversion, and in masculinity or femininity, manifested its judging or perceiving bent by orienting itself to one of these four functions. As the person developed a particular type of personality, he was to some degree unable to integrate the other functions since they were incompatible. Consequently, the "inferior" functions were relegated to the unconscious. They continued to influence behavior, but usually in a negative fashion because they were never permitted to mature and their influence was usually colored by other unconscious elements. A few individuals found the means of reconciling all these incompatible forces into a smoothly integrated adjustment. Others succeeded in life because, while there were incompatible and immature attitudes present, their dominant orientation was not so rigid as to block all foreign expression, or at least it could endure in spite of contradictory trends. In some cases a secondary function was combined with the dominant one in a supportive capacity. This secondary function was never antagonistic to the dominant one: if a rational function was dominant, then the secondary function must be an irrational one, and *vice versa*. For example, if a person were a thinking type, he could not focus on feelings, but he could think about sensations or intuitions. Two functions could only be of equal dominance in an underdeveloped personality where some potential was not realized.

The dominant function directed the course of the individual's life by siphoning off irrelevent aspects of experience and delimiting the kinds of relationship the person could have with others and himself. Furthermore, the functions were motives calling for certain actions. While natural drives such as sex or power initiated activity, the functions formalized and channeled the activity into certain actions toward specific goals. They were the basis of all social and personal attitudes about these goal objects.

A brief sketch of each of the dominant types will assist in clarifying Jung's type theory. However, these sketches, like all textbook examples, are abstractions, pure cases which are likely to be distorted by extraneous factors when observed in real life.

The extroverted thinking type was guided by objective, intellectual prescriptions which dominated him, and through him, all of his associates. This domination of the personality by its convictions could become tyrannical, and when this happened the tyranny was passed on to the individual's family and followers. Such a person's views were firm and idealistic and provided for no exceptions or extenuating circumstances. This type of person strove for perfection and demanded it of others. If his views were broad, his effect on the world could be most beneficial, because he was a man of action who could get things done and inspire others to follow his bidding. If his views were too narrow or rigid, he became a grumbling, self-righteous crank. The thinking type person repressed all feelings, so that he was emotionally shallow. In spite of repression, unconscious feelings remained as influential forces. Their primitive qualities, merged with other unconscious material, were mildly disruptive in normal states and could become bizarre in extreme cases. The repressed attitudes might appear, for example, as selfish, petty acts in one who prided himself on his altruism, or as smirches upon the face of the moral zealot. When other functions were dominant, the thinking of the extroverted individual retained its uncompromising, materialistic character without its clarity. Thus, a function that might be a conscious asset was an unconscious hazard.

The introverted thinking type was equally sure that his was the right way, but his was the realm of intellectual theory. He avoided society, even as the extrovert sought people as followers. While the introverted thinker might be courteous and friendly, he was ill at ease with people because he did not know how to deal with them. People did not understand him, and he could not make himself understood. In fact, although he expounded upon his ideas, he did so for the sake of the idea, and not for the sake of communication. Because he was dogmatic and uncommunicative, he got along poorly with his colleagues, except for those who knew him well enough to penetrate his guard. He tended, however, to be especially uncomfortable with the opposite sex. In extreme cases, the introverted thinking type became rigidly fixed in his beliefs and completely unsympathetic to other people, a sort of hermit. His thoughts grew so tortuous and remote that he could no longer express them at all. He became emotional and sensitive as a result of the intrusion of the repressed feelings which he fought.

The extroverted feeling type, ordinarily a woman, was guided by feelings, but feelings so formulated as to be the proper and correct ones. Her spouse was chosen because she loved him, but she could only love proper persons. She was conforming in behavior, an excellent wife and mother in conventional situations. She was often a social leader and excelled in diplomacy. However, her conventional feelings were not real or deep feelings, and if convention demanded too great a deviation from nature, the overt manifestation was confusion. Being determined by convention, her feelings were variable depending upon what she viewed as acceptable in the particular situation. If she found herself pushed to lengths where she could not behave consistently and appropriately because of the distortion of her true feelings, she might become reserved, but this would lead to a greater need for people, and therefore to greater distortions in order for her to maintain her version of propriety. Thinking in such a person was so repressed as to appear only in a very primitive form, loaded with unconscious content.

The introverted feeling type, ordinarily a woman too, might have been the subject of the proverb "Still waters run deep." She was reticent, perhaps melancholy, and socially inconspicuous. She might seem calm and exert a sweet, peaceful effect on others, but if she were a little more drawn into herself, she would seem to be indifferent. In either case, she would repel other's efforts to establish a closer relationship and would remain cool to the outer world. Yet her inner feelings were deep, and while she seemed unsympathetic, her concern for the misery of some other person might lead to a truly heroic outburst. She had a hidden need to overpower and control others which was usually manifest only in her relationship to her children, or in the slight stifling effect she had upon those around her. Extroverted men were especially fascinated by this forcefulness because of its appeal to their unconscious. If she adopted the superior air of the extrovert male by virtue of her relationship with him, she could develop a tendency to arrogance, vanity, tyranny, cruelty, or unscrupulous ambition. Her thinking was primitive, and when the dominant tendency became too exaggerated, her unconscious contributed a strong paranoid element to her personality.

The extroverted sensation type was the gourmet, sensualist, *bon vivant*. He was engaged in a constant and never-ending search for fresh sensations. This person, ordinarily a man, did not see himself as controlled by senses, but rather as one who loves indulging himself; his morality was hedonistic. Whatever else he was, he was loyal to his pleasure. He was often quite appealing to others, either as the jolly good fellow or the charming gentleman, depending upon his degree of refinement. He scorned all inner preoccupations and oriented himself completely to objects. If he moved too far to the extreme he could become a crude pleasure-seeker, wishing only to stimulate sensation. If he repressed all but the sensory, his unconscious would then try to compensate for the imbalance, and the repressed intuitive function would lead to mystic, magical practices. His behavior might take on a compulsive quality, alternating between indulgence and ritualistic compensatory efforts.

The introverted sensation type was immersed in his own responses to the world. He seemed calm, passive, and controlled because he was unconcerned with people and outside events. When he acted, it was in terms of his own subjective perceptions. He might be a creative artist, perhaps an impressionist painter. In the ordinary human being, however, he was simply an impressionist "behaver." While his influence on social groups might be disruptive insofar as he sought to direct it along the lines of subjective interpretations, he had no real defense against people and was often victimized. He would then take vengeance by inappropriate resistance and stubbornness. Thought and feeling were unconscious, and therefore his impressions were likely to be influenced by primitive ideas. Since he lived by impression, far removed from the object, his world was peopled with fairy tale-like creatures. Since he could not distinguish these fantasies from reality, he always behaved a little like *Alice In Wonderland*. In extreme cases, he might withdraw altogether into fantasy and psychosis.

The extroverted intuitive type lived in the world of possibilities, and was driven to wring the most from each of them. He threw himself into each new speculation with fervor, no matter what the risk. He had no reason or feeling to help evaluate a situation. He did have his own brand of moral conviction, namely, a firm belief in his own intuitions, but no element of judgment was involved. He was not concerned with his own or the welfare of others, nor had he any particular respect for human rights. He appeared to be a ruthless adventurer. Men of this type were gamblers, merchants, agents, speculators. Women, and there were more extroverted intuitive women than men, were shrewd social opportunists. This type of person could serve society in the role of a promoter of new ideas, movements, and commodities and could vitalize the cause he currently followed. However, because he must seize each new venture, he was never able to get ahead, for he spent his gains on his next project. His repressed thoughts and feelings, and his turning away from actual objects to intuitions about them often led to compulsive hunches which he was forced to follow to his own destruction.

The introverted intuitive type was a mystic dreamer, a crank, or an artist, depending upon what other forces acted upon him. The artist was perhaps the most probable example, for he utilized his intuitions to shape perceptions (and to convey them). He was a surrealistic artist, or at least not a member of the classical school, but he was capable of original work of great merit despite its distinctly other-worldly character. Those who were unable to achieve a creative shaping of their intuitive experiences could become weird geniuses or cranks, brilliant but divorced from the objective world, misunderstood and misjudged. If moral issues became intertwined with the intuitive processes, visions were no longer sufficient. The person must ponder their meaning for himself and the world. Such preoccupations produced the prophets of antiquity. The unconscious of the introverted intuitive centered about a primitive kind of sensation, so that he was subject to strong impulses and so tied to certain goal objects that he could not sublimate or re-direct his urges into some more acceptable action directly upon these objects; the result could be compulsive symptoms.

These manifestations of personality were determined to some extent by constitution, and more especially by genetic influences in the form of the racial unconscious, but the greater portion of personality could be traced to developmental experiences. Jung did not distinguish stages of development as Freud did. Rather, there was a gradual differentiation of self from parents, the kernel of which was not really formed until after the child was five or six. His first identity was an extension of his parents', and the personality growing out of this was markedly influenced by his parents and earlier ancestors. It was not so much what his parents and grandparents were which determined the child's personality, as what they might have been but were not. Those repressed potentials in themselves which the parents could not realize were often foisted off upon their children, bringing these potentials to fruition indirectly. This was ordinarily destructive to the child, for these potentials were aspects of their parents' personalities which had been repressed before they had an opportunity to mature.

As for childhood sexuality, Jung opined that Freud over-emphasized the role of sex in both children and adults. There were, of course, pleasurable activities and sensations, but these were not necessarily sexual. As for the Oedipus complex, there were emotional ties between parent and child to which the Oedipus myth might be an apt analogy. These desires were unlikely to reach the point of sexual desire for the parent, however, unless the parent was actively seductive. All in all, Jung found Freud's theory of the sexual and libidinal significance of behavior a little disgusting.

In children, then, neurotic symptoms were most commonly the reflection of the parents' unrealized potential. In the adult, as the review of personality types showed, it was the repressed and undeveloped aspects of the self which contributed the neurotic quality to behavior, the person having become lopsided in the direction of his dominant orientation. Of course, the real cause of neurosis was the same in both child and adult: characteristics (such as conflicts and tensions) passed on to the child by his parents and grandparents resulted in troublesome imbalances either in childhood or later in life.

Jung did not feel it was possible to derive a general theory of neurosis because the many complexities made a single theory impossible. One could only relate certain neuroses to certain personality types. For example, hysteria was to be found in the extroverted thinking and intuitive types, and in the introverted intuitive type; psychasthenia (nervous exhaustion) seemed to be most common in introverts, especially the thinking, feeling, and sensation types; compulsive neuroses were to be found in the sensation and intuitive types of both introversion and extroversion. In addition, one could describe certain phenomena like dissociation, and regression and the presence of conflicts which were universal to neurotic formations, but they had different roles and different qualities in each neurosis, just as flour has a different character in bread and in gravy. For each of Freud's laws of neurotic behavior, however, there were exceptions which this law could not explain. One could, for example, cite principles of repression which were perfectly valid as long as there was repression, but which could not explain what the cause might be when repression failed to appear. There were likewise valid principles to explain the absence of repression which could not explain those occasions on which it did appear. Jung therefore contented himself with investigating the nature of individual personality and in setting up a theory which he felt could explain what he observed.

Critique

Jung's philosophical and mythological speculations and his insistence on racial inheritance have led to limited applications of his theories. He is not widely known, is less widely followed, and is perhaps still less widely understood. The aspect of his theory which has received most acceptance within psychology is his theory of personality types. He described traits actually seen in people, traits psychologists find it easy to chart and measure, and which seem important and interesting as well as objective. In current usage personality traits are believed to be distributed along a continuum. Such a belief was not part of Jung's original theory. A person was either a masculine extroverted thinker or a feminine introverted intuitive; there was no question of degree. However, Jung was essentially the first person to describe personality in terms of traits dynamic enough to incorporate the richness of the individual. His proposals have sufficient import and validity to have become widely recognized, especially the masculine-feminine and extrovert-introvert distinctions. There have been borrowed for use in theories as diverse as the statistically derived factor studies and orthodox Freudian psychoanalysis. Indeed, extrovert and introvert are almost household words.

Another aspect of his personality theory is both significant and misleading. Jung held that a person was unconsciously the opposite of what he was consciously. It is true that what a person is on the surface is not necessarily what he is underneath, but it is not universally so, as Jung would have us believe. Even when it is, unconscious is not necessarily the opposite of conscious; it is just different.

Jung's approach to psychotherapy came into vogue in the late 1950's and early 1960's in several influential areas of the United States. Historically, it had always attracted a minor following in Europe but was more or less neglected in America. Its recent popularity may be due in part to growing concern with religion and conservatism, to both of which the content of Jung's theory would appeal. Perhaps its status is due still more to the fact that Jung's approach included a number of facets which have become almost sacred to psychotherapy. It exercised the method of psychoanalysis in the democratic atmosphere beloved of the Rogerians, and required the involvement of the therapist's personality and his unconscious in a manner similar to that suggested in some quarters of the Sullivanian and Adlerian schools (a matter we shall take up when these theories are discussed).

We complete our discussion of Jung with a touch of irony. Among theories of behavior this theory is one of the most mystical. Yet some of the traits proposed by Jung have been taken over by the tough-minded, empirically-oriented psychologists, while most of the more tender-minded analysts look askance upon his theories.

SUMMARY

Basic Unit; Field of Study. Same as Freud.

Methods of Investigation. Jung studied personality and/or administered psychotherapy by means of four methods: Association Method (word association), Symptom Analysis, Anamnestic Analysis (analysis of patterns in life history), and Analysis of Unconscious. In the latter method Jung proposed not to interpret symbols, but to accept the manifest content of dreams and fantasies at face value. These methods demanded much participation and involvement of the therapist. Therefore, it was essential that the novice undergo analysis before practicing it on patients.

Principles. The personality type of the individual was the determinant of all salient psychological activity.

Consciousness. The conscious aspects of personality were determined by whatever function of the personality was dominant. The rest of the functions, repressed early in life because they were incompatible, remained in a primitive state. The unconscious housed all sorts of potentials, not just bad things. Unconscious forces could exercise constructive effects equally as well as destructive ones; their nature depended upon whether the dominant function was able to integrate them or whether it had to distort them. In the unconscious, too, were housed all the wisdom of the ages, inherited as the racial or collective unconscious, and manifest in fantasy and dreams as archetypes—symbols of man's ancient experience.

Behavior and Personality. Personality was anchored in masculinity or femininity, and in extroversion (outer, objective orientation) or introversion (inner, subjective orientation). Around these two anchoring points the personality developed either its rational (cognitive) functions or its irrational (emotional) ones. The rational functions were thinking and feeling, the irrational functions were sensation and intuition. Whichever rational or irrational function became dominant forced the repression of its mate, for there was complete opposition between the two. It also forced the repression of the other aspects of function, but less completely because they were merely incompatible. However, an overbalance in the dominant direction led to the appearance of pathological (neurotic or psychotic) behavior. Personality was developed in the child in part from his constitution and in part from his racial heritage, but mostly by his experiences with his parents. In his early life the child was an extension of his parents' identity, and as such he was often most influenced by his parents' unrealized potentials, i.e., those repressed and incompatible functions whose influences were beyond their control. Jung did not formulate developmental phases; there seemed to him to be a gradual differentiation of the person into a distinct individual. Nor could he generalize to a universal theory of neuroses. There were too many complexities and exceptions. This did not prevent the possibility of understanding and treating the neurotic individual; it simply made it impossible to derive conclusive principles of neurotic behavior.

REFERENCES

Carl Jung

Jung, C. G., *Psychological Types or the Psychology of Individuation*. New York: Harcourt Brace, 1923.
———, *Collected Works*. New York: Pantheon, 1953.

CHAPTER 18

ALFRED ADLER: INDIVIDUAL PSYCHOLOGY (1927–1935)

ADLER was another of Freud's early students and another member of the inner circle until his views departed sufficiently from those of Freud that a break occurred. Adler then proceeded to develop his own theory of personality.

Basic Unit

As with Freud, Adler was not desirous of dissecting personality into elements. He was concerned, rather, with grasping its origins and functions, and approached it as a phenomenon to be studied in its own right.

Field of Study

Although he worked primarily with emotionally distressed persons, Adler believed it possible to construct a framework of generalities which would apply to all human behavior, normal as well as abnormal. A practicing clinician, he sought to understand his patients as individuals, but he did not believe each man was a law unto himself. He was convinced that everyone's behavior was lawful in the sense that all that people did and said could be understood in terms of their basic orientation toward life. He felt a consistent basic theme could be found, no matter how contradictory or inconsistent the behavior might seem on the surface. To this consistency he gave the name "style of life." In this concept were included the totality of habits, attitudes, feelings, and expectations about self and world derived as a result of the molding of an individual's biological propensities by his experience with his family and with society during the process of maturation. This focus on the evolution of a style of life, and its effects upon individual behavior, lent the name Individual Psychology to Adler's theory.

Methods of Investigation

Adler's methods of investigation were in no general sense different from Freud's, although his theory required subtle differences especially in its application to psychotherapy. These differences were important in the handling of patients, but need not concern us here. Suffice it to say that an Adlerian therapist may be quite directive, revealing to his patient his own thoughts and feelings and manipulating the patient's behavior. Such active steps would be justified by the hypothesis that personality difficulties were pathological modes of interaction with others based on unhealthy social experiences, and could best be treated by exposure to corrective influence. In contrast, the true Freudian analyst placed himself in the role of a blank screen, reflecting the patient's behavior back to him in much the same way as a mirror.

Principles

As with so many other theorists, Adler implied principles but did not spell them out. One can, however, infer that the following would comprise a set of basic laws:

Every human being began life in a state of biological inferiority and insecurity simply by being born an infant. Social (family) experience could reduce or magnify this inferiority.

"Life style" was the peculiar means used by the individual to cope with and compensate for inferiority. Most commonly it involved the effort to establish power over others, but whatever its goal, it was a result of the interaction between social experiences and one's biological constitution.

Consciousness

Adler did not separate mental life into Id, Ego, and Superego, but he did retain the tri-partite division of mental activity into conscious, preconscious and unconscious. However, the whole matter was given far less importance than in Freudian theory. Adler was more interested in behavior than in mental contents. His treatment of consciousness rendered it less a biological phenomenon and more a social and interpersonal one.

He noted the close connection between language and conscious thought and concluded that consciousness and thought both develop only as the child masters verbal communication. He equated consciousness with verbalization, actual or potential, so that for Adler, unconscious material was that which the person did not wish to, or could not, talk about. Threats to self esteem and security were repudiated and responsibilities avoided comfortably by the simple expedient of not recognizing them. Adler's use of the concept would seem to suggest a purposive element to unconsciousness, and to equate the unconscious with the unadmitted.

The preconscious was not different in any major way from the Freudian preconscious. Automatic processes such as walking or breathing which did not require voluntary control were not usually conscious, but the person could become aware of them if he so needed or wished.

Sensation, Perception, and Discrimination

Adler pointed out that all people did not necessarily react similarly to similar environmental experiences (sensations). Each person adopted an individual attitude, determined by impressions created in early childhood. Although the reality of the environment was a forceful factor, the person's subjective impression of it was actually more important. Thus Adler emphasized the significance of perception and minimized the importance of reality and sensation. The most decisive factor in behavior was not environment but the person's attitude toward it. The attitude was determined by, and in turn determined, perception. Perception was, then, an instrument for the enhancement of style of life and always took place in such a way as to be compatible with it.

Thinking, Cognition, and Memory

Even as preservation of style of life was the major function of perception, so it was the major function of all other cognitive functions. The person was forced to see and experience everything in accordance with his childhood biases, since it was on these that his style of life was based. This private, childish logic justified the person's mistaken ideas and guided him in continuing his irrational defensive actions. The person could learn from experience only when no bias was involved; otherwise, he merely perpetuated his earlier misconceptions.

The cognitive patterns of the individual were also influenced by certain guiding fictions or fictive goals which the person mistakenly believed would give him security. These goals were closely related to the life style but different from it in the same sense that the aim was different from the object in the Freudian theory of drives. While the style of life determined the way in which a person would think and act, the guiding fictions determined the direction of the person's problem-solving attempts, what his reasoning would accomplish for him. Guiding fictions complemented and implemented the style of life. Seen in this light, thinking was a defensive process. Any creative aspects of cognition could appear only in areas not involved in life styles and fictive goals.

A guiding fiction very common in the patients Adler saw was based on the high status of men in Western culture. Children recognized this high status and tended, from their own inferior position, to exaggerate it to the point of omnipotence and unquestioned superiority. Men were symbols of power. Women were perceived as weaker beings whose role was one of service and suffering. To compensate for inferiority could, under these circumstances, come to mean trying to achieve the role attributed to men (especially father). Treatment which lowered a person's value, making him (or her) less like the powerful masculine stereotype, was met by resistance in the form of a verbal or behavioral protest of masculinity, or to use Adler's term, a *masculine protest*. To strive to maintain masculinity (in this exaggerated sense) was a common guiding fiction not only in men, but also in women who found their assigned role intolerable and sought security in superiority and power.

Adler was less concerned with the mechanics of thinking than he was with the purpose it served. The "how" of thought took a back seat to the "why," just as it did in perception. Indeed, the matter of motivation was so central to the Adlerian theory that his handling of other concepts ordinarily took the form of explaining how they functioned to further the basic purpose of the individual.

Emotion and Motivation

It is in the area of motivation that the greatest difference between Freud and Adler can be found. Adler could not accept Freud's biological-sexual treatment of motivation. Sex was one source of motivation and conflict, but Adler saw more important determinants of personality. He stressed the fact that all human infants begin life under conditions of inferiority and insecurity, if for no other reason than their small size and complete dependency. Everyone had to cope with this inferiority, and the healthy person was the one who could achieve security in his relationships to other people in spite of it.

If the infant was born into a situation which reinforced his inferiority, he was indeed headed for trouble. Reinforcing influences included parental rejection, objective organic weakness, social discrimination, membership in a minority group, or an adverse position in family structure. This last factor received great attention from Adler. He believed he could predict the personality and social difficulties produced by each sibling relationship, e.g., oldest, youngest or middle child. He was especially convinced of the unfortunate status of the only child. So far, however, Adler's hypotheses regarding the influence of family position have not been substantiated. Historically, research has not been able to demonstrate any consistent pattern correlated with birth order. Recent studies (Becker & Carrol, 1962; Stotland & Cottrell, 1962; Stotland & Dunn, 1962, 1963; Stotland & Walsh, 1963) have reported personality constellations correlated with birth order, but these patterns are the result of empirical investigation, and there is no necessary relationship with Adler's predictions.

Whatever the source of inferiority, its effect was the same. A person feeling inferior tried to find some way to compensate, to make up for his inferiority. The most ordinary mode of compensation was a desire for power, domination, and superiority over others. The establishment of power-procurement not only set the style of the individual's life, but also provided his *life goal*, the central directive force which would thenceforward control his every move. Thus, Adler placed some external, acquired motive in the position of man's most dominant drive, in contrast to the biological emphasis of Freud.

Adler pointed out that the life goal was not necessarily realistic. The stronger the person's sense of inferiority, the more he needed some means of overcoming his handicaps. Unrealistic aspirations and interpretations arose out of the interaction between the environment and the person's feelings of inferiority and led to the distorted views and expectations to which, as we have already seen, Adler gave the name "guiding fictions." These distortions were present to some extent in everyone, representing the influence of motivation upon cognitive processes. The more disturbed the person, the more distorted were his guiding fictions.

Growing out of the same constellation of weakness and enforced dependency of human infancy which produced the inferiority complex was a need for association with other human beings. Even adults could not long survive in complete isolation. In the process of living with others, however, the infant soon discovered that his biological needs were in conflict with the (social) needs of those upon whom he had to depend. Not only man's needs, but also his conflicts were based on interpersonal factors. Moreover, his eventual solution was worked out in an interpersonal setting. Man's need for other men was manifested in his innate social interest in being with and doing for others. Adler gave this positive social drive tremendous importance in explaining the origin and continuation of society.

Adler did not find it necessary to deal with more specific biological or social motives since any need or desire became important only as it was utilized in compensatory efforts. His handling of sexual drives was somewhat of an exception at least insofar as emphasis was concerned. While he did not see sex as a prominent factor in personality, he nonetheless gave it individual attention instead of merely lumping it with other motives. Freud's emphasis undoubtedly fostered this attention to some degree. In his discussions of sexual impulses, however, Adler's approach was to render them, like all other motives, important only because they offered opportunities for compensation. Sex was a means by which a person exerted his power or superiority over others. It was not a problem in and of itself, but because of the secondary uses to which it could be put. From the Adlerian frame of reference masculine strivings in girls represented not penis envy but power envy. The Oedipal conflict was a struggle for the father's power. In like manner, sexual difficulties were a function of inferiority feelings, not Id-Ego-Superego conflict. Adler, it seems, did not wish to negate Freud's constructs: he merely re-cast them in a different frame.

Nature of the Learning Process

Adler dealt extensively with *what* is learned and where; he was far less concerned with *how* learning took place. He concentrated primarily upon the acquisition of social motives and the compensatory responses which served to further various fictive goals in a manner compatible with the life style of the individual. While he conceded that one could also learn material which dealt with facts and truths rather than fictions and defenses, he did not define how, nor if, the two were different. Indeed, he did not spell out the basis of learning at all. Insofar as what man learns was a means of reducing feelings of discomfort and insecurity, a reinforcement type of learning is implied. This thesis is not markedly different from that of Freud or other analysts, nor from reinforcement theorists in general.

Whatever the process, all essential learning took place early in the life of the individual, primarily in the family. Beyond this formative period, Adler did not believe the person could acquire new ideas or responses, short of intensive analysis. Thus, no essential learning occurred after early childhood.

Behavior and Personality

Adler's theory is mainly an account of the way in which a motive (need to reduce inferiority) influenced specific behaviors. Most of his theory has therefore been subsumed under earlier topics. However, there is some material specific to personality which we will deal with here.

Personality, Adler stated, was developed out of constant repetition of interpersonal difficulties, real or imagined, and the special ways the person used to meet these difficulties. It was equivalent to life style and was well fixed by four to six years of age. Personality types, as such, did not exist for Adler; people were merely similar or dissimilar, depending upon the experiences of the individuals involved in any comparison, (e.g., order of birth) and the varieties of compensation they employed.

All neuroses had a common origin. The neurotic was a person of burning ambition, but one who had lost courage and who feared his weakness and failure would be discovered. The appearance of neurotic symptoms gave the individual an excuse for withdrawal from responsibility, a reason for hiding. Neurosis was motivated activity, just as everything else was. The neurotic symptoms were compatible with the larger personality pattern. Timid, retiring personalities became anxiety neurotics, rigid individuals became compulsive. Each felt inferior and compensated in whatever way he could. Here, as elsewhere, the central theme of Adler's individual psychology was the way in which the inferior individual tried to undo his perceived status.

Critique

Adler did a great service to psychoanalysis by calling attention to the importance of other motives besides sex. He placed greater emphasis on the interpersonal setting of behavior, supplying a valuable counterpoint for Freud's intrapersonal emphasis. He appears also to have tied in broader factors, conceiving of interaction between the individual and the culture as an important formative influence on personality. For example, his concept of the masculine protest points out aspects of society which determine both the problems of the individual member and the solution he is likely to find. A matriarchal culture, for example, would produce a far different syndrome. Adler's emphasis on cultural influences set the stage for a new viewpoint in psychoanalysis, later seen in the work of Fromm, Kardiner, and Horney, as well as in the current interest among anthropologists concerning the relationship of cultures to personality.

Despite his good intentions, Adler could not avoid the psychoanalytic pitfall of emphasizing one aspect to the neglect of all else. Granted that inferiority and compensation are important aspects in understanding people today, these are not the only kinds of problems people face. They are not the core of all personalities and all symptomatology, as Adler would have us believe, any more than sexual difficulties, no matter how broadly conceived, can explain all man's ills. All too often, it seems, theorists fall victim to the disorder they are trying to correct.

SUMMARY

Basic Unit. Adler approached personality as a whole and did not find any smaller unit necessary.

Field of Study. Adler's "Individual Psychology" dealt with the development of distinctive styles of life and with efforts to adjust to the biological and social environment.

Methods of Investigation. Like all psychoanalysts, Adler used free association as a treatment and research technique.

Principles. Infancy was a state of biological inferiority. The environment could increase or decrease the degree, but in any case created sufficient insecurity to cause every person to attempt some means of compensation. Most often the person sought some form of power or superiority over others. This compensatory effort became the individual's style of life.

Consciousness. Consciousness could be equated with experiences which can be verbalized. Unconscious experience was really the "unadmitted," the things the person would not or could not talk about. Preconscious processes were those automatic events which ordinarily did not require voluntary intervention.

Sensation, Perception, and Discrimination. Perception was a matter of interpreting the meaning of the environment in the light of one's past experience, one's style of life.

Thinking, Cognition, and Memory. Thought proceeded according to a person's preconceived biases. It was more defensive than creative in function, preserving the life style by enabling the person to reach whatever false goals or maintain whatever guiding fictions might be required.

Emotion and Motivation. Born into an inferior biological and social status, the infant had an inherent need for security which only compensatory behavior could satisfy. The healthy person was able to achieve a style of life which compensated adequately, but the unfortunate infant born with physical disabilities or social handicaps had a great struggle ahead of him. The seeking of power was the most common compensatory effort, but whatever its nature, the goal of life style was the major directive force in behavior. Many of these compensatory goals were unrealistic, selected by the distorted thinking of the insecure individual, and leading him to strive after fictions rather than seeking some appropriate solution to his problems. Aside from the insecurity it created, the inferior status of the infant produced a need for human associations. The gratification of physiological desires or the exercise of compensatory mechanisms often conflicted with the person's acquired need for acceptance from his fellows, and difficulties in adjustment followed.

REFERENCES

Alfred Adler

Adler, A., *The Practice and Theory of Individual Psychology.* New York: Harcourt, 1927.

———, *Problems of Neurosis.* London: Kegan Paul, 1929. New York: Cosmopolitan Book Co., 1930.

———, "Individual Psychology," in C. Murchison, ed., *Psychologies of 1930*, Worcester: Clark Univ. Press, 1930.

———, "The Fundamental Views of Individual Psychology," *Int. J. Indiv. Psychol.* 1:5–8 (1935).

Dreikurs, R., *Fundamentals of Adlerian Psychology.* New York: Greenberg, 1950.

Personality and Birth Order

Becker, S. W., and Jean Carrol, "Ordinal Position and Conformity," *J. Abn. Soc. Psychol.* 65: 129–131 (1962).

Stotland, E., and N. B. Cottrell, "Similarity of Performance as Influenced by Interaction, Self Esteem, and Birth Order," *J. Abn. Soc. Psychol.* 64: 183–191 (1962).

———, and R. E. Dunn, "Identification, 'Oppositeness,' Authoritarianism, Self-Esteem, and Birth Order," *Psychol. Monogr.* 76: No. 528, ix (1962).

———, "Empathy, Self-Esteem, and Birth Order," *J. Abn. Soc. Psychol.* 66: 532–540 (1963).

———, and J. A. Walsh, "Birth Order and an Experimental Study of Empathy," *J. Abn. Soc. Psychol.* 66: 610–614 (1963).

CHAPTER 19

KAREN HORNEY (1937–1950)

HORNEY'S theory was derived by analytic technique and recognized such Freudian concepts as unconscious processes and defense mechanisms. Beyond this there was very little similarity to Freud. She emphasized cultural and interpersonal relationships and did not feel that sex and biological factors were more important than other aspects of personality. These characteristics place her formulation in the same camp as that of Adler and Fromm, far removed from the father theory.

Basic Unit and Field of Study

In view of previous theories, it is no surprise that Horney did not feel the study of personality could be divided into compartments or units. Personality was a result of the interaction of constitutional and situational forces of the past, present, and future, and could only be understood as a unified entity. It was this entity to which Horney's brand of analysis directed itself. This is not to imply that Horney sought to delimit psychology in any way. As an analyst, she spoke only for her own field, not for any other.

Methods of Investigation

Horney's theory developed out of her practice of psychoanalysis and therefore depended upon the common tool of free association. However, her application of this technique varied considerably from orthodox analysis and Neo-Freudian practice alike. She was less inclined to place emphasis solely on childhood experience, and much more likely to deal with the influence of a person's current situation upon his adjustment. Under certain circumstances she even had her patients engage in self analysis, using free association for a patient to explore his own problem, with only rare visits to the analyst's office.

Her alterations in both method and theory derived from clinical observations. Whatever else contributed to Horney's departure from orthodoxy, it seems likely that her extensive work with American patients was a significant element.

Principles

Basic to Horney's work was the idea (similar to Adler's) that the infant, being born helpless in a frightening world, would inevitably experience anxiety. The degree of anxiety, its duration, the means available to the infant and child for dispelling it, and the social situation in which the child lived, determined whether he would become normal or neurotic.

The prime determinant of behavior was the search for security. Neurotic resolutions of this basic anxiety reduced tensions momentarily, but eventually got the person into even greater difficulty because the behavior was unrealistic or ill-advised; these ultimate consequences made such resolutions unhealthy.

The common neurotic solutions involved the creation of secondary need structures (of anger, dependency, and fear) which must be gratified or relieved in order to preserve tenuous neurotic adjustment as well as to insure survival. If they were not fulfilled a sort of secondary anxiety was built up. These secondary characteristics formed on the basis of neurotic syndromes.

Consciousness; Sensation, Perception, and Discrimination; Thinking, Cognition, and Memory; The Nature of the Learning Process

Horney did not find it necessary to investigate many salient concepts of psychology. She was primarily interested in understanding personal adjustment. While she referred to such matters as perception, thinking, and learning, she felt no need to explain them. The phenomenon of consciousness was essential to her theory, but her handling of this concept did not depart from the Freudian tradition. The treatment given to motivation and to behavior and personality were the distinguishing features of her system.

Emotion and Motivation

Horney rejected the concept of instincts and was not concerned with the biological correlates of drives. She found it sufficient to consider only the psychological aspects of motivation, seeing the most important needs as social in nature. The prime determinant of behavior was the search for security and the reduction of anxiety. While anxiety was an inevitable result of an infant's status in the world and his lack of comprehension of his environment, it was produced and eventually relieved in a social setting.

Many things could threaten security and many means could be used to reinstate it. Among the multitudinous causes and effects, Horney felt she could isolate three common motivational patterns. While these patterns could appear in normal persons, they were ordinarily the basis for a neurotic adjustment.

The first neurotic constellation was a function of the helplessness experienced in the first few months of life. The fearful, inadequate infant was prone to resent his state and to lash out at the world to protect himself. He was punished for his anger and thereby threatened with more insecurity and further aggression. These conditions could produce a striving for some means of controlling the external world, a need which created problems in its own turn. So far the basic conflict was quite similar to that proposed by Adler, but similarity ceased at this point. Horney concentrated on the neurotic conflict whereas Adler treated the matter from the point of view of character structure. According to Horney, guilt was aroused over the hostile impulses, resulting in some people, in increased tension which could only be dispelled by increased striving and by increased guilt. A vicious circle was established. Insecurity led to striving and hostility, which led to guilt and insecurity.

Faced with the same circumstances in infancy, other persons reacted with an insatiable need for affection and a prevailing fear of disapproval. These new needs and fears manifested themselves in constant requests for attention, in demands to be loved and cared for, and in tendencies to become involved in a series of temporary and unsatisfactory sexual relationships. All these reactions were attempts to prove to one's self that he was acceptable, but their intensity and the impositions they placed upon others usually led to rejection or incomplete satisfaction, and to a neurotic adjustment.

The same fear of rejection which led to craving for affection could also lead to an inability to tolerate any close intimacy with people, and consequently to withdrawal from interpersonal relations. Finally, the desire for love and the fear of rejection could result in a desire to conform and submit to others.

Horney's treatment represented an addition to theory of motivation. The basic needs for security and well-being could create other needs, magnifying the problem of adjustment. The new needs, once established, must be satisfied not only in their own right but also to avoid a re-arousal of the primary needs upon which they were based. These need structures were the basis of personality.

Nature of the Learning Process

Horney handled learning, by implication, as a reinforcement based process. This was done in the style of the classic analytic theory.

Behavior and Personality

Horney, like Adler and Fromm, did not feel it necessary to refer to maturational levels. All three believed that personality was established as a result of the prolonged influence of a specific type of relationship to the environment evolving from a single complex of factors which acted continuously upon the individual. In contrast, the more biological theories of Freud, Erikson, and Sullivan required an account of how the varied physical skills of each new developmental phase provided the potential for several kinds of relationship. To them, personality matured irregularly, changing as relevant variables appeared or disappeared.

The single complex of factors which Horney stressed was in some ways quite similar to the set with which Adler dealt. Horney postulated that the infant was born helpless into an adult world and his personality grew out of his experiences in this world. The infant could not but feel helpless at first, no matter what the environment, and the environment could not but be frustrating and therefore hostile to some extent. It was impossible to minister to the infant constantly. He was bound to get hungry, wet, soiled, to fall, sneeze, get cold, etc. The unavoidable helplessness of the infant bred intense anxiety, called by Horney *basic anxiety*. In addition to normal helplessness, some infants were subjected to a lack of warmth and love, to actual hostility, or to parental adjustment problems. When this happened the stage was set for neurotic anxiety and for neurosis itself. The more intense and realistic the feeling of helplessness in a hostile environment, the more the infant (and later the child and the adult) must struggle to overcome anxiety.

From this basic anxiety developed the neurotic needs: striving for affection and power, hostility or fear of hostility, submission, and withdrawal. Once these patterns were established, it was not necessary to refer to the original anxiety situation as a cause. The newly created needs aroused anxiety apart from the original situation of helplessness and insecurity. Anxiety came to be a learned response.

The problem was complicated by the fact that any relief of anxiety was likely to be precarious. The action which removed the anxiety was likely to be anxiety-inducing itself, or to have eventual consequences which were anxiety-inducing. Recall the discussion of anger motivation; if a child struck out angrily at that which aroused his feeling of helplessness, he was likely to be met with more aggression. He was consequently made to feel more helpless, and a vicious circle was set in motion. Most neurotic conflicts eventuated in such vicious circles.

To cope with conflict situations the child developed what Horney referred to as safety devices (defense mechanisms). These provided a means of lessening existing anxiety without arousing too much new anxiety. It was the type of safety device the person employed which Horney used to diagnose, understand, and predict personality. Among the less pathological safety devices were such behavior patterns as constricted self-control, arbitrary self-rightousness, elusiveness, and cynicism. These were of minor importance, as were the classical Freudian defenses, in comparison to the broader orientations toward the environment which included syndromes growing out of the neurotic social needs. Horney described three such broad orientations.

One type of personality she characterized as *moving toward people.* This orientation was based on the compensatory need for affection and the fear of rejection which accompanied it. Such persons would abase themselves and sacrifice their autonomy to achieve acceptance. They felt weak and helpless and reacted with dependency.

A second type she characterized as *moving away from people* to live in isolation. Such a person distrusted himself as much as he distrusted others. Only in solitude was there safety. The withdrawal grew from the same need constellation as the search for love. Here, however, fear of rejection outweighed the desire for acceptance.

The final type she characterized as *moving against people*, feeling that the world was a "dog eat dog" place where everyone was hostile. This attitude was covered by a polite veneer, but underneath was a callous pursuit of self-interest and a need to control, dominate, and destroy others, based on the compensatory need for power over others.

Horney assumed that the normal person had something of all three orientations (as was appropriate to a given situation), while the neurotic could relate to others only in one or the other of these stereotyped modes. This set of concepts probably comprised the key to Horney's theory and the bulk of her contribution to systematic theory.

Critique

Horney seems to have taken Adler's concepts of the origin of anxiety and placed them in a cultural context similar to that suggested by Fromm (see chapter 21). However, she allowed for more flexibility than either Fromm or Adler because her system included several possible modes of adjustment, each broad enough to encompass numerous variations. Her speculations seem much more pertinent to present-day American behavior than Fromm's and Adler's. This is not surprising since she developed her theory in this country, while Fromm and Adler dealt primarily with European cultures.

Her concepts of secondary motivation and the vicious circle of the neurotic seem especially important contributions. Her hypotheses dealing with the process by which motives were acquired and come to have autonomy bear some interesting relationships to learning theory. The similarities might well be the source of much interesting research.

The broad adjustment patterns, *toward*, *away*, and *against* people, appear to be useful means of relating a great many different behaviors. The very breadth and simplicity which make this type of category useful, however, also make it dangerous. The system is vague and hard to define. Its predictive power is limited by the fact that the classes are so amorphous as to fit any prediction made. In like manner, one would find many of her other safety devices difficult to define. Such a criticism applies not to Horney alone, however. Vagueness is a common attribute of personality theories.

SUMMARY

Basic Unit and Field of Study. Personality could not be broken up into units but must be studied as a whole.

Methods of Investigations. Horney used the technique of free association. However, she believed that the current problems of the person were more important than their past history and therefore employed this classical analytic tool quite differently than the orthodox analyst.

Principles. The infant was a helpless creature born into a frustrating and frightening world. This inevitable state of affairs aroused anxiety and a need for security, which could be increased or decreased by the environment. The prime determinant of behavior was the search for security. If normal channels were unavailable, then neurotic solutions were found. These provided momentary relief, but created a set of secondary needs which must also be relieved, ordinarily resulting in tremendous complications.

Emotion and Motivation. Horney was not concerned with the biological correlates of drive and stressed instead the social concomitants. She saw the need for security as the central focus of motivation. The genesis of this need lay in the inadequate state into which an infant was born. To overcome this anxiety-evoking inadequacy the person might strive for power over others, seek affection from them, fear any contact with them, or conform inappropriately. These new needs originated from the desire to avoid anxiety but became autonomous motive states which had to be satisfied in their own right; if they were not, secondary anxiety was aroused.

Nature of the Learning Process. Learning, Horney seemed to imply, was accomplished through reinforcement, in the classic analytic style.

Behavior and Personality. Like Fromm and Adler, Horney could find no marked variation in personality which might correlate with stages of maturation. To her, personality evolved from long exposure to a universal set of social conditions, the unavoidable helplessness and basic anxiety of the infant. In learning to cope with anxiety and the needs it created, the person employed safety devices (defenses) which were usually organized into a consistent pattern of adjustment. Depending upon his dominant motivation he might move toward people, becoming dependent and submissive, move away from others, finding safety in isolation, or move against others in anger. The normal person was capable of all these types of reaction as they were appropriate, while the neurotic could respond only in one way. These broad orientations were the closest Horney came to speaking of personality types. Any more molecular typology was repugnant to her.

REFERENCES

Karen Horney

Horney, Karen, *The Neurotic Personality of Our Time.* New York: Norton, 1937.

———, *New Ways in Psychoanalysis*. New York: Norton, 1939.

———, *Self Analysis*. New York: Norton, 1942.

———, *Our Inner Conflicts*. New York: Norton, 1945.

———, *Neurosis and Human Growth*. New York: Norton, 1950.

CHAPTER 20

HARRY STACK SULLIVAN (1938–1954)

SULLIVAN'S theory might be called a *rapprochement* between European analytic theory (especially Freudian) and American concepts of personality dynamics. In his interpretations of the latter, Sullivan was heavily influenced by the psychiatry of William Alanson White and Adolf Meyer. Both White and Meyer, particularly the latter, maintained that man was a bio-social (biological-social) being. This emphasis became Sullivan's trade mark.

Basic Unit

Like most of the analytic theorists, Sullivan did not feel it was possible to subdivide personality or to extract its essence. The very concept of a basic unit was, in fact, incompatible with his idea of the nature of the fields of psychology and psychiatry.

Field of Study

Sullivan concerned himself with the course of events through which an organism became integrated with its milieu. An organism was a self-perpetuating *organization* of physiochemical processes, manifesting life in the form of purposeful activity. The interaction of organism and environment was the central factor in the development of personality. Although one or the other might be more influential at any particular time, neither could be considered without reckoning with the other.

Methods of Investigation

Sullivan chose to investigate this field with the common tool of psychoanalysis, free association. He employed this method somewhat differently than did the orthodox analysts and also recommended numerous changes in therapeutic technique. Beyond the fact that such changes render the therapist a more active participant in the therapeutic process, they need not concern us at present.

Principles

Sullivan's principles were nowhere definitely ennumerated, but were implied at various points in his writings. His basic tenet was the bio-social nature of existence. What man was, what personality was, resulted from the interaction between what his biology dictated and what his environment demanded or suggested. These two sets of forces were held in a dynamic equilibrium, constantly changing but perpetually balanced. Since man's environment was mostly social, the interpersonal relationships one experienced were the most salient factors in patterning personality.

Maturation was the process of adjustment to the changing biological and social demands and potentialities of the biological being. Since it was these demands which determined personality, it was to be expected that personality would be somewhat altered in the course of maturation.

The dominant motive of the human organism was to avoid anxiety and to seek security. In infants this could take the form of mastering skills to meet biological needs, but even here security was sought in an interpersonal context. After infancy, the social needs became the major sources of discomfort and insecurity, and therefore the main determinant of behavior.

Consciousness

Sullivan employed Freud's distinction between conscious and unconscious, but his concept of these processes differed from Freud's in at least two important ways. First, Sullivan assumed a slightly different content. The unconscious was not necessarily animal instinct, evil and antisocial. Unconscious material was rather that which could not be verbalized. Language was one of the most important instruments in the socialization of the individual, since it formed the basis of thought and rendered both thought and action subject to the control of society.

Second, Sullivan did not deal with conscious and unconscious in the animistic style of Freud. He did not recognize the Id, Ego, and Superego, nor did he imply armies of anthropomorphic forces inside the brain in constant battle over the possession of cognitive and motor outlets. He did accept the possibility that unconscious material might influence behavior, and it was in the nature of this influence that the distinction between conscious and unconscious could be found. Consciousness and unconsciousness differed only in their potential availability to social control, not in their roles in an intrapersonal struggle. They were equally important, but what was conscious could be controlled by the individual and his environment, while what was unconscious could not be controlled.

Sensation, Perception, and Discrimination

Sullivan gave little, if any, importance to raw sensation. He was much more interested in the interpersonal influences which acted to alter or interpret the incoming stimuli. He did not deal with perception as an entity in itself, but considered it among the cognitive processes. Perception is therefore subsumed under our next general category. The term "subsumed" should not connote that perception was in any way secondary. Sullivan simply saw no possibility of distinguishing any one aspect of cognitive functioning from any other.

Thinking, Cognition, and Memory

As an organism matured from infancy into adulthood, its skills for dealing with stimuli or experience became more complex and more adequate. Sullivan proposed three stages in the development of cognitive processes.

The first stage he called the *prototaxic.* The infant's world corresponded to the much-famed "blooming, buzzing, confusion." There were no definite impressions, but only a constant bombardment of meaningless stimuli. Gradually certain stimuli came to have some vague connotations of familiarity, or at least they stood out from the background as significant figures. There was no real meaning to these percepts; they came and went without apparent order or cause. Indeed, the infant in this stage was not yet aware of cause. The world about him was a vaguely familiar mass of floating experience.

As the infant matured he entered the *parataxic stage*. Here there was more differentiated perception and some interpretation of stimuli and realization of their relationship to other experiences. However, there was no organization of these percepts and concepts; they merely happened. There was a nascent awareness of cause and effect, but still with no real appreciation of causality and with much distortion of meaning.

Perhaps some of Jean Piaget's findings (1926, 1929, 1930, 1932) in regard to thinking in children will serve as an illustration. Piaget is in no way associated with Sullivan. He is a Swiss psychologist interested in studying the development of cognitive processes. The fact that his experiments validate a theory proposed by an entirely independent source serves to strengthen both theories. Among the material Piaget collected were children's answers to such questions as, "What is life?" "What is alive?" Very small children responded that all objects were alive and attributed motives and feelings to rocks, trees, and parents with equal abandon. Even the youngest of Piaget's subjects were probably well within the age range at which Sullivan would propose parataxic thought occurred. The distortions and misconceptions elicited by Piaget revealed the primitive quality of the cognition of this age group. Slightly older children believed that anything which moved was alive, including cars, bicycles, clouds. This would represent a later development of parataxic distortion, characterized by erroneous perceptions, over-generalization from experience, the influence of needs upon perceptions, and so forth. Only very late in childhood could the youthful subjects indicate anything like the common adult concept of life.

Sullivan suggested that the perceptual distortions which occurred in psychotherapy (such as interpreting neutral acts of the therapist as aggression, rejection, etc.) should be considered parataxes. What Freud called transference phenomena, Sullivan referred to as parataxic distortions. Sullivan's concept differed in one important aspect. He did not expect such distortion only from the analytic couch, but from the person's entire life. He believed such mistakes or misperceptions were a product of, and useful in, interpersonal relations. They were not solely the result of a person's childhood experiences with parents. Many other persons and events were involved. Perceptual distortions were generalizations based on what had happened in the past. They were useful in avoiding anxiety and achieving temporary security. However, they were misleading, and the security they produced was false insofar as it was founded on a mistaken premise.

The final and most mature level of development was known as the *syntaxic stage.* At this point the person thought and perceived in the manner common to his culture. He showed relatively few distortions and misconceptions. He was well aware of causal relationships and could utilize this knowledge to his own benefit. The appearance of the syntaxic or reality-oriented period was greatly aided by acquisition of language skills. Words enabled the child to compare his experiences with his peers, parents, and other people in general. In this way, he could check his impressions and beliefs against those of the majority. To use Sullivan's term, his experience was now open to consensual validation. Because language was required for consensual validation, and consensual validation was the instrument of socialization, language became an important tool in the development of personality. To Sullivan's mind it was the catalyst for the child's maturation.

While language accounted for the validity of thought and its power in producing conformity, other aspects of cognitive function had the opposite effect, that of distorting the person's experience. These distorting aspects, too, were affected by society and served in turn as a tool in social relationships and in avoiding anxiety and insecurity. One such aspect was *selective inattention.* In its simplest form, this was similar to oversight. It was a kind of suspension of awareness. Under certain circumstances there were things people just did not perceive. One might notice these things if something called them to his attention, and having noticed them could think about them, i.e., attach verbal symbols to the events. But ordinarily such materials were not conscious.

Sometimes selection occurred because the neglected stimuli were not crucial for ongoing activity. One does not usually need to be aware of his breathing, or the weight and texture of his clothing, for these are not likely to be significant. In a like manner, one can study with the radio going, or ignore street signs and traffic lights when riding in a taxi. Another factor which might produce selective inattention was the discomfort which might accompany awareness. Anything which was painful, aroused insecurity or anxiety, interfered with the feeling of well-being, or was socially taboo, might be "overlooked". One may forget a dental appointment, or not notice that his bridge score is lower than that of his bitter rival. One may not hear an off-color song or joke, or at least not realize it is off-color, because to do so would be embarrassing.

Regardless of the basis for selection, the distinguishing feature was a lack of awareness which could be terminated when the stimuli were pointed out, or when the internal or external state of the organism changed so as to make them significant.

Since Sullivan's discussion of selective inattention has much in common with Freud's discussion of pre-conscious, we may assume that the two concepts were similar. Sullivan's approach was more objectified and less animistic, definitely connoting a process, and not an entity as Freud's theory seemed to.

Another process which resulted in cognitive distortion was *dissociation*. Dissociation was similar to selective inattention in that there was no awareness, no possibility of attaching symbols to an experience, and thus no means of thinking about it. In the case of dissociation, however, the blackout was complete. The experience was rendered totally and permanently unavailable to symbols or language. Only in intensive psychotherapy (or some similarly dramatic situation) could the experience be recovered sufficiently to enable the person to talk about it. Material was dissociated either because the person lacked the means of conceptualizing it, or because recognition would seriously threaten security, produce anxiety, and interfere with one's self percept. Dissociation by virtue of a paucity of conceptual tools occurred in early childhood when the infant suffered some experience for which he did not yet have words. Therefore, he could not report it or think about it later. In a like manner, an adult could dissociate an incident he could not understand or for which he had no words. There are primitive languages, for example, which have no words for "before" and "after", or which lack prepositions or some other grammatical form. Our own language shows a dearth of non-technical, non-vulgar, everyday words for sexual acts, for genital areas of the body, etc. As proof, try to think of non-vulgar synonyms for "penis," or "vagina," or for excretory processes and products. In the face of such deficiency, dissociation can be expected.

The phenomenon of dissociation, or cutting off, of threatening experiences is described in many other theories. We have already encountered Herbart's discussion (Chapter 3) of the process of exclusion of material inappropriate to the apperceptive mass and Freud's formulation of repression. Even Pavlovian extinction bears some similarity. Sullivan's concept is perhaps most similar to Freud's, but the term dissociation excludes all connotations of libidinal energy transformation and sexual drives in the Sullivan theory.

There was still another cognitive process, empathy, which Sullivan believed to be an important tool. *Empathy* was an emotional contagion or communion between persons which enabled the perceiver to be aware, consciously or unconsciously, of the feelings and reactions of others and to respond to these, even though the others might not themselves be aware of what they were doing. This became in Sullivan's theory a rather mystical sixth sense in that it did not (necessarily) involve language and was assumed to be of greatest strength and importance between the ages of six months and twenty seven months.

Sullivan believed that empathy was a most important factor in early personality development, since the attitudes, values, and anxieties of the parents were communicated to the child by this means. The child, said Sullivan, first experienced anxiety and insecurity through his emphatic awareness of these reactions in his mother, an awareness which induced similar feelings in him. This was the prototype of all later anxiety, the birth place of *security operations* (Sullivan's term for defenses). In a study planned to demonstrate the existence and significance of empathy, a follower of Sullivan's Sibylle Escalona (1953), showed that tiny infants' taste for certain foods was highly correlated with that of the person who fed them. Although there was no communication on the topic and the adults tried to conceal any distaste they might have, each child soon manifested the same preference as his nurse.

Sullivan did not discuss the cues which might be utilized in one person's becoming aware of another's emotional state, nor the dynamics of the consequent response of the perceiver. Others have suggested that changes in muscular tension as the mother held the child, alterations in facial expression, voice, etc., might act as stimuli to the infant. Seen from this point of view, empathy was not a separate cognitive process, but merely a perceptual act. It seems possible that Sullivan may have had something different in mind, but his discussion was more concerned with the effects of empathy than with its cause. In his desire to employ the concept, Sullivan left the genesis and nature of empathy vague and more than a little mysterious.

Emotion and Motivation

The organism, according to Sullivan, was constantly striving to relieve tensions and to achieve a state of well-being or *euphoria*. Tensions arose from two sources, physio-chemical and interpersonal. The physio-chemical tensions were biological needs, e.g., hunger, thirst, sex, and elimination.

Their goal was bodily satisfaction. They might stem from some specific zone (as oral or anal) or they may relate to general, diffuse tensions affecting the whole body (such as fatigue, or the feeling of malaise which accompanies illness). Although they were genetic in origin, many of the goals and goal-seeking responses to physio-chemical tensions were learned. The acts of consummation had to be mastered, and certain secondary motives were eventually induced. For example, in addition to relief of tension from sucking on bottle or breast, the child soon learned to derive pleasure or well-being out of mouthing activities, thumb-sucking, chewing, or playing with his lips.

The interpersonal tensions were created by anxiety and insecurity. Their goal was achievement of security. Anxiety was acquired through social contacts; it was not biological. This origin distinguished Sullivanian anxiety from the Freudian approach, where anxiety resulted from dammed-up sexual energy or functioned as a warning of danger from intra-personal sources.

After the mastery of basic responses in infancy, the physio-chemical needs, except for sex, were ordinarily satisfied with great ease in the civilized world. The interpersonal tensions were, however, likely to be intensified in complex societies. Therefore most behavior was based on the drive for security.

Even when activated, the physio-chemical tensions were rarely pure in form. Most motivational states were a combination of the biological and social stimuli impinging on the person. Some particular combinations of biological and social needs were relatively enduring configurations in which energy was discharged in a characteristic fashion in an interpersonal situation; these patterns Sullivan called *dynamisms*. In this concept he included not only the motive itself, but its goals and the behaviors by which they were achieved. There was an *oral dynamism* which incorporated the needs and reactions of the Freudian oral period and the oral personality. In like manner, there was an *anal dynamism*, and a *sexual* or *lust dynamism*. There was also a set of needs and behaviors centering around the maintenance and enhancement of the self concept, the *self-dynamism*. These dynamisms were the central focus of personality development as it passed from stage to stage. They determined not only the mode of response, but also what was learned and when.

The Nature of the Learning Process

Since he attributed so much significance to interpersonal factors, it is not surprising that learning was a key concept to Sullivan. This is not to imply that he was a learning theorist. He did not concern himself with the whys and wherefores, the technical details of learning. It was enough for him that personality and behavior were almost entirely learned. His account of the variables which influenced this learning was rather sketchy.

One can assume that empathic transmission of emotion and value from parent to infant was an early learning process. At least, the infant *acquired* new behaviors as a result of this affective osmosis. Indeed, the lietmotif of the person's life was probably acquired by empathy; the infant exposed to the tensions and anxieties of his parents learned from these his all-encompassing need for security. But since Sullivan was vague as to the nature of empathy, it is impossible to say whether contiguity or reinforcement was the basis for empathic learning; it is equally impossible to describe its mode of operation, psychologically or physiologically.

As the child grew more experienced, he was able to discriminate between those activities which increased anxiety and those which diminished it. With this knowledge the child was able to alter his behavior so as to avoid anxiety and to maximize his security. This usually took the form of behaviors which prevented the parents' disapproval and perpetuated their acceptance. It was in this way that the child became socialized and established security operations. The type of learning involved in the later period of socialization was of a trial-and-error variety. Reward and punishment (decreasing or increasing tensions) were the necessary and sufficient conditions for learning at this stage, whether it were interpersonal or physical needs which motivated action. The naive child (or adult) upon arousal launched into some sort of activity, trying first one thing and then another until he accidentally found some means of relieving his tensions. Those acts were learned which were reinforced. Acts which were not reinforced or which had painful consequences were discontinued.

Sullivan accepted neither Freud's and Jung's idea of the racial unconscious, nor the concept of unlearned behavior. He believed instead that the biological organism was equipped with potentials which make certain kinds of action more or less probable, but that it was the interpersonal experiences which shaped these potentials. This shaping process was described in his conception of stages of personality development.

Behavior and Personality

While Sullivan's concept of developmental stages differed from Freud's in content, the idea underlying the concept of stages was similar to the orthodox analytic view. Each stage brought with it the possibilities of developing new skills, or maturing along different lines. Certain adjustment problems were posed in each period both by the biology of the human organism and by the society in which the person dwelt. Certain interpersonal experiences were possible in each stage which tended, within broad limits, to determine the progress of maturation.

Infancy. The newborn child was totally dependent upon persons in his environment, especially upon his mother or mother substitute. As the infant found relief in the mother's care of him, he experienced not only the physical relief, but also the tenderness which the mother displayed. The child gradually developed a need for such love or tenderness, and the first of many acquired motives came into existence. Not only did the child experience relief and love in the mother's care of him, but also he was exposed to her feelings of tension and anxiety through the empathic transfer of such emotions from mother to child. Through frequent exposures to maternal anxiety the child learned to be anxious and engaged in the first primitive struggles to achieve security and avoid anxiety.

Childhood. By the end of the first year to eighteen months of life, the child had developed the ability to move about and talk. He began to employ these abilities to solve his problems and to aid in interaction with his parents. His new-found skills enabled him to discover other means of avoiding anxiety. He could now assimilate some of the rules and values of his culture, and, being aware of these, could attempt to comform. This increased his security by allowing him to avoid punishment, disapproval, and possible rejection. The ways in which he modified his actions to suit social demands marked the inception of *security operations.* Any of the classical defenses might be learned. Sublimation was the most ordinary pattern of adjustment, according to Sullivan, but it had no sexual connotations; it merely involved the child's ability to express and satisfy his impulses in a socially acceptable form.

Juvenile Era. Ordinarily, around the age of five or six, the child had the first prolonged opportunity for independent social experiences with his own age group. The child's earlier experiences in avoiding anxiety and social conformity had established a sufficient number of habit patterns to form a kernel of individual identity. This identity was accompanied by a constellation of positive and negative feelings and expectations about himself. The distinctive habit patterns, the feelings and expectations, were organized into a *self-concept* or *self-system.* In his interpersonal relations, this constellation of attitudes about the self was reinforced because the child behaved in such a way as to maintain and enhance it. Having a self-concept which he needed to preserve, and an appreciation of social requirements, the child began to develop the capacity to censor his behavior and to evaluate it critically. What were previously the moral views of his adult associates now became his own personal values. This process compares with the development of the Freudian Superego.

During these first experiences with peers the child attempted further to define his status, role, and self. In doing so, he built up concepts and expectations about the behavior and attitudes of others which were quite stereotyped, and which might persist through life with considerable rigidity, especially if the maturational process were arrested at this point. There is nothing so rigid, for example, as the six or seven year old's adherence to the rules of a game; once learned, rules must be practiced exactly. Children of this age tend to be conservative, preferring familiar activities and rejecting novel experiences.

As a result of his contacts with adults outside his home and his growing knowledge, the child came to regard his parents more realistically, and less as omnipotent figures. He became less controlled by them and less demanding of them. He was eventually able to see both his own status and his father's and mother's in a clearer perspective.

Pre-adolescence. In the years just before puberty the child was capable, for the first time, of participating in a mutual love relationship with others. He began to establish intimate friendships with peers. He could develop a consideration of, and concern for, some other person than himself. A cooperative and egalitarian relationship appeared which had not been possible at earlier ages.

Adolescence. The last developmental stage began with the appearance of sexual feelings and the consequent problems of expression, satisfaction, and control of these feelings. Sullivan referred to the matrix of feelings, emotions, and actions accompanying sexual impulses as the *lust dynamism.* Adolescence was a particularly stress-filled time in our culture since there were prohibitions against direct sexual satisfaction, little opportunity for acquiring knowledge about these new-found potentialities, and a generally secretive and disgusted reaction to sexual topics on the part of adults. In spite of society's intolerance of his needs, the child's whole future depended upon his ability to master the expression of these impulses. Unless he was able to weld his sexual motives into a true love relationship, he was likely to become an eternal adolescent because he could not interact with people on a more mature level. If he could not integrate sex with other interpersonal relationships, neither sex nor social contacts were satisfying, and maladjustment usually resulted.

Self Dynamism. In each stage, the self was the focus of the developmental process. As has been indicated throughout the discussion of development, the attitudes, feelings, and values which composed a person's self concept were likely to reflect various maturational experiences, and in turn to determine the potential for further maturation. The idea of self first appeared in infants as a vague differentiation between what was and what was not "me". Gradually the child came to have more detailed ideas about "me"—"good me," "bad me," "big me," etc. These were reflections of the attitudes of significant persons in the child's world. Every effort was made to maintain the "good me" feeling by means of adopting socially approved acts and avoiding what was disapproved. Anxiety was roused if and when the environment valued the child differently than he wanted to be valued, and this anxiety about self was probably one of the greatest forces in socialization. It became the basis for many new motives and habits. The actions taken to preserve and enhance the self image could become the defenses which accompanied adaptation, or the symptoms which appeared in maladjustments.

Mental Health and Maladjustment. The normal or healthy person was able to sublimate, to conform without serious sacrifice of impulse gratification.

If socially acceptable forms of gratification were lacking, distorted forms were found; some persons moved off into a fantasy world, others were incorrigible, negativistic, ambition-ridden, lonely, asocial, inadequate, or homosexual. Sullivan seemed to accept the Freudian hypothesis that personality types represented either fixations of development at various stages or regressions back to less mature levels. Fixations or regressions occurred when the person encountered extreme difficulties with which he had no means of coping. They could also be expected when something happened to prevent his use or development of more mature skills. The point of fixation or regression was determined by the person's learning experiences during his development. Unhealthy social relationships at any one stage distorted subsequent development and impaired the individual's capacity for any more mature form of interpersonal interaction.

Critique

Sullivan sought to make Freudian theory less animistic while stressing the sociological and psychological implications. He appears to have been able to reach his goal in many cases, although it is often difficult to assess his meaning. While his efforts resulted in a theory which many people feel is more realistic and more applicable to the present day, Sullivan occasionally fell victim to the same errors he was attempting to correct. He was often hard to understand, and manifested a mystical bent. His treatment of empathy is a case in point. Because Sullivan is difficult to read, and because he used rather poorly defined terms, the casual reader is likely to find the works of certain of his colleagues, particularly Patrick Mullahy and Freida Fromm Reichman, more useful in clarifying Sullivan's concepts.

The impact of Sullivan's theory, whatever its weaknesses, can best be gauged by the fact that its popularity in American psychoanalytic circles is second only to Freud's. It seems to represent a growing force in the United States, perhaps because it is peculiarly applicable to our culture.

SUMMARY

Basic Unit. Sullivan followed most analytic theorists in rejecting the idea of a basic unit.

Field of Study. The sciences of psychology and psychiatry should concern themselves with organized flow of behavior produced by the interaction of man's biological nature with the social forces of his surroundings.

Methods of Investigation. Sullivan used the method of free association in deriving his system.

Principles. Personality resulted from the interaction between physiochemical and interpersonal forces. It was manifested in a social setting, as an adjustment to this setting. Maturation was the process of adjusting to the changing demands of biological and social forces as the child moved toward adulthood. The most important motive of the human organism was the avoidance of anxiety and insecurity. All behavior was oriented toward this goal.

Consciousness. Sullivan regarded the unconscious as composed of those experiences and reactions which a person could not verbalize. Because socialization took place in great part through action which could not be verbalized, unconscious material was not subject to personal or social regulation. This contrasted with Freud's belief in the forbidden nature of unconscious material and its constant struggle to free itself from Ego and Superego.

Sensation, Perception, and Discrimination. Raw sensation was in no way important to Sullivan. Perception was, on the other hand, very significant, but indistinguishable from cognitive processes as a whole.

Thinking, Cognition, and Memory. There were three stages in cognitive development. The first stage was called the prototaxic and corresponded to the complete lack of perception and comprehension of the infant. As life progressed, the world began to have some familiarity but was still a mass of floating experiences which were registered but not interpreted. In the second stage, the parataxic, there was some perception of the meaning of stimuli, but no organization and no appreciation of cause-effect relationships. Many of the perceptions were erroneous, overgeneralized, and strongly influenced by social and biological needs. The final, or syntaxic, stage was the most mature. It was characterized by accurate registration and interpretation, and by a sensitive awareness of causal relationships and an ability to utilize them. Words were now available to check the individual impression against the experience of others. Such consensual validation rendered the person's perceptions more valid and opened them to social restraint. While language increased the accuracy of thought and perception, other cognitive processes might act to distort experience in order to reduce anxiety and to increase efficiency. One of several mechanisms which might distort perception to avoid anxiety was selective inattention. Selective inattention was a cognitive device which enabled the individual to overlook painful or irrelevant events unless and until they became important. This corresponded in many ways to the Freudian preconscious. There was also a more permanent mechanism known as dissociation.

Sullivan also recognized a vague, non-verbal type of communication among people based on empathic awareness of another's emotional state and a consequent induction of a similar state in the perceiver. This could occur either consciously or unconsciously. Empathy was especially important in infants, for through empathy the child was influenced by its mother's anxiety, and itself experienced tension in response.

Emotion and Motivation. The organism was constantly striving to achieve a state of well-being or euphoria. This homeostatic state could be disturbed by physio-chemical tensions in the body which could only be relieved by an appropriate release or by gratification. There were also tensions arising from interpersonal circumstances which could be satisfied by achievement of security. The need for security was the primary motivation in human beings. The biological needs were ordinarily no problem once the basic responses were mastered. When activated they usually appeared in combination with a social motive. Some combinations were so common that Sullivan assumed they were universal and included them in a concept of dynamisms. There was an oral dynamism and anal one, a sexual one, and a self dynamism.

The Nature of the Learning Process. Sullivan stressed the importance of learning as the means by which interpersonal experiences could determine personality. He did not, however, account for the details of the process of learning, but merely emphasized the role. The first learning by the infant was probably based on a blind, empathic imitation of parental emotions. Later the person was able to engage in trial-and-error behavior in order to ascertain how to maximize security and relieve tensions under certain circumstances. Such an approach implied a reinforcement interpretation, as do most analytic theories.

Behavior and Personality. Sullivan proposed a number of developmental stages. First was infancy, a totally dependent period in which the main interpersonal experiences came through maternal ministrations. A need was soon created for social contacts in the form of love and tenderness which accompanied the mother's care. Empathically the child was infected with the environment's tensions, thus suffering anxiety for the first time. In childhood the infant began to realize that comformity to social demands could be a means of avoiding painful anxiety, and forms of behavior appeared which represented various defensive maneuvers or security operations. During the juvenile era the child began to participate in social relationships outside the home. Having developed a series of values and attitudes about himself, he sought to preserve these by internalizing moral values, by creating a conscience. The first appreciation of social rules was extremely rigid. By the pre-adolescent period the child was capable of mutual love relationships or friendships. This period ended with the appearance of sexual feelings which heralded adolescence. The mastery and integration of these impulses led to true maturity, but if such mastery were impossible, adult adjustment was negated. Throughout the years of development the self-concept was an important focus of adjustment. It was first evidenced in the infant's ability to distinguish between self and non-self. A little later certain positive and negative values were attached to the new-found self, and much behavior was initiated to preserve and enhance the feeling of well being in the self. Maladjustments were the result of improper learning, resulting in fixation or regression to immature modes of functioning.

REFERENCES

Harry Stack Sullivan

Sullivan, H. S., *Conceptions of Modern Psychiatry*. Washington, D. C.: William Alanson White Psychiatric Foundation, 1947.

———, *The Interpersonal Theory of Psychiatry*. New York: Norton, 1953.

———, *The Psychiatric Interview*. New York: Norton, 1954.

Sibylle Escalona

Escalona, Sibylle, "Emotional Development in the First Year of Life," in M. J. E. Senn, ed., *Problems of Infancy and Childhood. Tr. 6th conf. Macy Foundation*, New York: Macy Foundation, 1953.

J. Piaget

Piaget, J., *The Language and Thought of the Child*. London: Routledge and Kegan Paul, 1926. New York: Harcourt Brace, 1932.

———, *The Child's Conception of the World*. New York: Harcourt Brace, 1929.

———, *The Child's Conception of Physical Causality*. London: Kegan Paul, Trench, and Trubner, 1930.

———, *Judgement and Reasoning in the Child*. New York: Harcourt Brace, 1932.

CHAPTER 21

ERICH FROMM (1941 TO PRESENT)

ALTHOUGH Fromm is best known as a psychoanalyst, he is equally as much a philosopher, an historian, and an anthropologist. His professional life has been devoted to the application of these varied perspectives to the study of personality. He was critical of Freud because he felt Freud neglected the influence of culture upon personality; indeed, he felt Freud ignored it completely. He also criticized Freud for holding that sex was the main source of human emotional difficulty. The culture made the personality, Fromm believed, and depending on the culture any number of motives might become the axis of adjustment.

Basic Unit and Field of Study

For Fromm there was no basic unit. The most salient aspect in personality was the interaction of the individual with society. Psychology should study the social characteristics common to normal members of society. It should not concentrate on the deviant group and thereby hope to understand everyone. Theories must have general application, and this they could not achieve through concentrating on one select (abnormal) group.

Methods of Investigations

In contrast to psychologists who employ numerous experimental techniques and to psychoanalysts who employ clinical data in setting up theories, Fromm utilized a method combining naturalistic observation and speculative generalization. His theories are based on an interpretation of history and anthropological data and are not experimental. Indeed, experimental tests of such social concepts would be extremely difficult to make. Only further anthropological data, allowing for cross-cultural comparisons, can provide evidence which might validate or invalidate his theory.

Principles

Fromm's approach did not demand a formal set of principles, yet there was a set of implied propositions which shaped his theory.

Man's behavior was formed through the interaction of his social experiences, the requirements of his culture, and his biological tendencies. If large groups of people were exposed to similar social experiences, a common occurrence in any culture or class group, the similarity of experience should lead to similar types of character or personality.

Character types were the result of the social, political and economic forces acting on the individual. These forces created anxiety, insecurity, fear of responsibility, and doubts about one's own worth. The person might compensate for these pressures by hostility, dominant-submissive behavior, dependency, exploitation, hoarding, or efforts to sell himself to the world.

Consciousness; Sensation, Perception, and Discrimination; Thinking, Cognition, and Memory; The Nature of the Learning Process

Fromm approached the problems of psychology from a sociological frame of reference. He did not require specific concepts of consciousness, sensation, perception, thinking, or learning. On those rare occasions where he dealt with such aspects he did not differ appreciably from Freud. He was primarily concerned with motivation and personality, and to these areas we will now direct our attention.

Emotion and Motivation

Fromm placed little emphasis on biological variables, including sex. Insofar as man's biology was important to his personality, it was important because it determined or delimited the types of relatedness to others in which he could engage. If we say, as Freud did, that the anal character typical of the European middle class is the result of early experience with toilet training, we cannot present data as to why the correlation came about, nor how a certain technique of bowel training was ever established in the first place. If, on the other hand, we study toilet training as one means by which and through which the child is trained to relate to others, we can understand the isolation, narrowness, and hostility of this anal type of character. Toilet training was not the cause of particular personality pattern, it was merely a channel through which society impinged upon the individual, shaping certain responses in him. Toilet training in and of itself had no universal effect; the effect depended on the social overtones of toilet training. Such influence was equally true of any other biological need; eating, drinking, sex, physical illness, and safety all became important not because of their innate significance (which was easily fulfilled as a rule), but because they were targets for social modulation within the context of a certain society. Social modulation formed individuals into acceptable members of a society by the avenues it provided for expressing and gratifying various needs.

Motives, and the means which were taken to satisfy them, were the core of personality. They determined patterns of thought, feeling, and action. Most of the salient motives which directed an individual's response to his environment originated in his early experiences with other people and in the stresses and strains acting upon him during the period of socialization. The experiences and stresses were primarily determined by the culture in which the individual lived. Thus, society assumed a dominant role in personality development.

Behavior and Personality

Fromm emphasized that early training or experience *per se* was not crucial in personality formation. The family was merely the agent of society in transmitting society's requirements to the child. Since child training was the method of transmission, it could only be understood in terms of the kind of personality required for adjustment in a particular culture. Many methods could have the same result. It was the resultant product, therefore, and not the means by which it was produced, which was important.

In Western Europe (and later America) the collapse of the medieval society, with its rigid role prescriptions and automatic mechanisms for directing individual lives, engendered an atmosphere of insecurity, isolation, and doubt. Man, ill-prepared to become master of his own fate after the restrictions of the feudal system, found he had lost the structure for his life and had nothing to substitute for it. The problem was compounded by the Industrial Revolution and the political and economic reforms which accompanied it. The trends toward democracy and free enterprise stressed the individual's responsibility for his own actions; and out of the new philosophy came the religious movements of Calvin and Luther, based on the belief that man was responsible for his destiny and only failed because of his sinfulness. Man was now whatever he made himself. To be solely responsible in this manner was frightening and anxiety-inducing. He therefore sought some way of reducing his anxiety and found it in losing his personal identity, or "escaping from freedom" as Fromm called it. He identified himself with some powerful force which took over, spelled out his existence, and completely smothered his independence. This submission to a protective authority was partially a function of the same Calvinistic and Lutheran teachings which created the problem. If one gave one's self to God then one was saved; if one followed God (or some other authority) explicitly one could do no wrong. Man was fundamentally evil and weak and must humiliate and prostrate himself to gain God's grace. He could not let himself be so dominated, however, without some feeling of resentment. It was sinful to resent God and dangerous to resent authority. Some means of adjustment needed to be found which relieved the dread of such cosmic responsibility without creating a secondary problem of pent up hostility. Fromm described a number of behavior patterns which appeared to have been derived as solutions to the dilemma.

One such mode of adjustment was *masochism*; the person could avoid responsibility for himself by submitting to some higher power in the name of love or loyalty. Another more aggressive mode of adjustment was *sadism*, in which it was considered safe and acceptable to release one's resentment upon persons too weak to defend themselves, such as children, minority groups, paupers, and the physically and mentally defective. While sadism and masochism were separate modes of adjustment, they often appeared in a combination of *sado-masochism* which Fromm called the *authoritarian personality*. Such an individual surrendered himself to the social authorities above him, displacing his resentment onto those below him. He found the escape he required, and a means of venting the frustration his brand of escape aroused at the same time. Quite similar to the sado-masochistic mechanism were two other modes of adjustment which were more intense and more pathological manifestations of the authoritarian personality.

To escape responsibility some people sought to think, feel and act exactly like every other member of their group. To conform was the goal, regardless of what it might lead them to do. This orientation Fromm called *automaton conformity*.

Some people felt inferior in the social milieu in which they found themselves and became hostile and destructive to compensate for this weakness. Such persons were prone to attack anyone who offered competition for status or threatened their security in any way. This Fromm called the *destructive orientation*.

Fromm described several other personality types which were also typical of Western culture, but dealt less intensively with these, perhaps because he was less familiar with them. These additional types were more materialistic and object-oriented, in contrast to the person-oriented authoritarian. One would suspect that the authoritarian orientation was most prominent in Germany (Fromm's native country), Austria, and the Slavic countries, while the materialistic types would be more likely to be found in England, France, and America.

Fromm referred to one of these object-oriented personality types as the *receptive orientation*. Such an individual felt powerless to acquire any of the material or psychological supplies he required; and therefore he depended on outside sources to fill his needs. He could not give in return, but constantly demanded affection, attention, or gifts from others. (This is similar to what is commonly known as a dependent personality.)

In another type, the *exploitative orientation*, the material and psychological benefits were sought in a more assertive manner. Rather than passively beseeching others, the exploitative individual expected to have to wrest things from them either by force or cunning. All his relationships were an effort to exploit his fellows. In such a class were the "con man," the "sharp operator," and the shady businessman.

Sometimes individuals who found satisfaction only in the external world of people and objects sought security in possessing that which they valued. These persons were likely to manifest a *hoarding orientation*, and reciprocal relationships were impossible. This personality type was miserly, not only in material things which could be collected and saved, but emotionally as well. The hoarding person was unable to give of himself, yet sought to bind others to him. He did not use people, he collected them. While the "penny pincher" and the fanatic collector are of this type, so is the pretty girl who collects engagement rings. Her numerous boy friends are valuable only as possessions and proof of her attractiveness.

There were other personalities which felt that they must barter themselves, as if they were commodities, for favors and affection. They sought to create a good impression, much in the same way a manufacturer packaged his products for consumer appeal. Persons with this *marketing orientation* could find relief from anxiety only if they could get people to accept their advertising. They sold themselves to the highest bidder, hoping to achieve security in a sort of emotional prostitution. They had no well-defined personal characteristics since they altered themselves according to the laws of supply and demand. The glamor girl, the back slapping salesman, and the political opportunist were such personalities.

In contrast to these pathological orientations, the healthy person was one who could make some creative contribution in his job, in his community, and in his home. He was able to realize his own potential and to fulfill his own goals without misusing others. Fromm referred to this personality type as a *productive orientation.*

The origin of the healthy individual was not described except in Fromm's attempt to depict a Utopian society. Here, however, he left psychology to become a social philosopher. As such, he speculated about values and ethics at a level which is beyond the scope of a text on psychological theories.

Critique

Fromm's observations were most acute and sensitive, but like a case study they do not generalize beyond the situation to which they pertain. He offered a means of understanding the Western man, but his theory gives no basis for predicting the behavior of peoples with a different cultural heritage. Despite his belief that psychology should offer material which has application beyond the individual, he contributed less to understanding mankind as a whole than he may have hoped. In a way he was guilty of the sin of which he accused others, for he confined himself to one set of cultures. He further contradicted himself by dealing at length with pathological orientations to life, while he felt that one could learn more about personality by studying normal individuals. While one should not assume that the average or normal person is the epitome of mental health, it is also well to recognize that a majority of Western citizens are not so severely maladjusted as Fromm's types, even though they may display similar traits.

Fromm did not explain the origins of a culture, nor how the need for a particular orientation to life was created. He did not explain why or how different cultures led to different personalities, nor why the same culture could produce several "types". While these are matters which are more pertinent to the fields of anthropology and sociology, they are still vital to understanding the *national character*.

Although Fromm was guilty of many omissions, the basic character pattern which he hypothesized, the authoritarian personality, has stood up under scientific test and has become an important concept in personality theory. Moreover, his analysis of our culture serves as an illustration of his theory about the interaction of culture, child rearing, and personality, and its application to the understanding of social behavior and the forces which shape society and history.

SUMMARY

Basic Unit and Field of Study. There was no basic unit in Fromm's theory. He stressed the interaction between an individual and society, feeling that it was from this interaction that the personality was formed. The derivation of the normal personality was the proper concern of psychology.

Methods of Investigation. Fromm formulated his theories from his clinical, social and anthropological observations. Experimental testing of his hypotheses would not be practical or possible. Only further cross-cultural comparisons can provide evidence of their validity.

Principles. Behavior was the result of an individual's social experiences, his culture, and his biology. If large groups of persons shared similar experiences by virtue of living in the same society they were likely to have similar personalities. The typical Western personality displayed patterns of dominance-submission, dependency, hostility, efforts to sell one's self to the world, to exploit, or to hoard certain aspects of it.

Consciousness; Sensation, Perception, and Discrimination; Thinking, Cognition, and Memory; The Nature of the Learning Process. These matters were not considered by Fromm.

Emotion and Motivation. Man's biological heritage determined the means he could use in relating to others and defined the limits of interaction. Biological drives were of limited importance to Fromm, however, who saw the social experience of the individual as the source of his motives. These acquired needs were the core of personality.

Behavior and Personality. In the Western world after the Middle Ages the democratic political orientation, the value placed on the individual, the pressures growing out of industrialization, and the teachings of Protestant religions led to a tremendous emphasis on the responsibility of the individual for his own fate. This freedom was a source of fear and anxiety commonly relieved by allowing one's life to be dominated by an authority figure who could take over the burden of responsibility in exchange for submission. Domination, however, might also arouse resentment, which could only be vented on those weaker than one's self. Several modes of reaction were possible within this general orientation, including masochism, sadism, automaton conformity and destructiveness. Besides the authoritarian personality there were other common character types, the receptive or dependent orientation, the exploitative orientation, the hoarding orientation and the marketing orientation. These latter types grew out of Western materialistic values and the inability of the individual to fulfill his needs because of his inner emptiness.

REFERENCES

Erich Fromm

Fromm, E., *Escape From Freedom.* New York: Farrar & Rinehart, 1941.
———, *Man For Himself.* New York: Rinehart, 1947.
———, *The Same Society.* New York: Rinehart, 1955.

CHAPTER 22

ABRAM KARDINER: CULTURE AND PERSONALITY (1945 TO PRESENT)

IN GENERAL, Kardiner's interpretations of Freudian theory were well within the range of orthodoxy. It is appropriate to consider him at this point because of his interest in social as well as individual factors in personality. Kardiner is a practicing analyst who became interested in anthropology and collaborated in many field studies, using this training and experience to analyze cultures much as he analyzed the dynamics of his patients. Out of this work came a theory which was in many ways complementary to Fromm's

Kardiner dealt with such concepts as perception, thinking, motivation, and learning only as they pertained to personality. Therefore, his theory will be viewed entirely from that reference point. The entire theoretical treatment was sufficiently succinct as to be a statement of principles; no separate consideration of basic tenets is necessary.

Behavior and Personality

Kardiner proposed that early cultures developed from man's gregarious need to satisfy his basic urges without destroying or disrupting the group with which he lived. Indeed, society had to regulate behavior to survive. Customs arose as a means of formalizing direct need gratification or providing some indirect form of release. As the group continued to live together, the rules multiplied until a degree of social organization existed. The demands which the society placed on the person created new drives which the society must also find a means for fulfilling. These new drives often derived from the remnants of biological impulses frustrated or channeled by a culture. The new needs, although purely social in origin, were likely to become associated with the basic drives. Thus, all motives came to have a bio-social complexion.

Often society could not provide any perfect and complete gratification for man's needs without destroying itself. Out of this necessary frustration grew an aspect of culture which Kardiner called *projective systems*. These corresponded to the defensive maneuvers of individuals, with the difference that the factors which produced them were evident throughout the entire culture, and the behaviors comprising them soon became institutionalized. Like defenses, projective systems relieved anxiety and provided some socially acceptable outlet for repressed energies. Like defenses, these outlets were ordinarily indirect and unconscious, very often symbolic. They represented derivatives of the cultural conflict between needs of the individual and society. Once they appeared, they tended to be assimilated by the culture. Projective systems included religion, folklore, tribal rules, many forms of recreation, entertainment, art and literature, holidays and festivals. Kardiner was particularly interested in religions as projective systems, in our own as well as other cultures. The fear, awe, punishment-reward, dependency-love, and sexual elements to be found in various religious practices, plus the symbolic similarities to family constellations (such as God the Father and Mother Mary), illustrate the potentialities which religions have for the resolution of psycho-social conflicts.

The culturally prescribed means of impulse gratification combined with the socially created needs and the projective systems to produce a basic personality pattern common to a culture. This pattern was established in each individual through the socialization process. Socialization was much akin to acculturation. Through child-rearing techniques and pressures from various institutions outside the family, the child was initiated into the projective systems of his culture and instructed in the proper ceremonial behaviors.

The abnormal was just as institutionalized as the normal; a culture also prescribed the ways in which one could be maladjusted. This was accomplished by creating conflicts which normal action could not solve. At the same time it created potentials, as by-products of socialization, for certain kinds of action symptoms, thereby providing some release of otherwise unacceptable impulses, albeit in an inefficient and unhealthy way.

The portion of Kardiner's published works given over to the development of pure theory is quite small. He emphasized the testing and demonstration of his concepts through the analysis of anthropological studies of various societies. Aside from primitive groups (1945), Kardiner has examined several American sub-cultures, including the urban Negro (Kardiner & Ovesey, 1951) and the suburban Middle Western white (1939).

Critique

Kardiner, like Fromm, dealt with the concept of *national character*. Both accounted for the origin of such typical personality patterns through the interaction of human needs and the forces of society. The two are probably in basic agreement as to the means by which national character is established. Fromm tended to concentrate on the personality patterns themselves as they appeared in adult members of established cultures. He took cognizance of the fact that these patterns originated in child-rearing practices, and that the practices themselves originated in an interaction between man's biological and social needs. He did not spell out the mechanisms by which this might occur, but Kardiner seems to fill this gap, giving an account of how cultures originate and illustrating his point with anthropological data. Kardiner further hypothesized how personality be it normal or abnormal, was created.

Kardiner's theory was formulated around general principles which could apply to any society, while Fromm derived principles descriptive of only one culture. Kardiner, unlike Fromm, would be able to make predictions about mankind in general. Kardiner is, however, open to the criticism of overgeneralizing about the national characteristics he isolated, just as Fromm is. Both theorists assumed that motives were an important aspect of national character. Kardiner based his theory on Freudian biological impulses, which he said were tamed by the society they made necessary. The result of Kardiner's Freudian orientation may be an overemphasis on biology. Fromm's suggestion that man's innate needs limit and structure, but do not completely determine, his social interactions leaves more room for the role of acquired motivations and therefore places the various possibilities in a better balance. Paradoxically, however, Fromm as a social philosopher tended to appeal to more cosmic and impersonal forces in describing the appearance of social motives, and removed them from their human origins.

CULTURE AND PERSONALITY

Growing out of the work of theorists like Fromm and Kardiner is a new movement combining the skills of psychology, psychoanalysis, and cultural anthropology in an effort to study the relationship between culture and personality. Sometimes the effort is primarily anthropological in nature, using psychological theories to aid in understanding the culture, as in the work of Margaret Mead (1934, 1935, 1939, 1942, 1949, 1956) and Ruth Benedict (1934). Other theorists have used cultures to demonstrate psychoanalytic principles; Erik Homburger Erikson (see Chapter 16) is typical of this group.

Some, like Fromm, describe the personality of a society. Some, like Kardiner, have discussed the interaction of personality and society. While the movement is a lively, vital one, there is no organized approach, no one goal, no one doctrine or theory. The one identifying characteristic is a conviction concerning the necessary interaction between culture and personality. Most of the data collected by the practitioners of this persuasion is illustrative case study material which is of practical value, but not yet of sufficient generality to have meaning for further theory building.

SUMMARY

Behavior and Personality. Kardiner proposed that the culture which grew up to regulate the life of a group created a new set of drives for which the culture must also supply gratification in order to preserve itself. Certain institutions and customs (such as religion) arose as a means of supplying this gratification. Kardiner called these projective systems. The culture, the needs it aroused, and the means it permitted for gratification created a similar personality, the national character, in all of its citizens; it also created the patterns available for maladjustment. This type of approach has resulted in a new area of scientific endeavor, the study of the interaction of culture and personality.

REFERENCES

Abram Kardiner

Kardiner, A., *The Individual and His Society*. New York: Columbia Univ. Press, 1939.

——, *Psychological Frontiers of Society*. New York: Columbia Univ. Press, 1945.

Kardiner, A., and L. Ovesey, *The Mark of Oppression*. New York: Norton, 1951.

Culture and Personality

Benedict, Ruth, *Patterns of Culture*. New York: Houghton-Mifflin, 1934.

Mead, Margaret, *Sex and Temperament in Three Primitive Societies*. New York: Morrow, 1935.

——, *From the South Seas*. New York: Morrow, 1939.

——, *And Keep Your Powder Dry*. New York: Morrow, 1942.

——, *Male and Female*. New York: Morrow, 1949.

——, "The Cross-Cultural Approach to the Study of Personality," in J. L. McCary, ed., *Psychology of Personality: Six Modern Approaches*, New York: Logos, 1956.

PART VI

FIELD THEORIES

CHAPTER 23

GESTALT PSYCHOLOGY (1920 TO PRESENT)

THE NAME Gestalt Psychology was originally applied to two schools of thought. Max Wertheimer and his students, Kurt Koffka and Wolfgang Köhler, centered their activities in Germany while another, similarly oriented theory developed in Austria. To distinguish between these two, the names of their country of origin were attached as adjectives; thus they became known respectively as the German and the Austrian Gestaltists. Both sought to explain what might underlie sensory experience; both addressed themselves to the problem of discovering the nature of perceptual organization. Their explanatory hypotheses distinguished them from each other. The Austrian Gestaltists believed that perception was the result of processes within the brain working actively to combine a number of separate sensations into a meaningful experience. According to them, for example, the melody one heard when listening to a symphony was constructed by the brain from a series of individual neural impulses, one for each note. The German Gestaltists held that organization of experience occurred automatically as a result of the physiological functioning of the brain, particularly the sensory areas. Sensory reception and organization took place in the same step, rendering sensation and perception indistinguishable. For them the melody of a symphony was imposed on the brain by the prior workings of the nervous system.

From their interest in perceptual organization the German Gestaltists gradually moved to a consideration of behavior in general. Perhaps it was their interest in these more general applications which enabled the German Gestaltists to flourish while the Austrian group died out. In any event, the name Gestalt Psychology has come to apply to this group alone, and the Austrian group have become an historical curiosity.

The Gestalt theory of Wertheimer, Koffka, and Köhler arose from two sources. A rejection of the atomistic approach of other theories lent negative impetus, while Wertheimer's work with the *phi* phenomenon suggested an alternative.

Turning first to the negative pressures which fostered their work, the Gestaltists objected to Structuralism because it reduced mind to elements, and in doing so destroyed something very important, the patterning or organization of sensory events. Any attempt to dissect this pattern into its component parts was mechanistic, artificial, and, worst of all, misleading. The whole of anything was something more than its parts taken separately, and could only be understood by laws focusing on *gestalts* (organized wholes). Laws concerning components could supply only partial information. A second disagreement between the Structuralists and the founders of the Gestalt school was the *constancy hypothesis*. In brief, this was a philosophical controversy concerning the nature of reality. The Structuralists assumed that things were, forever and always, what they seemed to be. The behavioral or perceptual environment was identical, they said, to the physical environment in which the person found himself. They predicted a perfect, one-to-one correlation between stimulation and conscious experience. This prediction overlooked optical illusions, misperception, adaptation, constancy, and many other phenomena which pointed to discrepancies between perception and stimulation. Thus, for example, a red patch in different colors of illumination will be perceived as red so long as the person is given enough cues to compensate for the distortion of color produced by the different lights. This phenomenon is known as color constancy. If, however, the person is deprived of cues, he will no longer see red, but may report various shades of blue, purple, pink, or gray as the illumination changes. By concentrating on the raw feel of experience and disregarding the perception of its meaning or connotations, the Structuralists were led to exaggerate the validity of sensory processes and to neglect the importance of situational determinants in experience. They ignored the fact that cues influenced how red was perceived, and consequently were in the rather ridiculous position of trying to find out what red was when it wasn't red. To report an experience of red when a red object was viewed under colored light, i.e., to demonstrate constancy, was an error for the Structuralist but an accurate report of the situation to the Gestaltist, who recognized constancy as a naturally occurring event, the study of which could supply valuable information about perception.

The Gestaltists had equally strong criticisms to make of their contemporaries, the Behaviorists. It was commendable for the Behaviorists to be so objective, but in their objectivity they left out everything that intervened between stimulus and response, neglecting many important aspects of psychology purely because they could find no scientific way to investigate such things. The Gestaltists felt comfortable with speculation, and in contrast to the Behaviorists' S-R theory, they maintained an S-O-R (or pattern-of-stimuli——→ organism's-perceptual-organization——→ response determined-by-perception) approach. Their study of these "unscientific" topics provided many scientific insights which the reductionistic theories could never have produced.

Accusations of "analytic," "elementary," and "mechanistic" were also leveled at Thorndike, whose concept of trial-and-error learning was especially abhorrent to the Gestaltists. The whole concept was wrong; the errors which an animal made in a puzzle box were not blind errors at all. Errors did not occur accidentally, but were produced by the organism's perception of the field in which he was operating. Behavior was always appropriate to the perceived field. The problem was to discover what the field was; then one could understand the behavior. The Law of Effect was also mechanistic, suggesting a set of continuous but discrete improvements a result of each learning trial. The Gestaltists concentrated on insight learning and were convinced that learning was discontinuous, subject to abrupt changes. It also seemed erroneous to the Gestaltists to propose that reinforcement stamped associations in or out. Learning was a matter of appreciating perceptual relationships, and reinforcement was an event to be appreciated, not an instrument to aid in the appreciation of events.

These, then, were the problems the Gestaltists felt psychology was facing. They sought to remedy these ills with a new theory, based in great part on their work with the *phi phenomenon.* The phi phenomenon is produced when two small slits, at right angles to each other in an otherwise opaque screen, are lighted successively so that the bar of light appears to move from one position to the other (this same phenomenon accounts for the apparent movement in motion pictures; one sees the characters on the screen in motion but actually the sequence is composed of a series of discrete stimuli exposed very quickly, one at a time). As Wertheimer, Koffka, and Köhler studied this phenomenon, they were impressed with the effect of different patterns of stimuli on perception and concluded that such patterns must be the result of interaction among the neural processes within the brain. Having arrived at this conclusion, they devoted themselves to testing it and generalizing upon it.

Basic Unit

What we have already said is sufficient to indicate that the Gestaltists rejected the possibility of breaking psychological phenomena into units; analysis violated the nature of the gestalt. While the psychoanalysts also focused on the entire personality, they had no objection to examining components of behavior, and often did; but they always tried to find the meaning of these components for the rest of the personality, since they could not cure the symptom unless they also altered the context in which it occurred. To approach the subject matter in this way was practical. The Gestaltist's holistic approach, on the other hand, was essential to their philosophy of science. For them, the only plausible approach to scientific investigation was a molar one, considering the complex act or experience as the unit of significance, and not as some simple S-R sequence which might compose it.

Field of Study

The Gestaltists were best known for their investigations of perception and thinking, but they by no means limited psychology to these areas. As their theory developed, they became interested in many areas and eventually constructed a general theory of experience and behavior.

Methods of Investigation

The Gestaltists employed introspection in their studies of perception and to some extent in other areas. While they did use the naive introspection of the Structuralists, their more usual technique was phenomenal introspection, requiring the subject to report the meaning of the experience he was undergoing as well as its raw feel. The Gestaltists had no vested interest in method, however, and felt free to use or invent procedures as they were needed. In fact, they are noted for their ingenuity. For example, when the Gestaltists became interested in studying problem-solving and insight, they discovered no techniques suitable to the kind of study they had in mind. Consequently, they were forced to devise new methods. Insight, they said, was a change in perception such that new relationships were recognized. It was manifested by sudden alterations in behavior so that problem solution was achieved. To study this process, one must set up a situation where there was some sort of hidden, or at least not obvious, relationship which the subject must discover, and one where the discovery would be manifest in some change in performance.

One test situation which met these criteria was the barrier problem. A barrier was inserted between the subject and the goal for which it was striving. The subject must find out how to surmount or bypass this barrier and reach the goal. To do so the subject had to perceive the relationship of the goal to the rest of the field, including areas which were some distance away and apparently inappropriate to it. Only by venturing into these hitherto inappropriate parts of the field could the organism get around the barrier and reach its goal.

Another insight test was the inference problem. Within the field of the experimental subject there were one or more objects which the subject might use in reaching an otherwise unavailable goal. The potentialities of these various stimulus objects were not necessarily apparent; the subject had to figure out how the objects could be employed. Köhler's most famous experiments with apes were of this type. In the simplest of these the ape was placed in a cage with some fruit hanging from the ceiling high above his reach. Somewhere in the animal's cage was placed a stick long enough to reach the fruit. The ape had to perceive the stick as a tool before he could get the food. A more complex version of the same kind of problem supplied two sticks, each one too short to reach the fruit by itself but capable of being joined to the other to form a tool of sufficient length for the ape to achieve its goal.

A third method, the transposition experiment, was really a new type of experimental design developed bv Köhler (1918) as a crucial study, demonstrating whether a subject learned because of reinforcement of a particular response, or because of insight into the contiguity (relationship) of stimuli. The subject was taught to discriminate between two shades of gray, a lighter shade and a darker shade, by means of differential reinforcement: response to the goal object identified by the darker gray was reinforced with food, while response to the lighter gray goal was not. The subject, having learned the distinction, would approach the darker gray goal where he had been reinforced. After discrimination was established as evidenced by differential response, another set of goal identity cues was introduced. These new cues included the lighter of the two original stimuli and another still lighter shade of gray. It the subject had learned patterns or relationships among stimuli he would approach that shade which he had previously learned to avoid since it was now the darker stimulus. If, on the other hand, the subject had learned a specific response to a specific reinforced stimulus, he would avoid the same stimulus as before and seek food at the other goal, disregarding its new coloring. The subjects in the experiment always sought the darker stimulus, convincing Köhler that it was relationships rather than specific (reinforced) S-R bonds which were learned. While the experiment proved Köhler's point, it did not deal the death blow to reinforcement theory that he may have hoped for. Too many non-discriminatory types of learning could be cited as reinforcement-based by those who wished to support the S-R reinforcement argument. The technique, however, has become a classic for the study of discrimination and the learning of relationships.

Principles

Basic to all Gestalt theory was the law that the whole of anything was more than the sum of its parts. The principles derived by Wertheimer, Köhler, and Koffka to describe this patterning were developed by studies of perceptual organizations, but they had broader implications and have been generalized to many aspects of behavior, especially to thinking and learning. These organizational principles will first be discussed as they concern perception, and will then be generalized to other aspects of psychology as seems appropriate.

The first Gestalt principle was the Law of *Figure-Ground relationships*. Perception was organized in such a way that there were certain aspects of the field which stood out as figures against the background formed by the rest of the field. The Gestaltists believed that the figure-ground relationship existed aside from logic or causal conditions. Current interpretation, however, stresses figure as being that which is most salient or important at the time. As an example, the spaces surrounding each letter on this page are always background, never figure, as one reads. They are equally important to perception, yet never perceived. However, if it is important to see the space, figure and ground can be reversed. Imagine what would be perceived if one were asked to estimate the distance between words, or if the printer accidentally ran words together and one had to discover howtoseparatethem.

Figure-ground relationships were equally important in such matters as thinking and attention and could be applied to behavioral events within the body and outside it. Each act or event occurred in, and gained meaning from, the context in which it occurred. Given figure and ground, the remaining Gestalt principles explained how the patterning of the percept took place.

The Law of Similarity stated that things tended to be perceived in a pattern if they were similar to each other in some way. For example, in Figure 4 one perceives groups of circles and groups of squares. Since the two shapes are equidistant and of equal size, there is no reason for the grouping except that some figures are more similar to some of their neighbors than to others.

The Law of Similarity is very much the same as the Aristotelian principle of similarity in establishing associations. The relevance of the latter to thinking and learning has already been pointed out. The relevance of the Gestalt principle should be immediately apparent, generalizing from the treatment of similarity by Associationists.

The Gestalt Law of Contiguity held that things tend to be patterned or grouped if they are proximal to each other. In Figure 5 there is no good reason why the third and fourth figures should not be seen as members of a common group except that they happen to be farther apart than the second and third, or the fourth and fifth figures.

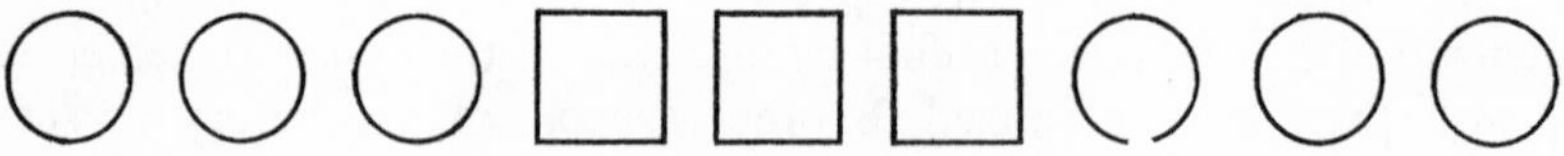

○○○□□□○○○

FIGURE 4

Patterning by Similarity

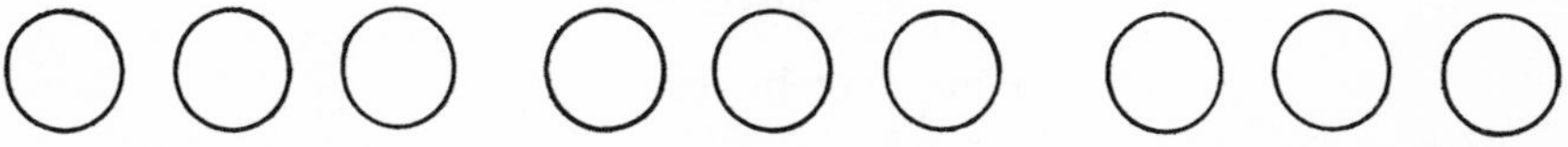

FIGURE 5

Patterning by Proximity

The Gestalt Law of Proximity had an obvious relationship to the Aristotelian Law of Contiguity. The significance of the contiguity law to learning theory has been stressed throughout this book, as has its pertinence to theories of thinking. Proximity has a similar relevance.

The remaining Gestalt principles describe peculiarly holistic phenomena which could only have been observed given the frame of reference of Wertheimer, Kohler, and Koffka.

The Law of *Pragnanz*, also known as the Law of Good Figure, stated that one perceived a pattern in such a way as to make it the best pattern possible. In Figure 6 the figures are roughly sketched, yet the casual observer will interpret them as squares and circles until he is told that the "round" figures are tomatoes, and the "square" figures are sheets hanging on a clothes line.

A related but less general principle was the Law of *Closure*. This principle stated that a figure which was incomplete was perceived as if it were a complete figure. One's first impression of the forms in Figure 7 is that they are complete, but closer examination reveals that they are not quite closed. Since closure could be predicted from the Law of Pragnanz, it was a secondary law. However, it describes an aspect of perception sufficiently important to achieve independent status.

Closure and Pragnanz appeared not only in perception but also in thinking, memory, and behavior. The manifestations of these principles in cognitive function usually involved altering a stimulus as it was thought about or remembered in such a way as to make it more nearly like one expected it to be, rather than representing it as it really was. Another cognitive and behavioral phenomenon which demonstrated the same set of principles was the so-called *Zeigarnick Effect*, named after the psychologist who discovered it. If a person were interrupted in the course of finishing some task, he would resume it later in preference to any other activity, other things being equal.

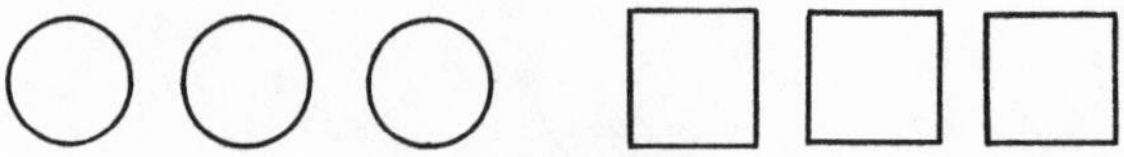

FIGURE 6

Patterning by Pragnanz

That is to say, he looked for closure. Likewise, he would be more likely to remember it rather than other tasks which he was allowed to complete, unless he was in an ego-involved situation where the incomplete task implied failure. Then, in conformity with the Law of Pragnanz, the person remembered in such a way as to enhance his view of himself.

Consciousness

Sensory experience was the topic of most interest to the Gestaltists. Experience must be conscious if one is going to introspect upon it. Consciousness was therefore an important phenomenon. However, it was important in the same way as conditioning was important to Pavlov; it was not significant in its own right, but because it was a window through which one might view the activities of the brain when it was aroused by some stimulus.

Sensation, Perception, and Discrimination

In Gestalt theory sensation was not raw material, as it was for the Structuralists and many other psychologists. Stimuli as they impinged on sensory organs were raw and unorganized, but the sensory organs and the

FIGURE 7

Patterning by Closure

reception centers in the brain automatically patterned them. The Gestaltists described the reception centers as *projection areas* and conceived of them as serving the same role as a projection screen upon which images were cast. The terms "images" and "projection" were more than analogies to the Gestaltists. For them the true nature of sensory function was similar to a projection of images. They postulated an *isomorphism* between sensory patterns and brain activity, such that each event which impinged upon the senses was represented in the brain field. In this representation the event was not reproduced point by point, but was transposed from a physical object into a pattern of neural excitation. The relationships between the event and the rest of the environment were likewise represented by relationships among patterns of neural activity.

The concept of isomorphism can best be explained by example, and the best example available is a map of some geographical territory. The map is isomorphic to the territory; it is in no way the same sort of thing as the territory; it is a representation of it. The spatial relationships are maintained, although they are translated into a different form. According to the Gestaltists, perception was a representation of the stimulus field in exactly the same way; perception was, then, much like map making. It was, furthermore, an indistinguishable aspect of sensation. It was not a separate operation at a higher level of cortical interaction which elaborated raw sensory data. It occurred as the stimuli first entered the nervous system. During the process of coding stimuli into neural impulses, patterning or organization was imposed by the nature of the nervous system. The forms these perceptual patterns might take were described by the Laws of Figure-Ground, Similarity, Proximity, Closure, and Pragnanz. The various processes by which these patterns were formed were called *peripheral factors*, since they were assumed to take place early in the sequence of events initiated by a stimulus impinging upon a sensory receptor.

In addition, Gestalt theory also hypothesized *central factors*, processes higher up in the nervous system which influenced one's interpretation of patterns, or altered the organization of them. These central factors included the set with which one entered the situation and one's past experiences.

Just as the environment could be conceived of as a field of forces, so could one conceive of a field of forces within the nervous system. The activity of this field was governed by the same laws as any other field. To preserve the field, the forces within it must be held in equilibrium. The organization of sensory data was a result of the interaction of the forces within the brain as they were brought into balance. The neural processes themselves conformed to the same principles of organization as the person's psychological experience. For example, the perception of closure was dictated by the fact that the representation of the imperfections of the original stimulus would disrupt the symmetry and thus the balance of the field. The forces in the brain acted to close the gap in the field caused by the incomplete figure. This action resulted in the perception of the figure as completed. In a like manner, proximity of activities in the brain led to interaction among them, and consequently to the meaningful percept or concept.

Thinking, Cognition, and Memory

Thinking for the Gestalists was a process of developing appreciation for relationships in the perceptual field. Thought was thus synonymous with insight. Insight was characterized by three attributes: it always resulted in sudden alterations of behavior (an attribute which Tolman also suggested as a criterion of what he called "inventive ideation"); once achieved, insight was well retained, even after long periods of disuse; and finally, it was easily transferred to other similar situations.

Insight was not a series of separate responses to separate stimuli. It was an integrated reaction to the whole situation. From a Gestaltist point of view any problem was a gap in the field produced by ignorance of certain relationships. Insight was a means of achieving closure of this gap, thereby regaining equilibrium. The result of closure on a cognitive level was the awareness of some relationship in one's surroundings which had not been previously noticed. Once this aspect was perceived, the forces which activated the problem could be allayed and resolved.

Emotion and Motivation

Although they used the concepts of force and equilibrium, the Gestaltists were more interested in the organization of behavior than in factors which produced it. Indeed, for all that force and equilibrium can be motivational concepts, they were not viewed in this light by the Gestaltists. Rather they were employed to account for organization and patterning. Among the field theorists, only Kurt Lewin considered motives, and his formulation is sufficiently distinctive from the classical Gestaltists to be a separate system, one we will take up in the next chapter.

The Nature of the Learning Process

For the Gestaltist learning was as inseparable from thinking as sensation was from perception. Insight involved the acquisition of new concepts, of retention and transfer from one situation to another. Consequently insight was learning as well as thinking. Gestalt theory rejected the concept of trial-and-error learning. As has already been stated, Gestaltists felt that errors were not accidental. They were dictated by the field as the person perceived it at the moment. When successful behavior finally appeared, it was because the last experience altered the field in such a way that the person's conception of it finally conformed to reality. A "gap" in perception had been filled and the person was now able to see all the various inter-relationships involved in the problem he was facing. If errors were the result of failures in the appreciation of the field, then trial-and-error learning could be reduced to problem-solving and development of insight, and reinforcement was an unnecessary and superflous concept.

Insight was a matter of perceiving relationships between stimuli, i.e., of becoming aware of the contiguity of stimuli. If contiguity led to insight, it led to learning as well, and was a sufficient condition for the establishment of learning.

Behavior and Personality

Koffka believed that behavior was governed by a field of interacting forces organized into dynamic patterns. The field in which the person operated was a psychophysical one in that both internal and external forces were active. The operations of this field could be approached from a molecular viewpoint insofar as they had some physical basis, but at the same time they were molar, including broad aspects of experience and behavior. It was the latter area which the Gestaltists felt was the proper study for psychologists. The former was left to the physical and biological sciences.

The Gestaltists felt that it was possible to take a negative approach to the historical view of behavior. Any act, they believed, was determined solely by the existing stimulus field. The field at any particular time included not only the persons perceptions of the present field, but also representations of the past in the form of memories and various desires, fantasies, and plans for the future. There was an interaction between these representations of past, present, and future, perception influencing memory, memory influencing perception, and dreams, based on both perception and memory and influencing both in turn. When the Gestaltists spoke of an historical approach, they did not mean one should neglect the effects of past and future, but rather that past and future affected behavior only through their effects on the present.

The Gestaltists stated that the behavioral field had two poles: the self, or ego, and the environment. Tensions could develop between these aspects of the field, thus sharpening the polarity and making the person more aware of the difference between self and non-self and disrupting the equilibrium of this field. Tensions could also develop inside the ego, or in the environment, again leading to disequilibrium. Moreover, behavior could be adjusted to the ego and yet not fit the real environment. This was true because the environment was not always what it seemed to be to the person. The person perceived and interpreted the field in which he functioned on the basis of his past experience and the relationships he was capable of perceiving at the moment. Insofar as his perceptions and the meanings which he attributed to them were inaccurate, the person could behave in a manner which was valid for him and yet invalid to the external observer who could see the situation objectively. The various neuroses and psychoses and other behavioral maladjustments were the results of this type of discrepancy; even mental illness was a Gestalt.

Critique

The Gestaltists formulated basic laws of perception and organization and applied these not only to sensory experience, but also to behavior in general. Most of what the Gestaltists said was not new, however; it was a restatement of ideas which had already been formulated by other psychologists and by philosophers. The Gestaltist contribution lay in being able to organize these ideas into a fresh approach, wherein they took on new and unforeseen connotations of vital importance to psychology.

The Gestaltists' use of the concepts of field and force, for example, was most instructive. These concepts presented a novel way of viewing experience and have initiated much fruitful research. Psychoanalytic theories have also implied the force concept with good results, but they have tended to restrict it to biological processes and to interpret its effects quite literally as forces of something which could be dammed up, overflow, be siphoned off, etc. The Gestaltists' application of the force concept was intended to be more operational, for even when they spoke of "forces in a field" they had in mind neural (electrical) forces in a neural (electrical) field. This translation of neural functions into physical (electrical) forces was most instructive. In like manner, the Gestalt emphasis on the organization of mental processes gave psychology a new vantage point. Furthermore, Gestalt theory provided a model for the derivation of neurological hypotheses insofar as it proposed an analogy between psychological and neurological principles.

Köhler, for example, was rather successful in demonstrating phenomena which could be produced only by some sort of field within the brain, but direct physiological experiments have been less supportive. Lashley (Lashley, Chow, & Semmes, 1951) inserted metal foil into the brain after training animals in an act which the Gestaltists said required a force-field explanation. Although the foil should have disrupted any existing field, and thereby distorted the behavior, no such disruption occurred. The post-operative behavior was intact. Whether or not this and future experiments confirm or negate the theory, the research itself has established a pattern.

The Gestalt theories have been criticized as vague about exactly what they intended the term "Gestalt" to connote. Did they mean "whole," as they sometimes used it? Did they mean "unity," another use of the term? Or did they mean "organization?" Apparently they meant all three definitions and did not find the multiple meanings incompatible. While the connotations are complementary, it is still important in a specific instance to know which meaning was intended; and the necessity of specificity is likely to be confusing.

The question has been raised as to how far the Gestaltists wished to carry their prohibition against analysis of experience. They obviously did not mean that one cannot break experience down at all, for they themselves never dealt with experience as a whole, since they found this much too large a unit for scientific study. They were not actually opposed to inspection of specific aspects of mental processes so long as these aspects arranged themselves into natural, compatible subgroupings of events so that artificial subdivisions were not created. It was analysis which destroyed the essence of groupings that they opposed, not the creation of meaningful classes of events.

However vague it may be on many points, the Gestalt theory has remained an important facet of both American and European psychology. It has the distinction of being able to avoid dogmatism, so that its adherents have found it possible to remain practitioners of science and not "retainers of the faith." As a result Gestaltists have been able to examine their own principles as critically as they examine those of other systems. Perhaps it is this capacity for self-examination and correction which accounts for the continuing vitality of the theory.

SUMMARY

Basic Unit. Experience and behavior could not be broken down into units, but must be approached as complex, organized entities, or gestalts.

Field of Study. Aside from specifying the focus, the Gestaltists did not delimit the field of application, although much of their own work was with perception or cognition.

Methods of Investigation. Gestaltists used introspection in their studies of perception and developed such techniques as the barrier situation, the inference problem, and the transposition experiment in their investigation of insight and learning, again without trying to restrict psychology to their own interests.

Principles. The whole of anything was more than the sum of its parts. It was a result of the patterning of the stimuli on the basis of figure-ground relationships, spatial proximity, the tendency to create the best pattern possible, and the tendency to fill in or finish incomplete forms.

Consciousness. Conscious experience was important as a means for examining the perceptual and cognitive functioning of an organism through introspection.

Sensation, Perception, and Discrimination. Raw sensation did not exist for the Gestaltists, who assumed that all stimulation was in some way organized and patterned in the sensory organs and the lower brain centers, so that the content of perception was an isomorphic representation of the stimulus field, coded into neural activities.

Thinking, Cognition, and Memory. Thinking was organized according to the same Gestalt principles as perception. It was a matter of developing insights into unforeseen relationships in the stimulus field. Development of insight was manifested by sudden alterations in behavior, and it was well retained and easily transferred to similar situations.

Emotion and Motivation. The processes which directed behavior did not concern the original Gestaltists, whose interests lay more in the organization of behavior than in its motivation.

The Nature of the Learning Process. Learning was a matter of acquiring and retaining insights, and as such it was indistinguishable from thinking. Learning was brought about by the contiguity of relationships existing in the field. Reinforcement was unnecessary to the establishment of learning.

Behavior and Personality. Behavior was governed by a field of psychophysical forces, and could be understood solely in terms of this field with no reference to past or future events except insofar as these were represented in the present by anticipation and memories. The behavioral field had two poles, the self and the environment. Conflicting forces within or between these poles were believed to be the cause of maladjustments.

REFERENCES

Ellis, W. D., *A Source Book of Gestalt Psychology*. New York: Harcourt Brace, 1938.

Kurt Koffka

Koffka, K., *Die Grundlagen dir Psychischen Entwicklung der Kinderpsychologie*. Osterweeck: Zickfeldt, 1921. Eng. trans., *The Growth of the Mind*, New York: Harcourt Brace, 1924.

———, "Mental Development," in C. Murchison, ed., *Psychologies of 1925*, Worcester: Clark Univ. Press, 1925, pp. 130–143.

———, "Some Problems of Space Perception," in C. Murchison, ed., *Psychologies of 1930*, Worcester: Clark Univ. Press, 1930, pp. 161–187.

———, *Principles of Gestalt Psychology*. New York: Harcourt Brace, 1935.

Wolfgang Köhler

Köhler, W., *Intelligensprufung an Menschenaffen*. Berlin: Springer, 1917. (A) Eng. trans., *The Mentality of Apes*, New York: Harcourt Brace, 1925. Excerpts 2nd Eng. ed. reprinted in W. Dennis, ed., *Readings in the History of Psychology*, New York: Appleton-Century-Crofts, 1948, pp 497–505.

———, "Abhandlungen der Preuss," Akad. D. Wissenschaft: *Phys.-Math. Kl.* 2, 1918.

———, "Intelligence in Apes," in C. Murchison, ed., *Psychologies of 1955*, Worcester: Clark Univ. Press, 1925, pp. 145–161. (A)

———, "An Aspect of Gestalt Psychology," in C. Murchison, ed., *Psychologies of 1925*, Worcester: Clark Univ. Press, 1925, pp. 163–195. (B)

———, *Gestalt Psychology*. New York: Liveright, 1929.

———, "Some Tasks of Gestalt Psychology," in C. Murchison, ed., *Psychologies of 1930*, Worcester: Clark Univ. Press, 1930, pp. 143–160.

———, *Dynamics in Psychology*. New York: Liveright, 1940.

———, "The Present Situation in Brain Physiology," *Amer. Psychol.* 13: 150–154 (1958).

K. S. Lashley

Lashley, K. S., K. L. Chow, and J. Semmes, "An Examination of the Electric Field Theory of Cerebral Integration," *Psychol. Rev.* 58: 123–136 (1951).

Max Werthermir

Werthermir, M., "Untersuchunger zur Lehre von du Gestalt," Psychol. Forsch. 4: 301–350 (1923). Excerpts in Eng. given in W. D. Ellis, *A Sourcebook of Gestalt Psychology*, New York: Harcourt Brace, 1938, pp. 71–88.

———, *Uber Schlussprogesse im Produktiven Denken*, 1920. Excerpts in Eng. given in W. D. Ellis, *A Sourcebook in Gestalt Psychology*, New York: Harcourt Brace, 1938, pp. 274–282. Also reprinted in *Drei Abhandlungen zur Gestaltheorie*, Erlangen: Philosophischen Akademie, 1925.

———, "Untersuchungen zur Lehre von der Gestalt," *Psychol. Forsch.* 1: 42–58 (1921). Excerpts in Eng. in W. D. Ellis, *A Sourcebook in Gestalt Psychology*, New York: Harcourt Brace, 1938, pp. 12–16, 71–88.

CHAPTER 24

LEWIN'S FIELD THEORY (1935 TO PRESENT)

WHILE the Gestaltists felt that their theory of perception and cognition was entirely adequate, they found it impossible to apply their methods and concepts to the study of such vital matters of human behavior as those which concerned psychoanalysts. Particularly, they found their system unable to cope with the problems inherent in the concept of motivation. It was left to Kurt Lewin (1890–1947) to expand Gestalt theory into this new area. He had become interested in working with motivation and tension systems about the time of World War I. At first this was a minor interest, but gradually he began to distinguish himself among his colleagues with his brilliant work and soon devoted more and more time to it. His efforts led to the development of a new formulation, known as *Field Theory*.

In order to study motivation, Lewin required some method of mathematical analysis and representation which could deal with the complex forces he postulated and yet satisfy the demands of scientific methodology. The search for mathematical tools suitable to complex data is not new. Geometry of plane surfaces is applicable to surveying, and geometry of spheres is useful for navigation, but Einstein had to turn to a geometry of four dimensions to handle his theory of relativity. Lewin faced the same dilemma in attempting to process complex psychological data. He found his solution in topological mathematics and vector psychology, and later in hodology, a new technique which he developed to fit the needs of psychology.

Topology is a non-metrical geometry of spaces in which such concepts as *inside*, *outside*, and *boundary* are used. The details of this geometry are beyond the range of this text, but the uses to which it was put are most pertinent. Lewin believed that psychological situations could be described topologically, and he proposed a number of concepts dealing with such psychological responses as behavior in space. Intrigued with early success,

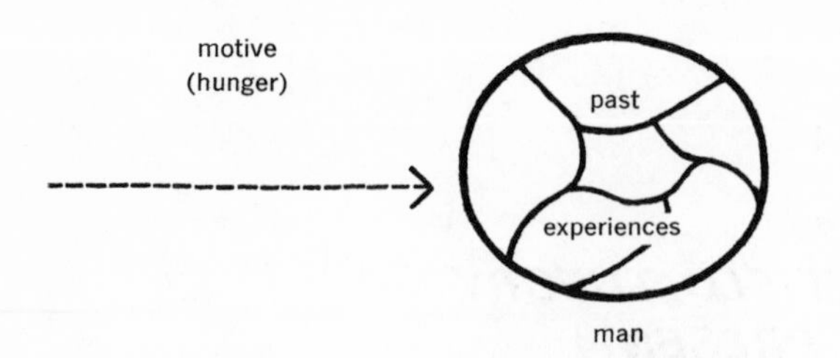

FIGURE 8

Simplified Representation of a Hungry Man
in the Manner of Kurt Lewin

Lewin proceeded to develop concepts concerning direction of behavior and the different possible courses of action within the life span. These directional concepts were beyond the scope of topology, and involved a geometry, sufficiently distinct for Lewin to coin the term *hodology*, or the science of paths, to describe his new technique.

To represent the effects of motivation Lewin borrowed the concepts of *vector* and *force* from physics and mathematics. Unlike topological concepts which are more or less descriptive, vectors are metrical, that is, they can be expressed as units or amounts of force.

Lewin found topology useful in representing the general situation or environment in which the organism operates. He employed vectors to show the various kinds of forces acting in and on the individual. Using these tools, he set up a model of the *life space*, an egg-shaped figure with subdivisions representing various vectors (the length representing intensity, and the direction representing the line and point of application). Figure 8 illustrates the application of topology and vector psychology to the representation of human behavior. Let us assume that a hungry man is roused to action to satisfy his need. His similar experiences in the past cause him to hurry home to dinner.

With these mathematical aids, and the conceptual innovations at which he gradually arrived, Lewin built a theory based on Gestalt principles, but with sufficient individuality to become a school in its own right.

Basic Unit

Like other Gestalt psychologists, Lewin did not believe that a basic unit was possible or necessary in psychology. The unit one must choose was the whole experience; to Lewin, then, the unit and the field of study were the same.

Field of Study

The appropriate place for psychology to exercise itself was in the examination of the individual in his life space. The life space referred to the psychological field in which the person moved. It is well to emphasize that this space was psychological, not physical. It was psychological in the same sense that Tolman's cognitive map was a psychological rather than a geographical concept. It could be represented by a spatial diagram (using topological geometry), but it did not thus exist as a spatial relationship. Space was used merely to represent various psychological *dimensions*. Life space was a hypothetical construct, an inference about what went on inside the human being or animal.

Within a person's life space, the person could move about, actually or psychologically. *Locomotion* was the movement from one point in the life space to another. The term was derived from the geometrical representation which Lewin employed and referred to the selection of alternative actions, the examining of possibilities, the setting out toward goals and the like. Locomotion could be symbolic as in thinking, or it could imply motor behavior. The meaning of these concepts can best be illustrated by diagramming a set of life experiences as Lewin might. Let us suppose that the situation represented in Figure 9 is that of a boy who wants to go to a circus. He is separated from the goal region by a number of regions with boundaries between them. The regions include (a) earning the money to go, (b) obtaining his mother's permission, (c) getting his neck and ears washed and putting on his best suit, (d) riding to the circus tent, and (e) getting his ticket. Each region is separated from the other by certain cut-off points. To traverse from his present position to his goal the boy must pass through each of these regions, successfully cross the border, and enter the next. If the boy instruments his plan, he will pass, or locomote, through all these regions before he enters the circus tent. At any time in his goal-seeking

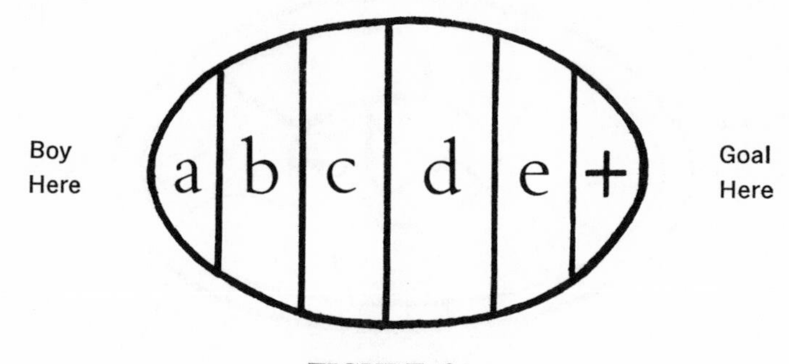

FIGURE 9

A Graphic Illustration of Locomotion through Regions

we can locate him somewhere in this life space. His goal-seeking can be marked off like a ship's position on its charts.

But the boy need not really go through all these maneuvers for this figure to represent his experience. The diagram is used to visualize his psychological status at any particular moment. If he is only thinking about and planning his adventure, the diagram still shows what his current position is in regard to paths, goals, and future overt behavior. Such diagrams represent implicit behaviors as adequately as they do explicit behaviors.

Lewin found that it was possible to represent the internal structure or environment in a geometric diagram, even as one can represent psychological environment. For Lewin, a person was made up of a number of interwoven layers of personality. There were some layers which were more superficial and therefore more observable by other people. Other layers were deeper and less accessible, but equally important. The layers represented regions, i.e., needs, ideas, goals, or any other mental activity. The structure of the personality differed in complexity from one person to another. Some personalities had more regions. Some had more interaction among regions, or more involved relationships. In some cases it was possible for the superficial and deeper layers to interact. In other cases they were cut off from each other, somewhat like the division between conscious and unconscious in Freudian theory. Again it is necessary to employ a Lewinian type of diagram to clarify the meanings of his concepts. Figure 10 is composed of an outer ring and several inner circles composed of cells. The outer ring represents perceptual and motor functions, processes which relate the person to his environment and must therefore be close to the surface where others can see them. The next circle represents certain objective but less noticeable factors such as individual mannerisms and traits. These needs, attitudes, and beliefs were less determined by the immediate situation in which a person found himself. Finally, there is a central core of personality

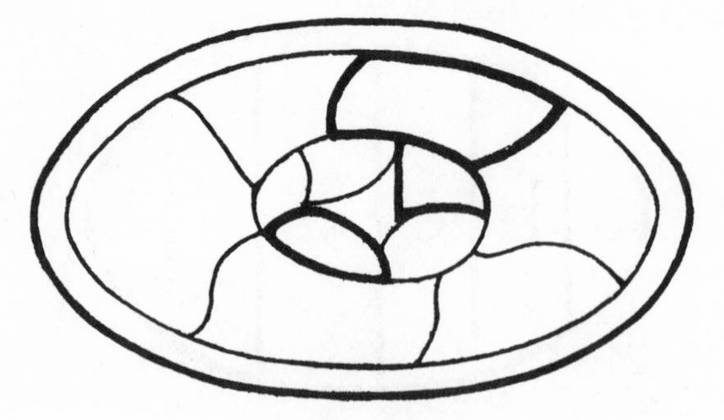

FIGURE 10

The Layers and Regions of Personality

seldom exposed except to one's most intimate associates, and very little influenced by outside events.

Some areas of the personality could interact with other areas; other processes were isolated into what was known as "logic tight compartments". In Figure 10 the lines drawn between regions indicate boundaries between processes. Heavy lines indicate impermeable areas, those which cannot be influenced by others. Light lines indicate borders over which interactions occur freely. In some people all boundaries were impermeable. In others all regions were open to influence from all others. The degree of interaction possible among various aspects of personality was one facet of a dimension of life space which Lewin called differentiation. Another facet was the number of regions which exist.

In a child there were a few simple, basic regions. With increasing experience, more and more needs, attitudes, and beliefs were established; that is, more regions were formed. In adults, there were a number of highly differentiated regions. The number of regions depended on the complexity of the individual. A feeble-minded person should have a less differentiated life space than a genius. But aside from complexity of personality, the degree of differentiation was also determined by the larger situation in which the person was functioning. A person under stress could find himself subject to such strong influence of one or two regions that, for the time being, it was as if his life space were made up only of these regions. Thus, the location of an individual's life space on the *dimension of differentiation* was a complex resultant from the individual's age, experience, capacity, and his present situation.

Besides differentiation, life space could be described in two other dimensions. There was, first, the *dimension of reality-irreality*. Occasionally, Lewin said, life space corresponded very closely to the real world, and the individual was said to be in touch with reality. At the other extreme there were individuals who lived in a world of fantasy; their life space was a complete distortion of the world about them. It was assumed that the life space of adults was more nearly a representation of reality than the life space of children, and that normal persons of any age were more realistic than the emotionally disturbed.

The third dimension of life space proposed by Lewin was *time perspective*. As a person became older he was able to exist in a broader time perspective, including his past, present, and future, while the small child lived completely in the present and determined his behavior only by the present situation. The span of time incorporated in one's life space, including remote causal events and future implications of acts, varied from individual to individual.

The field of study to which Lewin chose to address himself, the life space of an individual, was obviously a complex matter requiring not only special concepts, but also special methods. Indeed, the field was more complex than for most theories because the concepts and methods were mutually dependent upon each other.

Methods of Investigation

Lewin's main contribution to both theory and method was the adoption of special mathematical and geometric tools for representing life space. In testing his theory, once it was derived, he preferred natural experiments using everyday experiences and events. Abstract theoretical constructs were thus made practical and applied in a concrete manner. When he became involved in the study of group dynamics he used the same approach: first, abstract conceptual instruments, followed by concrete demonstrations and applications. The mathematics of Lewin's theory are so complex and technical that they can be understood only by a specialist, so that for our purposes it is sufficient merely to acknowledge their existence.

In addition to methods he developed, Lewin was well known as a critic of psychological theory and a commentator on scientific method. In a famous paper (1935, pp. 1–42), which appeared before the concern over the philosophy of science became so trenchant, Lewin attempted to stimulate a more scientific approach to psychology. In this famous analysis Lewin compared the state of science in general with the contrasting modes of thought represented by *Galilean* and *Aristotelian* physics and philosophical outlook. He considered Aristotelian physics "pre-scientific" because it classified objects into general groups or categories. In modern physics, categorical concepts have been replaced by more functional concepts. Physics no longer employs distinct classes composed of opposite types; it conceives of phenomena as describable in a number of dimensions, each dimension being represented along a continuum so that each event is varyingly similar and different from all others.

Another contrast is the criteria for lawfulness. To Aristotle lawfulness was based on frequency; if a thing occurred frequently, it was assumed to be lawful, and generalizations about its occurrence were scientific laws. Lawful things occurred regularly with no exceptions; therefore, something which appeared only once could not be lawful. Lawfulness, conceived of in this manner, was a census of vital statistics. In contrast, the Galilean approached equated lawfulness with the establishment of relationships between events. Ordinarily events are the result of several antecedent events in addition to the variable in question. A law derived merely by counting occurrences can easily overlook, or overemphasize, some of these events. Moreover, given variability of antecedent events, inconsistency can be as logical as consistency. From the Galilean point of view, things which can happen only once, or perhaps cannot take place at all, might not only be lawful, but may even be the best illustrations of scientific laws. For example, nobody has yet been able to produce a complete vacuum, yet speculation about what could come about under such circumstances has been very useful in helping physicists to understand much about the behavior of gases, the action of gravity, and many other physical phenomena.

In Aristotelian science, things were similar only if they appeared to be so on the surface. In Galilean physics, on the other hand, it is often possible to discover that two apparently different phenomena are actually subject to the same laws. Thus the action of a pendulum and the speed of a falling feather have little in common on the surface, but they are both a function of gravity. To develop the point further, Lewin appealed to genetics, from which he borrowed the terms *phenotype* and *genotype*. In genetics it is assumed that a person's appearance, his observable physical characteristics, are determined by dominant genes, and that in addition to these dominant characteristics there may be a number of other recessive characteristics represented in his genetic structure. These may be passed on to his child, but they are not observable in the individual because they are dominated by other stronger genes. An individual's appearance, then, is called his phenotype, and his genetic characteristics, overt and covert, make up what is know as his genotype. These two are not necessarily synonymous, for what a person looks like is not necessarily evidence of all the genes he possesses. Aristotelian science concentrated on the phenotype, Galilean on the genotype. The attempt to understand basic rather than superficial relationships obviated the necessity for classification and encouraged science to seek a new, more elastic interpretation of events in terms of a continuum of variation. The result was that the Galilean scientist was essentially oriented to observe function, and not structure or content. Things were categorized and explained on the basis of what they did, rather than on how they looked.

With the Galilean physicist's mounting aspirations for research into the nature of events, the task of describing individual cases became more important. This need for precise description was the real impetus to quantification in physics. Aristotelian scientists employed naturalistic observation in an effort to see things as they actually happened. They were not concerned with isolating and examining the pure case. When the Galilean physicists sought for pure cases, they found that control of external variables, manipulation of causal variables, and both quantitative and qualitative description were required to provide adequate answers to the questions they were asking.

Lewin pointed out that psychological theories tended to employ the rigid categorization, the statistical concept of lawfulness, the phenotypic as opposed to the genotypic approach, and observational, descriptive methods rather than controlled experimentation and quantitative measures. Lewin therefore concluded that much of psychology was prescientific.

Principles

In many ways Lewin's work represents a meta-theory, a theory about method and concepts, and not a body of speculation on some topic. Lewin was less interested in explaining psychological phenomena than in demonstrating how one might conceptualize and study psychological variables. The basic principle of Lewin's work was that these variables could be represented mathematically. The theory was characterized by the principle of multiple causation. Lewin and his followers did not believe that events were the result of one and only one cause. Events were usually formed by a number of interacting forces.

Lewin believed, moreover, that it was possible to understand a phenomenon without digging back into the past to discover the cause. If something happens in the present, it can be understood in terms of the present forces acting on the organism. The past and future might in some way be represented in the present life space and as such be influential, but for the most part Lewin preferred to overlook this representation and to propose a completely ahistorical explanation of causality.

Consciousness

Lewin did not speak of consciousness *per se*, but had much to say about the structure of the mind. He felt that the mind was composed of a number of regions, i.e., systems or processes. Some of these regions interacted and communicated with others, thereby making up a broader, more inclusive system within consciousness. Other aspects of mental phenomena were entirely isolated. For example, a person might have a number of interacting attitudes about social philosophies, legal developments, economic events, minority groups, labor, management, and so forth, all of which comprised his political attitude. This might be important in determining his behavior and might influence his reactions in many different spheres. On the other hand, he might have a certain attitude about chocolate ice cream which was activated only in situations where he was faced with chocolate ice cream and which did not influence him under any other conditions.

In discussing the structure of mind, Lewin stressed that earlier theories had spoken of the associative bond between mental processes as if it were a physical connection. Stimuli were believed to possess a kind of adhesion to certain reactions. This adhesion was regarded as determining the course of the event. In opposition to this, Lewin proposed that we could understand mental events only as a whole and could not break them down into parts that happen to adhere together. Thinking and behavior must instead be seen as a sequence of interacting and co-acting events which went to make up a pattern of incidents, that is, a Gestalt.

Sensation, Perception, and Discrimination

It has been difficult, in many of the theories which have been discussed, to separate sensation from perception, since they were made almost synonymous. Lewin, however, did assign a particular role to sensation, or rather to the concept of stimulus. In order for any process to occur, energy capable of doing work must be set free. One must therefore find out where the stimulus released energy by activating the sensory organ. This energy was transmitted through the nervous system until it reached various motor neurons and activated them.

Lewin pointed out that it was not the intensity or the physical characteristics of the stimulus which were important in determining response, but the psychological or social meaning of them. Stimulus or sensation must be judged in terms of its psychological reality rather than its physical intensity. Perception was the process by which the physical intensity or the physical reality was interpreted in terms of psychological reality. It was a process of reorganizing sensory input.

Perception of an object could create tension which did not exist before perception occurred; it could raise what was previously a relatively minor tension to dominance in the hierarchy. (Tension was equivalent to arousal of a motive state.) When this happened the object perceived was said to have *valence*, i.e. positive, approach-initiating value, or negative avoidance-initiating value. Valence arose according to whether the object was known to reduce or increase tension and operated in the same way as field forces did in the sense that it steered psychical processes. As the perceived environment led to some sort of action on the part of the organism, it made certain certain changes in its life space or its environment which it in turn perceived and interpreted in reference to its course of action. This interpretation guided the further action, determining whether it would be continued or altered. This was the concept of *feedback*.

In summary, besides organizing sensory input, perception functioned to direct behavior by rendering the organism aware of the value of objects in the environment, and later by helping the organism, by means of feedback, to orient itself to the consequences of its own action.

Thinking, Cognition, and Memory

In Lewin's terms, thinking was *locomotion* (symbolic or implicit). It was the means by which a person moved mentally from one region to another, i.e., the way relationships were perceived. It also referred to the same sort of process as Tolman's vicarious trial-and-error, wherein behavior was apparently tried out in one's mind before it was overtly performed. Locomotion in Lewin's sense had the connotation of mental manipulation of situations. It was a motivated act brought about by certain forces and directed by these forces to certain goals. Except for what excess meaning may accrue as a result of the new term, Lewin's theory of cognition was not markedly different from that of the Gestaltists.

Emotion and Motivation

Lewin assumed that the basic motivation in any organism was the need to maintain equilibrium. If something happened to disturb this equilibrium, locomotion, actual or psychological, was initiated and perpetuated until balance was restored. The principle of equilibrium applied only to the organism as a whole, however. Various part processes of the organism might actually be placed in a state of disequilibrium in order that eventual equilibrium might be restored as quickly as possible. Lewin illustrated this matter of disturbance in a part process for the purpose of maintaining equilibrium of the whole organism by reference to detour behavior. An animal faced with a barrier between himself and a goal might, under certain conditions, actually move away from the goal momentarily, thereby increasing the tension and disequilibrium in one region of his personality. This increase was necessary if the animal was to get around the barrier and achieve the total equilibrium which the goal offered.

Equilibrium did not signify a lack of tension or an absence of active forces. When there was equilibrium there might still be active forces of tremendous intensity in counterbalance, each checking and controlling the effects of the others. Organisms might, of course, establish equilibrium at low degrees of tension and probably were more comfortable there, but they could also establish equilibrium at very high degrees of tension. At least insofar as social phenomena were concerned, Lewin referred to these high tension states as *quasi-stationary equilibria* or *dynamic equilibria*. That is, a series of ongoing and interacting forces which co-act in such a way as to control each other mutually, and so maintain a balance. The organism was moving and dynamic but in equilibrium at the same time. The balance among directing forces was the product or resultant of their interaction. The smooth consistent flow of events was brought about by this balance.

The state in any one region was to some degree independent of the state in other regions. That is, there was not a perfect correlation among the conditions in all regions. If regions were related, they were more likely to be in the same state at the same time. Events which disturbed or enhanced the state of one region were likely to have the same effect on related regions, while they left unrelated regions alone, or affected them diversely. For example, if a person wanted money, had a desire for status, and enjoyed exercising his skills as a leader, a promotion from a job as a blue collar worker to a supervisory position would establish equilibrium in several regions but would not affect his enjoyment of fishing. The more regions brought to equilibrium, the more stable and predictable the person's behavior. To continue the example, if the person's new supervisory position allowed him to remain loyal to his union affiliations, he was more likely to remain on the job than if, despite its other rewards, the new position were incompatible with his union sympathies. In this latter case, equilibrium might be impossible and subsequent behavior eratic and inconsistent because a conflict had been created.

In addition to initiating forces, there was another aspect of motivation, the valence or value of the goal object. The concept of valence was introduced when we discussed perception, since valence derived from the way an object was perceived. The concept of valence was borrowed from chemistry and retained approximately the same meaning. In chemistry there are elements which have a positive charge and others which have a negative charge. The charge can be weak or strong, and can vary in its location (to translate atomic theory loosely). Psychological valences also had sign, intensity, and distribution, since various goal objects were located in different parts of the person's life space. The valence of an object usually derived from the fact that it was a means of satisfying a need or was associated with need satisfaction and accordingly led the person to approach or avoid it. The valence of goal objects for approach-type motives was of rather obvious origin. It corresponded to the concept of incentive proposed by other psychologists. It might at first seem inconsistent to state that avoidance motives also have goal objects. A moment's consideration, however, will reveal that different objects in a situation will offer varying degrees of possibility for escape or termination, and consequently will have differing positive valences (or incentive values), while the objects to be avoided will have negative valences of varying intensity.

Lewin spoke of the possibility of inducing valences. This aspect of the theory of valence seems to correspond to what is elsewhere called secondary reinforcement and secondary motivation. A goal with a very strong valence was so influential that all objects in the field surrounding it acquired value by being near it. Tools employed in reaching goals likewise came to have an induced value. If, for example, social conformity is seen as a means of achieving personal security, it will come to have value of its own. Valence, like reinforcement, demonstrated spread of effect, as indeed it should since both terms refer to the same general phenomenon.

Besides the driving forces and their goal objects, Lewin also recognized certain restraining forces which blocked movement toward or away from a goal. They also had a directive effect on behavior, stopping it entirely or altering its course, sometimes temporarily, sometimes permanently. An organism faced with a barrier might attempt to skirt the restraint, to engage in some substitute act or detour behavior, or it might become frustrated. Frustration led to anger, withdrawal, or in its extreme form to neurotic or psychotic behaviors. Barriers did not motivate behavior in the same sense as the various approach and avoidance motives. They simply altered whatever force was acting. A barrier could, of course, acquire negative valence, especially if it were frequently experienced, and through this induced or derived valence could come to have some secondary powers of avoidance motivation.

Driving forces and barriers had the potential to initiate or change behavior since they always led to locomotion as a necessary prerequisite to establishing equilibrium. This might be either motoric locomotion about the physical environment or cognitive activity in which the person worked out a problem in his mind. The forces acting on the person determined the direction of the locomotion and its strength through their *point of application.* Not only did motives determine what should be done and how, but also whether it was the person himself, some particular aspect of his self, or some environmental object which must be moved, altered, or manipulated.

To summarize briefly, any time that forces acted in contradictory directions they created disequilibrium and in turn motivated actions which reinstated equilibrium. The valence of goal objects present in the space determined the direction of this action although the action might be redirected by the presence of barriers. What was acted upon, the self or the environment, depended upon the nature of the activated forces.

It sometimes happened that the forces active at a particular time required more than one sort of action. If the actions were complementary, or if the forces had a neutral effect on each other, they might all be resolved at once if some act restored equilibrium to several regions at one time. Or, if one set of forces was much stronger than the other, then general equilibrium could be restored, albeit at a high level of tension, if and when the major force was resolved. But when aroused forces were approximately equal in strength and opposite in nature, the individual was in conflict and equilibrium could not be established.

Lewin conceived of conflict in much the same way as Neal Miller (Chapter 11) did. Both spoke of various types of conflict: opposition between two positive valences or forces (approach-approach conflict), opposition between negative valences or forces (avoidance-avoidance conflict), and opposition between positive and negative forces (approach-avoidance conflict). Lewin treated approach-approach and avoidance-avoidance conflict much as Miller did, but enlarged somewhat on the approach-avoidance conflict. He stated that if that latter type of conflict endured over any period of time, the negative force would gradually become stronger than the positive force. At this point the organism sought to go out of the field if it could. *Going out of the field* has more meaning when one recalls that Lewin was speaking of the life space as a field. The person presented with such a conflict situation attempted to escape entirely from this particular aspect of his life space. The approach-avoidance conflict could be solved if either force were changed by a large amount. Lesser alterations either postponed conflict momentarily or intensified it. A small reduction in avoidance or negative valence still left that motive active enough to interfere. Minor increases in the positive valence or the approach force built up the level of tension. They also made substitute behavior, or detouring, more difficult by rendering it harder for the person to turn away from the positive goal.

Lewin's treatment of motivation escaped the ordinary problems which beset concepts of drive, motive, or purpose, and at the same time provided a thorough coverage of the matter. It had the added advantage of equating human behavior with behavior of physical objects, although some theorists feel this destroys human uniqueness. However, the dignity of humanity is probably sufficiently restored in Lewin's theory of learning.

The Nature of the Learning Process

Lewin described four types of changes in behavior which he believed would correspond to different varieties of learning. First there was the acquisition of knowledge, which effected a change in cognitive structure, altering the patterning or the complexity of interactions in a particular region. A second type of learning involved changes in motivation. Still another type was the alteration of voluntary control of body musculature. Each of these, cognitive restructuring, motivational change, and motor control, were basic types of learning, described by different laws and referred to different aspects of the psychological field.

The final type, social learning, included the establishment or alteration of role behavior and the expectations one had of himself and others in interpersonal situations. It accounted for acculturation and identification with the group. Lewin did not believe that social learning was really a separate variety. Phenotypically it was somewhat different in that its content was distinctive, referring purely to the interpersonal sphere. Genotypically, however, it was a result of differentiating the social structure in which one lived, socializing one's motives, and bringing one's motor behavior under group control.

Cognitive Restructuring. Change in the cognitive structure ordinarily took place as a result of differentiation of life space. Objects or relationships which were not previously noticed became important; what was part of ground came to be figure. This type of learning was illustrated by the person who came to a strange town and gradually learned its geography: where the hotel is, where the streets lead, and so forth. It is by this same process that the newborn infant slowly learns to distinguish himself from his environment.

Sometimes a change in cognitive structure occurred without increase or decrease in the degree of differentiation. It was merely that the regions in the life space which had previously been separate could now be connected as a result of the perception of previously unrealized relationships (insight). The discovery that the action of a pendulum and the fall of a feather can be described genotypically by the same physical law is an example of this type of restructuring.

Another way in which cognitive restructuring could take place was through a change in the time perspective or in the degree of reality or irreality which the person attributed to some particular thought, idea, or region. In plain language, the person might come to see things as nearer or more distant in the future, or he might come to realize that some idea is not realistic, or that some erstwhile fantasy is true.

Cognitive restructuring was stimulus learning and was based primarily on contiguity. Reinforcement had secondary importance not affecting the learning process itself, but acting indirectly upon mechanical aspects which affect learning. Reinforcement influenced the motivational state, altering the valence of goal objects. Goals with positive valence were more vivid, and consequently easier to differentiate from the surrounding field. With continued reinforcement the drive state was altered, reducing valence and rendering a goal less attractive as it became less necessary. Aside from its effects on motives which indirectly influenced learning, reinforcement acted to protect the established cognitive structure from some inadvertent disruption. It kept the person in the situation, and maintained the act, thought, or perception until contiguity could bring about the necessary restructuring.

Motivational Change. Contiguity was also the basis for learning or changing motives. For example, a previously neutral object or act might come to be perceived as pleasant, and therefore desirable, since it was contiguous with pleasant stimuli (a case of induced valence). Because contiguity was based on induction, one could bring about changes in motivation by physically forcing a person to do something which he previously was not motivated to do. Thus he was gradually made aware of a new set of relationships in his environment, with the result that his motivational pattern was changed. This occasionally had the undesirable side effect of making the demanded activity more distasteful. It was therefore more effective to change motivation by positive appeal rather than force. In many cases, for example, instructing the person in the desirability of the new motive led to change. This instruction could be done best in a group setting where group change could support individual change.

The influence and efficacy of groups on acquisition of motive states led Lewin to conclude that much of what he classed as social learning was really a change in valence or motive. Motivational change became an important aspect of Lewin's learning theory.

Motor Learning. There was little to suggest that Lewin concerned himself much with the nature of motor learning. This is not surprising in a theory where cognitive and motivational aspects were the central focus.

Behavior and Personality

Although he developed his theory to deal with individual behavior, Lewin also found it applicable to the behavior of groups. As time passed he concentrated more and more upon this area, eventually creating a sub-science known as Group Dynamics, which is perhaps the major focus of those who follow Lewin's theories today. This is not to imply that the rest of the theory has fallen into disuse, for much research has been stimulated by it. But the emphasis of both research and theoretical developments is on groups. It is relevant to consider Group Dynamics here since it is that aspect of Lewin's work which involves the most molar view of behavior.

The groups Lewin dealt with were not composed of a number of loosely related persons, but rather of individuals acting as a unit, and therefore possessing certain structural properties characterized by relationships between parts. The group operated in a social field just as an individual operated in a life space. It was subject to a number of impinging forces and sought, like the individual, to maintain an equilibrium, ordinarily of the quasi-stationary or dynamic variety.

Perhaps a study done by Lewin, Lippitt and White (1939) will help to give an example of what was meant by the equilibrium and the changes of forces in a social group. These authors set up three experimental boys' clubs in order to study the effects of different kinds of leadership. One group was highly autocratic, one was democratic, and one was characterized as *laissez-faire*. The authors studied the level of aggression and the general quality of productivity of the boys in each of these conditions. They also studied what happened when they changed from one kind of leadership to another. In the autocratic group the boys behaved in a restricted fashion, showing relatively little aggressiveness except toward certain scapegoats within the group. When the boys changed out of the autocratic group into either of the others, their aggression mounted for some time. It seemed as if their frustration in the autocratic group, and the sudden removal of controls against reacting to it, led them to express an extraordinary amount of anger. Once the various forces acting within them returned to equilibrium, the aggressiveness disappeared and the productiveness of the boys increased. Boys placed in the autocratic group after taking part in one of the others tended to be rebellions, or at least to express temporary dissatisfaction, but gradually conformed to the leader. Boys taking part in the laissez-faire groups acted quite independently of each other. They appeared lost and confused. They started out being productive, but as the group fell apart the quality of their work was reduced. The democratic atmosphere resulted in the highest quality of work, and the members seemed to be less hostile and more friendly to each other. Morale was generally higher in this group and most, but not all, of the boys preferred it.

Other examples of the application of concepts of force and equilibrium to group situations are found in Lewin's work in industrial situations (1947A, 1947B). Factories are in some ways ideal laboratories in which to study group phenomena. Productivity and morale are ready-made criteria with which to demonstrate the influence of various forces. Productivity is held down by such factors as discontent, group norms determining production level, the strain of hard, fast work, or the desire to protect less adequate members of the work force from undue competition. Productivity is encouraged by the desire to make money, the need to improve status, or the recognition of society's need for the product. In a smoothly running plant the productivity of the various members usually became fairly constant. The constancy suggested to Lewin that an equilibrium must have been established among the various factors involved in production. If such an equilibrium existed, and it becomes necessary to change the level of production, one must first disrupt the original balance among the forces. This could be done by changing the intensity of the forces or the valences involved, and/or by introducing new ones. One must then establish a new equilibrium and freeze the forces into a new relationship.

How to change productivity became a problem Lewin set for himself in seeking some means of encouraging employees to adopt new work habits to cope with the emergency created by World War II. After trying a number of techniques, Lewin found that group decision was the most effective way. He would bring the workers in, have them discuss the situation in a democratic manner, and then vote on the request for higher productivity. The discussion concerning the necessity for higher production was seen in Lewinian context as a process of destroying or breaking down the old equilibrium. The request for a vote was a means of establishing the new equilibrium. Furthermore, since it was a group action in which all members supported the goal, the new level of productivity became a group value. To maintain one's membership in the group, one had to conform. Group decision tended therefore to solidify or freeze the new equilibrium.

The superiority of the group decision method over other methods of inducing group change has been demonstrated many times by Lewin and his followers. Besides industrial studies, the technique has been employed in persuading people to eat certain types of food, or to feed their children more codliver oil, more orange juice, etc. (Lewin, 1942, 1943B).

Lewin also utilized a related means of changing various social habits. In many cases there was a key member within the group who was instrumental in maintaining a certain kind of behavior. By manipulating this key member one could change the behavior of the whole group. Lewin's experimental work (1947C) with this technique involved changing food habits of families. It was assumed that the housewife was the key member, or *gate keeper* as Lewin called her, determining the family's taste in food. Lewin proposed that some means of changing the gate keeper's (housewife's) attitude would change the whole family's food habits. With this as a prototype, Lewin generalized that in any attempt to produce social change the first task would be to find the gate keeper and study his behavior, and then to establish the desired social change through him. Using the gate keeper as a lever is far more efficient than trying to change a group of individuals singly or collectively. The key person can produce change because of his status and function in the group and because of his access to those regions where change is to occur. He can induce change directly or can in some way create a role for himself which induces it indirectly.

While group dynamics was the major focus of Lewin's social psychology, he was also interested in other ears. In one paper Lewin (1948) contrasted the German and the American personality, pointing out the differences in the permeability of the boundaries in life space in the two countries. Germans, he said, have sufficiently firm boundaries that casual social acquaintances did not penetrate beyond the superficial regions. A German did not tell his income, personal problems, or marital discords to people he knew only slightly. In contrast, the inner regions of personality were easily accessible to those few persons who were really intimate with an individual. A German could reveal his "innermost self" to his friends without reservation. The American personality was the opposite, said Lewin. The outer, superficial regions of personality were completely open, so that one would discuss with casual acquaintances events of home and business life which were quite personal. At the same time, few people, if any, were ever admitted into the "inner regions." Indeed, these regions were often unknown to the individual himself.

Another area of interest to Lewin was the problem created by minority group status. Lewin was particularly concerned with Jewish culture in this respect. He pointed out (1948) that many Jews, because they grow up as a minority, come to accept the values of the majority group which surround them. Not only are the general social values taken over, but the majority group attitudes toward the Jews are also acquired. Consequently, many Jews come to feel they are members of an undesirable, distasteful group and perceive the majority group as more desirable. Such devaluing of one's self and one's group is likely to induce a wish to identify with the majority group. An individual in this frame of mind resents his group for holding him back, and hates his fellow Jews and himself for what they are said to be. Lewin called this phenomenon *negative chauvinism*. Unfortunately, leaders of a minority often came from this self-hating fringe. This had the effect of rendering the minority even less cohesive. A disorganized group had little to offer in a positive sense. The minority culture would deteriorate under these circumstances. At the same time, a minority individual striving for majority acceptance was a threat to the larger group and more liable to rejection than a defensively Jewish person, content to remain in the minority. By setting up some sort of cohesive group spirit in the minority, Lewin felt that the members would be less insecure and might gradually work out some healthy means of achieving group acceptance.

Critique

Much praise is due Lewin for his successful attempt to apply some quantitative technique to psychological data. In addition, he produced many useful ideas, particularly those dealing with the concepts of motivating forces and valences, and suggested a useful way of looking at people and the events that go on inside them. However, his attempts at mathematical quantification or description have not made his concepts easier to understand and communicate. Regardless of how simple the mathematical formulae may appear, it is very hard to tell anyone else what he is quantifying. For many psychologists terms such as *region, boundary, locomotion*, and *life space* take on popular or common sense meanings quite apart from those Lewin intended. Granted that this is a common hazard when trying to develop a psychological vocabulary, it can be intensified if the theorist provides only highly abstract definitions. Lewin's theory is a model, however, and the test of it comes not from how easily the neophyte can understand it, but from its usefulness and validity as a rich source of stimulating hypotheses. One's total impression is of a markedly successful record of validation of the theory.

Like all doctrines, Lewin's theory has inspired a religious and often missionary fervor. It is difficult for a person steeped in field theory to see the world and the people in it in any other light. This is true of, and detrimental to, any dogma, but when a scientific theory incorporates social values within its hypotheses, issues are likely to be clouded. For example, the ordinary follower of Lewin's theory of group dynamics is laudably democratic. But when persons brought up in different cultures do not respond to democracy, group dynamics cannot explain why, and both science and society suffer from the theoretical block imposed by a value-oriented formulation.

SUMMARY

Basic Unit. The basic unit for Lewin, as for any Gestaltist, was the whole experience.

Field of Study. Psychology should study the individual in his life space and how he moves (locomotes) from one thought or idea or perception or action (region of life space) to another. The individual personality was composed of a number of regions, some peripheral and easily observed, others covert. Some of these regions interacted, others were isolated. Life space possessed several dimensions: amount of differentiation, degree of reality, and time perspective.

Methods of Investigation. One of Lewin's greatest contributions was his technique of mathematical representation of life space. He also invented various means of studying dynamics of groups. In addition he played the role of critic, pointing out how psychology was in many ways Aristotelian, i.e., pre-scientific. These pre-scientific characteristics included psychology's penchant for dealing with rigid categories and its construction of laws based on frequency of an event under the assumption that what happens most often is lawful. Exceptions to a law were viewed as just that. They were seen as having no effect on the validity of the laws, whereas to a more Galilean (scientific) thinker they might suggest a need for revision of the law. Psychology was also Aristotelean in describing its subject matter phenotypically, according to surface appearances rather than to underlying seterminants; it neglected the need for controlled experiments; it avoided quantification. To these problems Lewin directed himself, as his principles reveal.

Principles. Most phenomena were caused by not one, but a number of forces. Events could be understood in reference to the present life space alone; past and future need not be considered. The phenomena of psychology could be described mathematically.

Consciousness. Mind was composed of a number of regions or processes, some interrelated, some isolated.

Sensation, Perception, and Discrimination. Stimuli released energy which activated a sensory organ and then entered the nervous system to initiate further reactions in the brain and motor centers. Perception was a matter of recognizing the social meaning of sensory input. The objects perceived attracted or repelled, initiating and directing behavior through the valence they possessed for the organism.

Thinking, Cognition, and Memory. Thinking was a matter of locomotion, or mental movement from one region to another.

Emotion, Motivation, and Purpose. The basic motive of any organism was to maintain equilibrium. Any disturbance aroused cognitive processes and motivated activities aimed at restoring balance. In the process of establishing equilibrium in the whole organism some regions might be disrupted for the total good. Equilibrium did not necessarily imply a complete lack of tension, for it might also connote a balance of forces. Beyond locating forces inside or outside the person, and describing their direction (approach or avoidance) and goal, Lewin did not catalog specific motives. He concerned himself instead with the role of valence, barriers, etc., in the motivational process. The valence of the goal object, he said, served as a secondary source of motivation. Valence was not only attached to goal objects, but could also be induced into previously neutral objects closely connected to the goal. Barriers acted to direct or alter a course of action and could acquire negative valence which gave them powers of secondary motivation. The motivating property of driving forces, valences, and barriers was their ability to initiate locomotion. If several incompatible forces acted upon the organism they propelled locomotion in several directions at the same time, and the result was a conflict. Lewin, like Miller, classed conflicts into approach-approach, avoidance-avoidance, and approach-avoidance.

The Nature of the Learning Process. Lewin conceived of several different types of learning. The first basic type was acquisition of knowledge. It came about through the restructuring of the cognitive field by means of differentiation or insight, or through alteration in perspective so that temporal or reality relations were perceived differently. Cognitive restructuring was a function of contiguity. Reinforcement had minor importance as a means of holding the person in the field and preventing him from varying his behavior. The second type of learning was a matter of altering motivations so that neutral objects came to have valence not attributed to them before. This type was also based upon contiguity. Motor learning, the third basic type, was not described in detail. A fourth variety of learning, social learning, was recognized but not considered basic. It was distinctive because it referred to acquisition of new thoughts, ideas, and actions in the interpersonal sphere. Its underlying process was, however, a matter of acquiring knowledge, motives, and motor habits.

Behavior and Personality. Although Lewin's theory was set up to describe intrapersonal phenomena, it was found to be extremely useful in prediction and control of group behavior. In point of fact, the applications of Lewin's theory of Group Dynamics are the most vital aspect of his theory today. The group was conceived as a Gestalt, subject to various external and internal forces which must be held in equilibrium if the group were to continue. The social field determined the attitude, the productivity, and the cohesiveness of the group. Values were easily changed in group situations because of the interpersonal support each member received in attempting his change. Sometimes the behavior of whole groups could be changed by altering the attitudes of one key member or gate keeper. Lewin also considered cultural variations, including the manner in which our society determines the availability of various regions for social intercourse, and the effects of minority group status on attitudes toward one's self and one's peers.

REFERENCES

Kurt Lewin

Barker, R. G., T. Dembo, and K. Lewin, *Frustration and Regression: An Experiment with Young Children.* Univ. of Iowa Stud. Child Welfare 18: No. 1 (1941).

Leeper, R., *Lewin's Topological and Vector Psychology: A Digest and a Critique.* Eugene, Oregon: Univ. of Oregon Press, 1943.

Lewin, K., *A Dynamic Theory of Personality.* New York: McGraw-Hill, 1935.

———, *Principles of Topological Psychology.* New York: McGraw-Hill, 1936.

———, "Psychoanalysis and Topological Psychology," *Bull. Menninger Clin.* 1: 202–211 (1937).

———, "The Conceptual Representation and the Measurement of Psychological Forces," *Contr. Psychol. Theor.* 1: No. 4 (1938).

———, "The Relative Effectiveness of a Lecture Method and a Method of Group Decision for Changing Food Habits," Committee on Food Habits, *National Research Council*, 1942.

———, "Defining the 'Field' at a Given Time," *Psychol. Rev.* 50: 292–310 (1943). (A) Reprinted in M. H. Marx, ed., *Psychological Theory*, New York: Macmillan, 1951, pp. 299–315.

———, "Forces Behind Food Habits and Methods of Change," *Bull. of Nat'l Res. Counc.* 108: 35–65 (1943). (B)

———, "Group Decision and Social Change," in T. H. Newcomb and E. L. Hartley, eds., *Readings in Social Psychology*, New York: Holt, 1947, pp. 459–473. (A)

———, "Frontiers in Group Dynamics. I. Concept, Method, and Reality in Social Science; Social Equilibria and Social Change," *Hum. Rel.* 1: 5–41 (1947). (B)

———, "Frontiers in Group Dynamics. II. Channels of Group Life; Social Planning and Action Research," *Hum. Rel.* 1: 143–153 (1947). (C)

———, *Resolving Social Conflicts*. New York: Harper, 1948.

———, T. Dembo, L. Festinger, and P. S. Sears, "Level of Aspiration," in J. McV. Hunt, ed., *Handbook of Personality and Behavior Disorders*, New York: Ronald, 1944, pp. 333–378.

———, R. Lippitt, and R. K. White, "Patterns of Aggressive Behavior in Experimentally Created 'Social Climates,'" *J. Soc. Psychol.* 10: 271–299 (1939).

PART VII

INDIVIDUAL PSYCHOLOGIES

CHAPTER 25

GORDON ALLPORT'S TRAIT PSYCHOLOGY (1937 TO 1967)

GORDON ALLPORT was not so much the founder of a separate system of psychology as a spokeman for a point of view concerning personality theory. In many ways his approach to psychology was eclectic. He took from all theories that which he found acceptable and welded a theory from this material, tying it together with co-ordinating concepts of his own. The final product contained recognizable elements of Behaviorism, Gestalt theory, Psychoanalysis, and much material from general and social psychology. His organization and the concepts he introduced, however, created a fresh and penetrating interpretation.

Basic Unit

Allport wished to develop a theory which could focus on the single case and allow for a scientific appreciation of its distinct individuality. The usual search for psychological elements in the form of needs, factors, or habits he found sterile because it neglected the individual and addressed itself to classes of behavior. Allport was aware of the necessity for some sort of descriptive concepts to apply to psychological data, but he wanted concepts which concentrated on the person rather than on some abstract aspect of behavior. Habit was too narrow and incapable of containing the rich connotations of individuality. The complete personality, taken at once, was too broad to be digested conceptually. The element which psychology must seek as its basic tool for understanding must be somewhere in between.

Allport found his answer in the concept of traits, not as adjectives describing static features, but as constructs inferred from behavior, describing some determining tendency or readiness to respond in a certain way, and appearing in behavior as habitual responses. Traits were generalized from an originally specific action to a series of related acts; they were self-perpetuating constellations of potentials for behavior, existing autonomously of the individual's biology but possessing the capacity to create new habits to gratify biological or personal needs. As determining tendencies, traits had something in common with motives, but they were expressive as well as directive. They also bore some resemblance to attitudes, except that they did not involve value and had no object of reference. The concept of trait as employed by Allport resembled many other psychological concepts, but had a distinctive flavor of its own. Allport summarized these qualities in his definition of trait:

> "a neuropsychic structure having the capacity to render many stimuli functionally equivalent, and to initiate and guide equivalent (meaningfully consistent) forms of adaptive and expressive behavior" (1961, p. 347).

Allport emphasized the fact that traits were individual characteristics, and as such were not comparable between one individual and another. When it was necessary to discuss human behaviors apart from individual persons, the trait concept could be employed if it were done in such a way as to avoid a travesty on the nature of individuals. To aid in the distinction between traits as general phenomena and as individual characteristics, Allport coined the terms *common traits* and *personal dispositions*.

Common traits were categories "for classifying functionally equivalent forms of behavior in a general population of people. Though influenced by nominal and artifactual considerations, a common trait to some extent reflects veridical and comparable dispositions in many personalities who, because of a common nature and common culture, develop similar modes of adjusting to their environments, though to varying degrees." (1961, p. 349) When a trait was measured across individuals, its distribution was dependent upon its origin. If the trait was biologically determined its occurrence was purely random, and therefore was distributed normally. If it was socially or culturally determined, on the other hand, it distributed itself in such a way as to represent the force toward conformity to a norm. Most of the individuals tested demonstrated that degree of the trait which was the norm. A few showed greater variation, but the curve tailed off rapidly. The resulting curve of conformity resembled a "J" in shape, and was therefore called a *J curve*.

What was seen in the majority of persons in a culture did not describe or explain what was found in an individual personality organization. The unique attributes of an individual were called *personal dispositions* in an effort to emphasize their uniqueness. Not only were they the jigsaw bits which together composed a distinct person, but they were also the source of direction and consistency, for the dispositions all functioned to actualize and enhance the self.

Within an individual one could not speak of a distribution of personal dispositions, for distributions implied a number of equally possible occurrences, while personal dispositions, once established, would always lead to the same occurrence. One could only catalog or describe the unity and organization among various personal dispositions, and it was this effort that led to Allport's concern with assessment of personality.

Field of Study

Allport took great pains to distinguish his orientation from other popular view points in psychology. Insofar as his theory was eclectic, it was necessary for him to delimit whatever he accepted from each interpretation. In criticizing other theories he enumerated his reasons for proposing a new approach and indicated by negative example what he thought the subject matter of psychology should be.

While Allport's formulation focused on the individual, he rejected the study of individual differences as the proper focus of psychology because the individual was viewed only as a means to an end. The ordinary study in differential psychology investigated individual differences as a means of deriving classes of behavior rather than of understanding individuality *per se*. Such a method was too simple. Furthermore, its source of data was test scores, and scores alone could never describe personality adequately.

Psychoanalysis, for all of its concentration on the individual, was equally unacceptable to Allport. It, too, sought universal laws and tried to explain the individual in terms of the general. It was dogmatic and not given to tolerating ideas from any other source. It was only interested in pathology, not in normality, and it neglected much important information in its insistence that the bulk of personality was unconscious.

Allport found Gestalt psychology more fertile, for it concentrated on intra-individual organization, was aware of the need for genotypic as well as phenotypic scrutiny, and looked beyond habit to a psychology of patterned behavior. The Existentialist philosophers and some of the teachings of Zen Budhism also incorporated many concepts concerning the necessity of focusing on the individual as a whole, an approach which Allport found highly praiseworthy.

Allport believed that, psychologist's convictions to the contrary, science and the individual were not antitheses. It was possible to evolve a science of the individual whose laws dealt not with invariate classes, but with natural uniformities. Such a science was not, of course, sufficient to cover the data of psychology. This *idiographic* approach (which concentrated on particular events) must be complemented by a *nomothetic* approach which sought general laws. Allport admitted that his idiographic emphasis on traits must be accompanied by a nomothetic psychology, focusing on the unity of the individual.

Methods of Investigation

Allport became widely known as an authority on techniques for the investigation of individual personality. Among methods which he adapted to his purpose were anthropological observations, medical records, and records of various social institutions (schools, etc.). He recommended use of personal data (such as letters, diaries, conversations) and expressive movements (writing, gait, positive, etc.). He described behavioral ratings, test scores, miniature life situations, laboratory experiments, prediction studies, model-testing studies, and synthesizing studies (where life histories, interviews, and a battery of evaluation techniques were used to reconstruct a portrait of the individual personality). He urged that these idiographic techniques be employed in preference to the nomothetic devices such as standard IQ and personality tests. He felt that descriptions, not scores, were the data from which theory should be derived.

Principles

Personality was persistent yet dynamic, continuously changing yet limited in its change by what it was.

Physique, intelligence, and temperament were the building materials of personality. These factors were genetically determined, and environment had little influence over them.

Adaptive mechanisms were developed to bring these genetically determined aspects into the most efficient and productive interaction with the environment. They were instruments of growth, brought about by learning.

Personality was the mode of adjustment by which the individual coordinated his drives with his environment. Personality was a broad determinant which structured the adaptive mechanisms and was thereby reflected in every activity of the individual. Once established, a mechanism of adjustment could become *functionally autonomous* and direct behavior in its own right.

Development was the process of establishing a sense of self-identity, self-worth, and a life plan for self-actualization. There were no distinct stages in this process, but a constant, consistent flow of events from birth to death.

Motives and adaptive mechanisms might become independent of biology, but they were never independent of the ego. The involvement and gratification of ego (self-concept) was the basis of the acquisition and persistence of behavior patterns.

Consciousness

Allport leaned toward a phenomenal interpretation of consciousness. Consciousness could not be appreciated or described as an entity. The individual experienced, and psychology had consequently to study, not consciousness but one *moment* of consciousness in a stream of moments. These moments were focused on some one particular aspect of experience.

There was a distinction between consciousness and self-consciousness. Consciousness was a meaningless awareness, a mere registration of events. It occurred but had no function, as in the infant who lacked any differentiated experience with the world but who still appeared to register what was going on. Self-consciousness was the awareness not only of the event but of its meaning to the ego. Self-conscious awareness was learned through exposure to internal and external situations and their outcomes.

Pain, in the form of a threat of isolation from the social world, was the origin of self-awareness and consequently of conscious experience. Whenever some unpleasantness arose it was a threat to the organism and had to be resolved by appropriate adjustment of the organism and its environment if the organism was to survive. To make such adjustments, the organism had to discover which things it could control directly (the self), and which indirectly, or not at all (the not-self).

There were certain anchor points to the self-conscious experience, and all the events of our lives were organized around these points. They included one's name, reference groups, social role and status, and possessions. Everything meaningful was centered around some aspect of the self, so that all of one's life was quite literally self-centered.

Sensation, Perception, and Discrimination; Thinking, Cognition, and Memory

Perception and thought must be part of the same process. Any attempt at subdivision was merely naming some way stations in the course of events. All cognitive function was veridical, i.e., it reflected what was "really" going on because man must adjust to reality to survive. Survival, however, required more than the mirroring of events. The individual must select, he must use his experience, he must look for what he needed, he must defend against certain dangers. These effects were exercised upon cognitive function through sets and attitudes, which remained latent in a preparatory or *tonic* state until aroused by some cue, and then roused into a *phasic* state, actively fashioning behavior. The mirroring aspect Allport called *perception*, while the shaping, selecting, organizing, aspects he called *proception*. In addition to the number and content and the general complexity of the sets, individuals varied in the breadth and elasticity of their cognitive styles. Only those whose cognitive function permitted broad and flexible limits were able to achieve healthy adjustment; others became cognitive cripples.

Emotion and Motivation

Biological cravings were most important in infancy. Infants differ from each other, and could be characterized as individuals by their *motility* (amount of activity) and *temperament* (amount of emotionality). From earliest infancy the patterns of motility and temperament were consistent and predictable. To the degree that any single factor could be important, the most salient biological forces arose from the sexual and nutritional needs.

Personality developed as a mode of survival. In the beginning, it was the individual's peculiar means of meeting his biological needs. Adaption mechanisms were acquired gradually, and as they were acquired they created needs which had in turn to be met. These needs soon surpassed the biological needs in their importance as directive forces. The personality itself was thus the source of the motives which directed life.

Allport pointed out that the conceptual tools for an adequate theory of human motivation have been difficult to devise. Hedonism, for instance, could never explain activities which persisted in spite of unpleasant results. The concepts that instincts motivated human behavior was equally inadequate because these inborn behavioral orientations were too uncommon in man. Other concepts, such as fundamental needs, dependable motives, and drives avoided the problem of innate behaviors, but they were still inadequate because they were too heavily oriented towards tension reduction. Their explanations of the unchanging biological urges of man were useful only in situations where tension was present and demanded release. Man's social motives, or adaptive devices, often persisted, too, and their gratification required tension arousal rather than tension reduction. Men could be good, loyal, polite, studious, all apparently without regard for immediate reward and even in the face of considerable discomfort. Moreover, these behaviors seemed to originate in the present, and not in the past as those theories would require which based all acquired motivation on secondary reinforcement of primary drives.

An adequate theory of human motivation which could explain the ever-changing needs of the organism for growth, exploration, competence, and self-actualization had, according to Allport, to allow for contemporaneity of the motive, i.e., it must permit the motive to be brought about by present circumstances. It must also allow for a plurality of motives in human behavior. It must recognize the dynamic force of cognitive processes. It must employ unique and concrete bits of behavior, and not abstract classes of activity: for example, it must permit explanations such as "seeking praise" rather than "need-nurturance," or "hoping to be elected" rather than "need for mastery." Allport proposed his concept of functional autonomy of adjustive mechanisms to satisfy these requirements. According to his theory, functionally autonomous mechanisms became drives which were independent of their original cause and connected to it only historically. Among the best examples of Allport's functional autonomy are: the miser, the retired sailor, now a banker, who maintains a love of the sea, and whose early life imposed thrift but whose present miserliness is not compatible with the fortune he has amassed; the hill dweller moved to the city who longs for his native mountains; or the genius who slaves night and day out of love for his work. Functionally autonomous values which became extensions of the self were necessary for maturity. Autonomous interests in, for instance, work or contemplation or loyalty accelerated the maturation process.

There were two levels of functional autonomy. The simplest autonomous acts were *perseverative*, i.e., were initiated, carried out, and repeated apart from any cause or result other than their own occurrence. These perseverative acts included odd bits of expressive behavior (such as a constant, inappropriate, and unconscious smile), circular activities (like babbling in babies), and addictions. These acts had no purpose; they simply seemed to occur and to continue. More important to the personality were the acts of *propriate autonomy*—the interests, sentiments, and values around which great portions of behavior were organized. These acts were both an expression of the self and a means of preserving the self.

Some types of behavior could never become autonomous. Drives, for example, could be guided in certain directions, but no drive could become autonomous of its biological base; and neither could reflexes or constitutionally determined behavior. Similarly, drive-initiated behaviors and drive-gratifying behaviors, because they were the product of reinforcement and could not exist apart from it, could not exist autonomously. By definition, something which was autonomous could not be controlled by reinforcement.

If autonomous acts could not be traced to reinforcement, how then did they originate? Allport proposed that they might originate, among other things, from mechanical factors of delayed extinction, from self-maintaining circuits, from the endurance of responses under conditions of partial reinforcement, from the motivating effect of novelty, from the establishment of tastes for certain kinds of goals, activities, or styles of activity (a neural "gating" process Allport hypothesized as something apart from secondary reinforcement), or from the capacity of the organism to provide a duplication of important mechanisms for survival (so that if one means were lost, another means could be substituted). Whatever the mechanical origin of autonomous acts, on the level of self-enhancement man needed to maintain a certain energy level in his function, so that given a dearth of stimuli in one situation he might be expected to seek out stimulation elsewhere. Moreover, man was compelled to strive for mastery or growth. Finally, man's nature sought unity and a solution to the eternal problems of existence, suffering, guilt, and death, which confronted him on all sides.

If these proposals seem cloudy and confused, perhaps it is because it is very difficult to account for learning after having excluded as unworkable, or of limited value, all of the known mechanisms of learning.

All matters of origin apart, we may inquire into how the autonomous act was energized, from whence it derived its power. According to Allport, what actually provided the directive force for autonomous acts was the individual's peculiar pattern of tensions. The major portion of a person's activity, except in some emergency situations, was determined by his various traits. Not all traits were equally significant motivators; some were more expressive of personality than directive. The expressive and directive qualities of a trait varied from situation to situation so that, for example, the trait of dependency might drive a person to seek help in time of emergency, but under ordinary circumstances would simply negate intense independent strivings and produce instead a clinging, infantile air.

The Nature of the Learning Process

The phenomena of conditioning, the Law of Effect, and the Law of Exercise were abstractions. Moreover, they misrepresented the growth process. No single mechanism operated in isolation. Thus conditioning could explain the increase in the kind and number of drive-arousing stimuli, but could not account for changes in response. Frequency and recency could account for the perfecting of a response, and effect could account for both selection and improvement of responses. A completely hedonic explanation of learning was, however, an over-simplification. The process of insight, as described by the Gestaltists, must be employed to account for complex behavior. However, it too could not explain all learning. Imitation (which Allport considered a special kind of learning) was the basis of social behavior. At first it was a blind echoing, later in life it involved empathy, and still later became elaborate copying, perhaps with insight into the means and ends to be achieved.

Allport seemed to be traditional in his use of conditioning and insight, but he re-interpreted the Law of Effect, framing it in a fashion he found more useful. The simple, hedonistic Law of Effect, referring to reward of response, probably described only the behavior of animals, infants, and some unimportant areas of adult behavior, he said. As a rule people did not repeat a successfully completed act without becoming bored. For example, having passed a test, we do not wish to take it again, or having had a pleasant trip we do not immediately travel the same road. Thus, the application of the Law of Effect seemed to be extremely limited. If, however, a person interpreted effect as reward to the ego or self, he could, according to Allport, understand the force of effect upon repetition of behavior. A person would repeat that type of response which was ego-gratifying, and thus the Law of Effect was secondary to the Law of Ego (Self) Relevance.

Behavior and Personality

Personality was Allport's central interest. He warned, however, that the term was much misused. The nature of the term invited misuse, of course. It was abstract, had no general referent, and had an excessive number of meanings, some technical, some colloquial. The popularity of the term made its use perilous. Allport therefore provided an explicit definition of personality to accompany his use of the term: "dynamic organization within the individual of those psychophysical systems that determine his characteristic behavior and thought" (1961, p. 58).

Development of personality was a process alternating between differentiation and specialization, and integration of what had been differentiated back into a more complexly organized process. Development took place in a smooth flowing pattern; there were no sudden switches from one level to another. Certain aspects of behavior gradually became sufficiently differentiated from the mass of experience because they were salient to the individual. But even while they were discriminable they were inseparably organized with the rest of the personality.

Allport's concept of development centered around the self. Between birth and age three the infant developed a sense of his bodily self as distinct from the rest of the world. He probably came to distinguish between self and non-self because in a collision only one of the two entities felt the impact. The child next proceeded to learn self-identity by developing an appreciation of "me" as a distinct individual. Once he understood his distinct separate existence, he was able to further his self interests through his own efforts in the simple skills of walking, talking, and manipulating things. These skills aided him in exploring, gaining independence from his parents, and achieving a sense of adequacy, or *self-esteem*.

Between the ages of four and six years, the child learned to extend and project his sense of self onto his possessions and family. This extension formed the basis for all later loves, loyalties, and devotions. A more complex concept of self was also established as the child gained the ability to be concerned with what he was and ought to be. These phases of development were called the *extension of the self* and the *self-image*.

From six to twelve years, as the child ventured out into the world and tackled the multitude of problems there, he began to develop a *sense of self as a rational coper*, as one who could think out solutions to the problems he encountered. By adolescence he was aware of the necessity for planning his life, selecting goals, and beginning to move toward them. These long range purposes Allport called *propriate strivings*, and the knowledge and attitudes one came to have about the self he called the *proprium*. Whatever alterations and additions to these strivings might be necessary to fit them to reality was the task of the adult years, for the actualization of the self was a lifelong project.

Healthy development from infancy to adulthood supplied the person with a number of qualities necessary for mature adjustment. It provided him with the capacity to extend his sense of self to outside interests, hobbies, family, career, etc. It provided him with the ability to relate warmly to others and to avoid over-reactions, and with emotional security and self acceptance.

It provided him with the ability to perceive realistically, and with adequate skills for solving the problems of living. It provided him with insight into his personality, and with enough humor to keep the self in perspective. It provided him with a unifying philosophy of life and with a defined set of values which gave direction and purpose to his activities. These qualities were so essential to maturity that Allport regarded them as criteria for assessing a person's level of maturity.

Since the philosophy of life and the values it defined unified an individual's perspective, Allport felt that values were the key to assessing and describing personality. Spranger's (1928) six ideal types offered him a basic hypothesis. According to Allport's interpretation of Spranger's types, people could be classified according to their orientation to life along several dimensions of value. These dimensions included the religious, the esthetic, the theoretical, the economic, the social, and the political. To assist in evaluating such master sentiments, Allport and Vernon (1931) developed a rating scale which tapped the salience of each set of value dimensions for an individual. Called the Allport-Vernon Study of Values, this scale permitted the psychologists to contrast the importance of each of Spranger's six values in the life of an individual.

Whatever the orientation of the individual, his personality was organized around his self or ego, and the maintenance of self-esteem was the central motive in life. This central motive accounted for the consistency and generality of the significant traits, for traits became the instrument by which self-esteem endured. The need for self-esteem was the reference point of all judgements, of all learning, of all memories. Self-esteem determined whether or not action would occur, and what the goal would be. The special traits of the individual governed the form of action.

Usually the mode of adjustment was less than ideally appropriate, and the integration of the personality less than perfect. Therefore, the personality easily became maladjusted, and regression or dissociation occurred. Adjustment to situations which vitiated achievement of esteem became a process of distortion of reality in order to preserve one's self concept. Persistent failure led to feelings of inferiority (as in Adler's theory), and to consequent compensation or over-compensation (again as in Adler). If compensation was impossible there appeared a substitution of goals, or some other defense to hide one's true feelings from himself and others. Allport did not dwell on pathological conditions beyond this point since they interested him less than the normal personality.

Critique

Allport's phenomenology was not greatly different from any similar approach. It was the conceptual tools Allport devised to instrument his phenomenology that were distinctive. Thus, his dynamic interpretation of traits served to reinstate them as phenomena worthy of psychologists' study. The idea of functional autonomy provided an invaluable means of dealing with acquired modes of behavior and helped psychology to realize the importance of adjustive mechanisms in directing and shaping further adjustment.

Allport was aware of one problem which functional autonomy raised. If some acts could become functionally autonomous, why didn't all acts? Why did only some action patterns become motives for further action? Allport tried to answer these questions by stating that those acts which were ego involved became autonomous and capable of initiating behavior. Acts which were in the process of being mastered where likely to be ego involved, and thereby to be motivating in their own right. Adults, he pointed out, rarely manifested functional autonomy in walking or talking. They had mastered the skill and now used it only to serve other ends; it was no longer ego involved. The toddler manifested autonomy and circular-motivation of these skills, walking and talking simply for the sake of the ego enhancement he achieved from mastering these new challenges.

This explanation may account for many functionally autonomous acts, but the most often cited examples, the ex-sailor with his autonomous love of the sea, and the city dweller who longed for his native hills, certainly do not fit the mastery explanation. One could, of course, suggest that their earlier environment had become an anchor point in their self-concept and was thereby ego involving. However, the psychologist who prefers a more tough-minded approach may find himself under great strain in trying to render these suggestions reasonable. Some tighter, more definitive explanation capable of generating testable predictions would be a valuable addition to the concept.

In his handling of learning phenomena and the establishment of functional autonomy, Allport attempted to avoid all the problems connected with conditioning, reinforcement, and mechanistic concepts of stimulus and response by altogether excluding these matters from his theory. In the end he virtually eliminated all known learning processes. This had the same unfortunate result as sitting on the limb of the tree while sawing it off. Allport was forced to fall back on a circular argument that growth took place because man had a tendency to grow, and that things were functionally autonomous because they were.

Elsewhere, Allport was so eclectic as to be all encompassing. He tended to incorporate every possibility, including those which logically excluded each other. The invariable result was a schizoid and indecisive scheme which spoiled the baby and the bath because it hesitated to throw out either one. Indivisible unity and elements, individual and group traits, reinforcement and contiguity, all-pervasive ego involvement and motives derived from other means, biologically determined innate mechanisms and acquired adaptive mechanisms—all these contradictory ideas were included, often without explanation of their apparent opposition. Nor were the psychological details of these constructs clearly formulated so that the critical student might attempt reconciliation on his own.

Although these comments point to faults, they also suggest solutions, for each criticism indicates areas where further development of the theory should take place. What seem like contradictions may really be conceptual gaps.

SUMMARY

Basic Unit. Allport felt that the single case, the individual, was the appropriate concern of psychology, and that traits as generalized determining tendencies provided the best conceptual tool for the study of the individual personality.

Field of Study. Psychology must study the individual in his own right, including both the numerous dynamic traits which characterize him and the final organization of these traits into personality.

Methods of Investigation. Allport was completely eclectic in his methods.

Principles. Personality was a dynamic process, internally consistent. It was originally based on biological factors such as physique, intelligence, and temperament, but the adaptive mechanisms set up to modulate between these biological aspects and the environment became functionally autonomous and capable of directing behavior on their own. Personality development was a continuous, consistent current of events, guided by the need to maintain self-esteem and the necessity to be consistent with the rest of the personality.

Consciousness. Allport provided a phenomenal formulation of consciousness, stating that it was a series of momentary foci in a smooth flowing progress. Consciousness *per se* was mere awareness, occurring without function. When awareness extended to the relevance of the event to the self, and was anchored to the individual, it became self-consciousness, an all-important directive force whose purpose was to maintain the self in the world.

Sensation, Perception, and Discrimination; *Thinking, Cognition, and Memory*. These matters must all be considered as cognitive processes, guided by sets relevant to self, need, and past experience, yet veridical enough to permit survival. The mirroring of events Allport called perception, while the selective and self-enhancing processes he called proception.

Emotion, Motivation, and Purpose. In the infant, the biologically determined factors of motility and temperament accounted for individual variations and for the consistent patterning of behavior. As the infant was forced to meet and gratify his biological needs, he acquired adaptive mechanisms which soon became functionally autonomous traits and assumed the role of motivating or determining variables.

The Nature of the Learning Process. No single mechanism, be it conditioning, frequency, recency, exercise, effect, imitation, or insight, operated in isolation as a basis of learning. The Law of Effect, stated as hedonistic law, was without important application. Only when it was assumed that effect involved enhancement of self-esteem was the Law of Effect applicable to adult behavior.

Behavior and Personality. Personality was a dynamic organization of psychophysical systems which determined the unique adjustment of the individual. It developed in a continuous progression in which the dual processes of differentiation and integration constantly interacted. Once basic skills were mastered the individual child began to learn how to cope with the world and other people. Maturity was reached when the person could be objective about himself, when his self-esteem had been extended to include socially desirable autonomous goals, and when he possessed a philosophy of life which acted as a master sentiment. Master sentiments included religious, esthetic, theoretical, political, social, or economic values, among others. Whatever the orientation, the personality was organized around the self as a reference point for all learning, all memory, indeed all activity. Usually the mode of adjustment was far from perfect and might disintegrate under threats to self-esteem, leading to a set of maneuvers designed to preserve one's self in one's own and the eyes of others by some deceptive means. Behavior under any conditions was both expressive and adaptive. However, the necessity for efficient actions tended to negate expressive style. Parts of social behavior were culturally determined, while other aspects were uniquely determined by the individual personality.

REFERENCES

Gordon Allport's Trait Psychology

Allport, G. W., *Personality*. New York: Hall, 1937.

———, *The Nature of Personality: Selected Papers*. Cambridge: Addison-Wesley, 1950.

———, *Becoming: Basic Considerations for a Psychology of Personality*. New Haven: Yale Univ. Press, 1955.

———, *Pattern and Growth in Personality*. New York: Holt, Rinehart, and Winston, 1961.

———, and P. E. Vernon, *A Study of Values*. Boston: Houghton-Mifflin, 1931.

Spranger, E., *Types of Men*, trans. by P. Pigors, Halle: Niemeyer, 1928.

CHAPTER 26

HENRY A. MURRAY'S THEORY OF PERSONOLOGY (1938 TO PRESENT)

MURRAY'S THEORY was devised with purpose aforethought. He intended to derive a system of psychology which would be an instrument for the organization of an intensive research project in personality. It has the distinction among psychological systems of being a planned child, not an accident of nature. As a planned child, its future was arranged even as it was conceived.

Basic Unit and Field of Study

The study of personality was the proper subject matter for psychology, or at least for that branch of it Murray called *Personology*. The life history of an individual was the gross unit of the field of study, but life history was too coarse a unit to digest scientifically. For purposes of investigation and formulation it must be divided into smaller units which Murray called *episodes*. An episode consisted of an initial or beginning situation which produced some action leading to an end situation. Murray reduced this sequence to the symbols B.S.⟶ A⟶E.S. and referred to his formulation as the *B—E form*.

Episodes, life histories, personality—all could be approached from one of two frames of reference, peripheral or central. *Peripheralists* concentrated on objective, observable S-R units; they defined personality in terms of motor responses and employed mechanistic, physiological explanations. Murray did not name names, but his discussion made it obvious that he was referring to the behaviorists as peripheralists. It was equally obvious that he considered such an approach less than ideal. Indeed, it seemed likely that Murray and his colleagues found it necessary to formulate their own theory to combat the peripheralist trends in psychology.

Opposed to the peripheralists, and preferred by Murray *et al.*, was the centralist position. *Centralists* were concerned with the organization and control of behavior by the central nervous system. They were not afraid to employ "subjective" concepts (although they preferred to be as objective as they could), as long as their concepts, whatever their nature, provided a dynamic and apparently valid explanation of behavior.

Methods of Investigation

The centralist position determined the conceptual tools of the Murray group and made certain methods appropriate. Given their orientation, a Skinner box or Pavlovian conditioning situation, a Rorschach test, or an analytic couch were all equally applicable as psychological methods. What was important was that there be some dynamic theoretical preposition to be tested. Method was determined accordingly. Whatever the method, its focus was personality, and not some mechanism or reflex.

To assess personality proper, method must involve observation of both objective and subjective factors. The objective factors included the reactions of the person to environmental and physiological changes and to his life. The Murray group (1938) devised questionnaires, interviews, and projective tests (the Thematic Apperception Test or TAT was an especially well known invention) for the assessment and evaluation of the objective and subjective factors appropriate to their interests. There was no intent, however, of limiting psychological method to these techniques. Any method which provided appropriate answers to appropriate questions was acceptable.

Principles

Psychology dealt with dynamic organisms. Its laws must therefore be dynamic, not static. It must approach its subjects as individuals, not as a class of creatures.

Each individual functioned as an organized unit characterized by continuous but changing patterns of activity from its birth to its death.

The individual could not be understood without reference to an environment as organized and dynamic as the individual himself. The environment could be understood from its effects on the individual, i.e., its *press*.

All responses of the organism were purposeful; it acted adaptively in order to survive. An adaptive incident was called an *actone*.

The organism's behavior was attributable to inner forces which, if not blocked, brought about activity; the effect of this activity was to negate the situation which initiated it. In the process of regulating these forces the organism sought certain press and avoided others; consummatory behavior occurred only when in the appropriate press. This coincidence of press and need in an episode was known as a *thema*. The success or failure of the organism correlating action and press into adaptive thema determined its developmental progress.

Life was marked by patterns of assimilation, differentiation, and integration in a continual process of refinement. There was a similarity of activity patterns throughout the life cycle because every situation left traces in the brain preserving past experience for future reference.

The brain coordinated the behavior of the individual, and thus it was the brain, and not the isolated responses, which was important to the psychologist. The dominant patterns of activity in the brain constituted *regnant* processes; the totality of dominant patterns active at any one time constituted the *regnancy*. All regnancies, active or potential, taken together made up personality.

What was conscious was regnant, but only some of the regnant processes were conscious at any particular moment. Some regnant processes could function unconsciously. Regnancies differed in organization from individual to individual and within an individual from time to time. Organized regnancies were said to be *conjunctive*; disorganized regnancies to be *disjunctive*. Regnancies became disjunctive with fatigue, in sleep, in conflict, or during intense emotion. The degree of conjunction among the regnancies was indicated by a number of factors: the degree of alertness; the efficiency of discrimination; the rapidity of learning; the endurance and the effectiveness of action; the coherence, relevance, and concentration of thought; the presence or absence of conflict; the degree of introspective awareness; and the degree of self-criticism.

Any aspect of the organism which was outside the regnancies could be considered an independent variable, whether the source was internal or external to the body, as far as psychological study was concerned. Regnancies and the rest of the bodily and environmental events continually interacted in dependent-independent variable relationship.

Man was a *time-binding* organism. By retaining the past and anticipating the future he could bring his behavior in accord with experience and so behave adaptively.

Consciousness

Consciousness and regnancy were closely related. Consciousness was the subjective aspect of a regnant process, the awareness of its influence. Many regnancies, of course, functioned permanently or temporarily outside consciousness. Consciousness was limited to what could be verbalized; and therefore early infantile experiences, and emotions so intense that all words were lost, could not be conscious. There were in addition incidents whose memory or recognition was inhibited. These, too, took place unconsciously. Finally, many events occurred automatically for the sake of efficiency, but a person could be consciously aware of them if he so desired.

Sensation, Perception, and Discrimination; Thinking, Cognition, and Memory

The raw sensory data was of relatively little import in behavior. Not until cognitive processes intervened to give meaning were external stimuli significant. The cognitive processes acted first to organize sensations into coherent patterns according to Gestalt patterns. Meaning accrued to sensation by way of the press of sensory events. The organism classified sensations (i.e., press) as to whether they were a threat or a promise to the individual and interpreted them in terms of past experience.

Murray described a number of aspects of interpersonal judgement which, though they were discussed in relation to a clinical psychologist's diagnostic judgements, seem to pertain equally well to the way the individual conceptualized his interpersonal experiences. First, an individual understood others through *empathy*, feeling himself into the place of others, so to speak, to see how they might feel. Also, he used his own feelings and experiences to guess at how others might feel, i.e., he projected onto others that which he had himself experienced. This was the basis of the Thematic Apperception Test. People projected especially easily upon ambiguous stimuli, and it was possible to learn about their experiences and attitudes by examining their projections.

Empathy and projection were useful interpersonal skills, but they could also be sources of distortion. A more mature understanding of others involved what Murray called *critical empathy*. Using empathy and projection as a source of hypotheses about the emotional responses of other individuals, the mature individual proceeded to check and test these hypotheses against the objective facts of behavior. He asked not only "How might I feel?" and "Could he feel as I do?" but "Does he really act like this is what's going on?"

In addition to these processes two other devices were used to evaluate the intent of others, and both centered on the reaction of the perceiving organism to the other person. There was first a *resonance* effect. The perceiver asked himself "What effect is this having on me? How does he make me feel?" It was assumed that the feeling induced in the perceiver was induced with intent. The individual could further evaluate the other person's intentions toward him by introspections concerning the drives aroused in him by the other's acts. He asked himself "What does he make me want to do about it?" This technique Murray called *recipathy*.

Murray did not mention perception or thinking as separate functions, and the preceding discussion makes it obvious that it would indeed be difficult to separate the two within the theoretical structure given by Murray. There is really no point in trying to distinguish perception from thinking or from apperception; all are part and parcel of cognition.

Emotion and Motivation

The concept of need was not entirely acceptable to (behaviorist) psychology at the time. Murray first proposed it as a valuable tool in personality assessment. As a result, Murray's presentation contained a certain proselytizing undertone, and a few almost apologetic harmonics. Thus, the material summarized in the next three paragraphs is not given by Murray as a discussion of the characteristics of need, but as behavioral evidence that a construct of need is necessary to a theory of psychology.

Need, Murray pointed out in the beginning, was a construct required to explain behavior. Need was initiated by a certain kind of stimulus situation, internal or external. It induced activity, random at first but later organized, which persisted in a certain direction and at a certain intensity until a certain kind of goal was reached. Needs accounted for the persistence of behavior, for the increase in activity if a course of behavior was blocked, and for the resumption of behavior when the block was removed. Actones did not occur when a need was not activated. Given an aroused need, objects could be employed in some unusual way, explainable only by such a construct as need. For example, a woman who wished to repair a broken object might use a hairpin as a fastener and the heel of her shoe as a hammer. A hungry person at a picnic might use a napkin for a plate if there were no other utensil available. With repetition, each need became associated more strongly with certain actones which led to certain goals so that eventually a simple habit pattern replaced the need-activity-gratification sequence.

Need was the result of some disequilibrium, some tension produced biologically or psychologically, which required resolution. The organism remained in disequilibrium until the initiating situation was changed. Need was not, however, a simple S→R mechanism. It was a complex press→ effect chain of behaviors. The many current bodily events involved in need were correlated within the brain. The brain also correlated the traces of earlier actones, paths, and goals which the present experience reactivated. This complex of experience, expectations, needs, acts, and objects was called the *need integrate*.

Needs could be variously classified. Some needs were unacceptable to the individual, so that although they continued to exist, they were not considered part of the self. These needs might be said to constitute the Id, and Murray called them *Id needs*. Some needs evoked by sudden press without any preceding intention or disequilibrium were instantaneously, impulsively, and emotionally acted upon. These were *emotional needs*. Some needs were actones which took place automatically without thought. In fact there often seemed to be a drive toward certain activities. These were *actonal needs*. A need could be Id, emotional and actonal, singly or in any combination.

Needs could also be classified as to origin, viscerogenic or psychogenic, and as to the situation which aroused them. *Viscerogenic needs* were evoked by bodily events which made them of primary import to the organism. They were periodic in occurrence; there was a refractory period, followed by an inducible or ready period, and finally by a period of activation, until they were eventually gratified. *Psychogenic needs* were not localized within the body, but were secondary to and derived from viscerogenic drives. (Murray did not state how they are derived.) They were not periodic in the same sense as their biological predecessors, but did show an alternation with other psychogenic needs which were their opposites. Dominance, for example, alternated with Deference, and Aggression with Abasement.

The viscerogenic needs included: *positive needs initiated by deficiency*—n Inspiration (oxygen), n Water, n Food, n Sentience (sensation); *negative needs initiated by distension due to secretion*—n Sex, n Lactation; *negative needs initiated by distension due to excretory pressures*—n Expiration (air), n Urination, n Defecation; *negative needs due to harm*—n Noxavoidance (contamination, noxious substances), n Heatavoidance, n Coldavoidance, n Harmavoidance.

The psychogenic needs included: *needs concerning inanimate objects*—n Acquisition, n Conservance, n Order, n Retention, n Construction; *needs for success*—n Superiority, n Achievement, n Recognition, n Exhibition; *needs for defense of status*—n Defendance, n Counteraction; *needs concerning human power*—n Dominance, n Deference, n Similance (empathy, imitation), n Autonomy, n Contrariance (non-conformity); *needs concerning sado-masochism*—n Aggression, n Abasement; *needs concerning avoidance of socially unacceptable behavior*—n Blamavoidance; *needs concerning affection for people*—n Affiliation, n Rejection, n Nurturance, n Succorance, n Play; and *needs concerning social interaction*—n Cognizance (to know, explore), n Exposition (to discuss, tell).

A need might not be completely satisfied by the actones it evoked. If not it perserverated as a *need set*. There was then a low threshold for arousal so that the individual could easily be set into need-related actones. Thus, the frustrated individual might show irritability long after his frustration or the child might play at his homework when called in from his games.

Needs often fused to form larger *need integrates*. One need could also be made subsidiary to another, so that it was activated in the service of the other need. A person might behave submissively to his boss to get a raise, or a child might conform to its mother's rules in order to continue receiving her affection. In more complex need patterns there might be several sub-needs with goals subsidiary to a dominant need. Need-activated behavior, therefore, was likely to be a progression from one sub-goal to another. Needs could alternate if they were not compatible, or they could come into conflict if they were evoked at the same time.

Needs differed in the degree to which they were *manifest* in their expression. Some were completely objectified or overt. Some involved imaginary acts toward real objects, or real acts toward imaginary objects as expressed in play, drama, ritual, and art. Murray called these *semi-objectified*. There were also completely *subjectified* needs expressed in fantasies, dreams, and vicarious actions. Semi-objectified and subjectified needs were *latent*, i.e., not openly expressed. Both manifest and latent needs could be conscious or unconscious.

Environmental situations or press included stimulating conditions, paths, and goals. They could be *positive* (offer promise) or *negative* (offer threat); they could be *mobile* (self-animated), or immobile (manipulable). Mobile press could either move themselves, being autonomous, or permit the individual to determine their movements for them, being *docile*. For example, a hungry man entering the kitchen at dinner time will be faced with a complex press, containing many aspects to which he will react differentially. The steak in his broiler will be positive and immobile. His wife, preparing the food, may be autonomous, but his docile son will fetch his immobile pipe and slippers.

The effect of the object determined its value for the individual, or in Murray's terms, its *cathexis*. A person made an emotional investment in significant objects, and as a result they had the power of determining his actions. Certain objects within a press were sought or avoided, or certain press were sought or avoided as a result of their affective value for the individual.

Needs, press, and cathexis clustered together into certain consistent patterns; when a particular press appeared, certain needs were aroused and certain cathected objects were sought (or avoided). Likewise, need arousal led the organism to seek various press. These patterns, whether of biological or social origin, were called *thema*.

Aside from specific motivational phenomena another factor influenced behavior. While not a motive in any particular sense of the word, it had some motive-like effects. Each individual organism sought out and maintained a certain level of energy expenditure. This level was a characteristic of the individual and varied from one person to another. It also varied according to the physical and mental state of the individual. When energy level was high, all drives were intense. Observation of this phenomenon led many people to suggest a generalized drive state which activated behavior as a whole. While Murray believed there might well be such a general drive state, he also hypothesized that various degrees of energy may be allocated to various specific aspects of function so that, for example, one individual may seem to possess a highly energized motor function while in another person the intellectual function may be the most energized aspect.

Murray saw emotion as a construct which referred to an excitatory state within the brain experienced subjectively, objectively, or both. Emotions were linked with tendencies toward action, but were not necessarily connected with either drive or gratification.

Affection Murray reserved to apply to hedonic tone. Positive hedonic tone was the result of activity pleasure, achievement pleasure, or effect pleasure (gratification). Negative tone accompanied the arousal of any need and derived from the deficiency, distension, harm, or threat which evoked the need. Behavior was induced to avoid the pain of the negative situation or its aftermath.

Knowing which need and emotion were active was not enough. It was also necessary to say something about the mode of behavior which the need called forth, i.e., what actones were involved, toward what objects they were directed, and in what manner directed. Actones were either motor (*motones*) or verbal (*verbones*). The action could be *focal*, focusing directly upon one object or a narrow group, or it could be *diffuse*, relating to a large number of objects. The action could be directed inwardly on the self (*intraversive*), or directed outwardly upon others (*extraversive*). It could serve the self only, being *egocentric*, or it could be of service to a larger group, being *sociocentric*. It could be directed toward inferior organisms (*infraversive*) or toward superior organisms (*supraversive*). An act could serve one or several needs. It could be objective or latent in expression. It could be conscious or unconscious. Need, then, was characterized by a typical direction and a typical mode of action which sought out certain press; it was accompanied by certain emotions, and eventually ended with a feeling of satisfaction in the achievement of certain effects. Murray's system for cataloging motivation included classification of all these facets of the need pattern.

The Nature of the Learning Process

Murray's theory did not attempt to explain how behavior was established. It rather sought a means of describing it as it existed. For all his interest in life history and the effects of action, Murray did not include in his theory more than the sparest account of learning. He pointed out that man was a *time-binding* organism, i.e., that he preserved past experiences and used them to anticipate future ones. Such time binding was presumed to be promoted by the Law of Effect and was obviously a vitally important factor of personality. Murray's desire to study dynamic behavior led him to concentrate on motivation and action, however, and he left learning phenomena to others who found it more to their research tastes.

Behavior and Personality

Adaption depended not upon specific actones but on their effect. Many different actones could have the same outcome or reach the same goal. For example, I could get to work many different ways. I could relieve my hunger by eating with a fork, chopsticks, or my fingers. I could be a success by working, by knowing the right people, by being lucky, or by cheating. Actions were replaceable; effects were constant and not replaceable.

Like Lewin (see Chapter 24) Murray used the term vectors, but his definition of it was different. Murray's *vectors* described the mode of interaction with objects. Vectors included *Adience* (approach), *Ingression* (withdrawal), *Adherence*, *Contrience* (attacking), *Abience* (avoiding), *Encasement* (walling self in), *Egression* (breaking out), *Locomotion, Manipulation, Construction, Reception, Acquisition, Ejection, Retention, Injection.* These vectors were related to Freudian psychosexual stages (see Chapter 15) and to Erikson's mode zone theory (see Chapter 16). Each need was more compatible with some vectors than with others. Aggressive needs, for example, were best satisfied by behaviors which struck out at the world, and hunger by acts which took on nourishment. Vectors were also the result of the individual personality. Thus personality revealed itself in the nature of the person's interactions with objects.

Personality was also revealed by the nature of the objects cathected, but one had to know the objects and the situation (press) to understand what was occurring. For example, it was not enough to know that a man hoarded his money. A sufficient description and history were also necessary in order to ascertain if he were a miser, were saving for something, were a deprived youngster, or were subjected to a traumatic toilet training. However important acts and objects might be, it is apparent that in Murray's theory needs were primary, and everything else could be understood in terms of how it fitted with dominant needs.

Critique

Murray and his group devised a widely useful means of classifying and objectifying behavior. Their system did not and was not intended to explain how behavior was established, nor did it permit predictions. It simply enabled the observer to encode what he observed. He might have difficulty at times with some of the subtle distinctions between types of needs or vectors, in spite of careful efforts at definition, but if he succeeded he found himself with a collection of information which told much about the interaction between motivating conditions, stimulus situations, and behavior.

The psychologist accustomed to the inclusion of genetic concepts is likely to find Murray's approach rather stilted and not so dynamic as its author supposes. Yet what the theory does, it does so well that it is a major source of concepts for those interested in assessing and classifying motivations. Indeed, Murray's work is a classic of tremendous significance and influence in the field of psychological measurement, and as we will see in Chapter 32, has provided the basis for many significant studies of motives and personality.

This success may not be as far ranging as Murray and his associates originally hoped, yet it is admirable in a science where few formulations can endure the criticisms of their peers.

SUMMARY

Basic Unit & Field of Study. Psychology, or rather that branch of psychology called Personology, should properly address itself to personality, utilizing the life history as a gross unit and subdivided into episodes for convenience in scientific digestion. An episode consisted of an initiating situation, an action, and an end situation. Murray did not intend this to connote an S-R, peripheralist position. He intended, rather, to take a dynamic, centralist position.

Methods of Investigation. A centralist position negated mechanistic methods. It required observation of objective and subjective facts, but did not prescribe the technique by which these facts were collected.

Principles. The individual was a pattern of rhythmic internal processes in interaction with dynamic environmental forces (or press) pushing for activity in some direction. The end result of need-directed behavior was a reversal of the internal tensions which gave rise to the activity. The brain coordinated the behavior of the individual in response to need and press with past experience. The dominant patterns of brain action were called regnancies. The totality of regnancies composed personality. What was conscious was regnant, but regnant processes could also occur unconsciously. Integration or conjunction of regnancies was indicated by efficient function, disjunction by disintegration. What was not regnant within or outside the body interacted as independent variables with the regnancies.

Consciousness. Consciousness was the subjective aspect of regnancies. It was limited to what could be verbalized. Thus non-verbal experience could not be conscious, and neither could repressed or inhibited events. There were some automatic actions which took place without awareness for the sake of efficiency, but these could become conscious if need required.

Sensation, Perception, and Discrimination; Thinking, Cognition, and Memory. Cognitive processes gave meaning to raw sensory data, first by organizing it in a manner described by Gestalt principles, later by empathy, projection, resonance, or reciprocity with other persons. Mature judgements utilized one's own feelings as a source of hypotheses concerning another person's reactions, hypotheses to be checked and tested against the person's behavior. In this sort of cognition perception, thought, discrimination, and memory were indistinguishable processes.

Emotion and Motivation. Need was a construct required to explain behavior. Initiated by internal events or external press, it produced activity (actones) directed toward a certain goal. This activity was persistent when need was active, but would not occur otherwise. Needs became more strongly associated with actones as a result of repeated experiences with the effect of the latter. Murray listed a large number of needs, viscerogenic and psychogenic, indicating in addition to their single effects that they could fuse into various combinations. Needs were accompanied by emotion, hedonic tone, and a cathexis which indicated preference for or aversion to goal objects. They might be latent or manifest and could concern objects which were positive or negative, mobile and autonomous or mobile and docile, or immobile. Behavior in response to need might be motor or verbal, focal or diffuse, directed toward self or others, inferior or superior, for self alone or for the social group.

The Nature of the Learning Process. Learning was a process of time-binding so that the past was preserved and the future anticipated in such a way as to guide present behavior. Learning occurred through the effect of various actions.

Behavior and Personality. The nature of a specific action was less important than its effect. Many acts could produce the same effect. Acts were consequently replaceable, while effects were not. Vectors were descriptions of the mode of interaction with objects. Murray listed a number of vectors drawn broadly from an analytic psychosexual mold. Vectors and objects revealed personality, but need was its primary determinant.

REFERENCES

Henry A. Murray's Theory of Personology

Murray, H. A., *et.al.*, *Explorations in Personality.* New York: Oxford Univ. Press, 1938.

———, "Some Basic Psychological Assumptions and Conceptions," *Dialectica* 5: 266–292 (1951).

———, and C. Kluckhohn, "Outline of a Conception of Personality," in C. Kluckhohn, H. A. Murray, and D. Schneider, eds., *Personality in Nature, Society, and Culture*, 2nd ed., New York: Knopf, 1953.

CHAPTER 27

PHENOMENOLOGY (1941 TO PRESENT)

ALTHOUGH there is no modern descendant of Structuralism, there is one theory which employs similar techniques to study somewhat similar problems. In its interpretation of psychological data, however, there is much which resembles William James, and some further parallels to the Gestaltists. This hybrid system is known as Phenomenology. While a number of persons could be loosely identified with this approach, few have attempted any broad discussion of it, with the exception of Donald Snygg and Arthur Combs. We will, therefore, consider their formulation as representative of those who hold to Phenomenological beliefs.

The *raison d'etre* of the Phenomenologist theory was a conviction that all other psychologies were normative, neglecting individual tendencies for group tendencies while the key to understanding lay in the opposite approach. One could only comprehend behavior by understanding the behaving individual. The knowledge thus acquired could be employed to explain behavior in the abstract and to derive norms for it.

Basic Unit

Snygg and Combs focused upon the individual's experience as an entity in itself and sought to understand human activity in the light of such an experience. This is essentially a non-reductionistic orientation which eliminates the necessity for a basic unit.

Field of Study

The experience to be examined was carefully specified to include the individual's *phenomenal field*, i.e., the external world and his own physical and psychological processes as he consciously experienced them. Like Wundt and Titchener, Snygg and Combs were interested in conscious experience, but with a different emphasis. They were concerned with the functional significance of the specific individual, and unlike the Structuralists they did not regard the composition of experience as important in and of itself.

Methods of Investigation

Since the phenomenal field was not open to direct observation and could be revealed only by the person who was experiencing it, introspection was the appropriate method. The classical objective introspection of Wundt and Titchener was of no use, however, in examining the phenomenal field since it was the individual's interpretation of his environment and experience which was of value. To this end Snygg and Combs employed a technique known as *phenomenal introspection*, wherein the person reported what he was thinking and feeling and what it meant to him.

The Phenomenologists were aware that introspection had certain limitations, and that the mere act of introspection changed a person's phenomenal field. This modification, sometimes slight, sometimes gross, had to be considered in interpreting data. For these reasons, in attempting to predict and understand behavior Snygg and Combs collected both the introspections of the subject himself and the reports of external observers. From these reports they inferred what the subject had experienced and what had determined his behavior. These inferences were checked against the introspective data. If the two corresponded, the findings were substantially valid. If they did not, the very lack of correspondence might hint at hitherto unsuspected factors operating to influence the individual's experience and suggest new ways of studying it.

Principles

The Phenomenologists held that the phenomenal field was organized on a figure-ground basis. The content of any experience was influenced not only by the figure itself but also by all the other things in the background at that particular time. The figure fused with or assimilated all else in the field, thereby acquiring undertones of meaning and the unique characteristics which distinguished it from all other similar experiences.

The organization of this field, once established, was maintained. According to the Phenomenologists, anything which threatened this organization was avoided if possible. If it could not be avoided, it was integrated into the existing organization with as little change as possible.

Any change in the organism, whether a change in perception, motivation, or cognition, was the result of differentiation of the field. As a result some new phenomena were incorporated into the field or some hitherto ignored aspect of the old figure became salient. In either case the basic organization was maintained, but was supplemented in such a manner that both the need for stability of phenomenal field and the demands of reality were served.

Consciousness

The Phenomenologists did not study the mind-body problem since to them the mind and body did not exist as separate entities. The phenomenal field encompassed both. Determination of all behavior was ascribed to one causal field.

Just as their approach simplified the mind-body problem, so the question of what constituted consciousness surrendered to easy solution. What was figure in the phenomenal field at any time was usually conscious; ground was usually not consciously experienced. This approach defined consciousness by means of the nature of its contents. How consciousness functioned or what made the phenomenon occur was beyond the scope of Phenomenology, since this knowledge was not part of the individual's phenomenal field.

The phenomenal field was the universe of naive experience in which the individual lived. It was what he took to be reality. This phenomenal field was private to each individual, but among individuals there were a number of common experiences. Everyone was born, and everyone was subject to a number of biological necessities. Within a cultural group people were exposed to the same general stimulus field. It was this biological-cultural commonality of field which permitted understanding and interaction between people and which enabled the Phenomenologists to predict group behavior from data collected in studies of individuals.

The phenomenal field was characterized by fluidity, and at the same time by a basic and enduring organization. Although the figure might change from moment to moment, the basic organization between various figures and ground was constant because the mode of differentiation or discrimination was the same. A person selected figure from ground in the same fashion in all situations; he was prone to focus on certain figures and leave certain other events in the background. What was in the field at any one moment was a function of the entire organization or personality of the experiencing person. The person could not achieve experiences of any type other than what he had because of the kind of person he was.

The phenomenal field was self-regulating, maintaining and preserving its organization. Events in the field were assimilated in such a way as to make them compatible with the existing organization. An example may help to clarify how this took place. The author commuted from town to town one winter with a gentleman whose conservative views on all political, economic, and racial questions were well known. One day while driving along a well-traveled highway, this gentleman happened to notice an old but well-preserved car in front of him. As he overtook the vehicle, he commented on what he presumed to be the character of its owner. He pointed out that anyone who cared for a car like that must be a worthy individual; he praised the cleanliness, conscientiousness, frugality, and wisdom of the owner because of the appearance of his car. As we passed the car, the gentleman glanced over to see what this laudatory person looked like. The driver was a Negro. As we drove on down the road, the gentleman continued, "As I was saying, that's the gaudiest black paint I ever saw! And look, two mirrors—one on the windshield and one on the door! And that radiator ornament—looks like a cross. Anyone who keeps his car polished like that must neglect his work." Those things which had previously been positive were now perceived negatively. It was impossible for the man to perceive a Negro as having any of the desirable characteristics he had previously attributed to the owner of the car. This example illustrates not only that the phenomenal field could be preserved, but also the means by which the preservation took place. The perception of events was altered until they could fit into the phenomenal organization.

Sensation, Perception, and Discrimination

Phenomenology did not require a concept of sensation, for it was impossible to sense something without also attributing some meaning to it, i.e., perceiving it. Meaning referred to the behavior which a stimulus suggested or required.

Meaning or significance was a function of a particular figure-ground relationship. Perception was a dynamic process, shifting focus from moment to moment. With each shift the field was altered so that a new figure predominated against a new ground. Shifts in perception could be due to changes in the environment so that the individual was exposed to a new phenomenal field, such as when he turned his head or snapped on a light in a dark room. Shifts could also be due to re-focusing of figure so that one became aware of different aspects. For example, in looking at a large crowd of people one person may stand out as figure; this person is much smaller than the original group, but one is aware of many details about him, his appearance and actions. The perception may shift so that the whole group becomes figure wherein no particular individual stands out, and one is only aware of a sea of faces. One might refocus again and see the group in a particular social or historical setting, e.g., a revolution or a parade.

Shifts of field and changes of focus were ordinarily temporary shifts in perception and were reversible. Permanent change occurred in a different manner; old figure-ground organizations were destroyed and new ones were substituted. The process was usually gradual. The properties of newly perceived objects emerged slowly from the background and became clear only with repeated exposure. There were frequent distortions and misinterpretations as a result of the ambiguity of the figure. Meaning was not yet isolated from the general stimulus field, so that it was likely to be influenced by the situation and not by the specific characteristics of an event. To demonstrate this gradual emergence of a significant figure one has only to listen to a three-year old recite a poem or sing a song. The words come out in a mangled version, a compromise between words the child knows and the real sounds. As the child becomes more and more familiar with the song and its meanings, his performance becomes more accurate.

Thinking, Cognition, and Memory

From the Phenomenologists' point of view, perception, thinking, learning, and memory were actually variations of a single process, differentiation. Each involved some slightly different aspect of the field, but the process as a whole was identical. It was possible, for purposes of discussion, to separate the variations, but the separation could only serve to show how difficult it was for Phenomenology to consider them apart.

Thinking differed from learning and perception in that it involved only auditory and visual modalities; the other processes could take place in any sensory mode. The actual nature of thought was not designated, but one can infer from examples and various passing references that it was aroused by a problem and was assumed to be a process of shifting the differentiation of figure-ground relations until cues to solution became available. Most frequently the individual sought to generalize from past experience so that several memories emerged as figures, each of which possessed some characteristic in common with the others and with the situation at hand. On the basis of this generalization or abstraction the individual developed a tentative new percept (percept is used in the same sense as "idea") to be tried and tested, using visual images to "see" or "conceive of" the field in the "mind's eye" as it might become if this percept (or idea) were valid. If the first trial percept failed to lead to a solution, another was constructed and tested, and another, and another if necessary. The information secured from each of these trials was integrated into the phenomenal field, which was re-organized to include it. Eventually a percept would be found which clarified the problem by differentiating figure and ground so that solution was apparent.

Memory was also a matter of the process of differentiation, differing from perception, learning, and thinking in that it was the result of enduring differentiations in that part of the field which represented the past. Forgetting occurred when the figure dropped back into the ground and lost its potency for determining behavior. This could happen because other figures were interfering with it, pushing it from its position as figure, or because of decay.

Emotion and Motivation

The maintenance of organization was the primary motive of any organism, for it was essential to the preservation of the phenomenal self. Contrary to most other theories where motivation involved physical survival, physical status was secondary to the Phenomenologist. One ate, drank, slept, etc., only to enhance the phenomenal self. Biology, from this point of view, was a psychological necessity. It existed only in order to allow psychological aspects to function. There were even times when an individual underwent physical discomfort in order to maintain a consistent image of himself: an artist might starve in an attic for the sake of his art; a woman might submit to all manner of painful procedures in order to make herself beautiful; a boy might fight every other boy on the block to prove his manhood.

Any situation which affected the organization of the field aroused emotion. Emotion was a state of tension, expectation, and preparation to act in such a manner as to preserve the organization of the field, either by fighting against or avoiding situations which threatened the organization of the phenomenal self (accompanied by feelings of anger or fear), or by approaching or seeking out situations which reinforced or enhanced the field (with a concomitant feeling of pleasure). The motivational and emotional tone of an experience determined what was perceived, what was learned, and what elicited a response.

The Nature of the Learning Process

The perceptual field changed in character as new attributes and entities were differentiated from the ground. Behavior was based on the perception of the situation at hand, and was effective only insofar as perception was precise and accurate. Learning was indicated by increased effectiveness in behavior, so that it could be defined as the emergence of more valid percepts. Errors were a function of the person's field at the time. An error was not a mistake or an accident, but was determined by what the person saw as figure, what he saw as ground, and the relationships between the two. A "wrong" response was no more incorrect, viewed in this manner, than a "right" response. Both were determined by the facts at hand and justifiable in terms of them. A person's phenomenological field at a particular moment might not represent all the relevant facts, and until it did he acted as best he could with the information he had.

The degree and direction of differentiation which led eventually to the establishment of valid percepts were determined by need and opportunity. Differentiation occurred because it was helpful in preserving the phenomenal self and because the person was placed in a situation where it was possible to make such a differentiation. The differentiation of a percept was accomplished by a series of approximations, the consequences of each trial percept being incorporated into the next version. This process involved a kind of shaping by reinforcement which had something in common with Skinner's concept. When the percept fit the requirements of both the phenomenal field and reality, learning was complete.

While learning was reinforcement based, repetition of an experience gave more opportunity for correct discrimination, providing the person was motivated. Similarly, other factors could encourage learning. If previous experience with a situation were recent, or either so similar to present field or so different as to contrast with it, learning was facilitated. If such a situation were the first of that sort one had faced, learning was easier. Finally, the learning process was more efficient if the figures to be differentiated or synthesized occurred close to each other in the phenomenal field either in time or place (i.e., were contiguous).

Snygg and Combs had little to say about most of the technical details of learning, with the exception of generalization. Generalization, they said, was a failure to differentiate between figures. Under some circumstances it might produce errors, but on the whole it was a useful process. In fact, it occupied a special position for Snygg and Combs; as we have already seen, it was essential to problem solving. As a result of generalization several remembered events could emerge simultaneously as figure, differentiated from their common ground by the fact that they possessed some common characteristic. Snygg and Combs equated this with abstraction, the process which enabled the individual to classify events and to comprehend basic relationships.

In conclusion, when one disregards the special vocabulary one discovers that Snygg and Combs employed a fairly standard trial-and-error approach to learning, albeit they dealt with only one variety, perceptual learning. However, since the phenomenal field determined behavior, perception determined behavior. No other sort of learning was necessary.

Behavior and Personality

Behavior occurred within the context of the phenomenal field and was governed by it. The person responded to the world as he saw it; what it looked like to others or what it might really be had no bearing on him. Likewise, all behavior was pertinent to the phenomenal field and was motivated by the need to preserve and enhance the organization of this field and of the *phenomenal self.* Goals became goals, i.e., were discriminated from ground as figure because they could assist the organism in achieving these ends. Some goals served this purpose directly, others served it indirectly by giving sustenance to the physical body. If goals were inadequately appreciated (discriminated) then physical and psychological function were blocked and illness and maladjustment resulted.

The individual must master behavioral techniques which would enable him to reach positive goals or avoid negative ones. When first learned, these techniques were crude and general, but they became more specific and more refined as the person became more experienced. The techniques that a person used in reaching one kind of goal were usually similar to those used in reaching other goals. This consistency of techniques supplied Snygg and Combs with a means of characterizing or typing personality. One group they described as constantly seeking to achieve goals by mastering or controlling the environment and the people in it. Another type found the means to goals by identifying with other individuals or groups, conforming to their demands, and thus living vicariously. A third type of person met life by changing himself and his phenomenal field in an effort to achieve desired ends.

Personality developed around the phenomenal self. The earliest discriminations the infant made were distinctions between what was him and what was not. From these early experiences, a crude concept of the self as a phenomenal entity was derived, and all further experience was interpreted in terms of its meaning for this entity. Everything was perceived in such a way as to enhance this view of the self, and anything which could not be so perceived was distorted or not perceived at all. This sort of selective perception reinforced the phenomenal self and at the same time reinforced its influence so that it became almost immutable. It could only be changed by a person's becoming aware of discrepancies between his beliefs and reality. The person tended to resist recognizing these discrepancies since they meant that some aspects of the self-concept must be revised. However, severe discrepancies led to distorted function, so that changes usually occurred. If they did not, illness resulted.

For example, a child who did poorly in school commonly came to include in his view of himself the characteristic of "dumbness" and would proceed to act accordingly. This unfortunate negative view would prevail unless some wise teacher or parent found a way of helping the child experience some academic success. Given a few such experiences, the child might gradually come to see the discrepancy between his idea of himself and what he could really do. Then he was likely to overcome the negative feeling and develop a new series of perceptions of himself and a new series of acts based upon them which would enable him to achieve adequate grades. If he were not so fortunate, the child's negative feelings about himself could be the foundation for a crippling neurosis.

The phenomenal self could also be changed if a person accepted a new role. For example, after the birth of his first child a man assumed a new facet to his phenomenal self, something that he did not have in his former role of a husband only.

Changes in the phenomenal self as a result of correcting discrepancies or assuming a new role were usually gradual. However, certain environmental trauma could produce sudden and violent changes in the content of the self. A person who lost both eyes in a hunting accident must suddenly incorporate into his self the idea of blindness. Likewise, the death of a father would demand many of changes in the self of a teen-age son. These sudden changes were likely to be difficult to assimilate.

Critique

It is indeed noble to try to appreciate the richness and warmth of an individual and at the same time to maintain sufficient rigor to express this richness in scientific form. It is also noble to attempt to reduce all psychological functions to a few processes. But one may soon come to feel that Phenomenology is a symphony of one note, repeated without variation and muffled to ambiguity by the lack of definition. To assume that differentiation alone could account for learning overlooked the associations or phenomenal meaning of a percept which was vitally important to the Phenomenologists themselves. It also overlooked the process by which all activities were learned and how they came to be combined with certain stimuli. While conceivably one could agree that all this is differentiation, it certainly makes differentiation into a lot of different processes and presupposes a number of independent variables which need to be defined.

Snygg and Combs tended to avoid dealing with such objective variables by addressing themselves only to what was experienced. They accounted for everything in terms of the phenomenal field and apparently permitted nothing to exist outside the mind. They exaggerated the subordination of the physical to the mental. They spoke of reality, and yet they would have had tremendous metaphysical problems in defining it because they would have had to refer it, like everything else, to the phenomenal field. This approach did, of course, relieve them of debating such things as the mind-body controversy, the technicalities of perception and cognition, and the nature of consciousness, but they seem to have solved these problems by means of a verbal sleight of hand.

In evaluating these criticisms, one must consider the fact that the Phenomenologists were not trying to formulate an explanatory theory. Snygg and Combs' intent was to understand the behaving individual. If this understanding were *post hoc* it was still better in their eyes than the approaches which negated the individual entirely. The type of understanding their theory provided was, in large measure, a means of describing individual experience and a set of concepts for classifying it.

Because it was descriptive, the problem of definition became important. We have already indicated that many of their concepts were lacking in objective referents, and our discussion of the concept of differentiation implied that further definition here was also necessary. But the most blatant areas of vagueness were exactly those which have plagued all theories of "mind." Phenomenal field, phenomenal self, naive experience, etc., all seem to have an excess of meaning which has resisted objective specification. Snygg and Combs have succeeded, of course, in dispelling this vagueness to some degree, and insofar as they have succeeded, their theory can provide those psychologists who study individual experience with a foothold in a more objective territory.

SUMMARY

Basic Unit. Snygg and Combs focused on individual experience as an entity to be studied in its own right.

Field of Study. The individual experience was called the phenomenal field and included the external world and one's awareness of his own internal circumstances.

Methods of Investigation. Phenomenological introspection, which tapped not only the raw feel of experience, but its meaning to the individual, was employed to study the phenomenal field and was carefully checked against an observer's impressions to validate any conclusions.

Principles. The phenomenal field was organized on a figure-ground basis with each aspect interacting with all others. The organism sought, above all, to preserve this organization. Changes in the field occurred as the result of differentiation of new figures from ground, and each change was made in such a way as to cause the least possible disruption of the phenomenal field.

Consciousness. All psychological activity was determined by the phenomenal field. Consciousness corresponded to what was figure in the field at any particular time. The phenomenal field constituted reality for the individual at any particular time, and was organized in a way which was compatible with the individual's personality and the social group in which he lived. It maintained itself by assimilating events in such a way as to make them compatible with the existing organization, altering perception to fit the field if necessary.

Sensation, Perception, and Discrimination. Perception involved the differentiation of some particular figure from the rest of the field and an appreciation of the meaning of this figure in terms of the behavior it permitted or required. Shifts in perception occurred when there was a new focus or a new field, or as a result of gradual changes in figure-ground differentiation through learning.

Thinking, Cognition, and Memory. All cognitive processes were primarily matters of differentiation. To solve a problem was to find some means of differentiating the field so as to permit the emergence of cues which led to a solution. These various possible organizations of the field were tested for validity "in the mind's eye" until an appropriate solution was discovered.

Emotion and Motivation. The primary motive of the individual was to preserve and enhance the phenomenal field and the self. Biological needs were important only because their satisfaction kept the body in good health so that it might better serve the self. Emotions were expectations or preparations to react in such a way as to enhance the field and the self.

The Nature of the Learning Process. Learning was a matter of establishing accurate perceptions through shifting differentiation of in the field. No percept or act was ever an error or accident, because it was always dictated by the phenomenal field, and correct in view of that field at the time it occurred. A percept was shaped (differentiated) over a period of trials until it fit both the field and reality. Reinforcement was the basis of this shaping, and thus of learning. In addition, learning (differentiation) was facilitated by a number of conditions such as repetition, frequency, recency, primacy, similarity and contiguity.

Behavior and Personality. Behavior was governed by the phenomenal field, and must be consistent with it, since the purpose behind every activity was to preserve the phenomenal self. The personality developed around the self so that the characteristic goals and means taken by individuals to insure such preservation could be used as a means of classifying the individual. Changes in the phenomenal self came about through the gradual resolution of discrepancies through the assumption of new roles, or through sudden traumatic events.

REFERENCES

Phenomenology

Smith, M. B., "The Phenomenological Approach in Personality Theory: Some Critical Remarks," *J. Abn. Soc. Psychol.* 45: 516–522 (1950).

Snygg, D., "The Need for a Phenomenological System of Psychology," *Psychol. Rev.* 48: 404–424 (1941). Pp. 409–415 reprinted in M. H. Marx, ed., *Psychological Theory*, New York: Macmillan, 1951, pp. 324–329.

———, and A. W. Combs, *Individual Behavior.* New York: Harpers, 1949.

———, and A. W. Combs, "The Phenomenological Approach and the Problem of 'Unconscious' Behavior: A Reply to Dr. Smith," *J. Abn. Soc. Psychol.* 45: 523–528 (1950).

CHAPTER 28

GARDNER MURPHY (1947 TO PRESENT)

EACH STUDENT of psychology has his own approach to his field and his own interpretations of various theoretical systems are made in light of this approach. Gardner Murphy's theory seems to have begun as such a personal view, and it has become recognized as a distinct theory not because he purposefully formulated a new system, but because the outcome of his efforts had sufficient originality and heuristic value that it earned its status.

Murphy maintained that psychology must take a bio-social approach to its subject matter by deriving concepts which were applicable to every level of consideration from the biological to the anthropological. Murphy had no particular criticisms of psychological theory. He simply thought about psychology and wrote about it. His theory was a collage of concepts from Hull, Watson, Freud, Gestalt, Allport, Murray, and others, interlaced with his own ideas.

Basic Unit

Murphy addressed himself primarily to personality, but his concept of personality was broad enough to include behavior in general. He did not use the basic unit approach to delimit psychology, but proposed that personality (and therefore behavior) could be approached from several different frames of reference. First, it could be approached as an entity of scientific interest when compared with other similar entities. This approach viewed the individual as a gross event, such as fat men or athletic women. It amounted to head-counting or census-taking. Second, personality could be regarded as a thing with a number of specific characteristics, each of which had a determining effect on behavior. This approach is seen in the trait theories of personality which treat the individual as if he were a living mosaic of neuroticism, introversion, masculinity, etc. Third, personality could be seen as a dynamically developing organization of inter-related characteristics, a view common to holistic theory, clinical practice, and the technology of projective tests. For example, the hierarchy of defenses manifested under increasing stress might be of interest to a psychologist operating at this level.

Psychology required information at all three levels. Which one the psychologist employed was determined by what he was studying, and by how abstract or holistic, dynamic or classificatory he wished to be.

Field of Study

Murphy's delineation of levels of analysis was a delineation of field as well. In addition to prescribing how to approach the subject matter, it prescribed what kinds of things psychology should address itself to at any level. A head-counting approach must count heads, a trait approach must catalog traits, and an organizational-interactive theory must study dynamic patterns of behavior.

Methods of Investigation

Each level of anlysis had its own methodology. The gross approach, with its biological underlay, was prone to use a genetic method (i.e., how things came about or developed), either cross-sectionally or longitudinally, since this was most appropriate to the events upon which it concentrated. The trait approach was most easily facilitated by a comparative methodology. Dynamic organizations were amenable to either genetic or comparative study, but could be most efficiently examined experimentally. In taking this position, Murphy was unique; it was commonly believed that the complexity of an integrative approach to personality would discourage the use of experimental controls. Murphy argued, however, that this very complexity made experimental controls necessary.

Principles

Personality was composed of three interlocking systems of attributes. One set was a group of general, undifferentiated, temperamental variables which affected all the individual's behaviors. A second was a series of specific trait-type characteristics. A third was the organizational processes which integrated the general and specific variables into a dynamic pattern.

Maturation was the process of differentiation of the gross variables into specific ones and then into an integrated whole. In maturation the preponderance of variables became differentiated and integrated, but some general characteristics could only remain general, e.g., temperament.

All aspects of psychological function were the product of biological variables tempered during maturation by the acquisition of experience within the environment. What was acquired was as much a result of the organism's biology as of the environment. Life could be viewed as a field of forces, "inner" biological and "outer" social events interacting in a complicated manner. The individual was a complex of biochemical tendencies which were the ultimate cause of activity. Structure, likewise, was a system of chemical units which maintained an appropriate relationship to the environment. Homeostasis was merely the process by which the structural integrity was maintained.

The uniqueness of the individual arose not from the special aspects of his behavior but from their organization into a special pattern.

Consciousness

Consciousness was a phenomenon which Murphy did not feel required special theoretical treatment. He employed a fairly standard psychoanalytic description of it when necessary, but was never confronted with having to find special status for it within his own theory. This perhaps reflects the attitude toward consciousness prevelant at the time Murphy was writing the bulk of his theory. Man had consciousness as he had a head and two legs, but what it was was a question psychology could not answer in the 1920's, 30's or 40's (although in the 50's and 60's some promising neurological correlates have been found).

The distinction between mind and body was likewise unnecessary to Murphy. He pointed out that the organism was a region in a field. To account for the organism either in terms of the field or of the forces within the region was equally misleading. Mind and body were simply different organs which participated in behavior in their own peculiar ways.

Sensation, Perception, and Discrimination

There was a stage in infancy (and to some extent in exposure to strange situations at any age) in which the individual knew nothing more than sensation. The earliest experiences with the mother provided the means for the initial differentiation of sensations into meaningful events. Stimuli connected with feeding and maternal ministration came to have connotations relative to food and care. When some aspect became differentiated, there was an *anchorage* process, i.e., an idea was anchored to the event now isolated from the morass of sensory events displayed to the infant. All percepts were eventually so anchored to meaning and event.

Form of an object provided a second means of anchoring a percept. The infant seemed to have a need for form in his percepts and struggled to impose form on experience. His success was the result partly of the stimulus itself, and partly of his own skill in achieving form. Still another anchoring point of perception was the self. Early perception was entirely self-centered. The self, its needs, and its experiences determined perception completely. The infant assumed that the world was as he saw it, and that everyone saw it as he did. Only when percepts based on such self-centered interpretation were negated by reality could they be extinguished and a more realistic view substituted.

Whatever the anchoring point, gratification of a motive fixed (anchored) a percept. Thus, all perception depended on past wants which made it *autistic* to the extent that needs influenced the appreciation of reality. It was not until integration of the whole organism took place that true autism occurred; affect could not distort until there was something to distort and some means of producing distortion. Early infantile perception was too vague to be influenced by need, and thus could not be called autistic.

Autism arose in ambiguous or confusing situations where the perceived objects were for some reason unable to provide clearcut meaning. Given these circumstances, the person sought some means of interpreting the object and eventually anchored it, i.e., found meaning for it, in his own needs, or in social norms of some sort. Because autism provided meaning and gratification it endured, perpetuating itself unless or until it was extinguished.

While autism served a purpose, it could also distort reality, the nature of the distortion depending on the source and function of the autistic percept. Affect produced distortion by anchoring the event to a series of inner and outer events which might not be truly correlated, as when one frightening experience produced a fear of all dogs. Moreover, this activation of need or emotion facilitated isolation and fixation, so that perceptual learning took place more rapidly. Affect could also contaminate perception by making an individual perceive as he feared or wished the situation to be. Another source of autism was the culture in which the person lived. Autistic views of the world and the people in it were a part of every society. A culture institutionalized certain ways of perceiving in order to regulate behavior (e.g., "it is wrong to hate"), insure conformity ("all policemen are good"), and provide a common ground for communication (e.g., a myth or superstition). The institutionalized views often served to distort perception so that the behavior of whole cultures could be based on some mistaken premise.

Perception followed the general pattern of maturity which the biology of the individual enforced. At first perception was vague, but as more differentiation occurred specific percepts were achieved and eventually integrated into the rest of the person's cognitive content. Maturation and experience provided the opportunity for this differentiation-integration process. Even in adults, however, not all the percepts were complex integrations. Different aspects of experience were perceived with different degrees of precision—a vague object led to a vague percept, and a complex one to a more complex percept. In addition, some percepts remained vague or became complex because of the peculiar experiences the person had had with them. In general, however, there was a correlation between level of maturity and complexity of perception. The maturation of a percept from one level of differentiation to another was a matter of developing insight, i.e., the placement of a percept in a new context such that new connotations emerged. Thus, the shading of perception into thinking and cognition was made quite explicit by Murphy.

Thinking, Cognition, and Memory

Sensory events perseverated in the nervous system after stimulation had ceased. As a result of this perservation (memory) past sensory events could be reinstated at some later time, without necessitating the outer stimulation. The reinstated events corresponded to images, and images were the stuff of which thoughts were made. They were neural representations of events in other parts of the field and anchored the meaning of those events. They also provided convenient handles for the nervous system to use in processing experience and solving problems.

The concept of image did not explain the origin of thought, however. Images were merely the vehicle which permitted its inception; motivation was the actual cause of thought. Motives provided the basis for the figure-ground context, gave rise to the occasion for thought, and guided its course. Personality was actually a system of drives. Need governed the establishment and recurrence of associations and beliefs; one thought about what one needed. Thinking led to the achievement of the desired end, by exploring the situation and rendering the whole affair compatible with the general need-style-belief structure of the personality insofar as reality permitted. Thus, a man's need for status made him unhappy in his present job and created a problem he had to solve. He thought about the problem and tried to find a way of achieving the status he needed. He believed it was wrong to quit what one had started, but that it was more wrong to oppose unbeatable odds. He decided to ask for a transfer to a related department. Another person with a different system of needs and beliefs might quit or quarrel with his boss, or he might plug away, blaming himself for his failure. Whatever he did, his behavior was dictated by his needs and the kind of person he was.

Emotion and Motivation

Motivation, or need, was ultimately based on cellular tensions which destroyed the optimal working balance of the self and thereby necessitated some sort of action. Seen on the cellular level, motives or needs were always present because there were always a few cells in some state of tension. When enough cells were so disturbed the entire bio-social system was disrupted, causing some generalized action to take place. Motivation was based on *tension gradients*; no sharply defined area was the locus of a drive, and need arose whenever a sufficient number of cells were in a state of tension, no matter where these cells were. While tension in any cell added to the gradient, the particular activity which eventually appeared resulted from the extent and source of the greater portion of the tension, since the content of activity was a source while intensity was a function of amount of tension.

Drives or motives produced activity by lowering thresholds for certain behavior patterns. Each potential pattern included both preparatory acts, which would lead the individual into a situation where gratification was possible, and consummatory acts, which finally produced the actual gratification. These behaviors were eventually triggered by the coincidence of tensions with certain events which Murphy called *adequate stimuli.* Only such a coincidence of tension, threshold, and cue could elicit constructive activity.

Murphy classified motives into visceral drives, activity drives, sensory drives, and emergency responses according to the kinds of tensions which produced them and the consummatory acts they required. *Visceral drives* included hunger, thirst, excretion, oxygen deprivation, vasomotor adjustment needs (temperature regulation), sexual tensions, and maternal tensions. These drives were the result of biological deficiencies, the presence of alien materials, or some other identifiable biological event. They were characterized by periodicity, facilitation of each other, and fusion, so that the individual drive was often indistinguishable in the final motive state or behavior. The intensity and frequency varied from individual to individual and from time to time.

The *activity drives* seemed to be produced by tensions in the muscles. If one considered visceral drives only, or motivation from the tension-release point of view, it was possible to conclude that all organisms ultimately desired to be inactive, and that they roused to activity only to rid themselves of that which prevented them from maintaining nirvana. Living beings would seem, from this point of view, to be active only so that they could be inactive. Murphy rejected this conclusion. Actually, he said, both motor and nervous systems needed to maintain a certain level of activity, and the need became manifest in activity drives. Activities, both general and specific, were sought out by the individual to restore or maintain the optimal function of his muscles and neurons. Activity drives could facilitate each other and fuse, just as visceral drives did, and there were individual differences in their intensity; but they were not periodic in appearance, and tended to remain constant for each individual over a long time.

Just as all drives did not arise from the necessity of discharging tension, so all drives did not arise from the viscera either. *Sensory drives* were needs for certain kinds of certain intensities of stimulation. They seemed to involve a "stimulus hunger" wherein the person sought out certain kinds of sensations, e.g., music, beauty, kinesthetic contact. The sensory drives, like visceral and activity drives, could facilitate each other and fuse, and like activity drives were aperiodic.

In addition to the internally aroused drives, Murphy also recognized emergency responses, which were drive behaviors roused by external stimuli and resulting in the mobilization of the organism for fight or flight.

Whatever their origin, internal or external, motives were a biological phenomenon. They could be altered and molded by experience and culture, but they could not be created. Culture and experience, indeed, originated from need satisfaction and were themselves the product of need. It was the interaction of biologically based phenomena with social phenomena which Murphy sought to explain in his bio-social approach.

The Nature of the Learning Process

Needs, which began as vague yearnings and random activity, became specific because they were satisfied in particular ways. By means of a process Murphy called *canalization*, cues were learned and preparatory responses fixed so that consummatory behavior was facilitated. Canalization was limited by innate preferences, and its appearance was dependent on the frequency of reinforcement. Once established, a canalization persisted. New, more dominant canalizations could be added, but the older ones remained in the background (the reader will note that canalization has some similarity to Allport's functional autonomy). Murphy attributed great significance to canalization in accounting for behavior, but he did not describe the nature of the process or its basis beyond defining it as "progressive shifts in differential response to the various means of satisfying a drive" (1947, p.981).

Murphy recognized conditioning as another variety of learning. He described the conditioning process as follows: "A response elicited by a stimulus which is ordinarily biologically inadequate to arouse the response, but which, having been presented along with a biologically adequate stimulus, has come to be an effective substitute for the biologically adequate stimulus" (1947, p.982).

While canalization involved learning stimulus and preparatory response, conditioning resulted in a new stimulus, being capable of arousing preparatory and consummatory responses; the responses themselves were unchanged. The conditioned dog will salivate to the bell, for example, but does not try to eat it. His preparatory response is roused by the new stimulus, but his consummatory behavior is unaffected.

Conditioning was based on contiguity, according to Murphy. When tension was aroused, activity was initiated; the person moved to some new aspect of his surroundings. These new aspects acted on the individual while the tension was still high, so that the stimulus energies from the situation converged into the neural channels which were common to the tension stimuli. As a result of this merger, the new external situation was able to induce the same movements as the tension state. It was the tension system (motive) which was altered, and not the reflex which was conditioned.

In contrast to the persistence of canalization, conditioning was easily broken down. The extinction of a conditioned response was a product of changes in response dominance. Another response took over because it was stronger. Discrimination and spontaneous recovery were likewise products of dominance.

Generalization of a conditioned response could extend as far as there were reinforcing results, i.e., as far as culture or reality permitted it to go. Theoretically there was no physical limit to generalization; it could continue to occur as far from the original stimulus as did the reinforcement—but no farther. Then some other response became dominant.

Murphy hypothesized that second order conditioning was the source of many aspects of social behavior, values, and attitudes. Behavior based on second order conditioning could be expected to remain stable as long as it was reinforced, but it would be extinguished when reinforcement ceased. There appeared to be survival value in the high morbidity of higher order CRs; the individual was spared the necessity of excessive or useless behavior.[1]

Behavior and Personality

Biological traits were the basis of personality. Depending upon the maturity of the individual, these biological traits could appear as broad, undifferentiated tendencies, specific differentiated behaviors, or patterned integrated responses. The breadth, diffusion, and complexity of the organic traits were determined by the kinds of organs which participated in their formation. The vague general traits were the result of such general influences as hormones; the specific behaviors were the product of specific organs or organ systems; the integrated chains were produced by coordination of many organs, usually via the nervous system. There was, then, a high correlation between maturity, complexity of behavior, and complexity of the biological substrate.

No matter what happened in the course of an individual's life, the organic traits always underlay, limited, and instrumented behavior. Therefore, a distinction between functional versus organic was meaningless. All activity involved the biology of the individual and took place through biological mechanisms. Experience could supplement or alter stimuli and consummatory behavior, by conditioning and canalization of needs, but it could never take its place. Psychological traits were merely tissue responses to (cultural) stimulation. They determined the form of expression of a need in

[1] Murphy's hypothesis that fears were higher order conditioning and should extinguish easily has been contradicted by more recent studies in avoidance learning (see Chapter 32). These more recent findings do not negate the validity of his remarks concerning the survival value innate in the morbidity of higher order conditioning, however.

a particular individual. Theoretically, acquired behaviors were limitless, i.e., anything could be acquired. In each individual case what was learned was shaped by needs and culture.

Of the various environmental influences which formed behavior, symbols (language) were among the most powerful. The infant acquired symbolic language in two ways. He learned by making sounds himself, at first randomly, later with purpose. Some of these sounds were reinforced and others were not. He repeated those with which he was successful and in this way learned words. This was the active aspect of verbal learning. The infant also learned language passively, through hearing others make sounds which he eventually came to connect with certain stimuli or responses. There were dominance relationships in language just as there were in any other conditioning. A symbol whose meaning was lost or negated was dominated by other symbols and other meanings, and so was dropped out of the hierarchy of symbols, or at least relegated to a lower status.

Symbols were a means of acquiring higher order conditioning. A symbol once learned as a response to a situation could become an adequate stimulus for another response. The child reacted to a symbol as if the real stimulus were present. His response could be another symbol, which called forth another response, and so on.

Thought was the process of signaling to one's self. Spoken words became thought words. Symbols were used as internal cues, for they set up tension systems in the nervous system and could arouse still other tension systems.

The symbol pattern was the instrument for supporting attitudes and values. First, it communicated (revealed) value systems to others. It organized and defined values by conditioning a value attached to one word to all similar words. Words themselves sometimes evoked values. Application of these words to situations tended to arouse and sustain value responses. Values arose originally from organic needs. Certain goals were canalized and came to be worth something when evaluated in some way. Likewise, certain stimuli were conditioned to the original goal object through symbols. Values were maintained by the fact that the symbols represented real events. Some values were the result of constant, ever-present tension and were thus constantly influencing the personality. Others were cued off only in situations which pertained to certain needs.

Learning accounted not only for language, values, and attitudes, but also for conflict. Conflict could not occur physiologically; physical tensions summated and interacted, but they could not oppose each other. The insoluble conflicts with which abnormal psychology dealt were aroused when signals were ambiguous, when two valued objects or needs were in opposition (conflicting canalizations), or when one object aroused two sets of values (conflicting conditioning), i.e., when their origin was psychological.

The effects for conflict and frustration (failure to achieve desired goals) were also the basis for disorganized behavior. Thus, again, we see the bio-social facies of personality.

While symbols, values, and conflicts shaped behavior, they had to act on or through something. This something Murphy said was the self. The canalization of the self was the principal root of social behavior. There were no feelings of selfhood in the infant, but the first glimmerings of self-concept developed in the vague and undifferentiated infantile phase. As a result, some aspects of an individual's self-concept were broad, diffuse attitudes remaining from this immature phase. The self-awareness of the infant began in his gradual discovery of his own body, its sensations and capacities. The concept of his worth and value and the other social aspects of self were derived from experience with other people. The child first saw himself as others saw him. If the views of other people were negative, the child came to see himself in a negative light. The child tried to adapt himself to the view of others by becoming like them (identifying with them) in order to insure their acceptance of him. As he grew older he adopted the role of others in evaluating his actions. At this point the self was still a perceptual object, something which one saw and heard but which was really imposed from without, and not from within. With maturity the self became a conceptual trait system, a set of ideas, beliefs, and attitudes. The self system was usually fairly well established by the elementary school years. However, adolescence, with its physical and social changes, made some aspects of this self-concept untenable; new versions of self had to be achieved. The individual was no longer a girl-child or boy-child, but a young man or woman who was sometimes expected to behave in semi-adult fashion, and sometimes in a child-like fashion. During the teen-age years these inconsistences were resolved, and an adult self gradually evolved.

Those aspects of self which concerned self-enhancement or self-defense were labeled *ego* by Murphy. Many of the self-enhancement and self-defense maneuvers had autistic colorations, so that Murphy's ego was more a means of maintaining a self-concept than of dealing with the world in general, as the Freudian concept of ego connoted. In dealing with self-enhancement, Murphy adapted the psychoanalytic theory of defenses, the Adlerian concept of life styles, and many of the Jungian traits. His treatment was a fairly literal rendition except for the occasional introduction of new concepts. For example, *secondary inferiority* was that feeling of loss of value which occurred when original means of dealing with the feeling of inferiority broke down. Another bit of embroidery dealt with *willing* vs. *unwilling introversion*; many people, Murphy said, were introverted not by nature, but by trauma which led to social withdrawal.

Murphy concerned himself with many other aspects of personality, but his concern adopted fairly intact concepts of traits from Allport, culture and personality from the anthropologists, and speculations from various economists and historians. At the time of Murphy's initial interest the emphasis on cultural and economic aspects in social psychology had not yet become so pronounced. What seems like the repetition of well known hypotheses to the student of psychology today was a fresh and vibrant viewpoint in the 1940's when Murphy wrote of these things.

Critique

Murphy's interpretation of personality was a combination of highly original and creative concepts and a smooth eclectism. Given Murphy's verbal facility, some fairly standard treatment of psychological phenomena could seem quite fresh and new. Murphy's approach seemed to call for being toughminded about tenderminded things such as Freudian theory, and tenderminded about such toughminded theories as Hull's.

One is struck in reading material Murphy wrote in the 1940's with the accuracy of his predictions and hypotheses about cultural and motivational influences on perception. What Murphy hypothesized has become the "new look" in perception. Many years and many scientists have been spent discovering what Murphy had already deduced.

Somehow Murphy's handling of social phenomena was of a different quality than his chapters on biology and individual behavior. In a bio-social theory all things should, it seems, receive equal treatment. Yet for Murphy the social and interpersonal aspects of life were more or less the frosting on the cake. The social seemed to an overlay on the biological without melting into it. In part, perhaps, this was because in the aspects of his theory dealing with organic traits, perception, and motivation he was called upon to do original thinking, while the parts of his theory involving personality and social factors were largely adopted from other theories.

Murphy's formulation seems to serve best as an overview and an organization of psychological material. It is probably not tight enough to be used directly in prediction of behavior. While it does contain numerous suggestions which have heuristic value, it would be necessary to explain more fully the logic of many of the hypotheses and the details of some of the mechanisms involved. This is probably as Murphy intended it to be, for he was attempting to clarify issues and content, rather than to build a complete system.

SUMMARY

Basic Unit. Personality could be studied as a gross unit, a series of specific traits, or an integrated entity. Each frame of reference was necessary to a complete science and was complementary to the other two.

Field of Study. Using these three frames of reference, psychology had to address itself to the biological functions, the individual traits, and the social behaviors of the individual. Each level, and the interactions between levels, had to be understood for psychology to be complete.

Methods of Investigation. The frame of reference the psychologist employed and the level on which he concentrated determined the method he used. Genetic methods, either cross-sectional or longitudinal, were most appropriate to the study of biological functions; the comparative method suited the study of traits, while experimental controls were necessary to examine social phenomena.

Principles. Personality was composed of three interlocking systems: diffuse tendencies, specific traits, and integrated patterns. Maturation was a process of differentiation of the diffuse tendencies into integrated activities. In every personality attributes from each of the three levels of maturity were found. All aspects of psychological function were biological products tempered by social experience. What was acquired was limited by the biology even as experience shaped the expression of biological forces. Life was a field of forces, based on biochemical tendencies, in a homeostatic equilibrium. Individual uniqueness arose not from specific traits, but from the organization of the personality.

Consciousness. Murphy never dealt directly with consciousness since his theory did not require such a concept. Neither did Murphy study the mind-body problem since his bio-social approach accounted for personality as a region in a field, with both region and field dependent on each other.

Sensation, Perception, and Discrimination. Perception began with the infant's ability to differentiate specific aspects from the mass of stimuli to which he was exposed. Usually the first percepts centered around the mother. Once differentiated, a percept was anchored to its objective referent, to a meaning, and to its form qualities. Most percepts were also anchored to the self. Early perception was entirely self-centered; there was no concern for reality until the infant was forced by failures of his self-centered percepts to learn more realistic interpretations of the world. Gratification of a tension by an object fixed the percept so that it was autistic (affect-influenced) to some degree. Autism could not occur, however, until there was a sufficiently differentiated and integrated perceptual system that a specific percept could be influenced by a specific tension. The social world was also productive of autism. To live in a society required that an individual acquire certain attitudes, and these social regulations could become shared autisms. Autism of either the social or the emotional sort was most likely to arise in ambiguous situations.

Thinking, Cognition, and Memory. Sensory events perseverated in the nervous system after stimulation in such a fashion that they could later be reinstated in the absence of the stimulus. These reinstated sensory events were images. Images, including words, were the tools enabling one to think, but words were not the sole basis of thought. They were mere anchors or symbols. To account for thought required both Associationistic and Gestalt principles, but the crux of thought was the motives which originally made it necessary and which then structured it and directed its course.

Emotion and Motivation. All motives were based on biological tensions. Drives were the result of lowered thresholds for certain types of activity and included preparatory acts and consummatory acts. A pattern of drive-induced activity appeared when a state of inner tension coincided with the appearance of an adequate external stimulus. Vegetative (or internally) aroused drives were of several varieties: visceral drives, based on periodic biological deficiencies, activity drives, and sensory drives, based on the need for maintaining a certain level of activity and for seeking out certain kinds of stimulation. In addition there were a series of tensions broadly described as emergency responses, fight or flight behaviors aroused by threatening external stimuli.

The Nature of the Learning Process. Needs became specific because they were satisfied in certain ways. Murphy called this process canalization. As a result of this variety of learning new stimuli came to arouse altered consummatory responses. Canalization was apparently the result of reinforcement and was also dependent on frequency of experience. Once established it was a persistent act, one which would not be extinguished. In addition motivation could be altered by conditioning; new stimuli acquired the power to arouse the preparatory responses but had no effect on the consummatory response. In conditioning, the motive not the biological reflex was altered. Conditioning was easily extinguished if other responses became dominant over it. Second order conditioning accounted for many of the fears, attitudes, and values so important in the socialization and interpersonal relationships of the individual.

Behavior and Personality. Personality was based on organic traits. No matter what experiences the person had, his biology always underlay and delimited his activities. Psychological traits were merely tissue responses to cultural stimuli, established by canalization and conditioning. Symbols were among the more powerful social acquisitions of the individual. Words were learned through active trial-and-error and through passive conditioning, and were a means of acquiring higher order conditioning, for they could act as stimuli as well as responses. They seemed to instrument thought, signaling to the self information about the environment and behavior, and they supported, organized, and delimited attitudes and values. Learning also accounted for conflict, for it was only the acquired aspects of motivation which could come into conflict as a result of opposition to values or ambiguity of meaning. Disorganized behavior resulted from insoluble conflicts. Symbols, values, and conflicts exerted their influence primarily through their effects on the self, which was the principal root of social behavior. The self grew from a vague undifferentiated body image in the infant into a perceptual object for the pre-school child, evaluated as his parents would view it, and finally became a conceptual trait, an integrated way of thinking and doing, in the adult.

REFERENCES

Gardner Murphy

Murphy, G., *Personality. A Bio-Social Approach to Origins and Structure.* New York: Harper, 1947.

PART VIII

PHYSIOLOGICAL AND NEUROLOGICAL MODELS

CHAPTER 29

CYBERNETICS (1948 TO PRESENT)

IN all of the social and biological sciences there is an historical controversy concerning the relative influence of nature and nurture in human development. Most social scientists, because of their specialization, tend to view human behavior as primarily the result of life experiences. Scientists trained in biology and physiology, on the other hand, are more likely to regard the content of their own field as most important in determining behavior. Were the controversy between professions alone, it might be concluded that it evolved out of each group's lack of understanding of the other. The disagreement persists, however, beyond the professions. Some aspects of behavior are taken for granted as the function of one or the other factor. But there are a number of behaviors where the underlying cause is not so clear, and these become the foci of conflict. There are, for example, constitutional theories of personality which attempt to account for all individual variations in terms of body type, genetic structure, and various intrauterine effects. On the other hand there are the theories in psychology which completely ignore physiology. One of the areas of greatest dissension is the emotional disorders. The search for physiological bases for psychoses, neuroses, and psychosomatic illnesses continues with somewhat uncertain success. There are numerous claims for hormones, special conditions in the nervous system, and various physiological malfunctions which correlate with mental illness, primarily schizophrenia. While some of these hypotheses seem very encouraging, none of them are at present established beyond question. At the same time, and this will not come as a surprise to any student of psychology, there are numerous theories which can account for neuroses and psychoses purely on the basis of a person's traumatic experiences in childhood or other stages of life. The results of studies arising from these theories are equally ambiguous, promising but not proven.

What this ambiguity seems to point out, and what the antagonists forget, is that whenever something happens to a person, it happens to him by way of his body. For any behavioral change there is a concomitant change in bodily functions, organs, muscles, glands, and nervous system. No matter how psychological an act may be, it must be mediated by physiological processes. Likewise, these bodily functions must be triggered in some fashion, and they must have some relationship to the rest of the organism, to his pattern of adjustment, to his past experiences, and to his environment. It seems, then, that psychology and physiology are simply different levels of studying the same behavior, with neither one having exclusive territorial rights.

So far we have considered only the psychological side. Many investigators are also interested in the mediating processes, the physiology of behavior, and have made some attempt to fit the two fields together. It is possible, of course to seek physiological correlates for each psychological phenomenon, and vice versa. The search could be conducted empirically, but to the extent that empirical studies cannot utilize theoretical foresight they are inefficient. An alternative to blind empiricism is the use of a theoretical model which guides the researcher toward the most likely sources of information. A model need not predict what is to be found, but rather can supply specifications of what sorts of mechanisms should be looked for. Such a model can be found in Cybernetics, although in all fairness it must be recognized that Cybernetics provides equally as many specifications for psychology as for physiology.

Cybernetics was originated by Norbert Wiener. The term had its root in a Greek word which might be loosely translated as "helmsman" or "guide." Its connotations suggest the general principle that the nervous system could be viewed as a controlling apparatus. Throughout his history on this planet, man has invented numerous machines for coping with his environment. As these machines have become more complex man has also invented apparatus for controlling them, to substitute for or perfect his supervision of their activities. The controlling apparatus works to direct, coordinate, and maintain the functioning of many units of the machine into a smooth, efficient operation. It performs automatically the same acts just as the human being would, but is capable of doing so without his intervention. A thermostat controls temperature by producing changes in the function of a furnace or refrigerator. An electric eye opens a door. An automatic pilot flies a plane. Aiming and firing mechanisms control the action of guns. Because of their services thse apparatus have become known as servo-mechanisms. Since these mechanisms were developed as a substitute for human control, and therefore copied after it, Wiener and his followers believed that if one were to attempt to construct a model of the human control apparatus, the nervous system, one might well use such mechanical operations as a guide. In the discussion which follows, the theory has been much simplified and translated into less technical form.

Basic Unit

Cybernetics concerned itself with the states of being that a *machine*, living or mechanical, was capable of maintaining. State-of-being was a technical term referring to what the machine was doing at any particular time. It would correspond to some broad class of behavior, and was conceived of as a dynamic process; when it ceased to be dynamic it ceased to exist. Cybernetics was also interested in how the machine arrived at this particular state and what would happen next; it therefore involved itself with what it called *transformations*, or changes from one state to another.

Field of Study

The transformations and states of being of any organism or dynamic object were appropriate subject matter for Cybernetics since its focus was universal. Cybernetics was presumed to be equally applicable to everything from thermometers and robots to people, groups, cultures, and history. Individual sciences were not defined within this field, but it was assumed that Cybernetics was applicable to all.

Methods of Investigation

While Cybernetics was a theory of behavior, it was not a laboratory science. The proponents of Cybernetics were theoreticians, dealing in formulae and abstract conceptualizations in an attempt to derive a common denominator for the description and prediction of behavior. Their main tools were logic and mathematics. Experiments were rare, and if they were conducted, they took the form of construction of physical models by which to demonstrate hypotheses. Testing predictions and deriving others was of minor concern with these models. Thus, for example, a set of batteries connected into a self-regulating circuit might be equated with some aspect of the human brain and observed to see if it conformed to the hypotheses concerning universal function.

Principles

The basic and single principle of Cybernetics was the assumption that the function of every dynamic system, be it mechanical or living, was governed by the necessity of maintaining itself and, further, that all systems went about this in the same general way.

Consciousness

As a universal theory of function, Cybernetics did not become involved in phenomena specific to any one field or system. Thus, except for habitual use of the word in informal discussions, and perhaps not even then, consciousness was never mentioned. Insofar as it resembled aspects of the behavior of servo-mechanisms in general, we can infer that certain general concepts of Cybernetics would apply. Consciousness must in some way be conceived of as a mechanical process involving transmission of energy from the sensory nerves to various brain centers and then out again to the periphery of the body. Since this was a change in the form of activity, consciousness could be studied as a *transformation*, or a change in process. Insofar as it was involved in decisions determining behavior it was a means of creating changes in the body and the environment, and thus a *means of inducing transformations*. It might also be viewed as a *channel* or path by which messages or signals were communicated from one point to another, having much the same function as a telephone line. Consciousness was also *input*, something being done to something else which caused a reaction, and as a result of neurological and physiological processes it was an *output* of these processes. In short, consciousness could be viewed as a process, a product, a means of creating changes within and without the body, or as a means of communication, depending upon the context in which it was considered.

These functions were not peculiar to consciousness, however; they were characteristic of the nervous system as a whole. What gave consciousness its special status was its role in feedback, or entropy. When any system expended energy a certain amount would rebound and affect the further action of that system. Just as a ball thrown against a wall bounced back, or a pendulum swung back toward the position from which it started (*entropy*), some of the energy expended by the nervous system affected the sensory organs, thereby supplying information as to what was happening. As a result, neural processes could track the movement of a muscle, guide it, and/or compensate for it. It seems fair to infer that consciousness would be a feedback mechanism of a highly specialized sort; as a corollary of this inference, consciousness could also be viewed as an information-processing device.

Sensation, Perception, and Discrimination

Where a psychologist would speak of stimulus, a Cyberneticist would be more likely to use the term *information*. That is, he would see a stimulus as having some meaning or indicating some fact. From this point of view sensation would most likely become a registration of information, and perception a matter of *coding* this information into some other form so as to render it useful for the function at hand. When a person read a book, for example, a series of patterns of activities in the nervous system was perceived or translated as words. When a person reached for an object, the object itself, the movement, and all the other information necessary to perform the act were translated from physical events into sensory impulses and other neural events within the brain. This translation was much like putting something into a different language or making a map of a particular geographic area. The two sets of events (physical and neural) would be equivalent in every way except that the form would be different. When an event, an object, or an idea could take several forms, each of the several equivalent representations was known as an *isomorph*. (The concept of isomorphism was also important to Gestalt theory.) Perception might be said to "code" raw sensory data into an isomorphic pattern representing a concept; the data itself was the same but was more useful in its new form. The uses made of this coded information involved various processes which in Cybernetics might be called *transformations* (changes in state-of-being) while the psychologist would call them cognition.

Thinking, Cognition, and Memory

Thinking was obviously a regulatory process and thus was one of the primary concerns of the Cyberneticist in seeking a model of psychological function. However, the process involved in thinking was the same as that involved in learning, since the latter was regarded more or less as problem-solving. The details of the theory of cognition will therefore be discussed under the category of the Nature of the Learning Process.

In a theory which was an attempt to describe and account for mechanical and human behavior with the same principles, the phenomenon of memory became a problem. To conceive of memory as a thing in the past somehow influencing present and future action was incompatible with the machine. To make a machine capable of memory, allowance had to be made for alteration in its make up. "Memory" must really be structural change. This is, of course, similar to what many psychologists have proposed, but its derivation points to the necessity for caution in formulating concepts of cognitive function lest we unwittingly permit animistic or teleological reasoning to hide in the robes of scientific constructs, e.g., memory as a place, or as an entity.

Emotion and Motivation

Dynamic systems, when functioning smoothly, operated in a state of homeostasis, and psychological systems were no exception. Motivation could be conceived of as a disturbance in this smoothly functioning equilibrium leading to a transformation from one state-of-being to another. Different amounts of disturbance had more or less intense effects. More than one disturbance could exist at a particular time, in which case they combined into some grosser force. The final coalescence of forces was known as a vector, the usage of the term being the same as that of Miller (see Chapter 11) and Lewin (see Chapter 24).

Motivation was caused by something and resulted in something else. It was either input or output, depending on whether one was trying to understand the behavior it caused, or the condition producing that behavior.

It is typical of a Cyberneticist's thinking that how one viewed a particular variable or factor depended upon what one was trying to do with it. Anything which caused something else was itself caused in turn, and the chain of cause and effect could continue *ad infinitum*. In attempting to study a particular causal relationship the investigator was merely isolating one link of the chain for his study. When he desired to study another part of this chain, the cause-effect link which he originally conceptualized in one manner must now be seen in a new frame of reference. Such matters were difficult to communicate and complex to understand, yet it was their very complexity which made them adequate to handle the material involved.

The Nature of the Learning Process

Most life situations were so indefinite and complex that learning to deal with one's environment became a matter of trying to anticipate which of a number of probable outcomes might be most probable and of responding accordingly. This made learning and problem solving part of the same process. Probability learning and problem solving could most likely be accounted for by some mechanical arrangement within the brain, such that when a particular stimulus occurred it aroused neural processes which formed the potential for transformation from the present behavioral state into several others. The eventual selection of one of the several states came about, according to Cybernetics, by trial-and-error. Whatever intervened had to be of sufficient simplicity as to apply equally to the behavior of machines and to human brains. There were, for example, numerous mechanical regulators which, when a behavior was disrupted, could hunt throughout their system until a satisfactory solution, one which returned it to stable function, was found. Thermostats, electrical timers, electronic brains, computers, and automatic automobile transmissions were capable of such apparently purposeful action. Moreover, having found a solution these machines could maintain it until external forces created some new problem, or longer if the machine had some means of storing data (computers, for example, store facts on tapes or as electrical charges).

Translating this into psychological terms, learning was approached from much the same point of view as it was by Guthrie (see Chapter 12) and some of the other empiricists. That act was retained which occurred at the time of cessation of a disturbance. It persisted until another disruption occurred. The persistence was a function of the construction of the machine, but Cybernetics did not feel impelled to explain how each different machine was constructed to do this. Similarly, storage took place, given the facilities and a means of coding information into the facility. This, too, was a result of the way the machine was constructed. Cybernetics inquired no further into the matter than to say that with recurrence of disruption the stored information would be used, providing the machine was constructed that way.

If disruption ceased again the act persisted; if it did not cease, other acts occurred. Learning was a mechanical process, and matters such as contiguity and reinforcement were too concrete and specific to one particular set of animate systems to be important to the abstract theory of Cybernetics.

Behavior and Personality

Although the Cyberneticists were interested in deriving principles of behavior as an abstract phenomenon, their approach was to try to comprehend it through the study of incidents or events. To understand the mechanics of a particular act, the Cyberneticist manipulated input, observed the consequent output, and then inferred what intervened. The inference was validated by repeating the manipulations, and by varying them in such a way that different outcomes should be observed if their inference was indeed correct. By this means a model or construct was derived and eventually so worked out as to become a specifiable intervening variable.

Behavior could be either fine or gross; it was behavior when an endocrine gland responded to some nerve impulse by altering its activities; it was also behavior when a person perceived an angry animal, became frightened, and ran. On any level of consideration, behavior had three functions. It could communicate or transmit information about the state of the system to other parts of it, or to the environment. It could change or transform the function of its parts or its environment. Most important, it could regulate or maintain the stability of the existing state and the equilibrium of the system. However, this regulation was not static, as the term may imply; it was a dynamic process which could involve cycles of activity, alternation of responses, or other types of variation which preserved and enhanced the current state.

When a disturbance occurred it moved the system from one state to another. It transformed it, to use the language of Cybernetics, into some new state of dynamic equilibrium which maintained its stability until another disturbance arose. One means of maintaining stability was by the feedback mechanism. Technically, feedback was a manifestation of *entropy*, i.e., the reflection of some amount of expended energy, or information in the case of feedback, back into the system from which it originated. Ordinarily, enough data was fed back to maintain ongoing behavior. If feedback was negative, i.e., if less information was given back to the controlling mechanism than it sent out, it would eventually lose its ability to guide and direct the ongoing behavior because available information was an inadequate base for the regulatory processes. If feedback was positive, more information was given back than was sent out. Under these circumstances behavior could not only continue but could also develop or mature.

Behavior was characterized by variety. Any act was one of a number of things which could have occurred and was selected by the controlling mechanism as the most appropriate. In well organized (automatic) behavior there was less possibility of variety because the behavioral pattern had been previously set and any deviation from it would destroy efficiency. In like manner, a malfunctioning system also suffered from a lack of variety in its actions because all the necessary states were not available to it. A system which could not vary at all was nonfunctional; if such a system had been an animate being, it was now dead. The variability of a machine was another aspect of the entropy concept. As a result of inadequate energy or information, negative entropy involved the loss of variety and adaptability. The gradual appearance of negative entropy was to be expected in the course of the life of a system until it finally wore itself out and could no longer regulate its own activities.

Critique

There is a danger that Cybernetics with its new vocabulary is simply calling old things by new names. On the other hand, the vocabulary of Cybernetics does render a number of unique connotations. If these connotations suggest new and fruitful hypotheses, then certainly there is more to the theory than new names for old things.

In the meantime one might question whether the theory is capable of handling the complexity of human and social behavior. There is no doubt about its capability to describe mechanical behavior, and insofar as human behavior is automatic or reflexive it can account for it. More important to psychology is whether it can contribute to the understanding of social behavior. When confronted with problem-solving behavior or complex regulatory action the theory tends to break down. It is given to saying that probabilities are taken into account, or that a machine can be developed which can select one of several responses. But too often it says no more. How can it be done? And how can this be translated into something equally significant about human brains and social behavior? The analogy is useful, but a theory that stops with the statement that something is analogous to something else and does not explain the analogy may have stopped where it should have begun.

Any theory which purports to equate man with machine is certain to be doubted as a sufficient explanation of the richness of the individual. Every theory in psychology is open to such doubt, but others do not invite attack on this point as Cybernetics does. Physics has solved this problem by contenting itself with atoms, molecules, and elements, leaving it to the engineer to apply the acquired knowledge to building bridges. Psychology either cannot or does not wish to avoid the problem of straddling the gap between abstract theory and everyday applications and will criticize any theory which restricts itself to either side. Cybernetics is an abstract theory whose proponents believe it is sufficient unto itself. In turning to more concrete physiological theories we shall have an opportunity to test this sufficiency.

SUMMARY

Basic Unit. Basic to the theory of Cybernetics were the various states of being an entity was capable of maintaining and the transformations from one state to another.

Field of Study. Cybernetics was a theory of behavior of anything, animate or inanimate, which was capable of activity. Its goal was to derive laws describing behavior in this general sense.

Method of Investigation. Cybernetics was not experimental, and therefore methodology in the usual sense was not a matter of concern.

Principles. All dynamic functioning could be described by the same laws, whether the function was human, animal, mechanical, or chemical.

Consciousness. Cybernetics did not concern itself with specific processes such as consciousness. It was more interested in the role a process played in a certain context. Thus, consciousness could be a means of producing change, a channel of communication, an output of physiological activities, or the input for other physiological activities depending upon one's frame of reference at a particular time. These functions were, of course, common to the entire nervous system; what made consciousness a special process was its status as the locus of the feedback mechanism.

Sensation, Perception, and Discrimination. Sensation was a registration of information; perception was the process of coding this information into a form usable within the nervous system.

Motivation and Purpose. Any disturbance in function which destroyed stability motivated a change of process.

The Nature of the Learning Process. Given a disruption in function, a self-regulating mechanism was capable of searching its system until it arrived at some state which returned it to stability. This state would then persist until some other disruption occurred. Information about this solution could be stored if the mechanism had storage facilities. Viewed in this light learning was a mechanical process, and matters such as contiguity or reinforcement were too specific to certain animate mechanisms to be important to such an abstract theory as Cybernetics.

Behavior and Personality. Behavior communicated to other parts of the entity or its environment information about its current state of being. It was a means of changing the state-of-being and the environment. Above all it served as a means of regulating and controlling the state of the machine.

REFERENCES

Cybernetics

Ashby, W. R., *Design for a Brain.* New York: Wiley, 1952.
Ashby, W. R., *An Introduction to Cybernetics.* New York: Wiley, 1956.
Wiener, N., *Cybernetics.* New York: Wiley, 1948.

CHAPTER 30

D. O. HEBB (1949 TO PRESENT)

DONALD HEBB is a physiological psychologist whose writings demonstrate how physiological theory and data can be used to answer questions put to it by psychology. Cybernetics prescribed the nature of things which physiology must account for. Hebb directed this inquiry further by describing the kinds of organic structures which would be required. Hebb's theory was a model, too; it was simply less abstract than Cybernetics. It described human functioning alone, and could thus formulate more specific hypotheses than was possible in a theory which attempted to deal with men, machines, and society. Hebb's work was perhaps all the more impressive because it was done before Cybernetics had much impact on the studies of psychology and physiology; and yet the processes that he proposed complement nicely those hypothesized on a different level by Cybernetics.

Hebb was trained partly in Canadian schools and partly in the United States, and he has been affiliated with universities in both countries. His interest in neurophysiological aspects of behavior arose from a study of the effects of major brain operations on intelligence and behavior. To account for the apparent lack of permanent damage which he observed, he developed a number of hypotheses about the nature of psychological processes out of which his theory eventually grew. Hebb believed, contrary to Gestalt theory, that within the brain there was some specificity of function. Although he accepted the Gestalt concept of the brain as a field of patterned activity, he did not feel that a pattern of activity in one part of the brain was necessarily equivalent to patterns in other areas. He postulated that certain areas had certain functions brought about by underlying structure. On the other hand, Hebb was critical of Hull and the other Neo-Behaviorists for proposing too much specificity. He also criticized Hull's learning theory for reasons which will become obvious when his own learning theory is considered.

Basic Unit

In his formulation Hebb was concerned with two types of units. The more molecular unit was the behavior of the individual neuron and its connections with other neurons. The second, more molar unit consisted of the patterns of activity in groups of neighboring neurons.

Field of Study

The activities of the molecular unit (the neuron) and the molar unit (groups of neurons) and the interrelationships between the two formed the body of Hebb's theory. Hebb would not dispute that generally psychology should be a study of behavior, animal and human. He was personally interested in what underlay behavior and tried to bring these phenomena within the scope of psychology. However, his theory did not confine itself to physiology, but also contained a number of formulations about the nature of behavior. He set up a model for physiology based on the needs of psychology, but he gave back to psychology a similar model dictated by the functioning of the nervous system.

Methods of Investigation

No particular method was prescribed by Hebb. His theory was originally founded upon his empirical findings derived through a number of techniques. As the theory developed, it generated in turn certain hypotheses and predictions which were exposed to empirical trial using whatever means were appropriate. Insofar as Hebb's concern was physiological, his experimental studies used the procedures of physiology rather than of pure psychological research. These procedures have permitted him to derive a number of principles of physiological functioning.

Principles

Hebb's most basic principle dealt with the establishment of connections between neurons. Among the neighboring neurons with which a particular nerve cell could be connected, those whose activities were simultaneous with its own became more strongly related to it. The development and strengthening of the connections could occur in several ways. First, there could be a general growth of the whole neuron in the direction of others which were active at the same time (neurobiotaxis). Second, there might be changes in the structure of the junction or synapse of neurons. (Hebb claimed to have discovered knob-like formations appearing on axons and on neighboring dendrites which seemed to serve to bridge the gap across the synapse, facilitating neural transmission.) Third, neural connections could be reinforced by certain hormone-like secretions from the nervous system such as adrenalin, noradrenalin, and acetylcholine, which further facilitated transmission from neuron to neuron. Fourth, there might be temporary outcroppings of the cell material at the synapse resembling synaptic knobs, though their brief duration made it more appropriate to refer to them as *ameboid growths*.

Not only were the connections between individual neurons strengthened by concurrent activation, but neurons which were consistently activated at the same time soon became so strongly connected to each other that they formed a sort of pattern. If one neuron of this pattern was activated, it tended to activate its neighbors even though they might not have been activated by the stimulus itself. This was known as *facilitation* of the firing of the other neurons. These patterns were formed so that physical proximity was less important than temporal contiguity. Neurons did not trigger off neighbors unless they were connected. They could activate very distant nerve cells if they had previously fired concurrently. Such interconnected groups Hebb called *cell assemblies* or *phase sequences*, depending on their complexity.

Much of what seemed to be native or natural in the adult could be shown by closer observation to be the result of primitive learning in the infant. Learning, perception, and motivation in the infant were different than in an adult. The early months of an infant's life were given over to learning how to perceive and interpret stimuli. In like manner, motivation began with a generalized disturbance of physiological functioning which was only gradually directed in a particular way as the organism learned to interpret its fine variations. The process of learning was itself different. The infant learned stimuli, the adult learned relationships; the infant learned how to make responses, the adult learned how to choose among them.

The organism sought to maintain homeostasis or equilibrium. Conflicts between patterns of neuron activity aroused by incompatible stimuli or environmental blocking of a particular act led to disturbance in neurological functioning, and consequently to changes in behavior.

Consciousness

Consciousness was thought to be a central process of long duration, the nature of which could not be specified. It was a self-maintaining process which organized and controlled behavior, making certain neural circuits available and blocking off others. It was characterized by selectivity and purpose. Familiar matters seemed to arouse neural patterns which circulated from beginning to end quickly and smoothly. Because of their efficiency these patterns required little conscious effort. For the most part unfinished, partly learned, or new experiences dominated the functioning of the nervous system and consciousness.

It will be noted that Hebb's formulation of conscious functioning was similar to Tolman's suggestion that consciousness arose when some problem appeared or when some decision had to be made. Consciousness mediated the perceptual and cognitive processes which permitted decisions to be made.

Sensation, Perception, and Discrimination

Except for a few constitutionally determined factors in the sensory centers of the brain which delimited and controlled the individual's perceptions, such as the figure-ground relationship), sensory experience (sensation) was raw data which the individual had to learn how to perceive. In addition to sensory data there were a large number of non-sensory influences coming from the life experiences of the individual which determined perception. Learning what to perceive and how to perceive it was a prolonged process.

Most of Hebb's theory of perceptual learning was generalized from research in vision. Visual perceptions involved not only the stimuli themselves, but also various motor processes. In viewing something for the first time or for the first few times the eye had not only to register what was given to the retina but also to trace the stimulus by moving about it. For example, if a person sees a triangle he sees the lines, but he also moves his eyes as he focuses on various aspects of it. Hebb believed that it was by such tracing with the eyes that the infant learned to perceive and to discriminate forms. This hypothesis was based on observations of perceptual learning in persons who had been blind until adulthood then somehow gained vision. These people underwent a considerable period of learning which Hebb proposed must resemble the evolution of perception in infants.

In the early stage of perception there occurred what Hebb referred to as the growth of the *cell assembly*, i.e., the patterning of discharge among a number of neurons. When a series of neurons were activated, two different kinds of traces could be noted after firing had ceased. First, there was some electrical activity in the neurons for an extremely short period after stimulation had ceased. Second, there was a structural trace, a more or less permanent change in the neurons as a result of their mutual activity. Hebb proposed that the electrical trace was maintained long enough to facilitate the structural change. This structural change in a neuron took place in such a way as to make it more likely that when one of the neurons in the series was again activated the others would also be aroused, either by direct interconnection or through some intermediary source which activated the whole series. Since these changes were the means by which neural connections were established, it was not surprising that they occurred at the junction (*synapse*) of one neuron with another. Hebb believed that the changed consisted of the growth of knobs on the axon (sending portion) of the nerve cell, or on any other part of the cell which was close to the dendrite (receiving portion) of other nearby neurons active at the same time. In some way these knobs connected the neurons, either by decreasing the distance between them or by making possible some trigger effect through the secretion of hormones like adrenalin and acetylcholine. While such structural changes could result from one occurrence of mutual activity, they were more likely to be established gradually as a result of a number of such occurrences.

In discussing the further development of perception, Hebb referred again to vision. In the part of the brain which received visual stimuli there was an area which might be called a projection center. Here the stimulus was represented isomorphically or topographically, i.e., each aspect of the stimulus as it impinged upon individual units in the retina was represented by neuronal firing. In the areas beyond this point of entry, however, there was no such organization among neurons or among patterns of stimulation. The neurons were connected with each other in a complex and unpredictable manner such that the one-to-one reproduction of a visual stimulus would be impossible. Hebb hypothesized that the visual pattern was represented by the concomitant firing of a number of neurons. After a number of firings of the several neurons a cell assembly was built up. This process characterized all the visual centers of the brain beyond the projection area. In the higher centers the cell assembly representing some visual stimulus became associated with cell assemblies representing other sensory, emotional, and physical states of the organism. It was at this point that the motor activity involved in the tracing movements of the eye became associated with the visual experience. The arousal of these cell assemblies was the basis for attributing meaning to a stimulus and for the anticipations a stimulus aroused. The patterns of cell assemblies composed still more complex neural constellations which Hebb called *phase sequences*. These were more or less synonymous with percepts. For example, the phase sequence which represented the percept of a triangle would involve cell assemblies fired by each individual aspect of the figure, the lines and angles, and by the eye movements which accompanied it. This information or phase sequence would be sufficient for an infant to recognize a triangle and match it with others. In the more mature person the phase sequence would become more complex, for it would include cell assemblies connected with the word and idea of a triangle and past experience with the nature of triangles. Phase sequences could also combine to produce even more complicated percepts.

A phase sequence tended to behave in a variable manner. A person might perceive the organized unit for a moment, and then the pattern might break up briefly so that some individual assembly, e.g., the lines of the triangle, was the focus of the percept. Then the phase sequence might reappear. This vacillation from cell assembly to phase sequence was probably most characteristic of the early stages of perception, though it never completely disappeared.

As perception became more facile the phase sequence could be aroused by the activation of fewer cell assemblies, so that the whole complex percept was worked out from a few significant cues. This process was known as *fractionation*, and was important in producing percepts quickly and efficiently.

The stability of the stimulus was also important to efficient perception. The more stable the stimulus pattern, the more readily it was identified. If the stimulus was extremely unstable, different cell assemblies were activated each time it was experienced. All these assemblies were reactivated each time it reappeared. A particular percept was the result of a particular set of assemblies, and thus varied in its appearance according to whether these assemblies or some other set had been activated. Each set had a certain probability of occurrence, depending on the stimulus and on past experiences, and each percept, therefore, had a similar probability of occurrence. Complex percepts almost always involved probabilities. The more complex or unstable the percept, the more probabilities were involved, and the longer the time required to organize the percept, neurologically speaking, or to learn it, psychologically speaking.

Thinking, Cognition, and Memory

Hebb proposed that thinking was a process of setting up hypotheses about relationships in one's environment on the basis of insight. As the insight improved the hypothesis also improved, becoming more and more valid. The improvement of the hypothesis involved learning, and the general insight-hypothesis process was really no different from learning. What differentiated thinking from learning was that thinking was more likely to result in temporary changes in the nervous system, while learning produced permanent alterations. Hebb believed that thinking might involve the ameboid growth of temporary knobs on the synapses of the nerve cells, temporary outcroppings of the cell material which apparently resembled the synaptic knob in every way except that they did not last as long.

Memory (and learning) could also be accounted for through synaptic knobs. So conceived, memory was not a thing which somehow floated around in the mind, but was a modification in the structure of the brain which facilitated connections between certain neurons or cell assemblies or phase sequences. (The reader will recall that this is what Cybernetics also proposed.) Given the hypothesis that memory was based on the appearance of synaptic knobs, forgetting could most easily be understood as the disappearance of these knobs through disuse. This proposal was in contrast to the more common belief that forgetting resulted from interference of newly learned material with the recall of earlier learning. It also contrasted with the suggestion that an inhibitory process could account for forgetting.

There is little more we can say about cognitive phenomena, since they were so closely bound up with learning. Having defined them and pointed out their relationship to learning, we postpone all discussion of conditions affecting them until we take up learning.

Emotion and Motivation

Hebb recognized two general classes of emotion. In one class were the pleasant feelings which led to behaviors tending to maintain or increase the original stimulation, having the apparent effect of enhancing functioning. In the other class were the aversive affects such as rage and fear wherein the response was one which sought to abolish or decrease the stimulus level, apparently in order to restore functioning. Aversive emotions were extremely disorganizing because they disturbed cortical patternings and aroused phase sequences which were incompatible with those already activated as part of some ongoing activity. Thus activity was blocked, but it blocked aversive actions in turn until one phase sequence or the other became strong enough to dominate and lead to avoidance (and aversive affect) or to relief of the aversion and continuation of the original action. If something happened to block avoidance without relieving the aversion, emotional disturbance developed. For example, a student upset by his inability to solve a problem might have an impulse to forget it all and go to a movie, and yet be unable to stop because he knew his grade depended on getting the work finished. He would remain mildly upset until he either solved the problem or comfortably extricated himself from it. If, however, he could do neither, he might eventually become very anxious, or very angry, or develop a headache, or tear up his notes and throw his books at the wall.

Aside from rage and fear, pain could cause emotional disturbance since it was not only a stimulus to aversive emotions, but also a source of cortical disorganization in its own right. However, when pain became a part of an organized neural pattern it no longer had such a disrupting influence. For example, experimental animals have demonstrated efficient learning on mazes and other laboratory apparatuses when a painful stimulus was used as a cue to indicate correct responses. It would appear that under the latter type of circumstance pain had in some way changed its character as a result of becoming a part of organized neural activity.

Another potential source of emotional disturbance was change in bodily processes. Hebb believed that in order to maintain smooth operation of the brain a certain level of activity must be maintained. He referred to this as sensory facilitation of cortical functioning, since by and large the optimal level of cortical function was brought about by impulses from sense organs reacting to the myriad stimuli in the environment. The constant influx of impulses acted as a priming device to the central nervous system; or perhaps a more apt analogy would be to the transmission of an automobile engine. Just as the engine can move the car only when it is geared to a certain speed and power ratio, so the brain was geared to a certain level of activity. If it had to handle more or less than its capacity it tended to become less efficient, and the entire organism was upset unless and until the nervous system "shifted gears" to produce an organization appropriate to the new level. Loss of facilitation, either because of sensory deprivation, or because of changes in those parts of the brain which served as activating systems, would lead to emotional disturbances. Experiments have shown that a person isolated in a darkened, sound-proof room and shielded from tactual stimulation with heavy gloves and thick clothing soon found his functioning extremely disrupted. People left in such a situation over a period of hours have been known to experience hallucinations and other bizarre phenomena.

Finally, changes in blood chemistry were a source of emotional disturbance. Variations in blood chemistry produced by toxic conditions of disease or drugs, physiological deprivation such as lack of food or oxygen, or any other intense drive affected the neuron, altering its firing pattern and destroying cortical organization.

The effect of drives on neural processes leads naturally to a consideration of the broader aspects of Hebb's theory of motivation. Some behavior, particularly in animals, was innately determined by physiological structure, i.e., was instinctual. Such instinctual activity was controlled solely by sensory influences, as opposed to the cognitive processes of higher brain centers. An organism with a very large part of its brain given over to sensory systems and having only a small *internuncial*, or association, area was subject to direct sensory control from the beginning of life. It was under these conditions that instinctual activity was possible. The larger the internuncial system, the less sensory control existed at first, and the slower it was established. More connections had to be built up, and more neural processes were involved. Given such a complex system, instincts were fewer, and acquired voluntary activity predominated. The size of the internuncial system was positively correlated with the organism's position on the phylogenetic scale. Man, who has the largest internuncial system and one of the smaller sensory systems, possesses very little instinctual behavior. Even in the lower animals instinctual acts might involve primitive learning, and in more complex animals expectations of the consequences of an act whose structure was itself instinctual could be of the utmost importance in determining whether or not the act occurred.

Although not cited by Hebb, Kuo's work with the development of chicks in embryo provides an example of how primitive learning influenced an instinctual act. Kuo's studies were described in detail in Chapter 9 in connection with Watsonian Behaviorism.

Motivation, even in instinctual acts, was not the arousal of activity in the organism by means of certain drive stimuli. It was rather a pattern of cortical functioning, an organized phase sequence. The sequence was characterized by specific direction and specific content, by persistence, and by stability of this direction and content. It controlled subsequent behavior, guiding it toward certain goals. The goals were selected on the basis of anticipations stemming from previous contacts.

Hebb postulated a common process underlying all motivated acts which he called the *central motive state.* Any physiological deprivation, Hebb said, affected the chemistry of the body and through this affected the brain, arousing a similar pattern of cortical disorganization regardless of the nature of the deprivation. The individuality of a motive was probably a function of the differential physiological effect of the specific deprivation. Depending upon the chemical and mechanical consequences of a physiological disturbance, some phase sequences were activated, and some were not. The activation or lack of it took place in addition to the general effects on cortical organization.

Motivation was independent of any special sensory stimulus which instigated the subsequent physiological and behavioral events. It was easy to mistake certain stimuli for drive stimuli because the same changes in blood chemistry which affected the brain also affected other organs of the body. For example, contractions of the stomach in hunger were not the cause of hunger; they were simply a correlate of a particular chemical status of the organism. What seemed on the surface to be specific drive stimuli were in reality effects of deprivation accompanying a more general disruption.

A motive did have the effect of sensitizing the organism to certain stimuli which were appropriate to gratification, however. The organism became vigilant, noting these stimuli more quickly than others and reacting to them more intensely.

In infants, the behavioral response to arousal of the central motive state was general restlessness and gross, undirected activity. The individual had to learn what he must do and what goals he must seek to satisfy himself. He also had to master the skills involved. Even the apparently innate consummatory acts (eating, drinking, etc.) were suspect to Hebb. He proposed that close examination would reveal learning here as elsewhere. In hunger, for example, the young organism must learn not only how much to eat in order to satisfy his needs, but also how to eat in the first place. Eating behavior was first elicited in the mammalian infant by stimulation of the lips, leading to a sucking reflex. Some things taken into the mouth produced unpleasant sensations and were consequently ejected. Those which did not seem unpleasant were mouthed and swallowed if possible. If the infant happened to suck on an appropriate object, the stomach contractions ceased and hunger stopped. After feeding, if no other stimuli were experienced the brain assumed a synchronous firing pattern which was so smoothly organized as to result in lethargy, lack of reactivity, or sleep. As hunger increased again, this smooth pattern was disrupted and cortical firing became disorganized. The infant grew restless and in its moving about was more likely to come in contact with the nipple. As the sequence was repeated the sensory stimulation was organized into assemblies of cells which facilitated certain motor behaviors. As organization increased still more, the appearance of a motive state was no longer disrupting, and the conceptual process which controlled eating became associated with other processes such as those representing the perception of food, the use of various utensils, etc. Integrated behavior of this sort was the result of an organized pattern.

If a motive state persisted unfulfilled beyond a certain time, so many cells were disrupted that no assembly could function in an organized fashion. At this point there occurred a change at the assembly organization level. This change in level would gradually affect the whole nervous system. If starvation occurred, for example, the assembly became organized and stabilized at a still lower level of activity, so that the organism was no longer interested in eating, at least until something forced him to do so. This apathetic state was brought about by the new organization of neural activity.

Occasionally, either as part of an organized act or through some external intervention, there was inhibition of activity. Inhibition consisted neurologically of a disruption of the pattern of neural activity in such a way that there was no longer facilitation among sequences. Under such circumstances one sequence could not initiate another.

Inhibition was particularly important in sexual behavior. Sexual excitation resulted in arousal of the central motive state, as did all other biological drives. The fact that it led to a different kind of behavior was due to certain differences in the general process. These details altered the central neural process, creating some sensory reactions and facilitating others. There was first a sequence of behavior which increased stimulation until a threshold was reached and orgasm was accomplished. This was followed by an inhibition of any further activity, apparently as a result of the interruption of the pattern of neural activity.

Waking and sleeping were also motivational phenomena. The neurological correlate of wakefulness was diffuse, generalized activity in the brain which seemed to function as a background for sensory, motor, and cognitive events. The neurological activity appeared to facilitate these events since they could not occur without its accompaniment. As sleep approached the diffuse activity seemed to abate and the firing of the nerve cells achieved a high degree of synchrony, or *hyper-organization* as Hebb called it. Such synchronous firing prevented integrated muscular control. In between the synchrony of sleep and the asynchrony of waking there appeared to be a state similar to emotional disturbance, produced by the incompatibility of the two levels of organization.

Waking, Hebb stated, was a motivated process. Old, familiar acts were performed quickly and automatically, requiring little involvement of the brain as a whole. Newer responses, however, demanded a good deal of cortical involvement. With the cortex so aroused, an asynchronous organization was maintained and the organism remained in a state of wakefulness. Hebb concluded that novelty was the motivating force for staying awake. He denied that fatigue was an important aspect of sleep, for a person tired of one task to the point of weariness could perform another with gusto. Hebb generalized from his observations on the effects of newness that growth and development in one's self, achieving some new synthesis or mastering some incipient neurological disruption, were the prototype for all feelings of pleasure. It was pleasure which kept us awake, and a lack of it which allowed us to sleep. Since pleasure kept us awake and variety led to growth and development, we may conjecture what effect such reinforcing factors had on the acquisition of skills and knowledge.

The Nature of the Learning Process

Learning was a lasting change in two or more specific neural structures which facilitated interaction between them. The learning process differed between infants and adults.

The infant organism had to learn to organize individual neural units into cell assemblies and then into phase sequences. Such learning had nothing on which to base itself. It had to create its own foundations by isolating events and then acquiring knowledge about them. Because it was the beginning of adjustment to life, infantile learning was slow and inefficient. The slowness was not due to poor motivation but to the necessity of building up basic percepts. Hebb suggested that the speed of early learning could be predicted by a ratio of the total size of the association areas of the cortex to the total size of the sensory cortex. In an organism which had a large area given over to sensory centers and only a small part of the brain involved in associations, learning could take place quickly because there was no room for establishment of more complex relationships. Organisms with large association centers learned slowly because in order to establish a percept a number of complex connections had to be made in the association center. The end result of such complexity was the ability to make finer and more varied distinctions about the environment. This was desirable even if it did leave the infant organism helpless in its environment for a longer period of time, since the numerous associations he could eventually form made him more adaptable. The lower the organism was on the phylogenetic scale, the more quickly it learned but the less flexible it was.

It was the nature of all early learning to be continuous. That is, there was a gradual establishment of some connection, or rather a series of connections, within the brain. Such connections allowed for environmental control of associative processes (including perception and cognition) and motor responses.

In contrast, later learning was discontinuous. It involved insights into relationships between objects, stimuli, phase sequences, etc. This type of learning could not be continuous beyond a point because once one saw a relationship the learning was established. There was, of course, the possibility of improving and refining such an insight, but for the purposes of distinction between the two phases of learning the continuous-discontinuous dimension was quite useful.

Learning in adults involved insight into relationships existing in the environment. Physiologically, insight could be equated with the association of cell assemblies into phase sequences, and of phase sequences into more complex patterns. Such associations were established because one or more cell assemblies or phase sequences were active at the same time, and a bond was created between them. Psychologically, insight could be equated with the appreciation of the meaning of the relationship represented by the bond, a matter requiring the exercise of intelligence. The process of insight was found all along the phylogenetic scale, but it was different for different organisms, simpler animals being capable of much simpler insights.

What Hebb meant by insight was not what the Gestaltists meant. Hebb's theory did not connote the sudden emergence of new concepts. It was rather the use of earlier learning to appreciate hitherto unsuspected possibilities. The hypotheses that preceded insight were based either upon expectancies recollected from previous experiences or anticipations founded on presently perceived material. Insight therefore required experience as well as intellectual capacity.

Insight and infantile learning were not the only aspects of learning to draw Hebb's attention. He also interested himself in incidental or latent learning, suggesting that this occurred when two different phase sequences unrelated to each other operated at the same time. A satiated animal placed in a maze might wander about showing no evidence of learning because the phase sequence governing his behavior was independent of any phase sequence established as he came to appreciate the maze and how it led to food in the goal box. Later, if a strong stimulus appropriate to the maze behavior appeared it would initiate the dormant phase sequence, making the earlier learning obvious.

As the treatment of latent learning implies, Hebb did not feel that reinforcement was necessary to account for learning. He pointed to the difficulties in finding the necessary physiological correlates of reinforcement, the traces which presumably must exist for some time after the stimulus in order for it to become associated with the reinforcement. Even if pleasure and pain were not necessary for learning, however, they did channel it along certain lines. Pain was avoided because of its disrupting qualities, and pleasure was sought after because it tended to prolong the organization of certain patterns of activities in the cortex.

From Hebb's objections to reinforcement and the implications of his descriptions of neural functioning, it seems that his theory of learning pointed toward contiguity as the underlying physiological process by which learning was established. A connection was made between two assemblies because they happened to be active at the same time. Learning, described in these terms, was a matter of physiological proximity and timing. The consequences of an act could keep the organism in the situation, or drive him away; they did not determine what he learned but they determined what he did.

Behavior and Personality

Hebb dealt at length with simple behavior, but had nothing to say about the higher processes of human activity and personality. He assumed that his descriptions and concepts applied to all behaviors, that more complex acts involved more complex organizations of phase sequences.

Behavior was conceived of as a series of self-maintaining sequences composed of numerous sets of cell assemblies. Hebb hypothesized that these sequences were made self-maintaining by virtue of being hooked into reverberating circuits, series of neurons so related to one another that activation of one resulted in the activation of all others in sequence, so that when the final neuron was set off it reactivated the first one. Arousal of one sequence within an organized pattern thus aroused all others, resulting in the appearance of a well-organized chain of behavior.

Behavioral sequences involved the process of *motor equivalence*. Depending on the nature of the environment the same stimulus might trigger one of several alternate acts, each leading to the same goal. The action most appropriate to a particular situation was the one selected. This act was equivalent to all its competitors in that it reached the same goal, albeit by a different means. If an organism were equipped with only rigid reflexes or instincts it could not vary its behavior in an appropriate manner, even when minute variations were called for. Each moment of life would require new learning.

Motor equivalence was a function of the association areas and its efficiency was correlated with the size of the area: the larger the space on the cortex given over to association the more equivalent actions the organism could set up. An organism with a small association area was limited by its mechanics; a better endowed one had capacity for greater variety.

Although Hebb ordinarily remained aloof from matters of individual experience, his interest in emotional disturbances and his desire to account for behavior in terms of physiological processes led him to consider neuroses and psychoses. He felt these disorders were the result of both experience and constitution, and were conditions of chronic emotional disturbance based either on present stimulation or upon some modification in the thought processes brought about by past experiences. In the ordinary process of maturation integrative behavior was learned as disintegrative behavior dropped out. With learning, such disruptive phenomena as fear and rage disappeared in familiar environments either because otherwise threatening stimuli came to be seen in a perspective with more calming events, or because preparatory actions were aroused and led to avoidance before the potential threat could act on the organism. If, however, avoidance was rendered impossible by some long-term condition, then a neurosis or a psychosis might appear. Or again, if the individual's past learning had been such as to prevent the acquisition of avoidance behavior, emotional illness was produced.

Critique

Hebb's was a double-edged theory. One focus was a prescription for physiological psychology describing what kind of structures and processes must exist in order to account for behavior. Many of the neural mechanisms he discussed are fairly well-established. Elsewhere his suggestions have resulted in vigorious programs of investigation. Even if it should turn out that he was not correct in all of his predictions, he will have given experimenters something to look for and helped them to discern what the facts really were. Many of the concepts such as cell assemblies and phase sequences will be difficult to demonstrate, however, because of the tremendous number of connections that exist within the nervous system.

The other aspect of Hebb's theory was a challenge to the psychology of learning, perception, and emotion. He developed a number of hypotheses dealing with the differences between infantile and adult learning and perception, the central motive state, the nature of thinking, learning, memory and forgetting. These predictions, different from those ordinarily made by psychology and research programs which try to consolidate them into psychological theory, should make sizable contributions to science.

Despite his actual and potential contributions, Hebb's theory tended to lose power when he attempted to apply his models to the more complex processes of thinking and behavior. He seemed to presume that he could explain them by merely pointing out that complex processes involved more complex organizations of simple neurological activities. Of this, obviously, there was no question, but to apply the formula of more complex phase sequences and interactions to behavior or thinking did not really explain the nature of act and thought. It is difficult, if not impossible, to describe an act or thought solely in neurological terms. A theory which implies that they are the result of complex interactions may be rather superficial. As more complex patterns occur, the nature of functioning or interaction could involve different or emergent phenomena within the brain. Only when one can understand more exactly what these complex relationships are can one really understand behavior and thinking on a physiological basis. It is all very well to talk of hypotheses and expectancies, and to suggest that these are phase sequences. But how is a hypothetical phase sequence different from an expectant sequence? Thinking and learning involve insight. But what is insight physiologically? What is motor equivalence in terms of neurons? How is selection made among alternatives? Some of these concepts were introduced casually with no particular indication of whether they were neurological or psychological. Others were equated to basic concepts and then apparently considered no further.

There are specific aspects of Hebb's theory of motivation which seem to need clarification. A central motive state plus certain peculiar physiological effects which differ from drive to drive might just as easily be called a set of different drives with some aspects in common. The description of sexual behavior as a cycle of excitement, orgasm, and inhibition seems to imply a longer or more complete state of inhibition than either animals or human beings are likely to demonstrate under many conditions. The description of sleep as an activity of boredom seems not to have considered that people can want to sleep or want to stay awake. How does this desire relate to the synchrony of cortical firing? Furthermore, it is possible to be in the midst of new and exciting stimulation and not be able to stay awake. There seems to be no room for exhaustion and fatigue in Hebb's theory.

Closely related to the theory of sleep was Hebb's concept of pleasure. The idea that pleasure always and only involved exposure to new content or creation of new syntheses does not necessarily include all the situations which one would introspectively find pleasurable. Also, many psychologists find themselves uncomfortable with any theory which implies a *growth principle*, that is, a force within the organism urging it toward improvement of itself. While such a reaction may indeed exist, its description in Hebb's theory is obscure. Why, from a physiological point of view, should self-improvement occur, and how does it take place?

Further inquiry into the concept of pain is also necessary. There are experimental studies showing that pain can have cue value. This would seem to validate in part the proposal that painful stimuli could lose their disintegrative effects when they occurred as part of an organized sequence. Still unexplained, however, is what happens to the pain. Is it now different neurologically? Is it dominated by other cortical activities, or does it interact with them? Is integration of painful stimuli harder to establish than integration of pleasant or neutral stimuli?

Turning from the nature of pleasure and pain to their functions within the organism, Hebb was unclear about the nature of learning. He often implied a trial-and-error sort of learning apparently based on reinforcement but he denied that the law of effect was applicable because of the lack of sufficient evidence for the establishment of traces. It seems quite possible that the trace systems he did allow for—either the electrical trace which seems to be maintained long enough for a structural change to occur, or the amoeboid growth of neurons under certain conditions—might well be used in accounting for reinforcement even as they were used in accounting for the theory of learning and thinking he proposed. If pleasure or pain act only as a means of channelling behavior, then there is the problem of how this channelling occurs, of how alternatives are chosen and represented neurologically. Hebb did not precisely define the relationship between such channelling and motor equivalence. One might presume that they are very similar if not identical.

It is a tribute to Hebb's theory that even the critical questions raised about it seem to point to important research possibilities. Any study designed to test it is almost sure to provide results of great significance to psychology, whether they support or contradict the theory.

SUMMARY

Basic Unit. Hebb's theory employed two types of units, one appropriate to molecular examination of neural function (the individual neuron), the other appropriate to molar examination (the pattern of neural activity).

Field of Study. Psychology was the study of behavior, behavior which could be understood in terms of its underlying physiological mechanisms.

Methods of Investigation. Hebb's theory was a model prescribing what neurological mechanisms would be necessary to account for behavior. He employed various physiological techniques in testing his speculations.

Principles. Connections between neurons were strengthened when the neurons were active at the same time. When several neurons were active simultaneously a pattern of cortical activity was formed. These patterns were the neurological underlay of perception, thought, and action. In the developmental sequence, the establishment of basic patterns proceded any more complex activities. Thus, infancy was given over to the patterning of activities in individual neurons. Later, relationships were built up among these basic units, and more complex behaviors were possible. The activities of the central nervous system were organized into a dynamic equilibrium. The arousal of processes which were incompatible with ongoing activities, or with the general organization, disturbed the equilibrium and consequently disturbed the functioning of the entire organism.

Consciousness. Consciousness was a process within the nervous system which organized and controlled behavior. Once an act was well established, conscious control was no longer required. Awareness was necessary only in novel situations or when problems arose.

Sensation, Perception, and Discrimination. Except for a few primitive organizational processes such as the figure-ground relationship which were innate, the structure and content of perception were acquired. Percepts were learned through the establishment of connections between several neurons so that when one was activated it could fire the others. The genesis of these connections lay in brief electrical traces which persisted in the nervous system after physical stimulation had ceased. In some way these traces produced permanent structural changes in the synapse. Hebb hypothesized that the changes took the form of knobs or growths on the neuron. As a result, neuronal activity was channelled into patterns known as cell assemblies. Constancy in a stimulus encouraged the development of stable cell assemblies, while variation impeded it, bringing many more nerve cells into the process and complicating its structure. As life progressed the number of cell assemblies increased, and more complex patterns evolved, based on interactions among simpler units. Hebb called these higher level associations phase sequences and considered them to be the physiological basis for percepts and concept formation.

Thinking, Cognition, and Memory. Thinking was a matter of achieving insight into relationships among concepts or objects. It could be equated with the establishment of temporary connections between cell assemblies or phase sequences. More permanent alterations in the structure of neurons accounted for memory, while the destruction or disappearance of the connections resulted in forgetting.

Emotion and Motivation. Emotions were divided into two classes: pleasurable feelings, accompanied by a desire to increase or prolong the originating stimulus; and aversive feelings such as rage and fear, accompanied by a desire to abolish or decrease the originating stimulus. Pleasant emotions were compatible with the pattern of neural activity and even enchanced the established organization, while fear and rage aroused competing activities and therefore interfered with cortical organization if they were not relieved. Emotional disturbances were brought about by anything which destroyed cortical organization, prolonged emotion, pain, an absence of facilitating processes necessary to cortical functioning, or alterations in blood chemistry.

Motivation likewise had a neurological basis. The so-called instincts were built into the brain structure in such a way that an appropriate sensory stimulus could trigger behavior automatically. In higher animals there was a relatively smaller area of cortex given over to sensory functions and relatively larger area given to association and inter-connections between cortical centers. Instinctual behavior was less possible under these conditions than in simple organisms because numerous associative connections had to be established before an act could occur. Any drive or motive, regardless of whether it was instinctual or not, affected the individual's physiology, and consequently his behavior, by altering the pattern of activity in the brain. Drives did not arouse neural processes; they changed what already existed.

There was a general, universal pattern or phase sequence which accompanied any physical deprivation. In addition, each specific deprivational state had some specific effects which allowed the organism to distinguish it from other drives. Unless and until the organism could discover some means of relieving a particular motive, it disrupted cortical organization and consequently disrupted normal functions. As some particular act of gratification was learned, integrative behavior was substituted for generalized disturbance and restlessness. Physiologically this meant that new phase sequences were created which organized the altered firing patterns into a smooth process. So long as there was threat of disorganization of cortical patterns from any source, the organism was wakeful, but when stimulus influx was reduced or when the flow of stimuli was familiar and not disturbing, cortical firing assumed a synchronous pattern and sleep followed.

The Nature of the Learning Process. Hebb defined learning as a lasting change in the facilitation between activities of neural structures. Learning in infancy and early childhood was slow, for it was at this time that perceptual and motor processes were organized. The larger the association area in the brain, the slower these basic units were established since more individual neurons had to be organized into assemblies. There was a gradual, continuous accretion, which contrasted to the quick, discontinuous course of later learning when mastery was a matter of gaining insight into relationships among stimuli, rather than of acquisition of basic facts. Insight called for the correlation of expectancies and recollection as a basis for deriving hypotheses about the environment; in other words, it was the result of association of phase sequences.

Behavior and Personality. Behavior consisted of self-maintaining sequences composed of large numbers of elements in a chain relationship. Arousal of one unit tended to arouse all others. Often in more complex behavior an act had to be selected from a number of alternative means to the same goal. The choice among the alternatives was made according to which response was most appropriate to the situation at hand. The existence of alternative means to a single goal was known as motor equivalence. Such equivalence led to an adaptability not possible in reflex and/or instinctual reactions. Personality could be understood as the result of still more complex patterns of neural organization. Maturation was the process by which neural activity was organized into the integrated pattern known as personality. Life began with relative neural disorganization but could not continue unless order was brought about. If for any reason there was a prolonged period of disorganization, emotional illness resulted. Neuroses and psychoses were conditions of chronic emotional disturbance caused either by the current situation or by the structural changes wrought by past difficulties.

REFERENCES

D. O. Hebb

Hebb, D. O., *Organization of Behavior*. New York: Wiley, 1949.
———, "The Role of Neurological Ideas in Psychology," *J. Personal.* 20: 39–55 (1951).
———, "The Motivating Effects of Exteroceptive Stimulation," *Amer. Psychol.* 13: 109–113 (1958).

CHAPTER 31

HANS SELYE (1956 TO PRESENT)

SELYE'S theory derived from his research in endocrinology, physiology, and medicine, and its primary relevance was to those fields. Its application to psychology (and psychiatry) arose from Selye's research with the reactions of an organism to situations of stress, including not only physical disease and injury, but also anxiety, worry, and emotional conflict.

Selye's first work with the idea of stress came as a medical student. He noted that despite the specific nature of the disease there were always a number of common symptoms such as fever, loss of weight, and a general feeling of malaise. This observation aroused his curiosity for a time as a student, but he soon forgot it as other matters occupied his attention. Not long after he began his career in endocrinological research he discovered what he thought was a new hormone. He inferred the presence of the hormone from certain physiological effects he observed when he infected an organism with his experimental preparation. In testing the composition of his "hormone," however, he found it to be nonspecific. Anything he injected into an organism would produce the same effects. This observation led him to suspect his discovery. Such an omnipresent influence is not an ordinary characteristic of hormones. To continue to regard the effect as hormonal under these circumstances seemed highly inappropriate. Indeed, the only commonality among the things he was injecting seemed to be the fact that they were alien substances which somehow must contaminate or disorder bodily functioning. These observations depressed him for a time until he recalled his earlier observations of the general pattern of reactions to physical illness and found that many of these characteristics seemed to correlate with his observations on his experimental animals. He concluded that the reactions he noted must be the result of exposure to stress, and became so intrigued with this idea that he launched upon a series of studies investigating it. From these his theory grew.

Basic Unit and Field of Study

Whenever a theorist chooses to concentrate on one set of phenomena, the distinction between Basic Unit and Field of Study loses its meaning. What become important under these conditions are the dependent and independent variables upon which the theory focuses. Thus, Freudian theories regarded personality as dependent upon a number of independent influences which they sought to specify and whose effects they tried to describe. Gestaltists likewise made the Gestalt their dependent variable and described the effects of various independent variables on the production of Gestalts. Selye's approach was a little different; rather than specifying the dependent variables and studying independent influences, he specified the independent influence, i.e., stress, and studied dependent effects, i.e., behavior.

Methods of Investigation

Selye's methods were those of endocrinology and medical research, and as such are not relevant to psychology in general. It may be of interest, however, to mention one of his ingenius techniques for inducing physical stress. While attempting to inject some irritant into an experimental animal, he discovered that injecting the substance just beneath the skin of his subject led to a localized abcess or pouch which enabled him to confine the reaction to some specific area, so that the specific effects of the disease or toxin did not cloud the general systemic effects of the stress their presence placed upon the organism.

Principles

Any organism reacted to stress by reorganizing its physiological and psychological processes in such a way as to delimit the stress to the smallest possible area of the body for as long as it could. In the meanwhile it adjusted its function in order that it could maintain its normal state in the face of the stressor.

These adjustive patterns included both defensive and offensive measures.

Consciousness; Sensation, Perception, and Discrimination; Thinking, Cognition, and Memory; Emotion and Motivation; The Nature of the Learning Process

These matters were not examined by Selye, whose work focused on physiological phenomena and their effects upon behavior.

Behavior and Personality

"Stress," as Selye used the term, had no one particular referent. It could be any condition which threatened the normal function of the organism. As we have already indicated, the primary law of adaption was that the effects of stress were limited to the smallest area of the affected organ, or to the smallest area of the body capable of meeting them. Thus a local irritant, whether a dirty splinter in the finger, a caustic agent on the skin, or a question of one's honesty, was followed by a local adaptive process. If this local reaction could not reverse the disruption, more and more of the organ and eventually the body became involved. Given sufficient stress it would affect the whole organism, initiating a sequence of reactions called the *general adaption syndrome* or GAS. Three separate stages could be distinguished within this sequence.

The first stage of a stress reaction was one of *alarm*, accompanied by changes in the adrenal glands, the intestines, and in other organ systems. As the stress continued there gradually appeared to be a return to normality, accomplished by virtue of alterations in normal function to compensate for the stress. Selye referred to this stage as one of *resistance* or *adjustment to stress*. If the stress situation persisted long enough, or was severe enough, the adjustive processes broke down and a stage of *exhaustion* was reached. The physiological reactions were the same as those of the alarm stage, but more intensive and more extensive. If they continued the organism would die or develop some pathology.

The physiological reactions of the alarm stage were the typical responses of an organism to an emergency situation. They were anticipatory, preparing the organism to advance against the threat, or to retreat from it. These responses, produced by the interaction of the sympathetic and the parasympathetic nervous systems, have long been known as the "fight or flight" syndrome.

The adaption to stress during the second stage was accomplished by means of defenses erected by the body as instrumentations of the fight or flight reaction of the alarm stage. These defenses included active aggressive reactions, the end result of which was the destruction or removal of the harmful agent, and avoiding or protecting maneuvers, the end result of which was the shielding of the organism.

Certain hormones produced by the adrenal cortex called *corticoids* appeared to activate both the initial preparatory reaction and the actual defensive responses. Corticoids were of two varieties: those which could activate potential aggressive actions such as inflammation, certain changes in blood pressure, lungs, stomach, intestines, and motor responses; and those which could activate protective actions such as retarding inflammation, certain changes in various organs of the opposite sort to the offensive reactions. Both hormones were present in the body in varying amounts, and their production and the reactions they controlled were coordinated into patterns of neural, physiological, and physical behavior. At any one time during a stress experience one or the other of the hormonal types was dominant.

The pattern of dominance, and in fact the entire coordination of reactions, was dependent on what Selye referred to as *internal conditioning factors* such as heredity and past experience. The heredity of the organism determined its capacity to produce hormones. Past experience could alter this basic ability to produce hormones in either direction. In addition, there were *external conditioning factors* such as diet, climate, and toxic substances which imposed their effects on the hormonal balance. These internal and external conditioning factors could enhance or distort. If they distorted, the end result was some pathology or imbalance in the offensive and defensive aspects of the adjustive pattern. Even tiny deviations in hormone production would disrupt normal functioning.

As a result of such deviations in hormonal balance, or because the organism was for some other reason unable to combat stress agents with adequate adaptive reactions, organisms might demonstrate *diseases of adaptation*. These were either offensive or protective responses inappropriate to the amount of stress, or reactions prolonged beyond the period of stress. In the former case, the organism was either too offensive or too protective, or else it responded with defensive behavior to a situation which was not a threat. In the case of persistence of defensive acts the response may have been appropriate at first, but was prolonged beyond need through the inability of the body to terminate the process. If this happened, the defensive response disrupted that which it had been initiated to preserve. Diseases of adaptation included diabetes, allergies, neuroses, and psychoses.

The third stage of the GAS was one of general breakdown in the defensive patterns, followed by severe illness and/or death. It came about because the organism either wore out after prolonged defense, or because its defenses were unable to contain the stressor. Whether the reappearance of alarm type of behaviors was a result of the now ineffectual defensive potentials remaining activated, or whether it was a reappearance of emergency actions is not made clear. The disorders seen in this phase were the result of breakdowns of adjustive behaviors, leaving the stressor to produce whatever physical phenomena were characteristic of it. These disorders were due to the absence of defense, in contrast to diseases of adaption which were exaggerations of defenses.

Selye was more interested in understanding the origin of stress reactions than in discovering therapies. However, there were certain peculiarities of the treatment of disease which attracted his attention. Aside from such obvious techniques as artificial interference with hormonal balance, or the application of forces to inhibit the pathological process, he noted that many of the treatments for diseases actually involved placing the organism in a situation of greater stress, causing it to produce an even more intensive adaptive response. Apparently such treatment had the effect of jolting the organism "out of its rut" in the case of a disease of adaption, or of forcing it to mobilize itself into a supreme effort in the case of adaptive failures. The ancient practice of bleeding patients, the treatment of syphillis by malarial infection, the use of electro-shock and insulin coma in the treatment of mental disorders are classic examples of this approach. (They also suggest that it is a rather crude approach and not as effective as more specific therapies in view of the fact that bleeding and malarial infection have all but disappeared from the medical scene.)

Critique

Selye's was actually more than a theory of stress. It was an account of adjustive and diseased behavior on a physiological level. It demonstrated how adjustment and disorder arose from the same circumstance. The reader will view the medical import of the theory according to his own interest. At the very least, he will be impressed with the suggestion that physical and psychological adjustment have the same general origin and are governed by the same general laws, and that illness, on no matter what level, is caused in the same general way. Selye's theory of physiological behavior is important to psychology. As a psychologist it is tempting to infer that when stressors are psychological, the GAS appears with certain modifications. Physical phenomena responding to disruption of physical equilibria (such as fever) would disappear, while psychological phenomena would appear in response to disruption of psychological equilibria. Thus, the alarm stage could include not only the endocrinological manifestations, but emotional reactions of anxiety, fear, anger, etc. The stage of resistance should include the appearance of psychological defenses. Selye proposed that neuroses and psychoses were diseases of adaptation, a proposal which can be compared with the current view in psychology that they are exaggerations of defensive maneuvers. His views have, moreover, added impetus to the search for physiological and endocrinological components of neurotic and psychotic reactions, although as yet no definitive findings have been reported. The parallel between psychological theory and Selye's proposals is equally clear at the third stage of the GAS. Psychologists and psychiatrists ordinarily assume that severe neuroses and acute psychoses are breakdowns in defensive maneuvers, an assumption which fits very well with Selye's belief. Thus, it is easy to see how theories of emotional disorders might appropriately borrow from Selye's theory.

SUMMARY

Basic Unit and Field of Study. This distinction was irrelevant since Selye concentrated on one set of phenomena. It is more significant to say that he regarded stress situations as independent (stimulus) variables and studied the effects of these upon the dependent (response) variables.

Methods of Investigation. Selye's methods were those of medical and physiological research. As his interest in the bodily reaction to stress grew, he found it necessary to develop techniques which enabled him to isolate the specific effects of an individual agent from its general effects as a stressor.

Principles. The organism under stress attempted to adjust by means of offensive and defensive reactions aimed at limiting the effects of this stressor to the smallest area. It could do so temporarily in such a way as to permit return to normal function, but eventually it would break down.

Consciousness; *Sensation, Perception, and Discrimination*; *Thinking, Cognition, and Memory*; *Emotion and Motivation*; *The Nature of the Learning Process.* Not relevant to Selye's theory.

Behavior and Personality. In responding to stress, either physical or psychological, the organism attempted to delimit the area of tension as far as possible and to deal with it locally. If this was impossible the organism initiated a three-stage general adaptation syndrome. First the organism reacted with a state of alarm, but as stress continued the organism eventually adapted to it for a period. Eventually, if stress was prolonged, the adaptation broke down and intense alarm reappeared. The period of adaptation to stress was characterized by the erection of physical and psychological defenses. Some of these processes were protective; others were offensive, intended to remove the source of difficulty. Occasionally something went wrong in the balance of offensive and defensive maneuvers and the organism reacted inappropriately by becoming too aggressive or too evasive. Selye called these distorted reactions diseases of adaptation. Emotional disorders seem to belong in this classification.

REFERENCES

Hans Selye

Selye, H., *The Stress of Life*. New York: McGraw-Hill, 1956.

PART IX

RECENT DEVELOPMENTS

CHAPTER 32

AN OVERVIEW OF PSYCHOLOGY AT MID-CENTURY

IN RECENT YEARS creation of broad new theories seems to have given way to the development and improvement of existing systems, particularly those related to the Freudian, Gestalt, and Neo-Behaviorist viewpoints, with the purpose of testing their validity and predictive powers and adapting their theoretical principles to new data in psychology, physiology, sociology, and anthropology. In addition, a number of so-called *miniature systems* have appeared. These deal with one narrowly defined area within psychology and attempt to set up some basic principles which apply to it and it alone. While several such theories may cover much the same territory, there is little effort by the majority of psychologists to seek any organization or coordination among them. Relating these theories to each other is an advisable, but difficult, task because each system is subject to rapid change as its author attempts to incorporate new facts and new concepts. Further difficulty arises because each theorist works in an isolated area, and even within specific areas there is a great deal of ambiguity and inconsistency. Thus, the individual worker must exert great effort to understand his own field and has little time for others which are not his speciality.

Basic Unit

The focus of the older theories has been considered earlier in individual chapters. As for the miniature systems now so prevalent, one cannot extract from them a focus which is basic to all; each directs itself toward that aspect with which it is concerned, regarding it as a dependent variable to be understood in terms of those independent variables which influence it. The aspects of psychology selected as topics around which to organize this text more or less define the range and focus of the multitude of systems, with each topic defining a field of study. Psychologists have tended to become specialists with such appellations as "sensation men," "learning men," "motivation men," and "personality men."

Field of Study

Psychology has come to be viewed as a behavioral science, wherein the reactions of animals and human beings, organs, individuals, groups and cultures are equally appropriate objects of study. There has been a growing interest in the application of psychology so that the pure scientist, who works in his laboratory unconcerned with how his knowledge will be used by society, is becoming a rarity. This is not to imply that psychology as a theoretical science is losing ground to psychology as a practical method. It simply means that as the world discovers more of psychology's practical applications, few psychologists find themselves able to resist its demands. There are many psychologists employed solely in applied fields, such as clinical or industrial psychology, who have no desire to engage in any role other than that of a practitioner. While there are persons at the other extreme who do only basic research, the majority of psychologists function in both roles to a greater or lesser extent.

Methods of Investigation

In a science characterized by a number of miniature theories and diverse interests there can be no one method generally recognized as the most desirable. As a matter of fact, psychologists seem to have abondoned the practice of prescribing method. As long as a particular technique meets the criteria of scientific procedure and produces reliable and valid information, it is acceptable. This broadmindedness suggests a certain degree of maturity.

Psychological Tests. One aspect of psychological method has become so significant to the entire field of study, and beyond psychology to many aspects of our society, that it has created several sub-specialties, just as engineering split from physics and gradually built up a number of distinct fields. Thus, psychological testing, which grew from psychophysical methods, now encompasses clinical diagnosis, educational measurement, personality assessment, and test construction.

While tests can be (and have been) developed purely from theoretical deduction, they are more commonly derived from empirical observations. Because a particular response to a particular question correlates with something else of practical interest to psychologists, educators, or consumers of these professional skills, (medical and psychiatric services, employers, army recruiting offices and training commands, advertisers, etc.), it is formalized as a tool for prediction, selection, or diagnosis. Whatever its derivation or purpose, a test is a means of sampling behavior relevant to some scientific, social, or personal goal. Tests provide ease and convenience in observing behavior, and they make possible greater control over what is observed than is possible in real life situations. They present a carefully devised stimulus in a standard manner, thereby controlling what factors determine the response.

Psychologists refer to the ability of a test to measure what it is supposed to measure as its *validity*, and to its ability to measure consistently as its *reliability*. A valid and reliable test of intelligence, for example, measures accurately how intelligent a person is, and gives the same result each time the same person is tested (unless the person has changed). Accuracy and consistency are not synonymous. A wrist watch, completely stopped, is only valid for two seconds a day, but it is highly reliable; whenever one looks at it he is certain to get the same answer. (The discerning reader will note that this example is not truly reliable, however, because time changes but the watch does not.) The same watch when wound may be highly accurate but very unreliable as an alarm clock, sometimes ringing at 5:00, sometimes at 10:00, and sometimes not at all.

Tests have been constructed to measure every conceivable human function, and merely to catalog them would provide no useful information. It is traditional to describe the field of testing by classifying tests according to their form of administration (group or individual) and their content.

Achievement tests (how-much-do-you-know), interest tests (what-do-you-like), aptitude tests (what-are-your-special-talents), attitude tests (what-do-you-believe), and trait scales (what-adjective-characterizes-you) are ordinarily group paper-and-pencil tests. So are many intelligence and personality tests. Such group tests are checklists, rating scales, questionnaires, multiple choice, true-false, sorting, matching, or essay-type items which the respondent must read and write or check. They are called group tests because they are more or less self-administering; the attention and instruction of an examiner is not required (but proctors are usually present for obvious reasons). Their self-administering qualities make it possible to give the tests to a group of subjects simultaneously. They are devised because some theoretical or empirically derived hypothesis makes certain kinds of items relevant. The items are ordinarily processed in some way to test their validity and reliability, scaled for intensity or difficulty if such scaling is appropriate, assessed for ease of administration, and so forth.

Each test gives rise to a set of data, and ordinarily to some interpretation of these data, such that a theory of sorts about each specific test comes into existence. These theories are important to the perpetrators of tests, but are less significant to our broad purpose.

The greatest value of group tests is as screening or gross selection instruments, or for general classification where specific information about a specific person is not required. Group tests are convenient and efficient, but the information they give has some marked limitations. One can never be sure that the testee really understands the instructions or the items, nor can the examiner be sure he understands what the testee meant by a certain answer. One can never be sure the testee is in the best possible frame of mind to take the test, or that he is completely honest and straightforward in his response. One cannot eliminate response sets toward acquiescence, social desirability, or a number of other factors (see section on Motivation in this chapter). Where one suspects misunderstanding, negative motivation, response sets, malingering, falsification, anxiety or confusion, or when one needs accurate information concerning a particular person, individual, tests are used.

Individual tests call for careful instruction, observation, and recording of the testee's response, conducted in an atmosphere of optimal rapport, with optimal communication between testor and testee. There are too many individually administered tests of intelligence and personality to list singly. We will content ourselves with discussing some of the better known tests and the miniature theories which have grown up around them. But first we must inquire into the origin of testing.

For all that individuals have long been recognized as distinctive entities, it was a discovery of some importance that individual differences existed in various motor and cognitive skills (Tuddenham, 1963). This discovery was not made until the 18th century in connection with the recording of astronomical observations. An astronomer noted that his assistant was recording times of occurrence of events which both had observed that were about a second slower than his own recordings. The astronomer promptly fired the assistant for incompetence. Another astronomer, Bessel, learned of the episode and began experimenting with various astronomical observers; and he found considerable variation from one individual to another. Interest in individual differences as a curiosity continued for some time until Galton demonstrated that they were a matter of importance to science and could be studied systematically. Galton (1883, 1889) collected a number of physical measures and applied statistical methods to describe a person's position on any measured variable relative to the distribution of his peers on the same variable. At about the same time Cattell (1890) described a series of mental tests, many of them laboratory psychophysical techniques, which he sought to administer to anyone who would take them, in order to ascertain their import and meaning. The goal of Cattell's tests was to study mental processes and their interrelationships. Interest in this sort of sensory-motor test continued in the United States for a few years, but waned when the tests contributed nothing to the introspective study of the mind.

In the meantime, Binet was working in France on tests of mental faculties similar to the Cattell items when the French Minister of Education decided to set up special schools for defective children. To assure that a child was truly defective enough to be a candidate for such a school, some sort of examination procedure was required. Binet was asked to help, and he complied, working with Simon (Binet and Simon, 1905a, 1905b) to devise a series of test items which became the first successful test of intelligence. As this test was given to more and more children it became apparent to Binet that one could classify test items according to age levels, i.e., some tests were consistently passed by average children of one age, others by average children of another age. The idea of age level subtests was incorporated into the next major version of the Binet test (Binet and Simon, 1908), so that there were a number of test items for each of several age levels. This concept proved to be of such value that it became the characteristic feature of Binet-type scales (Binet, 1911B). Each item was assigned a weight or score in the form of months of mental age, and the final score was the total number of months of mental age credit earned by an individual. But mental age was of little value unless one compared it to the child's real (chronological) age; only then could one tell if he were above, below, or the same as the average child of his age. This led Stern (1912) to suggest that a ratio of mental age (MA) to chronological age (CA) be devised in order to express the level of intelligence a particular score represented. Terman (1916) exploited this suggestion in his first version of the Binet Scale, devising the intelligence quotient (IQ),

$$IQ = \frac{MA}{CA} \times 100.$$

The multiplication by 100 was done in order to avoid decimals.

A child was assumed to increase in MA just as he did in CA, and furthermore, he was assumed to grow at an even rate. If he was an early developer (i.e., had a high IQ) at one age, he should continue to be an early developer as he grew older. Thus his IQ should remain constant, since as a ratio of mental to chronological age it was an index of developmental rate. The Binet scale was widely used in its original forms, and in various revisions by other psychologists. Terman's (1916) Stanford revision of the Binet was the best known of these revisions, and was itself revised in 1937 (Terman and Merrill, 1937) and again in 1960 (Terman and Merrill, 1960) to bring it up to date.

Despite its widespread use and general success, and despite the frequent and numerous revisions, the Binet tests presented some notable difficulties. First, most of the test items were verbal. They asked questions and required responses in words. People with limited vocabularies or non-verbal individuals suffer a handicap which causes them to score lower than their true level of ability. In addition, children stop developing in mental capacity as they approach adulthood, just as they stop growing bigger physically. They may be able to develop more muscles or put on weight, but their basic stature does not change once they reach full growth in their late teens or early twenties. Similarly, their mental stature will not change after age fifteen to twenty depending upon the type of capacity involved, although, of course, they can always learn more facts and ideas. Mental age in the adult becomes a rather meaningless concept, for an MA of 12, like a dress size of 12, is not necessarily a sign of immaturity in an adult. Just as a size 12 is quite common, so is an MA of 12.

To remedy the narrow coverage of the Binet tests, and to provide a more accurate basis for computation of adult IQ, Wechsler (1939) devised an intelligence scale for adults composed of a number of different types of verbal and "performance" items, the latter referring to tests which deal with objects other than verbal symbols. The Wechsler Verbal Scale consisted of tests of general information, reasoning, common sense, vocabulary, arithmetic, and immediate memory. The Performance Scale consisted of tests of capacity to make critical observations, social sensitivity, new learning skill, organizational ability, and model construction or pattern reading. These scales were scored along a distribution of standard scores. The total scores were then translated into IQ by references to a conversion table which weighted the scores according to norms for different age groups. To illustrate, a total score of 100 points was equivalent to an IQ of 140 for a child of 10, to an IQ of 101 for a youth of 20, and to an IQ of 115 for a person of 60. This illustration reveals another facet of the Wechsler test, the fact that it takes into account the gradual decrease in mental capacity with increasing age. Again this is a correlate of physical change.

The Wechsler test was so well received that a children's version was added (Wechsler, 1949), and the adult form was revised twenty years after its initial appearance (Wechsler, 1958A). Recently, a form for pre-school children was made available (1967).

Intelligence tests were derived empirically. Aside from selecting items which fit the author's definition of intelligence, there was no theoretical basis for item choice. Intelligence has been variously defined as "mental adaptability" (Terman and Merrill, 1960, p. 5), "capacity to act purposefully, to think rationally, and to deal effectively with . . . environment" (Wechsler, 1939, p. 3); but in all cases test items have been included, because of correlation with age, or school success, or the like, rather than because logical analysis made them seem reasonable. Indeed, the half jesting operational definition of intelligence as "what the intelligence test measures" has a grain of bitter truth. One cannot help but wonder if an intelligence test constructed from a complete theory of cognitive function, behavior, or personality might not produce some interesting results very much in contrast with present IQ tests.

Be that as it may, there is a body of theory concerning intelligence derived from studies of the correlations among distributions of IQs, or sub-test scores, and factor analyses of these correlations. Spearman (1904; 1923) proposed what he called the two factor version of intelligence, i.e., that intelligence was made up of a general factor (called *g*) of ability and a number of specific, idiosyncratic capacities (called *s*) peculiar to an individual and unrelated to his *g*. In contrast, Thomson (1920; 1951), Thorndike (1925), and Tryon (1935; 1959) have suggested that any general-specific interrelationship was really the result of chance sampling of random neural connections. Thurstone (1947) held that intelligence was composed of a number of correlated factors representing different kinds of intelligence, e.g., verbal comprehension, word fluency, computational facility, spatial visualization, associative memory, perceptual speed, and reasoning. Other studies have revealed other kinds of factors. It seems possible that intelligence may be made up of several kinds of ability which all correlate sufficiently that gross examination fails to distinguish components, while finer testing with appropriate measures will reveal a number of different aspects, plus some other qualities specific to each individual. However, because test construction is still a crude process and factor analysis is equally as sensitive to differences in experimental design and computational technique, we cannot yet be sure what these components are.

The widespread use of IQ tests has shown that whatever the test, it is difficult to control background, education, culture, motivation, and numerous other factors so that they do not contaminate the measure of ability. Even so-called "culture-free" tests administered under optimal conditions do not measure pure intelligence. The person's past experience still gives him a handicap or an unexpected advantage, the extent of which is impossible to assess. Thus, persons from underprivileged backgrounds or different cultures will tend to score lower than their actual ability level, while persons with a great amount of test sophistication and general knowledge may obtain spuriously high scores (Klineberg, 1963; Porteus, 1963). Furthermore, Masland, Sarason, and Gladwin (1959) have shown that most IQ tests do not really predict the capacity to adjust to life, but only what kind of performance to expect in school situations. Thus, many moderately retarded persons score low on IQ tests and do poorly in school, but in everyday life they cope quite adequately. These findings suggest the need to broaden the scope of abilities tapped by IQ tests and to assess potential functioning level as well as actual level.

Besides intelligence tests there are many individual personality tests. Some of these tests are objective, i.e., yield scores whose meaning is standardized. Others are "projective," and although they can be scored, they are usually viewed as samples of an individual's unconscious fantasies, or his personality, his conflicts, etc.; as such they are interpreted descriptively in terms of what they represent or symbolize.

Objective tests are numerous; questionnaires, self-rating scales, and check lists of all kinds have been developed. Two of the better known are the MMPI and the Q-Sort. The MMPI consists of a series of statements about feelings, ideas, actions, and beliefs which the subject is asked to sort according to whether or not they are true about him. His choices are then compared with various keys on which are recorded the typical responses of depressed, hypochondriacal, anxious, schizophrenic, masculine, or numerous other classes of persons. It is assumed that insofar as a choice resembles those of persons with certain disorders or characteristics, the rest of his behavior will likewise be similar. Behavioral correlates have been worked out for a large number of choice patterns and are described in textbooks, atlases, etc. (Hathaway and Meehl, 1951; Hathaway and Monachesi, 1961; Hathaway and Monachesi, 1963; Marks and Seeman, 1963).

The other objective test we will discuss here, the Q-Sort, was developed by the English statistician, Stephenson (1953), and is based on a statistical device for correlating an individual on lots of tests on two occasions (where the ordinary correlation technique employs lots of individuals on one test on two occasions). The Q statistic permits many kinds of tests to be used, and the Q-Sort was devised to take advantage of the statistic's peculiar characteristics. A Q-Sort consists of a number of statements which the individual is asked to sort into a number of piles according to some standard. The number of piles is so prescribed, and the number of statements to be placed in each pile is so arranged that the distribution of choices follows the normal curve. The statements can be about anything; in fact, their content could be random. In practice, however, they usually pertain to some aspect of behavior, feelings, attitudes, or symptoms which are relevant to the examiner's purpose in giving the test. The standard for making choices may be "what describes your personality (or feelings, behavior, symptoms, or attitude) best to what describes it least," or "what you like (or are interested in, or think about, or fear) most to what you like (etc.) least." Having individuals perform Q-Sorts before and after psychotherapy will indicate whether there is change in their behavior or in their symptoms but it will not show what the change is. Having a person perform a Q-Sort as it applies to his own interests, and then performing it as it applies to some one else's interests, or as he thinks someone else would sort them can indicate how much two people agree, or how much one sees himself as similar to another. Therapists can sort statements about patients to show whether progress has been made, as a criterion against which to compare a patient's sort for himself, as a way of finding out if patient and therapist think the same way, or to discover if one understands (or has insight into) the other or himself. It can be used in before-after attitude change studies, in comparing marriage partners, persons with similar illnesses or backgrounds. The individual can perform sorts under instruction which vary with his motives, his self-perceptions, his frame of reference, etc. As a result of its versatility, the Q-Sort has found wide acceptance as an objective measure of personality, social behavior, and behavioral change (in attitude studies and psychotherapy), and it is commonly used in both laboratory and clinical measurement.

Far different from these statistically derived, statistically interpreted rating devices are the projective tests. The term *projective* technique was coined by Frank (1939) as a class name to refer to a group of instruments for studying individual behavior based on the Freudian concept of projection, i.e., the attribution of one's own characteristics to someone or something else. In the case of projective tests, it is assumed that the test subject projects himself (almost as if he were a movie projector) onto some neutral medium where the expert can observe and interpret the production. Interpretation is required because the projection is assumed to be symbolic. The medium for projection can be any of a widely diverse group of stimuli which meet the criteria of having nothing about them which will form or determine response, of being ambiguous, with no socially defined reaction. Since the stimulus does not dictate the response, the subject's personality induces a reaction appropriate to itself.

The stimuli used as projective instruments include ambiguous pictures (TAT; CAT), ink blots (Rorschach), drawing tests (Draw-a-Person; House, Tree, Person), stage scenes (Make-a-Picture-Story Test), incomplete sentences, and other items so numerous that several books have been written to describe them (Bell, 1948; Anderson and Anderson, 1951). Techniques for analyzing and interpreting the projective tests are even more numerous than the tests themselves. Each expert on each different test seems to have his own system of evaluation and interpretation (Rorschach, 1921 and 1942; Beck, 1949; Klopfer, Ainsworth, Klopfer, and Holt, 1954; Klopfer and Davidson, 1962).

It is possible to distinguish among the numerous systems three general approaches to the matter. The first of these regards the projective material as symbolic in the same sense that Freud saw dreams and fantasies, and therefore to be interpreted (sometimes with the aid of the patient's or the examiner's free associations) in much the same way as dreams are, by describing the underlying psychosexual motives, their historical basis, and the defenses formed to insure psychic equilibrium. A second approach, at the other extreme, applies a formal scoring technique (such as the grammatical analysis of the TAT (Murray, 1943) or scoring Rorschach for location, movement, form, color, etc.) and then reads off interpretations from the scoring profiles indicated by some system of norms. A third method is a sort of compromise between the two extremes, and often appears as a complement to either of them. It employs a set of norms stating what is commonly responded and what it commonly symbolized, and regards these common responses as "signs" for a particular diagnostic entity or for a particular relationship among psychosexual (or other) processes. Given a sign (or several such signs) the tester may conclude that there is brain damage, schizophrenia, homosexuality, castration anxiety, sado-masochism, sexual impotence, Oedipal entanglements, etc.

In spite of the intense enthusiasm among practicing clinicians and their strong feeling that the tests possess great validity because it seems logical that they should (a concept known as *face validity*), the results of most validity studies are disappointing and often discouraging. Individual tests were developed to improve upon group tests, or upon predictions based on routine historical data. Predictions based on projective test data, in spite of the time and effort they require, cannot be proved more accurate than predictions based on paper-and-pencil tests, which in turn cannot be proved more accurate than actarial predictions based on age, education, marital status, etc. (Milholland, 1964; Gough, 1963; Meehl, 1954, 1956A, 1956B, 1956C, 1957, and 1960; Kelly and Fiske, 1951; Kelly and Goldberg, 1959). Meehl (1960) found these persistent claims for the clinical techniques even more disheartening than the evidence itself. Perhaps to some extent the clinician is a creature of habit, caught in a situation where he has only these tools and must place his faith in them blindly. Perhaps, also, the projective techniques contain the germ of something much more useful, something which could provide the means for improving predictions based on other sorts of data. Gough (1963) pointed out that while statistical, acturial techniques surpass clinical ones in accuracy, neither is really very good. He adds that while statistical procedures will undoubtedly continue to grow in importance as predictors of personal behaviors, the clinician and his tools have so far not received the same extensive validation as the statistical equations or actuarial items. Hirt (1962) also mentioned this, pointing out that significant interpretations seem to depend more on the examiner's skill than on the data themselves. Proper use of the clinician's acumen, Gough (1960) said, might supplement statistical prediction by aiding in the selection of the sort of material to be classified statistically. Also, the clinician can take account of factors in the specific situation which cannot be included in statistical formulae (for example, rain storms or broken legs). Moreover, while predictions about certain issues are better made by statistics (job success, school achievement, remaining in therapy), qualitative predictions (such as how dependency will be manifest, or how a person might feel about his spouse, or whom to select as a marriage partner) require sensitivity to the individual in question which cannot be programmed into a computer.

Experimental vs. Correlational Methodology. The controversy concerning clinical (intuitive) and actuarial prediction is paralleled by a more general diversity of approaches to psychology as a whole. Cronbach (1957) referred to these two approaches as the experimental method and the correlational method, and he wrote a broad critique of them. Experimental method, he said, involved isolation, control, and manipulation of variables in a laboratory situation. Correlational method, on the other hand, was used primarily in natural situations where control was not yet possible or might never be possible. It studied experiments of nature, using statistical means of isolation, control, and manipulation of variables.

The experimental method could handle only one variable at a time. If the experimentalist wished to evaluate some phenomenon involving several variables, these variables had to be studied separately. In contrast, the correlational method either could not or did not wish to, subject its natural data to artificial controls. Therefore it had had to find some means of handling several variables at once, and much effort was spent in perfecting the required tools: multivariate experimental designs and statistics capable of evaluating the effects of several interacting variables, whether these effects were expressed numerically or qualitatively.

The experimental method was rarely employed outside the psychological laboratory, since it was used in basic research on physiology, sensation, perception, thinking, motivation, and learning. The correlational method was most prevalent in studies where information had to be collected in the field in its natural state, as in investigations dealing with personality theory, or matters pertaining to clinical, social, and industrial psychology. The character of the data to be used and the general scientific maturity of the area determined the method used and the conclusions formed.

Conclusions based on correlational methods usually remained on an empirical level. The correlationists seemed not to have been very successful in setting up theory in spite of their statistical sophistication. The complexity of studying the whole person appeared to require an intricate technology which had not yet yielded enough well-founded facts to allow for theory making. The situation was the reverse in experimental aspects of psychology, where theories were advanced to an acceptable level of rigor while methodology, although chaste, remained simple and somewhat rigid. One wonders if improvement in theory does not decrease the demands made on method, and on the other hand if the rigidity of experimental method has limited the areas where theory can develop.

The experimental method manipulated stimuli as a means of controlling or standardizing responses. Experimental laws stated the effects of variation of stimulation on response. Individual differences interfered with the discovery of this type of law, and it was necessary to consider the intrusion of individual variation as an indication of poor control or of errors in measurement. The experimentalists' goal was to control or standardize the environment of their subjects so that everybody reacted in a predictable fashion. This goal was influential in their applications of their experiments to education and clinical and industrial work. They sought to discover the simplest, most efficient technique of teaching, treating, or supervising. They assumed that if they could find the right method, everyone, without exception, would learn, or adjust, or work.

What was error to experimentalists was the focus of the correlationists, who were interested in individual differences and found themselves confused when the stimulus situation varied because it distorted the individual's characteristic mode of response. Their technique called for varying the personality of the individual as a way of controlling response, and their laws were statements of the relation of responses to variations among individuals or within a single individual. The correlationists' goal was to discover what produced good or bad behavior, and then to select or change the individual so that he could adjust to the existing environment. This goal influenced the applications of correlational psychology to industrial and clinical work, just as the contrasting goal of the experimentalist influenced the applications of his view point. The correlationist practitioner tested candidates, patients, or applicants to determine the probable degree of success they might achieve in a given environment. Those individuals who did not show a high probability of achievement were dropped from the program or exposed to some remedial effort.

Both approaches conceived of behavior as an S → O → R (Stimulus → Organism → Response) sequence, but they disagreed as to whether S or O was the ultimate means of controlling R. Such disagreement could be reduced to whether the causes of behavior were distal or proximal to their effects.

Actually neither approach can exist apart from the other. While one might obtain some useful ideas through observation and correlation of natural data, these ideas can be translated into facts only if they are subjected to experimental test. On the other hand the experimentalists working with a single variable experiment were completely lost when asked to deal with matters which more nearly reflected the complexity of everyday phenomena. They could well make use of the multivariate methods and the factor analysis of the correlational approach in order to sharpen their research and extend its relevance.

The complex phenomena of perception, cognition, learning, and behavior which have so long evaded scientific explanation could yield to investigation only when the scientist had prior knowledge of the ecology of stimuli and responses which initiated and/or composed them. Ecology implied a catalog of the natural effects of stimuli and the varying degrees of their salient characteristics apart from what mental processing added. Similarly, it implied a catalog of the mechanical results of responses apart from the purpose or goal for which they might be performed, and a catalog of the individual differences in these effects.

The confusion surrounding many concepts would yield to experimentally controlled multivariate study conducted in the light of this ecological information. Consider, for example, the concept of rigidity. For some psychologists rigidity is defined as persistence of problem-solving responses which are either unnecessary, inefficient, or inappropriate. To other psychologists rigidity means persistence of a percept when the stimulus is changed. To a third group of psychologists, rigidity is persistence of an attitude (opinion) in social situations where it is inappropriate. Studies conducted from each of these points of view have yielded different relationships between rigidity and independent variables assumed to influence it. Furthermore, studies which compared individuals on problem-solving, perception, and attitude change have demonstrated no relationship between rigidity measured by one means and rigidity measured by another. An evaluation of the stimulus conditions involved and of the responses to them should reveal whether it is conceivable that these apparently divergent Ss and Rs are really the same or different. Moreover, laboratory controlled studies of the stimulus, and a multivariate assessment of the responses thereto, should reveal the extent to which behavior in one situation is correlated with behaviors in another.

Egon Brunswick made a similar plea some years earlier (1947), urging that psychology sample the various stimulus and response dimensions and combinations thereof, and test them for their purely mechanical effects which might otherwise be mistaken for phenomena of learning, perception, etc.

Principles

Within such a varied group of theories there is no one set of laws describing the data of psychology. However, it is possible to isolate a set of principles dealing with psychology itself. In recent years psychology seems to have become more self-conscious of its status as a science and has therefore struggled to set up guide lines to insure that its professional members perform as scientists. For the most part, dogmatic and unquestioning acceptance of any theory or any interpretation is unacceptable. The good psychologist is one who is open-minded; even though he might incline toward a particular theory, he rarely works with it alone. Rather, he examines other theories and empirical facts, deriving ideas and hypotheses against which to test and compare his own interpretations.

The primary goal in psychology is to be objective and scientific. Currently this takes the form of a great clamor for hyper-objectivity, a preference for mathematical and/or logical formulae, and a tendency to reject laws which are stated in words alone. The end itself is not new, but the particular means recommended for achieving it were not prominent in psychology much before 1930.

Accompanying this increased interest in objective and mathematical statements is an increased emphasis on parsimony. Many psychologists prefer a strictly empirical, non-theoretical science that makes no assumptions whatsoever. The supporters of this viewpoint believe that the facts should be sufficient to explain themselves.

These trends are well revealed in the recent theorizing on the various concepts selected here. In discussing these trends it is impossible to review all the literature pertaining to a particular aspect. The alternative is to attempt a broad general account of the current status in each area, citing studies which seem to illustrate this trend. There is no intent that any study cited should be viewed as necessarily more important than any omitted. Selection was made not for import alone, but for relevance as a demonstration of a point.

Consciousness

Consciousness is viewed as a process within the central nervous system. Its nature is not clearly understood, but enough is known to eliminate the mystical and metaphysical connotations which previously accompanied it. Despite our lack of knowledge about its physiological basis, consciousness is a matter of importance in social, clinical, and personality theories. It is considered to be that body of knowledge about the self and one's environment of which one is aware.

The Unconscious. Events, internal and external, can occur under certain circumstances without a person's being aware of them. Many phenomena occur automatically and need no conscious direction. The person becomes aware of them only incidentally. Into this category fall many physiological processes, drives and reflexes. In addition, voluntary activities can take place without the awareness of the person performing them. These acts may be unconscious because they are not appropriate or necessary to some ongoing chain of activity or because they are so well established that they require no conscious direction. Many phenomena are unconscious because the individual finds such feelings or impulses or reactions unacceptable and therefore does not permit himself to recognize them. This type of unconscious behavior is usually confined to the spheres of emotional and interpersonal reactions. In contrast to other kinds of unconscious events, it is often impossible for the person to become aware of these even if he should want to. The experiences have been repressed because they were incompatible with the individual's values or attitudes, or because he anticipated dire consequences if he should allow the experience to influence him. Before the individual can become consciously aware of repressed material his values and attitudes must be changed.

Physiological Studies. Recent studies in the neurological and physiological areas have suggested that eventually consciousness may be accounted for in terms of various activating processes within the nervous system. One process that is viewed as tremendously important for the production of consciousness is the reticular activating system in the lower brain (Adrian, Bremer, and Jasper, 1954; Lindsley, 1954; Magoun, 1952 and 1954; Papez, 1926, 1938, 1955, 1957; Proctor, 1958). It appears to have the function of priming the brain, as Hebb (1955) has suggested, creating a background of activity such that the brain can carry on its activities smoothly. It seems to induce a state of arousal and may be the key to the nature of consciousness. Another aspect of neurological functioning which could account for consciousness is the presence within the brain of metabolic gradients which affect differentially the processes by which the various areas of the brain utilize the chemical substances within the blood (Himwich, 1951). Some areas have different chemical reactions, some work at different speeds, some at different times. These differential gradients seem to be present in all levels of the brain.

In summary, current theory does not unduly emphasize consciousness and cannot really account for it, although it has some ideas on the subject. Generally the treatment given to the concept of consciousness is eclectic, incorporating all of the prominent historical theories.

Sensation, Perception, and Discrimination

Sensory Processes. Within psychology the term "sensation" refers to the basic sensory processes that occur in the sensory organs themselves and in the receiving centers in the brain. There are numerous detailed theories of vision, audition, and so forth. These theories usually combine physiological and psychological concepts in an attempt to account for the sensory phenomena. No one theory has been universally accepted as an explanation of the events in any sensory modality. Each theory is highly controversial and so technical as to be inappropriate for our present concern.

Social Perception. Perception is the process by which one interprets or gives meaning to sensory material. Such meaning is the result of the context in which the stimulus occurs (in the person and in the environment) and of one's past experience with similar sensory stimulation. Both the nature of perception and its functions in the social world are given great attention.

Among the persons best known for their work in social perception are Jerome Bruner and Leo Postman (Bruner, 1951; Bruner and Goodman, 1947; Bruner and Krech, 1950; Bruner and Postman, 1947A, 1947B, 1948A, 1948B; Bruner and Rodrigues, 1948; Postman, 1953A, 1953B, 1953C; Postman, Bronson and Gropper, 1953; Postman, Bruner and McGinnes, 1948; Postman, Bruner and Walk, 1951; Postman and Leytham, 1950; Postman and Miller, 1945; Postman and Schneider, 1951; Postman and Solomon, 1950.) They hypothesized that certain aspects of perception were determined by the structure of the sensory apparatus and the nervous system, particularly the brain. These they referred to as *autochthonous* factors. Figure-ground relationships, depth perception as a function of binocular vision, sound localization by differential stimulation of the auditory apparatus (sound reaching one ear before it reaches the other), closure, and other phenomena described in Gestalt principles were so determined. In addition to its structural aspects, perception was also influenced by the present stimulus field and by past experience. Bruner and Postman referred to these influences as *nonautochthonous* factors.

General and physiological psychology had long been concerned with the autochthonous variables; Bruner and Postman's work (1948A) opened the nonautochthonous phenomena to investigation, describing four processes which presumably could explain all perceptual behavior.

The first of these was selection. The brain was constantly bombarded with sensory impulses and had to choose from among these impulses which were to be noted and responded to and which were to be ignored. Given several equally clear and salient stimuli, some were less likely to be noticed than others. Bruner and Postman investigated this selective process by comparing the time it took to recognize a neutral or pleasant stimulus (word) with the time it took to recognize a threatening taboo stimulus (word). The stimuli were presented tachistoscopically, i.e., were flashed for varying periods on a screen until the length of presentation time was sufficient to allow for recognition. They discovered that one perceived that which fit with, or was reasonant with, one's needs, values, attitudes, and so forth. Certain threatening items in the environment were perceived at a level of intensity where ordinary stimuli would still be subliminal, that is, below the threshold of awareness. This process was called vigilance or subception. On the other hand, other threatening stimuli were completely overlooked even at levels of intensity where other stimuli were well perceived. Apparently in such a reaction the person avoided or ignored what was threatening in an effort to maintain a smooth adjustment unmarred by emotional disturbance. Therefore the phenomenon was called perceptual defense.

What determined whether a person would be vigilant or defensive in his perception was not immediately obvious. Research showed that past experience, general personality, adaptive mechanisms (defenses), and current needs contributed to selective perception, but the psychologist could not predict whether selection would result in greater accuracy or greater distortion.

The second nonautochthonous process described by Postman and Bruner was the organization of the sensory experience, putting together the neural impulses which flowed into the perceptual centers, and relating them to past experiences in such a way as to interpret the meaning of the current situation. In discussing research which demonstrated the organizing function of perception Bruner and Postman cited many examples, including Gestaltist experiments, Rorschach research revealing how personality influenced perception of ink blots, and many studies demonstrating how organization of ambiguous stimuli into percepts became affected by need, reward and punishment, past experience, and group pressures. Bruner and Postman themselves presented ambiguous pictures of buildings to subjects whose social and occupational interests were known. Each subject was asked to guess at the purpose of the buildings. It was found that the subjects viewed these ambiguous buildings as pertaining of their areas of interest. In another of their studies, subjects demonstrated far different preferences for, and impressions of, a fictitious person described by a list of adjectives including the word "warm," than for a second fictitious person described by the same lits of adjectives with the word "cold" substituted for "warm." Perception, it appeared, was organized to incorporate stimulus, social variables, and personality into a harmonious product

The third nonautochthonous process was the accentuation of certain aspects of sensory experience. What was important in a particular situation seemed to stand out from the rest of the sensory input. Those stimulus characteristics which had been reinforced in previous experience or were in some way necessary to person or the situation were accentuated. In like manner current needs caused accentuation of aspects of the environment relevant to their satisfaction. Several studies demonstrated this principle. Persons judging size of coins were found to be influenced by the value of the coin. The more it was worth, the more it was over-estimated (within certain limits). Similarly, in another study the size of a plastic disc was estimated quite accurately until it came to have some value by having a symbol put on it (dollar sign or swastika). In still another experiment children were asked to judge the size of a disc; then they were told that it was candy and asked to make another judgment. The second judgment was more distorted, the disc being perceived as much larger when its composition was known.

The final nonautochthonous phenomena Bruner and Postman described was fixation. As a result of fixation the recurrence of a stimulus was accompanied by the recurrence of the same perceptual experience it produced on its last appearance. To demonstrate this function Bruner and Postman referred to an experiment in which subjects whose interests and values were known were asked to guess the purpose (e.g., religious, business, educational) of buildings presented in incomplete pictures. The pictures were shown several times, each time in more detail. The subject was asked on each presentation to name the purpose of the building. It was discovered that the subjects resisted changing original guesses compatible with their own interests, but easily altered judgment irrelevant to these interests. Later studies led to similar conclusions.

The organizing, accentuating, and fixation processes proposed by Bruner and Postman have been generally accepted. The concept of selective perception, on the other hand, has been a source of disagreement. Howes and Solomon (1950, 1951; Howes, 1954A, 1954B) pointed out that vigilance and defense could be experimental artifacts; rather than avoiding recognition, the experimental subjects could easily have been less familiar with some of the stimuli than with others. Unfamiliar words would naturally take longer to recognize, and subjects would be slower to report taboo words even after they recognized them. Many studies aimed at testing this premise have shown that there is, indeed, a hesitance to report unpleasant pre-recognition hunches (McConnell, Cutler, and McNeil, 1958).

Vigilance and defense have also been challenged because they imply *subception*, i.e., they presuppose a perceptual process of some sort prior to perceptual recognition which cued off selection. Subception required a sensory center communicating with the rest of the brain on an unconscious level, functioning as a warning system. The implications of the subception hypothesis are not necessarily compatible with other theories of perception. So complex and obscure a process is difficult to explain, and to many psychologists it connotes a homunculus inside one's head acting as a watchman. Among those who accept the concept there is a general belief that subception need not be mystical. It is possible that prior to conscious awareness of a stimulus (a phenomenon of the cortex), emotional reactions (a function of lower centers in the brain) could occur which prepare the person to meet or avoid potential threat.

When the matter became vital to the whole theory of perceptual defense, Lazarus and McCleary (1951; Lazarus, 1954) designed what they believed would be a crucial experiment proving or disproving the existence of subception. They exposed threatening stimuli ("dirty" words) and neutral stimuli (ordinary words) at various subliminal speeds on a tachistoscope, gradually increasing exposure time until conscious recognition occurred. They measured the extent of the psychogalvanic reflex (palmar sweating) at each exposure of each stimulus. They found an increase in psychogalvanic reflex on all but the shortest exposures of threatening stimuli, while no such increase was noted for neutral stimuli. Lazarus and McCleary concluded that even though the person was not aware of a stimulus he could still react to any threat it might pose. Although these findings have been replicated numerous times, subception is still a controversial concept because no one has yet proved that the subject is really unaware of the stimulus, and because other factors could possibly intervene (e.g., unfamiliarity), and because the physiological mechanisms cannot be specified.

Bruner and Postman's original intent was to describe cognitive function and organization as manifested in perception. They had no intent of creating the "New Look" in perception, and as research accumulated showing that perceptual defense might be an experimental artifact, they were quite willing to concede that familiarity, probability of response, and censorship, word frequency and difficulty could certainly produce delays in perception (or in the report of it). They defended the logic of the construct of defense (Postman, 1953), but indicated that it was descriptive rather than explanatory.

Bruner (1957A) suggested that defense, vigilance, etc., were matters of perceptual readiness, the result of mechanisms of grouping and integration, access ordering, match-mismatch, signal utilization, and gating, all of which could be tied to neural processes (Bruner, 1957B). These mechanisms were the mediators of categorizing, differential threshold, cue search (hypothesis testing), and filtering, etc., and of cognitive processing of sensory data.

Having thus settled matters to their satisfaction, Bruner and Postman continued to pursue their interests in cognition (Bruner, Austin, and Goodnow, 1957; Postman, 1955; Goodnow and Postman, 1955). However, the concepts had in the meantime gained sufficient acceptance in some circles and sufficient antagonism in others that Bruner's disclaimer had no effect on the controversy. The dust has still to settle, but in the current status of the concepts was summarized by London and Rosenhan, who stated:

> When *S*s are grouped and predictions made in terms of their personality characteristics, some significant and stable differences in perceptual behavior occur. The problem that confuses the study of perceptual defense, as opposed to the generality of the differential interactions of personality and perceptual processes, seems to revolve entirely around the contamination of experiments by use of stimulus materials or conditions which are conducive to response bias by being embarrassing or otherwise difficult to report accurately (1964, p. 465).

Present-day research appears to be aimed at specifying the parameters of these other variables, and of the processes of vigilance and defense themselves.

Adaptation Level. Another theory relating to the constancy or stability of perception is Helson's *adaptation level* (Helson 1930, 1933, 1947, 1948, 1951, 1959; Helson, Blake, Mouton and Olmstead, 1956). The theory evolved in the context of research on object perception and was generalized to social perception as well. On the basis of his research, Helson concluded that in those cases where significant characteristics of an object varied with members of a class, so that, for example, some apples are bigger or sweeter than others, the individual perceived a particular object not as it really was, but as its characteristics compared to a subjective average (the adaptation level) of all similar characteristics experienced in the past. Thus, if one were shown an ordinary size apple and asked how big it was, one would make a judgement based not only upon the apple involved, but also upon the general size of apples he had known before. Under usual circumstances an individual's internal standard functioned very well as a guide for behavior. When conditions changed, however, the frame of reference was not altered immediately, and perception was distorted. If a person's past experience had been with extremely small or extremely large apples his internal standard or adaptation level would vary in such a manner as to cause a sizeable error. While the concept of adaptation level could not be related to any specific neurological process, it made sense psychologically, even to the extent of being amenable to mathematical expression which enabled the experimenter to predict the perceptions of experimental subjects whose relevant experience had been controlled or was known. The concept has been useful in explaining various unusual perceptual phenomena and appears to be a source of fruitful hypotheses about stereotypes, expectancies, and perception of social roles.

Thinking, Cognition, and Memory

Theory of Concept Attainment. Bruner's most recent efforts (Bruner, Goodnow and Austin, 1957) have centered upon what he called a functional study of thinking which was both a theoretical exercise and an experimental demonstration. It began with the premise that concepts, classes, laws, principles, etc., did not really exist as such, waiting for man to discover them. They were invented by man to impose order on his world and to provide a means of comprehending it. Concepts were generalities, groups of objects placed in a class by virtue of having attributes in common (*conjunctive* concepts), some mutual relationship to something else (*relational* concepts), or because something about them rendered them equivalent although they were not alike (*disjunctive* concepts). A class might include the attributes of being an animal which barks and has four legs (conjunctive); it might include the attribute of being related through a common ancestor (relational); it might include all persons who live in a city or who own property there but live elsewhere (disjunctive). To form a concept was to become aware of the existence of a way of grouping things, to discover some attribute or set of attributes which delimited a group of interest to the individual. A number of decisions had to be made in the process of defining a set of attributes. The information the individual had on hand allowed him to set up hypotheses about the aspects of the world relevant to his problem. He had to decide which of these hypotheses to test, when to test it, and how. Testing these hypotheses gave him more information. Each new bit of information called for decisions regarding its meaning, its use, and its relevance to the other information available.

There were numerous strategies for utilizing available information in making decisions. One could test all possible hypotheses simultaneously, considering how the information he had pertained to each one. One could systematically eliminate the potential solutions one at a time, concentrating on this narrow scope and ignoring whatever broader connotations the incoming information might suggest. One could exercise logic, focusing first on one aspect and then on another until he arrived at the solution deductively. One might gamble on a particular hunch either at the beginning, or after he had worked at the problem. Which of these strategies was selected depended upon which was the most effective approach to a particular situation and how much strain and effort it required. The degree of efficiency and the amount of strain expected, plus the person's estimate of the probability of various outcomes, formed the *pay-off matrix*, the subjective statistic that told the person what chance his various hypotheses had of paying off and which strategy was most economical. Errors made in problem solving were not so much mistakes as they were results of the strategy the person chose. Some strategies were inefficient, some invited miscalculations.

Sometimes a person relied upon misleading similarities or upon social and cultural biases, for culture and past experience determined the kinds of decisions he could make. Sometimes limited cues prevented him from perceiving accurate information. The choice of problem-solving strategy thus determined how easily and effectively the problem would be solved.

Bruner, Goodnow and Austin, attempted to demonstrate how concept formation occurred and how strategies varied with the situation by requiring human subjects to sort cards according to one or more attributes. As they predicted, strategy varied with the kind of problem, but wherever possible the subjects usually tried to pick the most likely hypothesis and utilize the information obtained to gain insight into other hypotheses at the same time, demonstrating an effort to deduce the solution rather than to discover it by trial-and-error.

Thought Disturbances. Another area of current interest is the thinking of psychotic persons. On one hand the Freudian theories have held that such thinking was a regression to a primitive mode of behavior, employing symbolic representations of conflict in much the same way that dreams did. On the other hand, bio-social personality theorists like Cameron (1938, 1947) have held that the disturbance was the result of prolonged social isolation, so that the individual never developed the thought and word patterns which would enable him to communicate with others. In the absence of communication, distortions developed which could not be checked against other people's interpretation, and idiosyncratic ideas were formed.[1]

Research aimed at testing or demonstrating these opposing views began in the 1930's and 40's but the controversy is still active almost 30 years later. Studies by Goldstein (1943, 1944; Goldstein and Scheerer, 1941, 1953; Bolles and Goldstein, 1938), Hanfmann and Kasanin (1942; Kasanin, 1947), Storch (1924), Werner (1940), and Vigotsky (1934A, 1934B) tended to confirm the Freudian hypotheses. Although they employed different terms, all these investigators concluded that the thinking of the schizophrenic was less abstract, more concrete, and more primitive in the sense of being like that of a child or primitive person. They maintained that the reasoning ability of the schizophrenic was so different in quality from normal thought that it seemed to be governed by separate and distinct laws of logic.

Not unexpectedly, the results of Cameron's research supported his (earlier) views that psychotic reasoning was impaired in the sense that the experience of the psychotic individual was so atypical that he did not perceive basic facts in the same way, and might not even have access to the same

[1] Cameron has recently (1963) published another book in which he offers an unmistakably psychoanalytic interpretation of personality dynamics and development, apparently as a result of personal experiences in working in an analytic setting and undergoing a training analysis which led him to retract his earlier bio-social views. His change of theories has not, however, changed the bio-social point of view; rather, one of the protagonists has changed to the other side.

body of fact. Henle, a logician, concluded (1962) that psychotic logic was not qualitatively different from normal logic.

Memory and Inhibition. There are no new theories about the nature of memory and forgetting, but there have been some realignments of emphasis based on experimental evidence. Despite the convictions and research of Hullian theorists, the concept of conditioned inhibition remains controversial. The questions at issue seem to pertain mostly to the nature of an inhibitory process and to whether forgetting and extinction could be explained without such a construct. A recent study by Underwood (1957) suggested that forgetting might not be due to newer experiences interfering with earlier learning, as in the commonly held belief, but rather to earlier learning interfering with later learned material, making it difficult to master and easier to forget. In technical terms, Underwood suggested that proactive inhibition was more important than retroactive inhibition in accounting for forgetting.

Emotion and Motivation

Physiological and Neurological Studies. With the appearance of the tranquilizing drugs a new tool was made available for research on motivation and emotion. Studies of the effects of lobotomies and other types of brain surgery used in the treatment of emotional disorders had earlier offered similar opportunities, but the operative procedures were more expensive, more difficult to perform, harder to control, and above all less available for human research since they involved radical attacks on brain tissues. Consequently they were not so practical a research tool as drugs. With pharmacological techniques it is possible to relate emotional and motivational events to various activities in the body and the brain. For all the time and effort that have gone into the development of tranquilizing, activating, and otherwise behavior-inducing drugs, psychopharmacology is still in its infancy. The development of drugs was obviously a medical activity; as safe and effective drugs were found, a need arose to study the mode and site of action and to evaluate their behavioral effects. As psychologists became involved in the study of various drugs, their interest began to broaden beyond the medical questions which initiated their work to include its relevance to psychology. It soon became clear that drug effects offered a valuable source of theoretical hypotheses as well as a tool for testing or demonstrating predictions. Indeed, drugs could be used to investigate matters which had little apparent relationship to physiology. Among the hypotheses which drug research has suggested, the response of depressed persons to various activators and tranquilizers led Ostow (1958) to speculate on the nature of motives in depression and the dynamics by which homeostasis was recovered when drugs were administered. Similarly, Carlton (1963) concluded from the results of numerous studies that the central nervous system was composed of two sub-systems, one arousing, the other inhibiting, which interacted in a complex manner. Stimulation of arousal or dampening of inhibition led to the disappearance of learned avoidance behavior, and to the appearance of variations in behavior previously held in abeyance by inhibition. Stimulation of inhibition or decrease in arousal prevented the appearance of new responses which might otherwise occur. The testing of such hypotheses should not only provide interesting data on the phenomena in question, but on the relationship of behavior, experience, and physiology.

Aside from drug studies, much investigation has been conducted in the physiology of motivation and emotion. Research has demonstrated that individual variations in these physiological processes can often be correlated with personal histories. Thus, according to some studies, people with certain types of disorders which involve changes in blood pressure tend to come from certain kinds of religious orientations (King and Funkenstein, 1957), and certain kinds of life situations seem prominent in asthmatic attacks (Funkenstein 1950, 1953). These studies are suggestive, but there are as yet no definitive results.

Closely related to this type of study, and actually antedating it, are the studies conducted at the Boston Psychopathic Hospital by Funkenstein and his associates (Funkenstein, 1956; Funkenstein, Greenblatt and Rost, 1950; Funkenstein, Greenblatt and Solomon, 1950, 1951, 1952, 1953; Funkenstein, King and Drollette, 1953, 1957; Meadow and Funkenstein, 1952; Sloane, Lewis and Slater, 1957). These workers found that individual reactions to the injection of adrenalin compounds and other drugs predict whether or not emotionally disturbed persons can best be helped by electroshock or by insulin coma. They also demonstrated a relationship between physiological processes and various personality traits and family experiences. This work was purely empirical; no explanations of the results were given, and no effort was made to relate them to any theory. The fact that some correlation was observed and could be useful in treating patients was far more important to these clinical investigators than theoretical accounts of its basis.

Neal Miller and his co-workers have carried on extensive investigations of the neurological correlates of motivation. Among their findings was the isolation of centers within the brain which seemed to regulate thirst and hunger (Bower and Miller, 1957, 1958; Delgado, Roberts and Miller, 1954; Miller, 1958, 1961A, 1961B; Miller, Bailey and Stevenson, 1950).

Stimulation of these centers produced eating or drinking in the absence of food or water deprivation. They also found that stimulation of certain areas of the brain could be used as reinforcement for learning, while stimulation of other areas was punishing and disrupted established behaviors. Research based on these findings led Olds to develop his theory of central pleasure states and central pain states (discussed in Chapter 7). Miller's work has demonstrated, beyond question that whatever the distal causes of motivation, the proximal or immediate cause of emotions and motivations was a series of events in the central nervous system, and that the initiation of these events could be traced physiologically (Miller, 1956; Miller and Bailey, 1952; Miller, Berkun and Kersen, 1952; Miller, Sampliner and Woodrow, 1957).

Assessment of Social Motives. There has been a growing interest among psychologists in the description and classification of various specific motives. The motive to be studied is first isolated by devising some test which measures its salient characteristics. This test is then used to investigate the natural history of the motive, how it influences behavior, how it interacts with other motives, how it is influenced by other internal and external conditions, and how it relates to the broader aspects of psychological functioning and personality. This type of study amounts to a cataloging of the characteristics of a motive state.

The approach probably began with Henry Murray's classical work (1938 and 1943: See Chapter 26 of this volume) in which he set up a system describing and classifying needs as a key to understanding personality. He evolved the Thematic Apperception Test or TAT designed to elicit imaginative interpretations of ambiguous pictures of social situations. These interpretations or stories were analyzed in such a way as to provide an indication of what kinds of motives were attributed by the subject to persons in the pictures. It was assumed that similar motives had been aroused in the individual by similar situations, and that these motives had affected the person's perceptions and thus his performance on the test, thereby providing a sample of the spectrum of needs and their function in behavior.

McClelland and Atkinson, selecting from Murray's list, attempted to set up separate tests for specific needs. They elected to begin with need for achievement and devised a set of standards for evaluating the degree of arousal of this motive as manifested in stories to TAT cards, similar pictures and various fantasy materials (Atkinson, 1954, 1958; Clark and McClelland, 1956; Birney, 1958; DeCharms, Morrison, Reitman and McClelland, 1955; French and Thomas, 1958; Krumholtz and Farquhar, 1957; McClelland, 1955; McClelland, Atkinson, Clark and Sowell, 1953; Miles, 1958; Parrish and Rethlingshafer, 1954). Having carefully derived, defined, and validated these evaluative criteria, they set themselves to the task of studying the behavioral manifestations which accompanied varying degrees of arousal of this need, its effects on other aspects of behavior, and how numerous independent variables affected it. They and their associates have found, for example, that there are sex differences in the appearance of need for achievement, girls being less likely to show achievement motivation than boys (Moss and Kagan, 1961; Lesser, Krawitz and Packard, 1963). Ego involvement tended to heighten the intensity of need achievement (Atkinson, 1953; Atkinson and Raphelson, 1956), but there was a complex interaction between ego involvement, fear of failure, and achievement, such that persons with high need for achievement were less likely to take great risks than persons with strong fear of failure, but were more likely to select harder tasks (Atkinson, 1957), unless some other motive intervened introducing goals inappropriate to achievement (Smith, 1963). McClelland employed the scoring criteria they had developed to evaluate children's stories, etc., thereby attempting to trace historical influences on social motives (1961) and social influences (Krebs, 1958; McClelland, Rindlisbacher and De-Charms, 1955; McClelland, Sturr, Knapp and Wendt, 1958; Samelson, 1957; Wertheim and Mednick, 1958; Bending, 1958).

Atkinson and McClelland's success with assessing need achievement led them to attempt similar techniques for assessing *need for affiliation* (Atkinson, Heynes and Veroff, 1954; Shipley and Veroff, 1952) and *need for power* (Veroff, 1957). As before, they developed standards for evaluating the degree of such motivation as manifested in response to selected TAT cards (or other productions). These scoring techniques are still being perfected; information concerning the attributes of these needs must await validation of the measuring instruments.

Another approach to assessment of motives was Taylor's scale of Manifest Anxiety (TMAS, Taylor, 1953). This scale is not a projective test, but a list of statements describing feelings, acts, and symptoms which the subject must sort (or check off) as true or false descriptions of his own feelings. The items were originally part of the MMPI, the Taylor Scale merely being another empirically derived key for obtaining patterns of judgements about MMPI items, in this case patterns which correlated with some objective index of anxiety. Taylor's original purpose was to provide a means of testing Spence's hypotheses about anxiety as a drive, and about drives and learning (Farber, 1954; Hill, 1957; Silverman, 1957; Spence, 1958; Spence and Farber, 1953; Taylor, 1956). Anxiety seemed not only to have the drive-like qualities Spence predicted, but to be an important determinant of the learning phenomena that interested Spence (Goodstein and Farber, 1957; Grice, 1955; Hunt and Schroder, 1958; Spence and Beecroft, 1954; Spence and Farber, 1954; Spence, Farber and McFann, 1956; Spence, Farber and Taylor, 1954; Spence and Ross, 1957; Spence and Taylor, 1951, 1953; Spence, Taylor and Ketchel, 1956; Taylor and Spence, 1952, 1954). It also provided a useful tool for other learning theorists (Bendig and Vaughn, 1957; Mednick, M. T., 1957; Mednick, S. A., 1967; Stevenson and Iscoe, 1956).

The simplicity and objectivity of the scale attracted the attention of students of motivation and personality, who adapted the scale so completely that it became one of their standard tools, even as it was one of Spence and Taylor. Many hunches about anxiety as a motive and its relationship to personality have been validated (Bendig, 1958A, 1958B; Ericksen, 1954; Ericksen and Davids, 1955; Jessor and Hammond, 1957; Kerrick, 1955; Levey and Kusz, 1957; Martin, 1958; Shore, 1958; Smith, Powell and Ross, 1955; Wenar, 1954). Short forms were developed to make the procedure even briefer (Christie and Budnitzhy, 1957).

However, anxiety as measured by the TMAS was soon discovered to be somewhat different than anxiety measured by projective tests, self-rating, or clinical observation. Therefore a number of other tests of anxiety were developed. The best known of these was a scale worked out by Sarason (Cox and Sarason, 1954; Gordon and Sarason, 1955; Mandler and Sarason, 1952; Sarason, 1950; Sarason, Davidson, Lighthall, Waite and Ruebush, 1960; Sarason and Gordon, 1953; Sarason and Mandler, 1952; Sarason, Mandler and Craighill, 1952). In contrast to Taylor's and Spence's belief that anxiety was a general motive state, Sarason proposed that anxiety was produced by specific situations and present only in reference to that situation. A person could, of course, be anxious about several different situations, each to a different degree. Thus Sarason hypothesized a number of specific anxieties, and not one universal condition. He pointed out that to assess the individual's motivational state one must gauge the amount of anxiety produced by each source. To demonstrate his hypothesis, Sarason devised a check list somewhat like the Taylor Scale, but with items specific to test situations. Research demonstrated some degree of correlation between the Sarason Test Anxiety Scale and the Taylor Scale, as one might expect for two tests dealing with similar areas, but the small size of the correlation indicated that the two areas were distinct (Gordon and Sarason, 1955). Sarason established the construct validity of his scale by means of studies in which persons achieving high and low scores on his Test Anxiety Scale were found to have distinctly different test behavior, different personalities, and different life histories, all understandable in terms of their level of anxiety. For example, test-anxious persons were more rigid, had more trouble with problem-solving, and seemed to have more difficult social experiences (Sarason, Davidson, Lighthall, Waite & Ruebush, 1960).

Sets and Response Bias. In an area given over to a survey of the characteristics of motives there would seem to be little reason for controversy. For some years this was true, and while many fields of psychology were riven with contention there was tranquil progress in the area of motivation (except for certain questions about drive and tension-reduction constructs). Then the effects of set or frame of reference on test results, long recognized but never fully evaluated, began to be investigated. These studies demonstrated the profound effects of social desirability of test items and responses, and the equally profound effects of the tendency toward acquiescence or its opposite (Berg, 1955; Cruse, 1963; Hesterley, 1963; Holtzman, 1965; Iscoe and Harvey, 1963; Lunneborg, 1963; Sechrest and Jackson, 1963). Many other sets were also found to affect test scores. As a result, it has become necessary for many researchers to concede that much of what had appeared to be characteristic of a particular motive was really the result of one or more of these test-taking sets. Actually, of course, insofar as sets influence and orient behavior, they are closely related to motives. The problem is to re-evaluate earlier findings in order to attribute them to the correct source, and to evaluate the interaction of long recognized motives and recently discovered sets.

We can summarize the status of motivation concepts by stating that new evidence concerning physiological and neurological aspects of drive has aided in advancing theory, but at the expense of some of the older tension-reduction concepts. Likewise, progress in measurement of motivation has unseated old concepts, even as it has suggested new ones. This state of affairs is well documented in the review of motivation theory and research by Cofer and Appley (1964).

The Nature of the Learning Process

Current research and theory in the area of learning are characterized by a trend toward questioning and re-evaluation of all concepts. Few aspects of learning theory have remained untouched, many are radically altered, and some have been discarded altogether. Any statement made about learning is likely to be supplanted in a short time by another. Perhaps the most far-reaching alterations are Spence's revisions of the Hullian concept of *incentive* (amount and type of reinforcement) and the consequent changes in Hull's theory of learning.

Spence's Revisions of Hull's Theory. Incentive was important to Hullian theory because once an organism had been exposed to a reinforcing situation it was predicted that he would be influenced in similar situations by an anticipation of recurring reinforcement. It seemed to Hull that the subject responded to this expectation to a certain extent as he would to the goal itself. At least it made him strive harder for the goal, becoming an additional stimulus directing behavior toward a specific goal. Hull called this phenomenon the *fractional anticipatory goal response*.

As Spence continued the work that Hull began, he came to reason that if an anticipatory response was a stimulus to behavior and was produced through association with the reinforcing or incentive stimulus, then it was also a matter of relating two stimuli rather than relating a stimulus and a response, i.e., a matter of contiguity association as opposed to the S-R reinforcement learning proposed by Hull. Spence's convictions led him to propose a two-factor learning theory (Spence, 1956) in which he assumed that reinforcement accounted for classical conditioning while contiguity led to the establishment of instrumental acts which involved anticipatory goal responses. It should be noted that Spence's interpretation is exactly the opposite of Mowrer's (1947) original theory that instrumental behavior was learned through reinforcement and conditioning was a contiguity process.

Reinforcement vs. Contiguity. The problem of finding a physiological counter-part has already led many theorists to abandon the idea of reinforcement altogether and turn instead to contiguity to account for learning. Only a few still hold to a pure reinforcement theory of learning; those who do must find some way to make it fit with physiological data. Miller, a major proponent of pure effect learning, attempted to do this by defining reinforcement as a reduction in stimulus intensity. This solution avoided all physiological problems, but it had to reckon with the question of habitual behaviors which seem to heighten stimulation (e.g., exciting activities).

The most popular current position is some approach which utilizes both contiguity and reinforcement. McClelland (1953, 1955) proposed a two-factor theory, interpreting reinforcement in a manner similar to Miller (1951; Miller and Dollard, 1950) and including contiguity as a separate process. At one time Mowrer (1947, 1950) held a dual theory of learning, but he has revised it (1956), so that while it remained a two-factor theory, all learning was interpreted as sign learning or contiguity. Instead of dealing with avoidance and instrumental learning as previously, he dealt with what he called *incremental fear conditioning* and *decremental fear conditioning*. Incremental fear conditioning was an acquired or conditioned fear. Decremental fear conditioning was a conditioned hope, an expectation that certain acts or goals would reduce the fear.

The general emphasis on the need for a simple objective theory, the general questions that have been raised about reinforcement, and the doubts about all theories of learning have led to a renewed interest in Guthrie's approach (see Chapter 12) and others like it which offer a means of describing learning while making no assumptions as to what underlies it. The statistical or mathematical learning theories have evolved from this orientation.

Statistical Theories of Learning. Although statistical descriptions of learning phenomena are a recent development, it is easy to see in Ebbinghaus's learning curves (see Chapter 3) the roots from which a theory grew. Learning, more than many other psychological functions, lends itself to this form of expression. Whatever the mathematical basis of the theory, the content involves mathematical statements of formulae which indicate the increasing probability of certain kinds of behavior under certain conditions. A number of statistical theories have been derived, of which the best known are Estes' (Burke and Estes, 1957; Burke, Estes and Hellyer, 1954; Estes, 1950, 1954; Estes and Burke, 1953; Estes, Burke, Atkinson and Frankman, 1957; Estes and Johns, 1958; Estes and Straughan, 1954; Lauer and Estes, 1955) formulation derived from differential calculus, and Bush and Mosteller's stochastic model (1955; Bush and Wilson, 1956) derived from probability mathematics. Like all statistical theorists, Estes, Bush and Mosteller describe behavior but do not explain it. Because of the logic inherent in their derivation, the formulae extend beyond any specific situation, enabling the theorist to make predictions about relationships to stimuli, drive conditions, etc., which might not otherwise be apparent from the phenomena observed. These predictions are not speculation, but deductions, inevitably logical once the basic descriptive statements have been made.

Most of the statistical theories are models rather than theories proper. They become theories only when they are translated or interpreted from symbols into psychological terms. To a certain extent the various theorists have inadvertently abandoned their models for theory and attempted to talk in psychological terms on the basis of mathematics without first discovering whether their translation of mathematical symbols to psychological concepts is valid. This, says Walker (1957) is their weakest point, for these theories are meaningless until they are interpreted, and their adequacy can never be greater than the adequacy of their interpretation. In a similar vein, Hilgard (1956) pointed out that while the models made good mathematical sense they did not necessarily make good psychological sense, and by themselves could not be expected to. Mathematics was a tool and could not become a concept.

Avoidance Learning. In a field beset by doubts and controversies, one small area of relative calm is the subject of avoidance learning, perhaps because it is a late-comer whose basic parameters have not yet been completely investigated. Avoidance learning is a special variety not only because of its aversive content, but also because once established, it is difficult to extinguish. Solomon and Wynne (1953, 1954; Wynne and Solomon, 1955) described how they had found it virtually impossible to extinguish after large numbers of trials. They proposed that continued avoidance was reinforcing because it reduced the anxiety roused by the threat of punishment. If the organism lagged in responding, his anxiety would heighten and induce a response. Since the anxiety was anticipatory, aroused *before* punishment took place, avoidance was also anticipatory. As a result, an organism never experienced an unreinforced trial; escaping anxiety provided reinforcement and the organism never permitted itself to remain long enough in the situation to discover that the typical punishment had disappeared. If forced to remain in the situation long enough to make the discovery that physical punishment had ceased, the organism experienced the emotional punishment of anxiety, and its avoidance was reinforced in spite of the experimenter's design. One kind of aversive stimulus had been substituted for another. This view was supported by most research findings (Berkun, 1957; Dinsmoor, 1954, 1955; Kimble, 1955; Miller and Kraeling, 1953; Miller and Murray, 1952; Mowrer and Aiken, 1954; Mowrer and Lamoreaux, 1942; Mowrer and Solomon, 1954; Murray and Miller, 1952) until the advent of tranquilizers offered a new tool.

Tranquilizers proport to remove anxiety. If they indeed have this function, then an individual trained in avoidance behaviors motivated by anxiety should, when his anxiety is reduced by a drug, show a reversal of avoidance. Similarly, if the individual's original experience is one of anticipatory anxiety learning, then if he is subjected to avoidance learning situations while under drugs he should not learn to avoid because he is not anxious. So far, experimental results (Arbit, 1957A, 1957B, 1957C; Auld, 1951; Berkun, 1957; Brady, 1956; Bullock, 1957; Carlton, 1963; Coppock and Hood, 1956; Coppock, Maloney, Pacheco, Yearwood, Coppock and Maloney; Feldman, Liberson and Neet, 1957; Kornetsky, 1958; Kornetsky and Humphries, 1957; Kornetsky, Humphries, and Evarts, 1957; Kosman and Gerard, 1955; Moyer and Bunnell, unpublished; Payne, 1958; Steinberg, 1954; Wenzel, 1957; Whitehead and Thune, 1958) have been ambiguous; either the tranquilizers do not remove anxiety, or experimental techniques do not induce it, or the theory of avoidance learning has some inaccuracies.

Behavior and Personality

Much of the present-day study of behavior and personality centers around the testing of predictions based on established theories, especially the psychoanalytic ones. If such study is carried out in an objective and controlled manner it makes great contributions both to the theory involved and to psychology in general. It is often the case, however, that such investigations are conducted by persons with vested interests (either pro or con) who somehow act to prove rather than to test their point of view, and this detracts seriously from their potential value.

Along with the testing of personality theories, there is a growing interest in the application of personality theory to education, social problems, and most of all to clinical practice. Such applications are sometimes made as the result of cautious investigation, but equally as often they may be adopted with no consideration for their appropriateness. This need not be a criticism of the investigator, who has no other means of establishing a foothold on new territory. The application of theory to a practical situation can be beneficial to both if conducted properly: it can serve not only society but also the theory, testing it and suggesting areas where revisions are necessary. But disservice is done if a theory which is itself untested and perhaps invalid is literally transferred into situations in which it was not intended to operate and to which it may be irrelevant.

Factor Analysis Studies. Aside from these general trends, several new approaches to personality have appeared. The first to be considered are the factor analytic studies and the trait listings which usually result from them. Factor analysis is a statistical device which allows for the administration of a large number of tests which may then be correlated and manipulated statistically to reveal any relationships among them. The technique divides an array of isolated facts or scores into classes or categories called *factors*, which are formed or bound together by their intercorrelations. The experimenter attempts to abstract from this group some essence or general characteristic which makes it psychologically significant. It is not surprising that such an analysis should be adapted to the study of personality and behavior. A large number of tests exist or can be developed which can divulge some aspect (or trait) of personality, but no one really knows how these aspects relate to each other or to the total picture of human behavior. Many theorists have felt that an objective survey of all traits would demonstrate the dimensions of personality and the laws of interaction among them. Early psychologists occupied much of their time devising lists of traits. As Freudian theory became more influential, traits were felt to be too static, not reflecting the seething forces which give rise to individual personality. Traits seemed to be rather cold and meaningless pigeon holes, and interest in them lagged in spite of theorists like Jung (see Chapter 17) and Allport (see Chapter 25) until factor analysis made it possible to reconstruct traits from bits of behavior and to relate these bits to others, many of which might not appear to be related on superficial observation. The fact that it could reveal genotype relations beneath the surface provided a means of considering the dynamic aspects of behavior which the older trait theories could not supply.

The extensive investigations of Cattell (1946, 1950A, 1950B, 1953, 1956A, 1956B, 1957A, 1957B, 1958A, 1958B; Cattell and Baggaly, 1958; Cattell, Beloff and Coan, 1958; Cattell, Dubin and Saunders, 1959; Cattell and Scheier, 1958; Cattell and Stice, 1954; Cattell, Stice and Kristy, 1957) and Eysenck (1947, 1951, 1952A, 1952B, 1952C, 1953A, 1953B, 1954A, 1954B, 1954C, 1955, 1956A, 1956B, 1957; Eysenck, Granger and Brengelmann, 1957) are perhaps the best known applications of factor analysis to the study of personality. Both of these psychologists have isolated a number of factors or groupings within personality and have, after studying the nature of the test items within such a group, proposed various names for them. While the composition of these factors and the names applied to them differ, they bear some general resemblance to neuroticism, emotional spontaneity, extroversion-introversion, and dominance-submission. A number of other factors have been suggested but are less well validated.

One of the appeals of the factor analytic type of study is the fact that it may appear to be letting the phenomenon under study dictate the findings, rather than being distorted by some inaccurate theory. Granted that theory, or at least the experimenter's thought patterns, enters into the naming and interpretation of the findings after they are isolated, nature presumably makes the findings, not man. Once the factors have been isolated they can be incorporated into an inductive theory and used to predict behavior. For example, Eysenck has explored how his traits affect learning, forgetting, and many other facets of personality.

The reliance on empirical data is, however, more apparent than real. Actually the factors are dependent upon the tests from which they are derived, and tests are only derived to tap what an investigator is interested in or aware of, and are only appropriate to his idea of how these things should be tested and how they relate to behavior. Factor analysis cannot bring out of the data anything that has not already been put into it by the investigator.

Further problems in the use of factor analysis inhere in the fact that there are a number of computational techniques. Results with one technique differ to some extent from results computed by another. Even using the same method, different groupings appear with replication, and factor components change from one study to the next.

Authoritarian Personality. The trait and factor approach is paralelled by an effort to isolate patterns of traits or social adjustment. A number of personality types have been described, mostly by Freudian clinicians (discussed in Chapter 15). Another personality syndrome which has received much research attention (Christy and Cook, 1958) is the authoritarian personality. Acting on the hypothesis that persons who manifest strong prejudice toward minority groups were also similar in other aspects of their personality, Adorno, Frenkel-Brunswick, Levinson, and Sanford (1950) conducted an historic investigation. In addition to using most of the standard means of assessing personality, these investigators introduced several new methods. Principal among these were a test of ethnocentrism, the E scale, and a test of authoritarian orientation known as the F scale (F stands for Facist attitudes). The findings were highly significant.

Case histories and projective tests revealed that the authoritarian personality was developed in a particular family constellation which was conducive to the child's learning to see his parents as authority figures, strict and over-controlling. Being so constricted, the child developed a strong feeling of resentment, but the authoritative temperament of his parents prevented him from expressing this resentment openly. Instead it was displaced to some other person. The child was trained to admire strength and to detest weakness. These attitudes toward strength were a reflection of his perception of parental dominance and his own weakness. He learned to be entirely non-accepting of weakness both in himself and in others. Thus the persons or objects upon whom he displaced his anger were likely to occupy some powerless status. These persons were selected out of a generalized dislike and because they could not retaliate and would probably submit. The most likely place to find such a powerless, submissive person was in a racial or religious minority, and the resentment usually generalized to include minority groups as a whole, taking the form of an unreasoning prejudice.

In addition to their need to dominate others, the authoritarians had a strong need to be dominated and usually sought out some authority to guide and direct their activity. They were, of course, ambivalent, resentful of this domination even as they sought it, and this ambivalence probably increased their need to dominate others. Their inability to act without external guidance made them unable to tolerate ambiguous situations. They tended to jump to conclusions about problems or other aspects of their environment, and having once interpreted a thing in a certain way they resisted change. This resistance to change affected not only their problem-solving and general social adjustment, but also their attitudes regarding politics, economics, etc. Anything new or different, be it a social issue or a kind of person, was displeasing and threatening to them. In other words, political conservatism, prejudice, and a peculiarly rigid, authority-oriented personality formed a pattern of social and personal maladjustment.

Further observations suggested that there were personalities who were similar in every detail except for the fact that their social and economic attitudes were at opposite ends of the liberal-conservative continuum. Since the F scale measured only authoritarianism of a conservative nature, Rokeach (1960) developed measures of dogmatism as opposed to measures of conservatism, and with these tests was able to show the relationship of the so-called authoritarian of the political left to the previously studied authoritarian of the right. The dogmatism scale developed by Rokeach isolated what its author believed was a purer culture of authoritarianism than the F scale.

The authoritarian personality was also described by Fromm (1941) and Jaensch (1938). The latter, working in Nazi Germany, used more positive adjectives, but the general findings were the same.

A personality type which was in many ways the reverse of the authoritarian was given the equally value-laden name of *democratic personality* by Adorno, Frenkel-Brunswick *et al.* According to their findings, democratic personalities were tolerant, flexible, and prone to independent action. They were much more directly hostile and often a little rebellious or nonconforming. Their early years were in many ways just the opposite of the authoritarian child's. Since the study of the authoritarian personality was conducted to account for prejudice, and since the so-called democratic personality was not prejudiced, the latter was originally conceived to be more normal and healthy. However, it seems quite possible that in the extreme democratic personalities would be equally pathological either as social rebels or as completely ineffectual individuals. At least this is how Jaensch, the German psychologist, saw them (1938). However, this group has not been studied sufficiently for either its extremes or its more moderate variations to be understood in detail.

The clarity of the early findings by Frenkel-Brunswick, *et al.* has been clouded by the finding that the tendency to behave in an acquiescent fashion can account for much of the high F scale score of the erstwhile authoritarian orientation. The question therefore arises as to whether the authoritarian or the passive acquiescent attitude is the basis for many of the research findings. The study of acquiescence has become sufficiently salient to achieve the status of a separate area of investigation, and the issue has yet to be settled.

Newcomb's Theory. The group investigating authoritarian personality were social psychologists, concerned with the impact of the individual's make-up upon the social phenomena about him. Social psychology has made another contribution to personality theory in the work of Newcomb (1950), who attempted to understand the development and change in personality as a function of the various roles that a person was expected to play in a society. He placed great emphasis on the opinions of other people as a factor the individual's evaluation of himself and more particularly as a means of developing his personality. Newcomb also stressed the importance of communication between individuals as a means of developing personality and implementing interpersonal relationships. Newcomb's theory was, however, more concerned with social action than with individual behavior, seeking to account for the various attitudes and other social phenomena that a person demonstrated in a social situation by virtue of his earlier social experience.

Psychology in Other Countries

Our discussion of the current theoretical situation applies mostly to psychology as it exists in the United States. Some of these trends are evident in other parts of the world, but there are also many differences (David and von Bracken). The emphasis on theories and scientific methodology is typically American, while psychoanalysis, physiology, and philosophy form the milieu in which European psychology thrives.

Psychoanalysis in Europe is either of the orthodox variety or some minor deviation therefrom. Neo-Freudian theories are less significant; although the theories of Fromm and Adler were European in origin, their impact has probably been greater in America. One exception to the orthodox orientation is Jungian theory, which is more popular in Switzerland and France than it is in America. In England the theories of Anna Freud and Melanie Klein determine the analytic climate, creating more or less competing philosophies. Anna Freud and her co-workers stress the Ego, defense mechanisms, and orientation to reality, while Klein concentrated on the Id and sexual symbolism.

In England there has also been a growing interest in Group Dynamics. This work is closely allied with the psychoanalytic movement although it retains its Lewinian flavor.

Psychoanalysis and Group Dynamics are primarily important in the applied areas of psychology. Much of the experimental psychology in

Europe is physiological in nature. In Germany laboratory research follows the tradition of Wundt modified to suit a more modern body of fact. Classical studies of sensation and perception are numerous not only in Germany, but also in Italy, and to a lesser degree in France. There is also much interest in neurological problems.

Psychology in Russia is governed by political movements. For many years it was not an acceptable field of study. Eventually, however, the philosophy of the state altered to some extent and it found the Pavlovian theories of conditioning compatible with its new goals. A psychology largely centered on conditioning has grown up in recent years. It is closely allied with physiology and neurology, and in combination these fields constitute a larger science of bodily functions.

Philosophy has always been important in Europe, and the atmosphere which fathered the science of psychology still exists on the continent. Particularly in Germany there is often a close alliance with philosophy. Much of German and Italian psychology concerns itself with *characterology* (a study of character traits), ethics, morality, and personality, apparently stimulated by the same forces which gave rise to psychoanalysis. The foundation of this study is philosophical, but it has led to the construction of various tests and measures of traits. There is also a lively interest in the style or patterns of action which characterize an individual's behavior and outlook, and a concentrated effort to utilize handwriting, motoric functions, and many other behavioral phenomena as a way of demonstrating the richness of the individual. The Rorschach Test originally developed because of the interest in the perceptions of the individual, and its use is still heavily influenced by this emphasis. French psychology, especially that part which is influenced by the Existentialist movement, is deeply involved in the nature of self and the meaning of existence, experience, and of life itself. Experiments are rare in such an approach, for it strives more for emotional comprehension than objective understanding.

Elsewhere in the world psychology tends to follow the European approach of tender-minded, delicate reasoning, the American hyper-objective, hyper-statistical orientation (Australian psychology seems to be a hybrid of these two), or to be a physiological brass-instrument study (as in Japan).

SUMMARY AND CRITIQUE

In a chapter which is itself a summary, a further abbreviation of the material appears to be unnecessary. We can provide a general summing up, and at the same time set the tone for the critique of current trends by referring to some comments made by Hebb:

Psychology has sometimes in the past been too free in postulating special processes to explain behavior. Now it is doing penance by going to another extreme, scientifically just as sinful. This current misconception of scientific method makes any hypothetical entity somehow disreputable. Psychologists now seem to feel that it is risky indeed to depart from statements of fact; nothing should be mentioned which is not operationally demonstrable. . . . At the same time the context in which the definitions appear makes it obvious that the writer has in mind something inferred from behavior, not the behavior itself.[2]

The current trend in psychology seems to be related to broader events. Following the First World War there was a great spurt in the growth of psychology, particularly in applied fields. During the economic depression of 1930's psychology went through a sort of scientific depression at which time it was forced to question and revise many of its earlier opinions about testing, behaviorism, psychoanalysis, etc. With the Second World War came another spurt of growth, followed by a second period of questioning.

It would seem that pressure from the larger realm of society, in the form of social disorganization and wars, creates demands for inventions which will allow society to adjust itself. Consequently there is a tremendous development in all sciences. Pure science, as well as its applied branches, benefits from such needs and support, but the benefit is a mixed blessing, for a science under so much pressure is likely to overgeneralize. It must later go back and check on itself before it can continue.

Each science must, it seems, pause for an occasional moment in its progress to consider where it wants to go, if it is really moving in that direction, and why it needs to go there. Looking from a new vantage point often reveals new variables, or new complexities which require a certain maturity to perceive. Such new information can shake the very foundations of a science, pulling its air castles down around its ears. The science undergoing such a reorganization must be cautious, however, lest it destroy its solid edifices along with its wilder fantasies.

REFERENCES

Methods of Investigation

I. *Testing*

Anderson, H. H., and G. L. Anderson, *An Introduction to Projective Techniques*. Englewood Cliffs, N.J.: Prentice-Hall, 1951.

Beck, S. J., *Rorschach's Test*, Vols. I and II. New York: Grune & Stratton, 1949.

Bell, J. E., *Projective Techniques*. New York: Longmans, Green, 1948.

Binet, A., *Les Idées Modernes sur les Enfants*. Paris: Flammarion, 1911. (A)

———, "Nouvelles Recherches sur la Mésure du Niveau Intellectuel chez les Enfants de l'Ecole," *Année Psychol.* 17: 145–210 (1911). (B)

———, and T. Simon, "Méthodes Nouvelles pour le Diagnostic du Niveau Intellectuel des Anormaux," *Année Psychol.* 11: 191–244 (1905). (A)

[2]Hebb, D. O., *Organization of Behavior*. New York: Wiley, 1949, p. 162.

———, and T. Simon, "Applications des Méthods Nouvelles au Diagnostic Chez des Enfants Normaux et Anormaux d'Hospice et d'Ecole Primaire," *Année Psychol.* 11: 245–336 (1905). (B)

———, and T. Simon, "Le Dévelopement de l'Intelligence chez les Enfants," *Année Psychol.* 14: 1–94 (1908).

Cattell, J. McK., "Mental Tests and Measurements," *Mind* 15: 373–381 (1890).

Frank, L. K., "Projective Methods for the Study of Personality," *J. Psychol.* 8: 389–413 (1939).

Galton, F., *Inquiries into Human Faculty and its Development.* London: Macmillan, 1883.

Gough, H. G., "Clinical Versus Statistical Prediction in Psychology," in L. Postman, ed., *Psychology in the Making*, New York: Knopf, 1963, pp. 526–584.

Hathaway, S. R., and P. E. Meehl, eds., *An Atlas for the Clinical Use of the MMPI.* Minneapolis: Univ. of Minnesota Press, 1951.

———, and E. D. Monachesi, *An Atlas of Juvenile MMPI Profiles.* Minneapolis: Univ. of Minnesota Press, 1961.

———, and E. D. Monachesi, *Adolescent Personality and Behavior.* Minneapolis: Univ. of Minnesota Press, 1963.

Hirt, M., *Rorschach Science; Readings in Theory and Method.* Glencoe, Ill.: Free Press, 1962.

Kelly, E. L., and D. Fiske, *The Prediction of Performance in Clinical Psychology.* Ann Arbor: Univ. of Michigan Press, 1951.

———, and L. R. Goldberg, Correlates of Later Performance and Specialization in Psychology: A Follow-Up on the Trainees Assessed in the VA Selection Research Project," *Psychol. Monogr.* 12: 75 (1959).

Klineberg, O., "Negro-White Differences in Intelligence Test Performance," *Amer. Psychologist* 18: 198–203 (1963).

Klopfer, B., M. D. Ainsworth, W. G. Klopfer, and R. R. Holt, *Developments in the Rorschach Technique*, Vols. I and II. Yonkers-on-Hudson: World, 1954.

———, and H. H. Davidson, *The Rorschach Technique: An Introductory Manual.* New York: Harcourt, Brace & World, 1962.

Marks, P. A., and W. Seeman, *The Actuarial Description of Abnormal Personality.* Baltimore: Williams and Wilkins, 1963.

Masland, R. L., S. B. Sarason, and T. Gladwin, *Mental Subnormality: Biological, Psychological, and Cultural Factors.* New York: Basic Books, 1959.

Meehl, P. E., *Clinical Versus Statistical Prediction.* Minneapolis: Univ. of Minnesota Press, 1954.

———, "Clinical Versus Acturial Prediction," in *Proceedings, 1955 Invitational Conference on Testing Problems*, Princeton: Educational Testing Service, 1956, pp. 136–141. (A)

———' "The Tie That Binds, " *J. Counsel. Psychol.* 3: 163–164, 171–173 (1956). (B)

———, "Wanted, A Good Cookbook," *Amer. Psychologist* 11: 236–272 (1956). (C)

———, "When Shall We Use Our Heads Instead of the Formula?", *J. Counsel. Psychol.* 4: 268–273 (1957).

———, "The Cognitive Activity of the Clinician," *Amer. Psychologist* 15: 19–27 (1960).

Milholland, J. E., "Theory and Techniques of Assessment," *Annual Review Of Psychology*, Berkeley: Annual Reviews, 1964, pp. 311–346.

Murray, H. A., *Thematic Apperception Test.* Cambridge: Harvard Univ. Press, 1943.

Porteus, S. D., and A. J. Gregor, "Studies in Intercultural Testing," *Percept. and Mot. Skills* (Monogr. Supp. 7–V16): 705–724 (1963).

Rorschach, H., *Psychodiagnostik.* Bern: Huber, 1921. 2nd ed., 1932.

———, *Psychodiagnostics.* New York: Grune and Stratton, 1942.

Spearman, C. "'General Intelligence' Objectively Determined and Measured," *Amer. J. Psychol.* 15: 201–293 (1904).

———, *The Nature of "Intelligence" and the Principles of Cognition.* New York: Macmillan, 1923.

Stephenson, W., *The Study of Behavior: Q-Technique and Its Methodology.* Chicago: Univ. of Chicago Press, 1953.

Stern, W. L., "Uber die Psychologischen Methoden der Intelligenzprufung," *Ber. V. Kongress Exp. Psychol.* 16: 1–109 (1912).

Terman, L. M., *The Measurement of Intelligence.* Boston: Houghton Mifflin, 1916.

———, and M. A. Merrill, *Measuring Intelligence.* Boston: Houghton Mifflin, 1937.

———, and M. A. Merrill, *The Stanford-Binet Intelligence Scale.* Boston: Houghton Mifflin, 1960.

Thomson, G. H., "General Versus Group Factors in Mental Activities," *Psychol. Rev.* 27: 173–190 (1920).

———, *The Factorial Analysis of Human Ability.* 5th ed. London: Univ. of London Press, 1951.

Thorndike, E. L., *The Measurement of Intelligence.* New York: Bur. Publ. Teachers College, Columbia Univ., 1925.

Thrustone, L. L., *Multiple Factor Analysis.* Chicago: Univ. of Chicago Press, 1947.

Tryon, R. C., "A Theory of Psychological Components—an Alternative to Mathematical Factors," *Psychol. Rev.* 42: 425—454 (1935).

———, "Domain Formulation of Cluster and Factor Analysis," *Psychometrika* 24: 113–136 (1959).

Tuddenham, R. D., "The Nature and Measurement of Intelligence," in L.

Postman, ed., *The Making of Psychology*, New York: Knopf, 1963, pp. 469–525.
Wechsler, D., *The Measurement of Adult Intelligence.* Baltimore: Williams and Wilkins, 1939.
———, *The Wechsler Intelligence Scale for Children.* New York: Psychological Corp., 1949.
———, *Wechsler Adult Intelligence Scale.* New York: Psychological Corp., 1958. (A)
———, *The Measurement and Appraisal of Adult Intelligence.* 4th ed. Baltimore: Williams and Wilkins, 1958. (B)
———, *Wechsler Preschool and Primary Scale of Intelligence.* New York: Psychological Corp., 1967.

II. *Experimental versus Correlational Methodology*

Brunswick, E., *Systematic and Representative Design of Psychological Experiments*. Berkeley: Univ. of Calif. Press, 1947.
Cronbach, L. J., "The Two Disciplines of Scientific Psychology," *Amer. Psychologist* 12: 671–684 (1957).

Consciousness

Adrian, E. D., F. Bremer, and H. H. Jasper, eds., *Brain Mechanisms and Consciousness*. Oxford: Blackwell Scientific Publications, 1954.
Hebb, D. O., "Drives and the C.N.S. (Conceptual Nervous System)," *Psychol. Rev.* 62: 243–254 (1955).
Himwich, H. E., *Brain Metabolism and Cerebral Disorders*. Baltimore: Williams and Wilkins, 1951.
Lindsley, D. B., "Physiological Psychology," *Annual Review of Psychology*, Palo Alto: Annual Reviews, Inc., 1956, pp. 326–334.
Magoun, H. W., "An Ascending Reticular Activating System in the Brain Stem," *A.M.A. Arch. Neurol. and Psychiat.* 67: 145 (1952).
———, "Brain Stem and Higher Centers. Nerve Impulse," New York: *Tr. 5th Conf. Macy Foundation*, Vol. 5, 1954, pp. 11–93.
Papez, J. W., "Reticulospinal Tracts of the Cat," *J. Comp. Neuro.* 41: 365 (1926).
———, "A Case of Epilepsy," *Arch. Neurol. and Psychiat.* 39: 150 (1938).
———, "Central Reticular Path to Intralaminar and Reticular Nuclei of the Thalamus for Activating EEG Related to Consciousness," *Electroencephalog. and Clin. Neurophysiol.* 8: 117 (1955).
———, "Path for Nonspecific Diffuse Impulses to Cortex for EEG, Related to Consciousness," *Dis. New. System* 17: 3 (1956).
Proctor, L., *et. al.*, eds., *The Reticular Formation of the Brain.* Boston: Little, 1958.

Sensation, Perception, and Discrimination

I. *General References*

Allport, F. H., *Theories of Perception and the Concept of Structure.* New York: Wiley, 1955.

McConnel, J. V., R. L. Cutler, and E. B. McNeil, "Subliminal Stimulation: An Overview," *Amer. Psychologist* 13:229–242 (1958).

II. *Social Perception*

Bruner, J. S., "One Kind of Perception: A Reply to Professor Luchins," *Psychol. Rev.* 58: 306–312 (1951).

———, "On Perceptual Readiness," *Psychol. Rev.* 64: 123–152 (1957). (A)

———, "Neural Mechanisms in Perception," *Psychol. Rev.* 64: 340–358 (1957). (B)

———, and C. D. Goodman, "Value and Need as Organizing Factors in Perception," *J. Abn. Soc. Psychol.* 42: 33–44 (1947).

———, Jacqueline Goodnow, and G. A. Goodnow, *A Study of Thinking*. New York: Wiley, 1957.

———, and D. Krech, *Perception and Personality: A Symposium*. Durham: Duke Univ. Press, 1950.

———, and L. Postman, "Emotional Selectivity in Perception and Reaction," *J. Personal.* 16: 69–77 (1947). (A)

———, and L. Postman, "Tension and Tension-Release as Organizing Factors in Perception," *J. Personal.* 15: 300–308 (1947). (B)

———, and L. Postman, "An Approach to Social Perception," in *Current Trends in Social Psychology*, Pittsburgh: Univ. of Pittsburgh Press, 1948. (A)

———, and L. Postman, "Symbolic Value as an Organizing Factor in Perception," *J. Soc. Psychol.* 27: 203–208 (1948). (B)

———, and J. S. Rodrigues, "Some Determinants of Apparent Size," *J. Abn. Soc. Psychol.* 48: 17–24 (1953).

Dulaney, D. E., and C. W. Erikson, "Accuracy of Brightness Discrimination as Measured by Concurrent Verbal Responses and GSRs," *J. Abn. Soc. Psychol.* 59: 418–423 (1959).

Eriksen, C. W., "Unconscious Processes," in M. R. Jones, ed., *Nebraska Symposium on Motivation, 1958*, Lincoln, Nebr.: Univ. of Nebraska Press, 1958.

———, J. L. Kuethe, and D. F. Sullivan, "Some Personality Correlates of Learning Without Verbal Awareness," *J. Personal.* 26: 216–228 (1958).

Goodman, C. D., *Evidence for a Tri-Factorial Theory of Perception*, Honors Thesis. Cambridge, Mass.: Radcliffe College Library, 1946.

Goodnow, J. J., and L. Postman, "Probability Learning in a Problem-Solving Situation," *J. Exp. Psychol.* 49: 16–22 (1955).

Howes, D., "A Statistical Theory of the Phenomenon of Subception," *Psychol. Rev.* 61: 98–110 (1954). (A)

———, "On the Interpretation of Word Frequency as a Variable Affecting Speed of Recognition," *J. Exp. Psychol.* 48: 106–112 (1954). (B)

———, and R. L. Solomon, "A Note on McGinnes' 'Emotionality and Perceptual Defense,'" *Psychol. Rev.* 57: 229–234 (1950).

———, and R. L. Solomon, "Visual Duration Threshold as a Function of Word Probability," *J. Exp. Psychol.* 41:401–410 (1951).

Lazarus, R. S., "Is There a Mechanism of Perceptual Defense: A Reply to Postman, Bronson, and Gropper," *J. Abn. Soc. Psychol.* 49: 396–398 (1954).

———, and R. A. McCleary, "Autonomic Discrimination Without Awareness: A Study of Subception," *Psychol. Rev.* 58: 113–122 (1951).

London, P., and D. Rosenhan, "Personality Dynamics," *Annual Review of Psychology*, Palo Alto: Annual Reviews, 1964, pp. 447–492.

Postman, L., "The Experimental Analysis of Motivational Factors in Perception," in *Current Theory and Research in Motivation*, Lincoln, Nebr.: Univ. of Nebraska Press, 1953. (A)

———, "Perception, Motivation, and Behavior," *J. Personal.* 22: 17–32 (1953). (B)

———, "On the Problem of Perceptual Defense," *Psychol. Rev.* 60: 298–306 (1953). (C)

———, "Association Theory and Perceptual Learning," *Psychol. Rev.* 62: 438–466 (1955).

———, W. C. Bronson, and G. L. Gropper, "Is There a Mechanism of Perceptual Defense?", *J. Abn. Soc. Psychol.* 48: 215–224 (1953).

———, J. S. Bruner, and E. McGinnes, "Personal Values as Selective Factors in Perception," *J. Abn. Soc. Psychol.* 43: 142–154 (1948).

———, J. S. Bruner, and R. D. Walk, "The Perception of Error," *Brit. J. Psychol.* 42: 1–10 (1951).

———, and G. Leytham, "Perception Selectivity and Ambivalence of Stimuli," *J. Personal.* 19: 390–405 (1950).

———, and G. A. Miller, "Anchoring of Temporal Judgements," *Amer. J. Psychol.* 58: 43–53 (1945).

———, and B. H. Schneider, "Personal Values, Visual Recognition, and Recall," *Psychol. Rev.* 58: 271–284 (1951).

———, and R. L. Solomon, "Perceptual Sensitivity to Completed and Uncompleted Tasks," *J. Personal.* 18: 347–357 (1950).

III. *Adaptation Level*

Helson, H. "The Nature and Problem of Perception," in R. H. Wheeling, ed., *Readings in Psychology*, New York: Crowell, 1930.

———, "The Fundamental Propositions of Gestalt Psychology," *Psychol. Rev.* 40: 13–32 (1933).

———, "Adaptation-Level as Frame of Reference for Prediction of Psychophysical Data," *Amer. J. Psychol.* 60: 1–29 (1947).

———, "Adaptation Level as a Basis for a Quantitative Theory of Frames of Reference," *Psychol. Rev.* 55: 297–313 (1948).

———, "Perception," in H. Helson, ed., *Theoretical Foundations of Psychology*, New York: Van Nostrand, 1951.

———, "Adaptation Level Theory," in S. Koch, ed., *Psychology: A Study of a Science*, New York: McGraw-Hill, 1959.

———, R. R. Blake, J. S. Mouton, and J. A. Olmstead, "Attitudes as Adjustments to Stimulus Background and Residual Factors," *J. Abn. Soc. Psychol.* 52: 314–322 (1956).

Thinking, Cognition, and Memory

I. *Theory of Concept Attainment*

Bruner, J. S., Jacqueline Goodnow, and G. A. Austin, *A Study of Thinking.* New York: Wiley, 1957.

II. *Thought Disturbances*

Bolles, M., and K. Goldstein, "A Study of the Impairment of 'Abstract Behavior' in Schizophrenic Patients," *Psychiat. Quart.* 12: 42–65 (1938).

Cameron, N., "Reasoning, Regression, and Communication in Schizophrenics," *Psychol. Monogr.* 50, No. 1 (1938).

——— *The Psychology of Behavior Disorders.* New York: Houghton Mifflin, 1947.

———, *Personality Development and Psychopathology: A Dynamic Approach.* Boston: Houghton Mifflin, 1963.

Goldstein, K., "The Significance of Psychological Research in Schizophrenia," *J. Nerv. and Ment. Dis.* 97: 261 (1943).

———, "Methodological Approach to the Study of Schizophrenic Thought Disorder," in J. S. Kasanin, ed., *Language and Thought in Schizophrenia*, Berkeley: Univ. of California Press, 1944.

———, and M. Scheerer, "Abstract and Concrete Behavior: An Experimental Study with Special Tests," *Psychol. Monogr.* 53, No. 2 (1941).

———, and M. Scheerer, "Tests of Abstract and Concrete Thinking," in A. Weider, ed., *Contributions Toward Medical Psychology*, New York: Ronald, 1953.

Hanfmann, Eugenia, and J. S. Kasanin, "Conceptual Thinking in Schizoprenia," *Nerv. Ment. Dis. Monogr.* 67 (1942).

Henle, Mary, "On the Relations Between Logic and Thinking," *Psychol. Rev.* 69: 366–378 (1962).

Kasanin, J. S., ed., *Language and Thought in Schizophrenia.* Berkeley: Univ. of California Press, 1944.

Storch, A., "The Primitive Forms of Inner Experience and Thought in Schizophrenia," *Nerv. Ment. Dis. Monogr.* 36 (1924).

Vigotsky, L., *Thinking and Speech*, Moscow: Socekgrz, 1934. (A)

———, "Thought in Schizophrenia," *Arch. Neurol. and Psychiat.* 31: 1063–1077 (1934). (B)

Werner, H., *Comparative Psychology of Mental Development*. New York: Harper, 1940.

III. *Memory*

Underwood, B. J., "Interference and Forgetting," *Psychol. Rev.* 64: 49–60 (1957).

Emotion, Motivation, and Purpose

I. *General References*

Hilgard, E. R., *Theories of Learning*. 2nd ed. New York: Appleton-Century-Crofts, 1956, pp. 426–433.

Cofer, C. N., and M. H. Appley, *Motivation: Theory and Research*. New York: Wiley, 1964.

II. *Physiological and Neurological Studies*

Carlton, P. L., "Cholinergic Mechanisms in the Control of Behavior by the Brain," *Psychol. Rev.* 70: 19–39 (1963).

Ostow, M., "The Biological Basis of Human Behavior," in S. Arieti, ed., *American Handbook of Psychiatry*, Vol. I, New York: Basic Books, 1958, pp. 58–87.

III. *D. H. Funkenstein*

Funkenstein, D. H., "Psychophysiologic Relationships of Asthma and Urticaria to Mental Illness," *Psychosomat. Med.* 12: 377 (1950).

———, "The Relationship of Experimentally Produced Asthmatic Attacks to Certain Acute Life Situations," *J. Allergy* 24: 11–17 (1953).

———, "Nor-Epinephrine-Like and Epinephrine-Like Substances in Relation to Human Behavior," *J. Nerv. Ment. Dis.* 126: 58–67 (1956).

———, M. Greenblatt, and S. Rost, "A Test which Predicts the Clinical Effects of Electro-Shock Treatment on Schizophrenic Patients," *Amer. J. Psychiat.* 109: 889 (1950).

———, M. Greenblatt, and H. C. Solomon, "A Test which Predicts the Clinical Effects of Electrical Shock Treatment on Schizophrenic Patients," *Amer. J. Psychiat.* 106: 889–901 (1950).

———, M. Greenblatt, and H. C. Solomon, "Autonomic Changes Paralleling Psychologic Changes in Mentally Ill Patients," *J. Nerv. Ment. Dis.* 114: 1–18 (1951).

———, M. Greenblatt, and H. C. Solomon, "Nor-Epinephrine-Lik and Epinephrine-Like Substances in Psychotic and Psychoneurotic Patients," *Amer. J. Psychiat.* 108: 652–662 (1952).

———, M. Greenblatt, and H. C. Solomon, "Psychiatric Treatment," in *Proceedings of the Association for Research in Nervous and Mental Disease*, XXXI, Baltimore, Williams and Wilkins, 1953, pp. 245–266.

———, S. H. King, and M. Drolette, "The Experimental Evocation of Stress," *Symposium on Stress*, Washington, D. C.: Army Medical Service Graduate School, 1953.

———, S. H. King, and M. E. Drolette, *Mastery of Stress*. Cambridge, Mass.: Harvard Univ. Press, 1957.

King, S. H., and D. H. Funkenstein, "Religious Practices and Cardiovascular Reactions During Stress," *J. Abn. Soc. Psychol.* 55: 135–137 (1957).

Meadow, A., and D. H. Funkenstein, "The Relationship of Abstract Thinking to the Autonomic Nervous System in Schizophrenia," in P. H. Hoch and J. Zubin, eds., *Relation of Psychological Tests to Psychiatry*, New York: Greene and Stratton, 1952.

Sloane, R. B., D. J. Lewis, and P. Slater, "Diagnostic Value of Blood Pressure Responses in Psychiatric Patients," *Arch. Neurol. Psychiat.* 77: 540–542. (1957).

IV. *N. E. Miller*

Bower, G., and N. E. Miller, "Paradoxical Rewarding and Aversive Effects from Stimulating the Same Place in the Rat's Brain," *Amer. Psychol.* 12: 464, (1957) abstract.

———, and N. E. Miller, "Rewarding and Punishing Effects from Stimulating the Same Place in the Rat's Brain," *J. Comp. Physiol. Psychol.* 51: 669–674 (1958).

Delgado, J. M. R., W. W. Roberts, and N. E. Miller, "Learning Motivated by Electrical Stimulation of the Brain," *Amer. J. Physiol.* 179: 587–593 (1954).

Miller, N. E., "Effects of Drugs on Motivation: The Value of Using a Variety of Measures," *Ann. N.Y. Acad. Sci.* 65: 318–333 (1956).

———, "Central Stimulation and Other New Approaches to Motivation and Reward," *Amer. Psychol.* 13: 100–108 (1958).

———, "Learning and Performance Motivated by Direct Stimulations of the Brain," in D. E. Sheer, ed., *Electrical Stimulation of the Brain: Subcortical Integrative Systems*, Austin: Univ. of Texas Press, 1961. (A)

———, "Comments on the Implications of the Olds' Reward Effect for Theories of Reinforcement," in D. E. Sheer, ed., *Electrical Stimulation of the Brain: Subcortical Integrative Systems*, Austin: Univ. of Texas Press, 1961. (B)

———, and C. J. Bailey, "The Effect of Sodium Amytal on an Approach-Avoidance Conflict in Cats," *J. Comp. Physiol. Psychol.* 45: 205–208 (1952).

———, C. J. Bailey, and J. A. F. Stevenson, "Decreased 'Hunger' but

Increased Food Intake Resulting from Hypothalamic Lesions," *Science* 112: 256–259 (1950).

———, M. M. Berkun, and M. L. Kersen, "Hunger-Reducing Effects of Food by Stomach Fistula versus Food by Mouth Measured by a Consummatory Response," *J. Comp. Physiol. Psychol.* 45: 555–564 (1952).

———, G. Hubert, and J. B. Hamilton, "Mental and Behavioral Changes Following Male Hormone Treatment of Adult Castration, Hypogonadism, and Psychic Impotence," *Proc. Soc. Exp. Biol. Med.*, article 9925 (1938).

———, R. I. Sampliner, and P. Woodrow, "Thirst-Reducing Effects of Water by Stomach Fistula versus Water by Mouth Measured by both a Consummatory and an Instrumental Response," *J. Comp. Physiol. Psychol.* 50: 1–5 (1957).

V. *Assessment of Social Motives: H. A. Murray*

Murray, H. A., and collaborators, *Explorations in Personality*. New York: Oxford: 1938.

———, *Manual of Thematic Apperception Test*. Cambridge, Mass.: Harvard Univ. Press, 1943.

VI. *Need Achievement, Need Affiliation, and Need Power*

Atkinson, J. W., "The Achievement Motive and Recall of Interrupted and Completed Tasks," *J. Exp. Psychol.* 46: 381–390 (1953).

———, "Exploration Using Imaginative Thought to Assess the Strength of Human Motives," in M. R. Jones, ed., *Nebraska Symposium on Motivation 1954*, Lincoln, Nebr.: Univ. of Nebraska Press, 1954.

———, "Motivational Determinants of Risk Taking Behavior," *Psychol. Rev.* 64: 359–372 (1957).

———, *Motives in Fantasy, Action and Society: A Method of Assessment and Study*. Princeton: Van Nostrand, 1958.

———, R. W. Heyns, and J. Veroff, "The Effect of Experimental Arousal of the Affiliation Motive on Thematic Apperception," *J. Abn. Soc. Psychol.* 49: 405–410 (1954).

———, and A. C. Raphelson, "Individual Differences in Motivation and Behavior in Particular Situations," *J. Pers.* 24: 349–363 (1956).

Clark, R. A., and D. C. McClelland, "A Factor Analytic Integration of Imaginative and Performance Measures of the Need for Achievement," *J. Gen. Psychol.* 55: 73–83 (1956).

Birney, R. C., "The Achievement Motive and Task Performance," *J. Abn. Soc. Psychol.* 56: 133–135 (1958).

De Charms, R., H. W. Morrison, W. Reitman, and D. C. McClelland, "Behavioral Correlates of Directly and Indirectly Measured Achievement Motivation," in D. C. McClelland, ed., *Studies in Motivation*, New York: Appleton-Century-Crofts, 1955.

French, E. G., and F. H. Thomas, "The Relation of Achievement Motivation to Problem-Solving Effectiveness," *J. Abn. Soc. Psychol.* 56: 45–48 (1958).

Krebs, A. M., "Two Determinants of Conformity: Age of Independence Training and N Achievement," *J. Abn. Soc. Psychol.* 56: 130–131 (1958).

Krumboltz, J. D., and W. W. Farquhar, "Reliability and Validity of N Achievement," *J. Consult. Psychol.* 21: 226–231 (1957).

Lesser, G. S., R. N. Krawitz, and R. Packard, "Experimental Arousal of Achievement Motivation in Adolescent Girls," *J. Abn. Soc. Psychol.* 66: 59–66 (1963).

McClelland, D. C., ed., *Studies in Motivation.* New York: Appleton-Century-Crofts, 1955.

———, *The Achieving Society.* Princeton: Van Nostrand, 1961.

———, J. W. Atkinson, R. A. Clark, and E. L. Lowell, *The Achievement Motive.* New York: Appleton-Century-Crofts, 1953.

———, A. Rindlisbacher, A. and R. De Charms, "Religious and Other Sources of Parental Attitudes toward Independence Training," in D. C. McClelland, ed., *Studies in Motivation*, New York: Appleton-Century-Crofts, 1955.

———, J. F. Sturr, R. H. Knapp, and H. W. Wendt, "Obligations to Self and Society in the United States and Germany," *J. Abn. Soc. Psychol.* 56: 245–255 (1958).

Miles, G. H., "Achievement Drive and Habitual Modes of Task Approach as Factors in Skill Transfer," *J. Exp. Psychol.* 55: 156–162 (1958).

Moss, H. A., and J. Kagan, "Stability of Achievement and Recognition-Seeking Behavior from Early Childhood through Adulthood," *J. Abn. Soc. Psychol.* 62: 504–513 (1961).

Parrish, J., and D. Rethlingshafer, "A Study of the Need to Achieve in College Achievers and Non-Achievers," *J. Gen. Psychol.* 50: 209–226 (1954).

Samuelson, F., "Conforming Behavior Under Two Conditions of Conflict in the Cognitive Field," *J. Abn. Soc. Psychol.* 55: 181–187 (1957).

Shipley, T. E., and J. Veroff, "A Projective of Need for Affiliation," *J. Exp. Psychol.* 43: 349–356 (1952).

Smith, C. P., "Achievement-Related Motives and Goal Setting Under Different Conditions," *J. Personal.* 31: 124–140 (1963).

Veroff, J., "Development and Validation of a Projective Measure of Power Motivation," *J. Abn. Soc. Psychol.* 54: 1–8 (1957).

Wertheim, J., and S. A. Mednick, "The Achievement Motive and Field Independence," *J. Consult. Psychol.* 22: 38 (1958).

VII. *Taylor's Manifest Anxiety Scale*

Bendig, A. W., "Manifest Anxiety and Projective and Objective Measures of Need Achievement," *J. Consult. Psychol.* 21: 354 (1958). (A)

———, "Identification of Item Factor Patterns within the Manifest Anxiety Scale," *J. Consult. Psychol.* 22: 158 (1958). (B)

———, and C. J. Vaughn, "Manifest Anxiety, Discrimination, and Transposition," *Amer. J. Psychol.* 70: 286–288 (1957).

Christie, R., and S. Budnitzhy, "A Short Forced-Choice Anxiety Scale," *J. Consult. Psychol.* 21: 501 (1957).

Ericksen, C. W., "Some Personality Correlates of Stimulus Generalization Under Stress," *J. Abn. Soc. Psychol.* 49: 561–565 (1954).

———, and A. Davids, "The Meaning and Clinical Validity of the Taylor Anxiety Scale and the Hysteria-Psychosthenia Scales from the MMPI," *J. Abn. Soc. Psychol.* 50: 135–137 (1955).

Farber, I. E., "Anxiety as a Drive State," in M. R. Jones, ed., *Nebraska Symposium on Motivation 1954*, Lincoln, Nebr.: Univ. of Nebraska Press, 1954.

Goodstein, L. D., and I. E. Farber, "On the relationship Between A-Scale Scores and Digit Symbol Preference," *J. Consult. Psychol.* 21: 152–154 (1957).

Grice, G. R., "Discrimination Reaction Time as a Function of Anxiety and Intelligence," *J. Abn. Soc. Psychol.* 50: 71–74 (1955).

Hill, W. F., "Comments on Taylor's 'Drive Theory and Manifest Anxiety,'" *Psychol. Bull.* 54: 409–493 (1957).

Hunt, D. E., and H. M. Schroder, "Assimilation, Failure-Avoidance and Anxiety," *J. Consult. Psychol.* 22: 39–44 (1958).

Jessor, R., and K. R. Hammond, "Construct Validity and the Taylor Manifest Anxiety Scale," *Psychol. Bull.* 54: 161–170 (1957).

Kendell, E., "The Validity of Taylor's Manifest Anxiety Scale," *J. Consult. Psychol.* 18: 429–432 (1954).

Kerrick, J. S., "Some Correlates of the Taylor Manifest Anxiety Scale," *J. Abn. Soc. Psychol.* 50: 75–77 (1955).

Levy, L. H., and R. B. Kurz, "The Connotative Impact of Color on the Rorschach and its Relations to Manifest Anxiety," *J. Personal.* 25: 617–625 (1957).

Martin, B., "A Factor Analytic Study of Anxiety," *J. Clin. Psychol.* 14: 133–138 (1958).

Mednick, M. T., "Mediated Generalization and the Incubation Effect as a Function of Manifest Anxiety," *J. Abn. Soc. Psychol.* 55: 315–321 (1957).

Mednick, S. A., "Generalization as a Function of Manifest Anxiety and Adaptation of Psychological Experiments," *J. Consult. Psychol.* 21: 491–494 (1957).

Shore, M. E., "Perceptual Efficiency as Related to Induced Muscular Effort and Manifest Anxiety," *J. Exp. Psychol.* 55: 179–183 (1958).

Silverman, R. E., "The Manifest Anxiety Scale as a Measure of Drive," *J. Abn. Soc. Psychol.* 55: 94–97 (1957).

Smith, W., E. K. Powell, and S. Ross, "Manifest Anxiety and Food Aversions," *J. Abn. Soc. Psychol.* 50: 101–104 (1955).

Spence, K. W., "A Theory of Emotionally Based Drive (D) and its Relation to Performance in Simple Learning Situations," *Amer. Psychol.* 13: 131–141 (1958).

———, and R. S. Beecroft, "Differential Conditioning and Level of Anxiety," *J. Exp. Psychol.* 48: 399–403 (1954).

———, and I. E. Farber, "Conditioning and Extinction as a Function of Anxiety," *J. Exp. Psychol.* 45: 116–119 (1953).

———, and I. E. Faber, "The Relation of Anxiety to Differential Eyelid Conditioning," *J. Exp. Psychol.* 47: 127–134 (1954).

———, I. E. Farber, and H. H. McFann, "The Relationship of Anxiety (Drive) Level to Performance in Competitional and Noncompetitional Paired-Associates Learning," *J. Exp. Psychol.* 52: 269–305 (1956).

———, I. E. Farber, and E. Taylor, "The Relation of Electric Shock and Anxiety to Level of Performance in Eyelid Conditioning," *J. Exp. Psychol.* 48: 404–408 (1954).

———, and L. E. Ross, "Experimental Evidence on the Relation Between Performance Level in Eyelid Conditioning and Anxiety (Drive) Level," USN Office of Naval Research, *Tech. Rep.*, No. 5, 1957.

———, and J. A. Taylor, "Anxiety and Strength of the UCS as Determiners of the Amount of Eyelid Conditioning," *J. Exp. Psychol.* 42: 183–188 (1951).

———, and J. A. Taylor, "The Relation of Conditioned Response to Anxiety in Normal, Neurotic and Psychotic Subjects," *J. Exp. Psychol.* 45: 265–272 (1953).

———, J. A. Taylor, and R. Ketchel, "Anxiety (Drive) Level and Degree of Competition in Paired-Associates Learning," *J. Exp. Psychol.* 52: 306–310 (1956).

Stevenson, H. W., and I. Iscoe, "Anxiety and Discriminative Learning," *Amer. J. Psychol.* 69: 113–114 (1956).

Taylor, Janet A., "The Relationship of Anxiety to the Conditioned Eyelid Response," *J. Exp. Psychol.* 41: 81–92 (1951).

———, "A Personality Scale of Manifest Anxiety," *J. Abn. Soc. Psychol.* 48: 285–290 (1953).

———, "Drive Theory and Manifest Anxiety," *Psychol.* Bull. 53: 303–320 (1956).

———, and K. W. Spence, "The Relationship of Anxiety Level to Performance in Serial Learning," *J. Exp. Psychol.* 44: 61–64 (1952).

Werner C., "Reaction Time as a Function of Manifest Anxiety and Stimulus Intensity," *J. Abn. Soc. Psychol.* 49: 335–340 (1954).

VIII. *Sarason's Test Anxiety*

Cox, F. N., and S. B. Sarason, "Test Anxiety and Rorschach Performance," *J. Abn. Soc. Psychol.* 49: 371–377 (1954).
Gordon E. M., and S. B. Sarason, "The Relationship Between 'Test Anxiety' and 'Other Anxieties,'" *J. Personal*; 23: 317–323 (1955).
Mandler, G., and S. B. Sarason, "A Study of Anxiety and Learning," *J. Abn. Soc. Psychol.* 47: 161–173 (1952).
Sarason, S. B., "The Test Situation and the Problem of Prediction," *J. Clin. Psychol.* 6: 387–392 (1950).
———, K. S. Davidson, F. F. Lighthall, R. R. Waite, and B. K. Ruebush, *Anxiety in Elementary School Children*. New York: Wiley, 1960.
———, and E. M. Gordon, "The Test Anxiety Questionnaire Scoring Norms," *J. Abn. Soc. Psychol.* 48: 447–448 (1953).
———, and G. Mandler, "Some Correlates of Test Anxiety," *J. Abn. Soc. Psychol.* 47: 810–817 (1952).
———, G. Mandler, and P. G. Craighill, "The Effect of Differential Instructions on Anxiety and Learning," *J. Abn. Soc. Psychol.* 47: 561–565 (1952).

IX. *Sets and Response Bias*

Berg, I. A., "Response Bias and Personality: The Deviation Hypothesis," *J. Psychol.* 40: 61–62 (1950).
Cruse, D. B., "Socially Desirable Responses in Relation to Grade Level," *Child Developm.* 34: 777–789 (1963).
Hesterley, S. O., "Deviant Response Patterns as a Function of Chronological Age," *J. Consult. Psychol.* 27: 210–214 (1963).
Holtzman, W. H., "Personality Structure," *Annual Review of Psychology*, Palo Alto: Annual Reviews, 1965 pp. 122–127.
Iscoe, I., M. Williams, and J. Harvey, "Modification of Children's Judgements by a Simulated Group Technique: A Normative Developmental Study," *Child Developm.* 34: 963–978 (1963).
Lunneborg, P. W., "Relations Among Social Desirability, Achievement, and Anxiety Measures in Children," *Child Developm.* 35: 169–182 (1963).
Sechrest, L., and D. N. Jackson, "Deviant Responses: Their Measurement and Interpretation," *Educ. Psychol. Measmt.* 23: 543–561 (1965).

The Nature of the Learning Process

I. *General References*

Cf. the *Annual Review of Psychology*. Palo Alto: Annual Reviews, 1950–present.

Estes, W. K., S. Koch, K. MacCorquodale, P. E. Meehl, C. G. Mueller, Jr., W. N. Schoenfeld, and W. S. Verplanck, *Modern Learning Theory*. New York: Appleton-Century-Crofts, 1954.

Hilgard, E. R., *Theories of Learning*. New York: Appleton-Century-Crofts, 1948, 2nd ed., 1956.

II. *Spence's Revision of Hull's Theory*

Mowrer, O. H., "On the Dual Nature of Learning—A Reinterpretation of 'Conditioning' and 'Problem Solving,'" *Harvard Educ. Rev.* 17: 102–148 (1947).

Spence, K. E., *Behavior Theory and Conditioning*. New Haven: Yale Univ. Press, 1956.

III. *Reinforcement versus Contiguity*

Dollard, J., and N. E. Miller, *Personality and Psychotherapy*. New York: McGraw-Hill, 1950.

McClelland, D. C., "Toward a Theory of Motivation," in *The Achievement Motive*, New York: Appleton-Century-Crofts, 1953.

———, "Notes for a Revised Theory of Motivation," in D. C. McClelland, ed., *Studies in Motivation*, New York: Appleton-Century-Crofts, 1955.

Miller, N. E., "Learnable Drives and Rewards," In S. S. Stevens, ed., *Handbook of Experimental Psychology*, New York: Wiley, 1951.

Mowrer, O. H., "On the Dual Nature of Learning—A Reinterpretation of 'Conditioning' and 'Problem Solving,'" *Harvard Educ. Rev.* 17: 102–148 (1947).

———, "Further Evidence for a Two-Factor Theory of Learning," in *Learning Theory and Personality Dynamics*, New York: Ronald, 1950.

———, "Two-Factor Learning Theory Reconsidered with Special Reference to Secondary Reinforcement and the Concept of Habit," *Psychol. Rev.* 63: 114–128 (1956).

IV. *Statistical Theories*

Burke, C. J., and Estes, W. K., "A Component Model for Stimulus Variables in Discrimination Learning," *Psychometrika* 22: 133–145 (1957).

———, W. K. Estes, and S. Hellyer, "Rate of Verbal Conditioning in Relation to Stimulus Variability," *J. Exp. Psychol.* 48: 153–161 (1954).

Bush, R. R., and F. Mosteller, *Stochastic Models for Learning*. New York: Wiley, 1955.

———, and T. R. Wilson, "Two Choice Behavior of Paradise Fish," *J. Exp. Psychol.* 51: 315–322 (1956).

Estes, W. K., "Toward a Statistical Theory of Learning," *Psychol. Rev.* 57: 94–107 (1950).

———, in *Symposium on Psychology of Training Basic to Military Training Problems*, Washington, D. C.: Research and Devel. Board, 1954.

———, "Theory of Learning with Constant Variable or Contingent Probabilities of Reinforcement," *Psychometrika* 22: 113–132 (1957).
———, and C. J. Burke, "A Theory of Stimulus Variability in Learning," *Psychol. Rev.* 60: 276–286 (1953).
———, C. J. Burke, R. C. Atkinson, and J. P. Frankman, "Probabilistic Discrimination Learning," *J. Exp. Psychol.* 54: 233–239 (1957).
———, and M. D. Johns, "Probability-Learning with Ambiguity in the Reinforcing Stimulus," *Amer. J. Psychol.* 17: 219–228 (1958).
———, and J. H. Straughan, "Analysis of a Verbal Conditioning Situation in Terms of Statistical Learning Theory," *J. Exp. Psychol.* 47: 225–234 (1954).
Lauer, D. W., and W. K. Estes, "Successive Acquisitions and Extinctions to a Jumping Habit in Relation to Schedule of Reinforcement," *J. Comp. Physiol. Psychol.* 48: 8–13 (1955).
Walker, E. L., "Learning," *Annual Review of Psychology*, Palo Alto: Annual Reviews, 1957, pp. 113–138.

V. *Avoidance Learning*

Berkun, M. M, "Factors in the Recovery from Approach-Avoidance Conflict," *J. Exp. Psychol.* 54: 65–73 (1957).
Dinsmoor, J. A., "Punishment: I. The Avoidance Hypothesis," *Psychol. Rev.* 61: 34–46 (1954).
———, "Punishment: II. An Interpretation of Empirical Findings," *Psychol. Rev.* 62: 96–105 (1955).
Kimble G. A., "Shock Intensity and Avoidance Learning," *J. Comp. Physiol. Psychol.* 48: 281–284 (1955).
Miller, N. E., and Doris Kraeling, "Displacement: Greater Generalization of Approach than Avoidance in a Generalized Approach-Avoidance Conflict," *J. Exp. Psychol.* 43: 217–221 (1952).
———, and E. J. Murray, "Displacement and Conflict: Learnable Drive as a Basis for the Steeper Gradient of Avoidance than of Approach," *J. Exp. Psychol.* 43: 227–231 (1952).
Mowrer, O. H., and E. G. Aiken, "Contiguity vs. Drive Reduction in Fear Conditioning: Temporal Variations in Conditioned and Unconditioned Stimulus," *Amer. J. Psychol.* 67: 26–38 (1954).
———, and R. R. Lamoreaux, "Avoidance Conditioning and Signal Duration — A Study of Secondary Motivation and Reward," *Psychol. Monogr.* 54, No. 247 (1942).
———, and L. N. Solomon, "Contiguity vs. Drive Reduction in Fear Conditioning: The Proximity and Abruptness of Drive Reduction," *Amer. J. Psychol.* 67: 15–25 (1954).
Murray, E. J., and N. E. Miller, "Displacement: Steeper Gradient of Generalization of Avoidance than of Approach with Age of Habit Controlled," *J. Exp. Psychol.* 43: 222–226 (1952).

Solomon, R. L., and L. C. Wynne, "Traumatic Avoidance Learning: Acquisition in Normal Dogs," *Psychol. Monogr.* 67, No. 4 Whole No. 354 (1953).

———, and L. C. Wynne, "Traumatic Avoidance Learning: The Principles of Anxiety Conservation and Partial Irreversibility," *Psychol. Rev.* 61: 353–385 (1954).

Wynne, L. C., and R. L. Solomon, "Traumatic Avoidance Learning: Acquisition and Extinction in Dogs Deprived of Normal Peripheral Autonomic Functions," *Genet. Psychol. Monogr.* 52: 241–284 (1955).

VI. *Effects of Drugs on Avoidance Learning*

Arbit, J., "Effects of Drive Strength and Chemical Black of Autonomic Impulses Upon Maze Learning and Retention," *Psychol. Reports* 3: 91–94 (1957). (A)

———, "Skeletal Muscle Effects of the Chemical Block of Autonomic Impulses and the Extinction of Fear," *J. Comp. Physiol. Psychol.* 50: 144–145 (1957). (B)

———, "The Chemical Block of Autonomic Impulses and Learning," in proceedings of the *Amer. Psychol. Assoc.*, New York, September, 1957.

Auld, F. Jr., "The Effects of Tetraethylammonium on a Habit Motivated by Fear," *J. Comp. Physiol. Psychol.* 44: 565–574 (1951).

Berkun, M. M., "Measurement Problems in Animal Work on Drugs," in proceedings of the *Amer. Psychol. Assoc.*, New York, September, 1957.

Brady, J. V., "Assessment of Drug Effects on Emotional Behavior," *Science* 123: 1033–1034 (1956).

Bullock, D. H., "Drugs and Behavior Theory: One Man's Opinions," *Psychol. Newsletter* 9: 58–62 (1957).

Carlton, P. L., "Cholinergic Mechanisms in the Control of Behavior by the Brain," *Psychol. Rev.* 70: 19–39 (1963).

Coppock, H. W., and W. R. Hood, "Retardation and Retraining Following Alcohol Injections in Rats," in proceedings of the *Midwest. Psychol. Assoc.*, St. Louis, April, 1956.

———, W. M. Maloney, E. Pacheco, and E. J. Yearwood, "Phenobarbitol Prolongs Conflict During Retraining," in proceedings of the *Amer. Psychol Assoc*, Chicago, September, 1956.

———, and W. M. Maloney, "Subanesthetic as well as Tranquilizing Drugs Prolong Negative Transfer during Shock Escape Training," in proceedings of the *Amer. Assoc. Advance Science*, Tuscon, 1957.

Feldman, R. S., W. T. Liberson, and C. C. Neet, "Effects of Reserpine and Chlorpromazine on Behavior Fixation in Rats," in proceedings of the *Amer. Psychol. Assoc.*, New York, September, 1957.

Kornetsky, C., "Effects of Meprobamate, Phenobarbital, and Dextro-Amphetamine on Reaction Time and Learning in Man," *J. Pharm. Exptl. Therap.* 123: 216–219 (1958).

———, and O. Humphries, "The Relationship Between the Effects of a Number of Centrally Acting Drugs and Personality," *Arch. Neurol. Psychiat.* 77: 325–327 (1957).

———, O. Humphries, and E. V. Evarts, "A Comparison of the Psychological Effects of Certain Centrally Acting Drugs in Man," *Arch. Neurol. Psychiat.* 77: 318–324 (1957).

Kosman, M. E., and R. W. Gerard, "The Effect of Adrenalin on a Conditioned Avoidance Response," *J. Comp. Physiol. Psychol.* 48: 506–508 (1955).

Moyer K. E., and B. N. Bunnell, "Effect of Injected Adrenalin on an Avoidance Response in the Rat," unpublished manuscript.

Payne, R. B., "An Extension of Hullian Theory to Response Decrements Resulting from Drugs," *J. Exp. Psychol.* 55: 342–346 (1958).

Steinberg, H., "Selective Effects of an Anesthetic Drug on Cognitive Behavior," *Quart. J. Exp. Psychol.* 6: 170–180 (1954).

Wenzel, B. M., "Differential Effects of Reserpine on Approach and Avoidance Behaviors," in proceedings of the *Amer. Psychol. Assoc.*, New York, September, 1957.

Whitehead, W. A., and L. E. Thune, "The Effects of Chlorpromazine on Learning in Chronic Psychotics," *J. Consult. Psychol.* 22: 379–383 (1958).

Behavior and Personality

I. *Factor Analysis Studies: R. B. Cattell*

Cattell, R. B., *Description and Measurement of Personality.* London: Harrap, 1946.

———, *Personality: A Systematic Theoretical and Factual Study.* New York: McGraw-Hill, 1950. (A)

———, *An Introduction to Personality Study.* New York: Hutchinson's Univ. Lib., 1950. (B)

———, *A Universal Index for Psychological Factors.* Champaign, Ill.: Lab. of Personality Assessment and Group Behavior, 1953.

———, "Validation and Intensification of the Sixteen Personality Factor Questionnaire," *J. Clin. Psychol.* 12: 205–214 (1956). (A)

———, "Second-Order Personality Factors in the Questionnaire Realm," *J. Consult. Psychol.* 20: 411–418 (1956). (B)

———, *Personality and Motivation, Structure and Measurement.* Yonkers: World Book Co., 1957. (A)

———, "The Conceptual and Test Distinction of Neuroticism and Anxiety," *J. Clin. Psychol.* 13: 219–233 (1957). (B)

———, "The Dynamic Calculus," in G. Lendzey, ed., *Assessment of Human Motives*, New York: Rinehart, 1958, pp. 197–238. (A)

———, "Extracting the Correct Number of Factors in Factor Analysis," *Educ. Psychol. Measurement* 18: 791–838 (1958). (B)

———, and A. R. Baggaly, "A Confirmation of Ergic and Engram Structures in Attitudes Objectively Measured," *Australian J. Psychol.* 10: 287–318 (1958).

———, H. Beloff, and R. W. Coan, *The IPAT High School Personality Questionnaire*. Champaign, Ill.: Institute for Personality and Ability Testing, 1958.

———, S. S. Dubin, and D. R. Saunders, "Verification of Hypothesized Factors in One Hundred and Fifteen Objective Personality Designs," *Psychometrika* 19: 209–230 (1954).

———, and I. H. Scheier, "The Nature of Anxiety: A Review of Thirteen Multivariate Analyses Comprising 814 Variables," *Psychol. Reports* 4: 351–388 (1958).

———, and G. F. Stice, "Four Formulae for Selecting Leaders on the Basis of Personality," *Human Relations* 7: 493–507 (1954).

———, G. F. Stice, and N. F. Kristy, "A First Approximation to Nature-Nurture Ratios for Eleven Primary Personality Factors in Objective Tests," *J. Abn. Soc. Psychol.* 54: 143–159 (1957).

II. *H. J. Eysenck*

Eysenck, H. J., *Dimensions of Personality*. London: Kegan Paul, Trench and Truber, 1947.

———, "The Organization of Personality," *J. Personal.* 20: 101–117 (1951).

———, *The Scientific Study of Personality*. London: Routledge and Kegan Paul, 1952, New York: Macmillan, 1952. (A)

———, "Personality," *Annual Review of Psychology*, Palo Alto: Annual Reviews, 1952. (B)

———, "Schizothymia-Cyclothymia as a Dimension of Personality: II. Experimental," *J. Personal.* 20: 345–384 (1952). (C)

———, *The Structure of Personality*. London: Methuen, 1953. (A)

———, "The Logical Basis of Factor Analysis," *Amer. Psychol.* 8: 105–114 (1953). (B)

———, *A Dynamic Theory of Anxiety and Hysteria*. London: Institutes of Psychiat., Maudsley Hospital, 1954. (A)

———, "Abord Statistique et Experimental du Probleme Typologique dans la Personalitè Neurotique, Psychotique et Normale," *L. Evolution Psychiat.* 3: 377–404 (1954). (B)

———, "Zur Theorie der Personlichkeitsmessung," *Z. Diagnostische Psychol. u. Personlichkerlsforsch* 2: 87–101, 171–187 (1954). (C)

———, "Cortical Inhibition, Figural after Effect, and Theory of Personality," *J. Abn. Soc. Psychol.* 51: 94–106 (1955).

———, "The Inheritance of Extraversion-Introversion," *Acta Psychologia* 12: 95–110 (1956). (A)

———, "Reminiscence, Drive, and Personality Theory," *J. Abn. Soc. Psychol.* 53: 328–333 (1956). (B)
———, "Drugs and Personality," *J. Mental Sci.* 103: 119–131 (1957).
———, G. W. Granger, and J. C. Brengelmann, *Perceptual Processes and Mental Illness.* Maudsley Monographs, No. 2, London: Chapman and Hall, 1957.

III. *Authoritarian Personality*

Adorno, T. W., E. Frenkel-Brunswik, D. J. Levinson, and R. N. Sanford, *The Authoritarian Personality.* New York: Harper, 1950.
Christie, R., and P. Cook, "A Guide to Published Literature Relating to the Authoritarian Personality through 1956," *J. Psychol.* 45: 171–200 (1958).
Fromm, E., *Escape from Freedom.* New York: Farrar and Rinehart, 1941.
Jaensch, E. R., *Der Gegentypus.* Leipzig: Barth, 1938.
Rokeach, M., *The Open and Closed Mind.* New York: Basic Books, 1960.

IV. *T. M. Newcomb*

Newcomb, T. M., *Social Psychology.* New York: Dryden, 1950.

Psychology in Other Countries

David, H. P., and H. von Bracken, eds., *Perspectives in Personality Theory.* New York: Basic Books, 1957.

INDEX